PURNELL'S Concise
Encyclopedia
IN COLOUR

Published by Purnell Books,
Berkshire House, Queen Street,
Maidenhead, Berkshire

© 1970 Purnell & Sons Ltd.
S. B. N. 361 01542 9

Made and printed in Great Britain by
Purnell & Sons Ltd., Paulton (Avon) and London

Reprinted 1971
Reprinted 1972
Reprinted 1973
Reprinted 1974
Reprinted 1975

PURNELL'S **Concise**

Encyclopedia

IN COLOUR

Michael W. Dempsey B.A.

Purnell

Contents

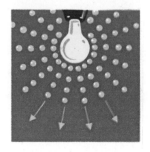

The Restless Sun

The Sun is a star. It is the star round which the Earth and other planets revolve. Compared with the millions of other stars we know about, the Sun is small and of average brightness. But because it is much nearer than any other star it appears larger and brighter.

The Sun is a mass of hot gases, more than a million times as large as the Earth and over 300,000 times as heavy. It is about 93 million miles away. Light from it takes about $8\frac{1}{2}$ minutes to reach Earth. Light from the next nearest star (Proxima Centauri) takes more than 4 years.

Without the Sun, life as we know it would be impossible. It is practically our only source of light and heat.

The Sun's heat and light is produced, as in any other star, when hydrogen atoms inside it join together to form atoms of helium. Eventually, in millions of years' time, the Sun will have used up all its hydrogen. Astronomers believe that before then the Sun will swell until it becomes a vast red star, larger than the Earth's orbit.

The temperature at the Sun's centre has been estimated to be about 20 million degrees Centigrade. At its surface, the temperature is 6,000° C.

The Sun rotates on its axis, but as it is not a solid body the time for a complete revolution is less at the equator (about 25 days) than at the poles (about 34 days).

Sunspots

From time to time dark patches appear on the Sun, usually in pairs or in large clusters. These patches are called *sunspots*. They are areas where the Sun's surface is slightly cooler than normal: 4,000° C. instead of 6,000 C. Most sunspots last for about 20 days before disappearing. Some measure as much as 50,000 miles across.

Sunspots are probably caused by magnetic disturbances deep inside the Sun, but astronomers have not yet been able to explain exactly how they are formed. Nor do they know why there are more sunspots at certain times than at others.

Every 11 years or so, sunspots are very common, and there may be many groups visible at the same time. Following a peak year, sunspots appear less and less frequently, until the Sun may be completely free of them for several days at a time. Then their number increases towards the next peak year.

Particles of atoms shot out of sunspots may approach the Earth, and can cause interference to radio transmissions. They sometimes produce displays of polar lights (*aurorae*) in the upper atmosphere.

Solar Eclipse

Sometimes the Moon in its path round the Earth passes between the Sun and the Earth. Its shadow falls on the Earth, blotting out the Sun's light. This is called a *solar eclipse*. If the Sun is completely hidden, the eclipse is said to be *total*. When only part is hidden, it is *partial*.

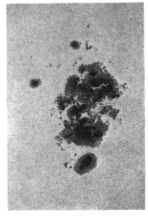

Above: A photograph of sunspots on the disc of the Sun. Sunspots usually occur in pairs or clusters. They generally last for about 20 days before disappearing.

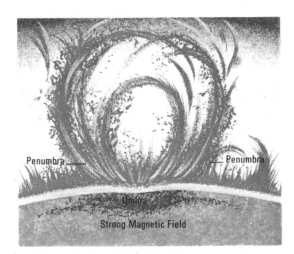

Penumbra — Penumbra

Umbra

Strong Magnetic Field

Above: Cross-section of a sunspot, showing the umbra and penumbra. Sunspots are thought to be due to magnetic disturbances in the Sun.

Below: The visible disc of the Sun is called the *photosphere*. Surrounding it is an envelope of crimson gas, the *chromosphere*. Great flares of luminous gas (*solar prominences*) leap out thousands of miles from the chromosphere. Beyond the chromosphere is a pearly-white halo of gases, the *corona*. The photosphere is so bright that the other features can only be seen during an eclipse.

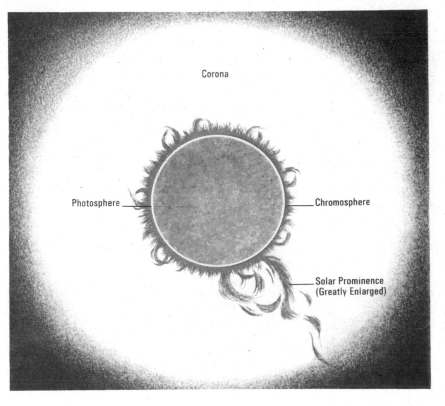

Corona

Photosphere — Chromosphere

Solar Prominence (Greatly Enlarged)

The Solar System

The Solar System in which we live consists of the Sun, the planets and their satellites (moons), and the thousands of other smaller heavenly bodies, such as asteroids, comets, and meteors. The Sun is the centre of the Solar System. It holds together, by its force of gravity, all the bodies that revolve around it.

Only the Sun has any light of its own. The planets and moons shine by reflecting this light. The radius of the Solar System is more than 3,500 million miles, representing the distance from the Sun to the furthest known satellite member of the system, the planet Pluto. The nine planets, in order of their distance from the Sun, are Mercury (the smallest), Venus, Earth, Mars, Jupiter (the largest), Saturn, Uranus, Neptune, and Pluto.

Comets orbit the Sun in long, oval paths. As a comet approaches the Sun it glows brightly and develops a luminous tail which may be up to 200 million miles long – more than twice the distance of the Earth from the Sun.

The asteroids, or minor planets, circle the Sun just like the larger planets, but are nearly all grouped together between the orbits of Mars and Jupiter.

The comets also circle the Sun, but their orbits are very *elliptical* (oval), so that their distances from the Sun vary much more than those of the planets do. Some comets pass between the Sun and the Earth and then travel right out past Pluto.

It is unlikely that ours is the only such system in the Universe. There are probably many other stars with systems of planets.

There have been many theories attempting to explain the origin of the planets. One theory suggests that early in its life the Sun was surrounded by gases and solid particles. As these revolved with the Sun, separate masses of matter developed. These drew more particles to them, forming solid cores which slowly grew into the planets. There are other theories which suggest a sudden beginning rather than a gradual process. One such theory supposes that the Sun was once one of a pair of stars. Its partner exploded, throwing out matter, some of which was captured by the Sun's gravitational field and eventually formed the planets. The force of the explosion would have shot the remains of the other star into space.

Below: The planets and their moons drawn to scale in order from the Sun: Mercury, Venus, Earth, Mars, Jupiter, Saturn, Uranus, Neptune, Pluto (distances between them are not to scale). Pluto sometimes crosses Neptune's orbit and is shown beneath that planet.

THE PLANETS

Planet	Distance from Sun (million miles)	Diameter (miles)	Volume (Earth=1)	'Day'	'Year'	Satellites
Mercury	36·0	3,100	0·06	59 days	88 days	None
Venus	67·2	7,700	0·91	3–4 months?	224·75 days	None
Earth	93·0	7,927	1·0	23 hr. 56 min.	365·25 days	1
Mars	141·5	4,200	0·15	24 hr. 37 min.	687·0 days	2
Jupiter	483·3	88,700	1,312	9 hr. 50 min.	11·86 yr.	12
Saturn	886·1	75,100	763	10 hr..14 min.	29·46 yr.	10
Uranus	1,783	29,300	50	10 hr. 49 min.	84·01 yr.	5
Neptune	2,793	27,700	43	14 hr.	164·79 yr.	2
Pluto	3,666	3,600	?	6 days 9 hr.	248·43 yr.	None

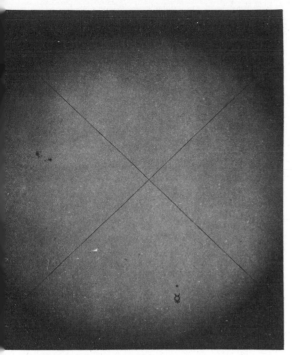

Above: Mercury sometimes moves between the Earth and the Sun. During these *transits*, it can be seen as a small dot against the Sun.

Below: Mars has polar 'ice-caps' which grow during the winter and shrink during the summer. As the 'ice-caps' melt, part of the surface changes to a greenish colour. This led some astronomers to believe that plant life existed on Mars. Recent space-probes, however, suggest that Mars is arid and lifeless.

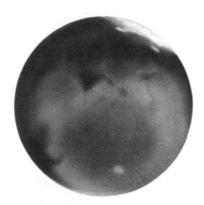

Above: Meteors are fragments, usually smaller than grapes, which circle the Sun. Sometimes they plunge into the Earth's atmosphere. Then friction makes them glow white-hot. Some meteors move round the Sun in shoals, and when the Earth passes through them they produce a *shower* of shooting stars. There are a number of showers every year. One of the biggest occurs in late July and early August. Another occurs at the beginning of January.

The Family of the Sun

Mercury is the smallest planet in the Solar System and the one closest to the Sun. It also has the shortest 'year', taking only 88 Earth-days to orbit the Sun.

Mercury is a difficult planet to see, since it is usually hidden by the Sun's fierce glare. When it can be found, it appears either low in the western sky, just after sunset, or low in the eastern sky, just before sunrise.

Temperatures on this airless planet vary tremendously. During the long day it is so hot that lead would melt. At night it is far colder than anything experienced on Earth.

Venus is often visible as a brilliant white 'star', sometimes low in the western sky after sunset *(Evening Star)* and at other times low in the eastern sky before sunrise *(Morning Star)*. Venus appears bright because it reflects more of the Sun's light which falls upon it than any other planet.

Although Venus approaches the Earth more closely than any other planet, astronomers have been able to discover little about it because the surface is always hidden by a dense layer of cloud. Information sent back to Earth by space-probes indicates that the surface temperature is about 400°C.

Moon The Moon is our nearest neighbour in space, some 239,000 miles away on average. It is bleak and has no air or water. Its surface is covered with hard, loose dust and pitted with craters up to 150 miles wide. It has great, dry plains, known as *seas*, and towering, jagged mountains. On the Moon, days are extremely hot and nights extremely cold. Our knowledge of the Moon has been greatly increased by information from space-probes and astronauts who have landed on its surface.

Mars is the only planet having conditions even remotely similar to those on Earth. But the Martian atmosphere contains much less oxygen and water vapour than the Earth's atmosphere, and temperatures vary greatly. At noon on Mars' equator, the temperature may reach 25°C. (77°F.). At night it falls to about minus 40°C. (minus 40°F.).

Like Earth, Mars has two white polar caps which shrink during the summer. These are possibly layers of frost an inch or so thick. As the frost melts, parts of the surface change from brown to green in colour. This led some astronomers to believe that there may be simple plant life on Mars. Photographs taken by recent space probes, however, have shown no signs of life. They have also disproved the idea that a network of 'canals' criss-crosses the Martian surface.

Asteroids are lumps of rock and metal whose paths round the Sun lie mainly between Mars and Jupiter. Over 2,000 have now been found. The largest, Ceres, is only 480 miles across.

Jupiter is the giant of the Solar System, more than ten times as wide as the Earth and almost twice as large as all the rest of the planets put together. Thick clouds hide its surface, but Jupiter may be a ball of rock encased in a layer of ice 16,000 miles deep.

One curious feature of Jupiter is the 'great red spot' which grows and shrinks from time to time. It is believed to be a mass of helium (containing metals that give it the reddish colour) floating on heavier gases.

Saturn is the only planet with a system of rings around it. Viewed edge-on, the rings appear as an extremely thin disc, measuring 170,000 miles across and between 10 and 40 miles wide. Saturn has ten known moons. It may once have had one more but it is thought that the innermost moon broke into pieces which now make up the rings. The nearest of the remaining moons, Janus, is only 98,000 miles from the planet's centre. Saturn is much larger than the Earth, but it is made up of very light material. If you could plunge Saturn in water it would float.

Uranus was discovered in 1781 by the British astronomer William Herschel. Through the telescope it looks like a pale greenish disc marked with faint bands. Like the other outer planets, Uranus is intensely cold and is surrounded by an atmosphere of poisonous gases.

Neptune was discovered in 1846 after irregularities in the orbit of Uranus led astronomers to suspect the presence of another planet comparatively nearby.

Pluto is the outermost known planet in our Solar System. Through the most powerful telescopes, it appears as little more than a yellowish spot. Irregularities in the orbit of Neptune led the American astronomer Percival Lowell to predict the existence of another planet, but he died without finding it. In 1930, Clyde Tombaugh photographed part of the night sky while continuing Lowell's search. He compared photographs taken on different nights and noticed that one point of light on them had changed its position. Pluto had been discovered.

Comets are collections of gas and dust a few miles across which travel round the Sun in long, oval paths. A comet is normally invisible, but when it approaches the Sun it appears in the night sky as a bright ball of light with a long glowing tail. It is the Sun's rays that cause the gas to glow and form a tail. Most famous of all is Halley's comet which appears every 76 years. It was last seen in 1910 and is expected to return in 1986.

Meteors On its journey round the Sun, the Earth collides with millions of small fragments in space. Many of these are dust particles left behind by comets. As the fragments plunge through the Earth's atmosphere, friction makes them white-hot. The result is a *shooting star*, or *meteor*, a bright line of light that flashes for a moment across the sky. Most meteors burn up as they race towards the Earth, but a few are large enough to reach the ground. These are called *meteorites*. In Arizona, U.S.A., there is a crater almost a mile across made by a meteorite which struck the Earth in prehistoric times.

Stars and Galaxies

Year after year the stars seem to remain unchanged in the sky. The constellations looked much the same to the Ancient Greeks as they do now.

Even so, stars do not last for ever. In the year 1054 a brilliant star suddenly appeared in the sky. For two years it shone so brightly that it was visible during the day. Then it faded away. All that remains now is a mass of faintly glowing gas – the Crab Nebula.

This was one of the first recorded *supernovae*, stars that end their lives in a tremendous explosion. By no means every star ends its life as a spectacular supernova, but every star has a definite beginning and a definite end.

The Birth and Death of a Star
Stars are formed from vast clouds of dust and hydrogen gas in space. Gravitational attraction between the atoms of gas gradually draws them together, and the huge cloud, called the *protostar*, begins to get smaller.

As the protostar shrinks, the temperature at its centre rises. When it reaches 1,000,000°C., the star settles down to a steady and much slower process of 'middle age'.

During the middle age of a star, atoms of the gas hydrogen are continually combining to form atoms of a heavier gas – helium.

Above: Astronomers believe that the Universe is expanding and that the distance between the galaxies is increasing, rather like spots painted on a balloon move farther apart as the balloon is inflated.

Right: The 'death' of a star, a nova in the constellation of Perseus. The fronds are the outer layers of the star which are being ejected into space.

Below: Stars are still being 'born' in the dark clouds of dust and gas obscuring part of the Orion Nebula.

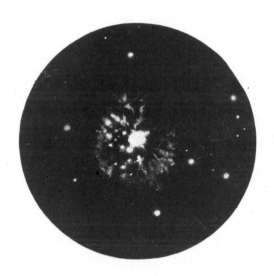

Each time an atom of helium is formed from hydrogen, a little energy is released in the form of light and heat. Many millions of tons of hydrogen must be converted into helium each *second* to make the vast amount of energy produced by a star.

Most of the star's energy is given off into space, but a little is retained, causing the star to grow hotter. When the temperature at the centre reaches 100,000,000°C. the star expands, and helium atoms start to join together to form heavier atoms.

If this process takes place too quickly, the star explodes, shooting matter into space. Such an occurrence, the *supernova* stage, is rare. More often, the star expands slowly into a huge red star, called a *red giant*. Finally, when all the hydrogen 'fuel' has been used up, the star shrinks again to

become a *white dwarf*, and 'dies' as it cools and grows fainter.

The birth and death of a star takes thousands of millions of years. The process is studied by observing thousands of stars, all at various stages of their lives. The Sun, for instance, has been releasing heat and light for about 5,000 million years and is halfway through its middle age.

Size and Magnitude
Some stars are so large that if the Sun were at their centre the Earth would also be inside the star. Other stars are much smaller than the Sun.

The brightest stars are a thousand million times brighter than the dullest ones. The brightness of a star in the night sky is called its *magnitude*. It is not a reliable guide to the star's real brightness, because the farther away a star is the fainter it looks. Bright stars are of magnitude 1, and the faintest stars visible without a telescope are of magnitude 6. Some stars are so bright that they have *negative* magnitudes. The Sun has a magnitude of −26·72. Stars whose brightness continually changes are called *variable stars*.

Galaxies – Islands in Space

On a dark night, a faint band of light can be seen stretching across the sky. Its appearance to the naked eye is the reason for its name – the Milky Way. When seen through even a pair of binoculars, the 'milkiness' disappears, and the light can be seen to come from millions of stars clustered closely together.

The Milky Way is a *galaxy*, a slowly rotating mass of stars, dust and gas 100,000 light years across. (A *light year* is the distance travelled by light in one year – 5,880,000,000,000 miles.) The Sun and its family of planets belong to this galaxy, along with some 200,000 million other stars.

The whole galaxy is shaped rather like a flattened disc with a central bulge of closely packed stars. The disc is composed of wispy, spiral arms of stars, gas and dust. People on Earth get an end-on-view of the disc of the Milky Way because our Solar System is itself part of the disc.

For a long time astronomers called the Milky Way 'the galaxy'. But it is by no means the only galaxy in the Universe. There are millions of others. One of the most famous, the Andromeda galaxy, appears to the naked eye as a fuzzy patch of light beyond the stars which make up the constellation of Andromeda. This galaxy is 2,000,000 light years away from our own.

The Ten Brightest Stars

Star	Constellation	Magnitude
Sirius	Great Dog	−1·43
Canopus	The Ship	−0·73
Alpha Centauri	Centaur	−0·27
Arcturus	Herdsman	−0·06
Vega	Lyre	0·04
Capella	Charioteer	0·09
Rigel	Orion	0·15
Procyon	Little Dog	0·37
Achernar	The River Eridanus	0·53
Betelgeux	Orion	variable

The Ten Nearest Stars

Name	Magnitude	Distance in Light Years
Proxima Centauri	10·5	4·2
Alpha Centauri	−0·3	4·3
Munich 15040	9·7	6·2
Lalande 21185	7·6	8·1
Wolf 359	13·5	8·1
Sirius	−1·4	8·7
Innes Star	11·7	9·6
B.D. −12° 4523	9·5	9·9
Cordoba Vh. 243	9·2	10·2
Ross 248	13·8	10·2

Edwin Hubble (1889-1953) classified galaxies according to their structure. He distinguished three main types: *elliptical*, *spiral* and *barred spiral*. About 60% of all galaxies are spirals. Galaxies which fit into none of the three main types are called *irregular*. The photographs show various types of spiral galaxy. S stands for spiral. The letters c, b, and a denote the importance of the central nucleus relative to the spiral arms.

1

2

1. Type Sc. The central nucleus is small and there is a marked spiral structure.

2. Type Sb. The central nucleus is larger and the spiral structure less marked.

3. Type Sa. The central nucleus is very large and the spiral structure insignificant.

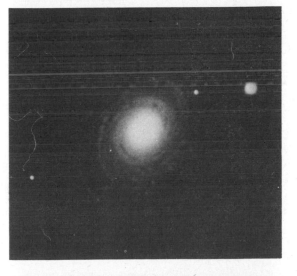

3

4. Type So. This is a connecting point between the main types of galaxy. It has no spiral structure but is more flattened than the elliptical galaxies.

4

13

The Constellations

For thousands of years men have looked at the stars and picked out recognizable shapes and patterns. One group of stars reminded them of a hunter, another suggested the outline of a lion, and so on. Soon they built up stories which connected these groups, or *constellations*.

The Chinese, Arabs, Babylonians and Egyptians were some of the first people to give special names to the constellations and to use them as guides to sailors and travellers. The Ancient Greeks knew of 48 constellations which they named after their heroes and gods. But it was the Roman astronomers who gave the constellations the Latin names by which we know them today.

The most famous of all the constellations is probably Ursa Major, the Great Bear, whose seven chief stars form the Plough, or Big Dipper. Two of the Plough stars are known as the Pointers, because they always point to Polaris, the Pole Star. This is the star immediately above the Earth's North Pole around which all the other stars seem to revolve.

Today astronomers know of 88 constellations. The 23 constellations in the far south of the southern hemisphere were first named by astronomers in the 18th century.

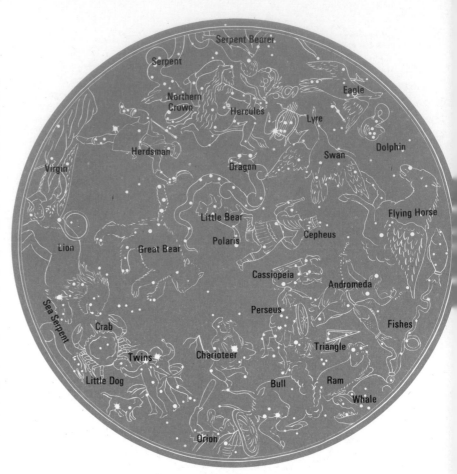

Constellations of the Northern Hemisphere

Perseus   Andromeda

Legends in the Sky

There are many famous legends about the constellations. One concerns a King Cepheus and Queen Cassiopeia who had a beautiful daughter, Andromeda. Cassiopeia foolishly boasted that her daughter was more beautiful than the Nereids, or sea nymphs. The Nereids complained to their father, the sea god Neptune, who sent the monster Cetus to terrorize the land of the boastful Queen.

Wise men told King Cepheus and Queen Cassiopeia that the only way to save their people was to sacrifice their daughter to Cetus. Reluctantly, they chained Andromeda to a rock on the sea shore and left her to await the monster.

Meanwhile, the hero Perseus was returning home with the head of the wicked Gorgon, Medusa. Medusa, who had snakes in place of hair, had been able to turn any living creature into stone with a single glance. As Perseus flew over the place where Andromeda was chained, he saw the monster approaching. Quickly he swooped down on the back of his winged horse Pegasus. He pointed Medusa's head at the monster which promptly turned to stone. All the figures in this legend are to be found in the sky.

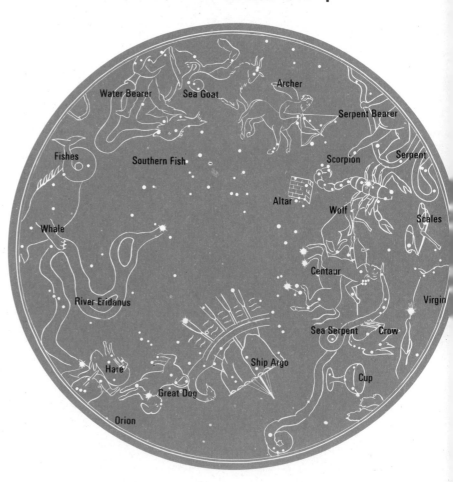

Constellations of the Southern Hemisphere

14

The Earth in Space

The Seasons

Like the other eight planets in the Solar System, the Earth circles the Sun, and it takes one year to complete this journey. At the same time, it is spinning on its own axis, completing one revolution about every 24 hours. If the axis were at right-angles to the plane of the Earth's orbit round the Sun, each part of the world would have 12 hours of daylight and 12 hours of darkness the whole year round. Seasons would not exist. But the Earth is like a great tilted top spinning through space. The axis is constantly inclined at an angle of 66½° to the plane of the orbit. It is this 'tilt' which produces the seasons.

At one point in the Earth's orbit the North Pole leans towards the Sun and northern lands have their summer. At the same time, the South Pole leans away from the Sun and southern lands have their winter. Six months later, the Earth has travelled to the other side of the Sun. Now

Above: Seasons are caused by the tilt of the Earth's axis as it circles the Sun. Northern and southern lands have their seasons at opposite times of the year.

Right: The phases of the Moon. We see only that part of the Moon which is illuminated by the Sun. When the Moon is between the Earth and the Sun, virtually none of the illuminated side can be seen (new Moon). When the Moon is at the other side of the Earth, the whole of the illuminated side can be seen (full Moon). Between these two positions we see varying amounts of the illuminated side.

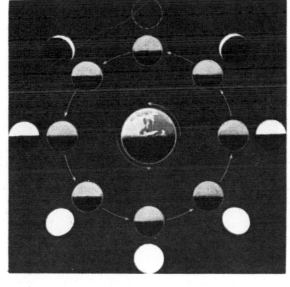

the North Pole leans away from the Sun while the South Pole leans towards it. Northern lands have their winter and southern lands have their summer.

Time

Early man realized that time can be measured in three natural units: the *solar day*, the *lunar month* and the *solar year*.

A solar day is the time taken for a point on the Earth's spinning surface to revolve and come back to its original position facing the Sun. The Solar day (measured by sundials) varies in length. The day we measure by our clocks is the average of these variations and is called the *mean solar day*.

A lunar month is the time between full moons and is equal to 29½ days. It is not used in modern calendars because it does not divide equally into the solar year. This is the time taken for the Earth to orbit the Sun and is almost 365¼ days.

The Romans invented the calendar that we use today. In 46 B.C., Julius Caesar decreed that the year be divided into 12 months, each of 30 or 31 days except February which had 29 days and 30 days every fourth year. One day was later taken from February and added to August.

The Julian calendar worked well for over 1,500 years. But the calendar year was slightly longer than the solar year, and by 1580 it was 10 days out. In 1582, Pope Gregory XIII decreed that 10 days be removed from the calendar, and made a small change in it: every 100 years, February would not have an extra day, except for the years 1600, 2000, 2400 etc. The Gregorian calendar is the one we use today. It is accurate to 26·3 seconds per solar year.

Right: Owing to the spin of the Earth, various parts of the world experience day and night at various times. When it is midday at one point on the Earth, it is midnight at the opposite side of the Earth.

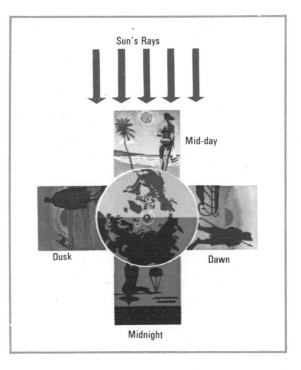

Astronomy

Astronomy is the scientific study of the stars, planets and other heavenly bodies. For thousands of years men have sought answers to such questions as: What are the stars made of? How far away are they? Does the Earth move? How did the Universe begin? Today, astronomers can answer many of these questions.

In modern observatories astronomers study the nature of the Universe. They plot the stars; they search the sky for new stars; and they study the composition, movement, distance, colour, brightness and size of the heavenly bodies. They also study the nuclear reactions that take place inside stars and produce such vast amounts of heat and light.

Telescope and Spectroscope

The astronomer's most important instrument is the telescope which makes distant objects seem nearer. It does this by forming an image of the object being viewed and then magnifying this image. Some of the largest telescopes are used as cameras.

Another valuable instrument is the spectroscope which is used to analyze stars. When the starlight passes through the spectroscope, the astronomer sees it broken up, as a prism divides white light into a rainbow band of colours. By studying the variously coloured light it is possible to tell a great deal about the composition of the star itself.

Radio Astronomy

Radio waves are sent out by all galaxies and many stars, including the Sun. These waves are invisible, and so cannot be discovered by ordinary telescopes. But they can be picked up by receiving aerials, just like any radio broadcast. The waves start small electric currents flowing in the aerial. These currents can be turned into sound. But it is more usual when picking up radio waves from space to use specially designed receivers in which the currents are automatically recorded on a paper strip as a wavy line. These receivers are called *radio telescopes*.

Some big radio telescopes have a large bowl-shaped reflector, or 'mirror', which can be moved to point at any area of the sky. In front of the reflector is an aerial on which all the waves are drawn together so that the currents they produce are large enough to be recorded.

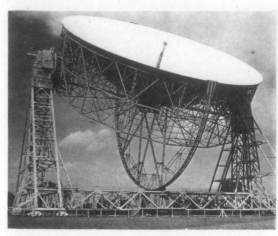

Right: The giant bowl of the radio telescope at Jodrell Bank, Cheshire, England, can be steered to point at any part of the sky. As well as recording radio waves from space, this telescope has been used to track artificial satellites and space-probes.

Radio telescopes can detect far more distant objects than optical telescopes. Radio-astronomy is used to pin-point an area of space from which strong signals are received. Optical telescopes then search this area in order to discover the source of the signals. *Quasars* (very powerful and very distant sources of radio waves and light) and *pulsars* (stars that produce regular pulses of radio waves and light up to 30 times a second) were both discovered by radio astronomy.

Below: The revolving dome of the 100-inch Hooker reflecting telescope at Mount Wilson, California, U.S.A. When this telescope came into operation in 1917, it opened up entirely new fields of research and more than doubled man's knowledge of the Universe.

Clocks and Watches

The earliest means man had of measuring the passage of time during the day was the position of the Sun in the sky. When he noticed that the shadow of a tree or a stick moved in a semi-circle from sunrise to sunset, the idea of a sundial was born.

The Ancient Egyptians invented *waterclocks* at least 4,000 years ago. In the simplest of these, the water level in a leaking vessel indicated the time. *Sand-glasses* similar to the egg-timers in use today were also widespread in ancient times.

Mechanical clocks probably came into use in Europe during the thirteenth century. The earliest ones consisted of a weight attached by a rope to a drum. As the rope unwound, the drum turned and moved a mechanism which struck a bell at regular intervals. Dials and a moving hand to indicate the time did not appear until the 1400's.

Above: An egg-shaped watch of the late 16th century with a gilt bronze case.

Above: the anchor escapement invented in the 17th century. The arm has two teeth which engage with the teeth of the escape wheel and by rocking to and fro allow it to move tooth by tooth.

Left: An ancient sundial. The sundial measures solar time but the length of a natural day varies. The time measured by a clock is the average of these variations – mean solar time.

SUN DIAL
MADE BY PHAEDRUS, SON OF ZOILUS, OF THE PAEANIAN DEME.

At about the same time, the *coil spring* was invented as an alternative to the weight for driving clocks. This meant that clocks could be much smaller.

In all mechanical clocks, some device is needed which allows the system, or *train,* of gear-wheels driving the mechanism to move slowly. Otherwise the weight would fall or the spring uncoil in seconds. Such a device is called an *escapement.* The earliest type was the *verge escapement* where a kind of rocking bar allowed a toothed escape wheel at the end of a train of gears to move tooth by tooth. The present form of escapement—the *anchor* or *recoil escapement*—was invented in the 17th century. This also has two teeth which engage with the teeth of the escape wheel and by rocking to and fro allow it to move tooth by tooth.

Another essential part of any timepiece is a device to control the release of the escapement. For a clock to be accurate, the escapement must be released regularly. In early clocks the movement was not regular. Then, in 1581, Galileo discovered that the time of swing of a *pendulum* is constant. This led to the use of the pendulum as the regulating device in clocks. Today, watches and small clocks have a regulator in the form of a *balance wheel* which is made to swing back and forth at a steady rate by a delicate *hairspring.* The spring which powers the watch is called the *mainspring* to distinguish it from the hairspring.

A very accurate modern clock is regulated by the vibrations in a quartz crystal. Some electric clocks are regulated as well as driven by the alternating electricity supply Most accurate of all are atomic clocks which depend on the vibrations of atoms to regulate them. They are used by scientists who measure time extremely accurately.

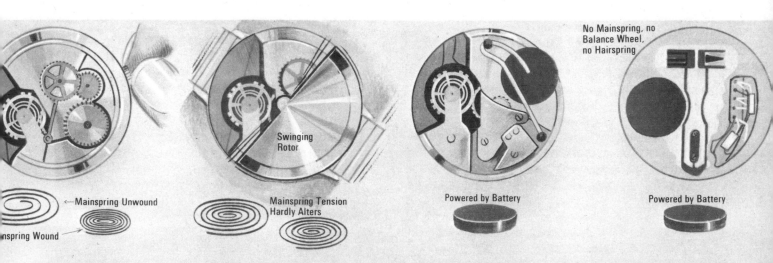

No Mainspring, no Balance Wheel, no Hairspring

Swinging Rotor

←Mainspring Unwound

Mainspring Wound

Mainspring Tension Hardly Alters

Powered by Battery

Powered by Battery

Ordinary watches have to be wound up once a day to give them energy which is stored in the mainspring.

Self-winding watches have a rotor that swings as the wrist moves and keeps the mainspring constantly wound.

Electric watches contain a small battery that provides power to drive the watch, replacing the mainspring.

Electronic watches contain a battery to drive a tuning fork that vibrates at a constant rate to regulate them.

Man in Space

Astronautics is the branch of science which deals with the many problems of space flight. The Space Age began with the launching of the artificial satellite *Sputnik 1* on October 4, 1957. Already, man has reached the Moon and unmanned *probes* have been sent to other parts of the Solar System.

Astronauts receive intensive training to prepare themselves for space flights. For example, they spend a long time in a machine called a *centrifuge* which whirls them round rapidly and reproduces the kind of forces they can expect during take-off and landing. The astronauts also train in dummy spacecraft which can be made to do many of the things a real one would do in space.

After months of training, the astronauts climb into their spacecraft and are blasted into space on top of a massive rocket. The rocket gives the spacecraft the high speed needed to escape the Earth's gravity (about 25,000 m.p.h.). The astronauts lie on their backs during the launch, since this is the best way to withstand the great forces of acceleration.

Out in space there is no effective gravity, and the astronauts, like everything else, are weightless. Nothing keeps them 'down' and they can float around freely. Eating and drinking are very different from on Earth. Food and drink must be squeezed right into the mouth.

Above: A Vostok spacecraft on top of its launching rocket. The spacecraft is about 35 feet high.

Above: The blast-off of a U.S. multi-stage rocket.

Right: A scientific satellite for measuring radiation from outer space. The 'paddles' contain the solar cells which generate power from the Sun's rays.

Left: An astronaut 'walks' in space tethered to his spacecraft. He carries a jet pistol to move himself around.

Rockets

Rockets burn fuel to produce a jet of hot gases which shoot out backwards and drive the vehicle forwards. (The forward thrust is produced by the *reaction* to the jet of gases.) Rockets can operate in the vacuum of space because they carry their own oxygen as well as fuel. The substance that provides oxygen to burn the fuel is called an *oxidant*. Both fuel and oxidant are called *propellents*. They can be either liquid or solid.

Liquid propellents are usually the more powerful. They are used in the rockets which launch spacecraft. Liquid hydrogen and kerosene (paraffin) are widely used as rocket fuels. Liquid oxygen is the favourite oxidant. Solid propellents are used in guided missiles and in retro-rockets.

A single rocket cannot by itself launch a heavy load into space. A number of rockets must be linked together, one on top of the other, to provide enough power. Rockets built in this way are called *multi-stage*. Most space vehicles have a massive first stage, or *booster*, and two smaller stages. Each stage fires in turn and thrusts the vehicle higher and higher. The vehicle gets lighter and lighter as each spent stage separates and falls away.

The crew cabin of the spacecraft is connected to what is known as a *life-support system*. This provides gas under pressure for the astronauts to breathe, removes stale air and moisture, and keeps the temperature steady.

Returning to Earth is one of the most dangerous aspects of space flight. If the spacecraft is in orbit round the Earth, *retro-rockets* are fired to slow it down and gravity draws it towards the ground. The capsule containing the astronauts then separates from the rest of the craft. As the capsule re-enters the atmosphere the air acts like a brake, slowing it down and heating it at the same time. The base of the capsule glows red-hot, but it is specially designed as a *heat-shield* to protect the astronauts. As the capsule falls lower, parachutes open and gently carry it down to the ground or the sea.

Re-entry after a round trip to the Moon is even more difficult. The capsule is travelling at almost 25,000 m.p.h., and it must enter the atmosphere through what is called a 'window', only a few miles long. If it misses the 'window', it will either burn up or 'bounce' back into space.

American astronauts set foot on the Moon on July 21, 1969.

Steps in Space

1232 Chinese soldiers used rockets during their war against the Mongols.

1660s Johannes Kepler developed his laws of planetary motion.

1687 Sir Isaac Newton described his theory of universal gravitation and his laws of motion.

1903 Konstantin Tsiolkovsky, a Russian schoolmaster, published a paper suggesting the use of rockets for space flight.

1926 Robert Hutchings Goddard fired the first liquid-propelled rocket in the U.S.A. It used petrol and liquid oxygen as propellents and rose almost 200 feet in the air.

1957 The U.S.S.R. launched *Sputnik 1*, the first artificial satellite, weighing 184 pounds, on October 4.

1958 The U.S.A. launched its first satellite, *Explorer 1*, weighing only 31 pounds, on January 31.

1959 *Lunik 1* (U.S.S.R.) and *Pioneer IV* (U.S.A.) were the first space probes launched to the Moon. *Lunik 3* sent back a picture of the far side of the Moon which is never seen from Earth.

1961 Yuri Gagarin (U.S.S.R.) in *Vostok 1* became the first man in space on April 12. making one orbit of the Earth.

1962 John Glenn in *Friendship 7* made three orbits of the Earth on February 20 to become the first American in space.

1963 Valentina Tereshkova (U.S.S.R.) became the first woman cosmonaut.

1964 The U.S.A. launched *Ranger 7* Moon probe, which sent back close-up television pictures of the Moon before crashing on the surface.

1965 Alexei Leonov (U.S.S.R.) made the first 'walk' in space on March 18, when he spent just over 20 minutes outside his two-man spacecraft *Voshkod 2*.

1966 Luna 9 (U.S.S.R.) made the first true soft Moon landing in January and sent back a series of close-up pictures.

Gemini 8 made the first successful docking, or link-up manoeuvre, with another vehicle in space, an essential step for subsequent space flights.

1968 In October, a three-man team in *Apollo 7* made a successful 10-day flight in orbit, rigorously testing the *Apollo* craft. In December, Frank Borman, James Lovell and William Anders in *Apollo 8* became the first men to travel to the Moon and back.

1969 In March, *Apollo 9* was launched into an Earth orbit to test the Lunar Excursion Module designed for the actual Moon landing. *Apollo 10* repeated the separating manoeuvres of *Apollo 9* in a Moon orbit. *Apollo 11* repeated the Moon trip, and on July 21 Neil Armstrong stepped from the lunar module on to the Moon's surface. On November 19, American astronauts again landed on the Moon.

1970 In April, an explosion in *Apollo 13* almost brought disaster to the mission. In November, the USSR soft-landed a robot space-probe, *Luna 16*, on the Moon.

1971 In February, *Apollo 14* made another Moon trip. In May, three Russian cosmonauts were killed by the depressurization of their re-entry capsule. In August, American astronauts drove a battery-powered vehicle over the lunar surface. In November, a Russian probe soft-landed on the surface of Mars.

1972 *Apollo 16* (April) and *Apollo 17* (December) completed the Moon programme.

1973 In May, U.S. launched Space Station *Skylab* into a near-Earth orbit. It was visited by two teams of astronauts for 28 and 59 days respectively.

1974 American astronauts spent a record 84 days in orbiting *Skylab*.
U.S.S.R. launches *Soyuz 14* (July).

1975 First international manned space link-up between *Apollo* and *Soyuz* spacecraft.

The Plant Kingdom

Living things are divided into two main groups – plants and animals. Most plants are fixed to one spot, but the majority of animals can move from place to place. Plants do not have a fixed shape, and they go on growing throughout their lives, whereas animals do have a definite shape and they stop growing when they reach a certain point. But the most important difference between plants and animals is in the way they get their food. Plants can make food from simple materials in the air and the soil. Animals cannot do this; they have to obtain ready-made food from plants or from other animals that have eaten plants. This is what is meant by the biblical saying 'all flesh is grass' – all flesh must come from plant material and all animals therefore depend upon plants. This is so even in the sea, where the bulk of the plant life consists of millions of tiny floating plants called plankton.

Photosynthesis

The food-making process of plants is therefore the most important process in the world. It is called *photosynthesis*, which means 'making by light', because it uses the energy of light. Most of the energy comes from sunlight, and photosynthesis normally takes place only in the daytime, although it can proceed in artificial light.

The biggest difference between plants and animals is that plants can make their own food while animals cannot. Plants make their food from carbon dioxide in the air and from the water and nutrient salts in the soil. They can only do this in sunlight, or, occasionally, in artificial light. The sun's energy is trapped by chlorophyll, the green pigment in leaves. The following formula is much simplified:

$$6CO_2 + 6H_2O + e \rightarrow C_6H_{12}O_6 + 6O_2$$

carbon dioxide + water + sun's energy → carbohydrate + oxygen

The food is stored in stems or roots.

Most plants are fixed to one spot, and consist of roots, stems and leaves.

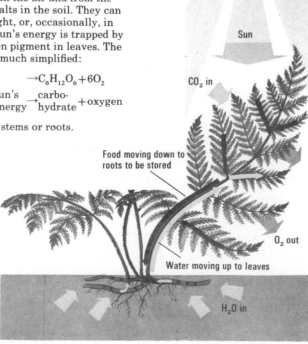

Food moving down to roots to be stored

CO₂ in

Sun

O₂ out

Water moving up to leaves

H₂O in

Light falling on the plant is trapped by the green pigment called *chlorophyll*, which is found mainly in the leaves. The leaves of a plant are therefore arranged so that they receive as much light as possible – no leaf completely overshadows another, and there are no wasteful gaps between the leaves. In this way, the plant makes the best possible use of the sunlight and makes as much food as it possibly can.

The raw materials used in photosynthesis are water and carbon dioxide gas. Water is obtained from the soil and carbon dioxide is obtained from the air. Inside the plant, the light energy trapped by the chlorophyll is used in a complicated series of reactions. The end result is that the water and carbon dioxide are joined together to form glucose sugar. Oxygen is given off during the process and returned to the air.

The glucose sugar provides the plant with energy for growth, but the plant cannot build new parts from sugar alone. It must also have minerals, such as nitrates and potash, which it obtains from the soil. These minerals are combined with the sugar to form proteins, which are the basis of all living material. The proteins are used to build new plant material and they may be converted into animal material if the plant is eaten by an animal.

The Carbon Cycle

The amount of carbon dioxide in the atmosphere stays constant at about 0·03%. This means that every 10,000 gallons of air contains about 3 gallons of carbon dioxide. Huge quantities of carbon dioxide are removed every day by plants and yet the total remains the same. How can this be? The answer is that carbon dioxide is being returned to the air all the time. When animals breathe, they take in oxygen (which is given out by plants) and give off carbon dioxide. This is the most important route by which carbon dioxide returns to the air. Plants also breathe, but their carbon dioxide is given off only at night: during the daytime it is used up in photosynthesis. A great deal of carbon dioxide is released when things decay, and man also returns large quantities to the air when he burns wood, coal and petrol.

This whole system of carbon dioxide being taken from the air by plants and then returned by various routes is called the *carbon cycle*. It is vital to all living things because if the carbon dioxide were not returned the plants would soon exhaust the supply. The plants would all die, and the animals would all die, too, because they would have no food.

Algae

The simplest members of the plant kingdom are the *algae*. These are flowerless plants which include all the seaweeds and the tiny floating plants called plankton. They range from microscopic cells and threads to huge seaweeds more than 100 feet long. Many of the smaller algae live in ponds and streams, and they often form a thick green scum on the surface. Some seaweeds are brown or red, but they still contain chlorophyll and make food in the normal way. Seaweeds may have a *holdfast* which attaches them to the rocks, but there are no real roots or stems or leaves and one part of the plant looks very much like any other.

Fungi

Moulds and toadstools belong to a group called *fungi*. These plants have no chlorophyll, but they are so like the algae in general structure that there is no doubt that they are plants. Because they have no chlorophyll, they have to get food from other organisms. Most fungi live in the soil and get food from dead leaves. Some grow on living plants. Fungi are made up basically of slender threads, and the familiar toadstools are composed of threads packed densely together. Fungi have no flowers or seeds and they reproduce themselves by scattering clouds of dust-like spores.

Mosses and Liverworts

The *mosses* and *liverworts* are all small green plants, living mainly in damp and shady places. Most of them have stems and leaves, but there are no real roots and the plants are held down by hair-like outgrowths. These plants usually grow in clumps and form 'mats' or 'cushions' on the ground. There are no flowers or seeds and the plants scatter tiny spores from capsules which grow up above the leaves. The spores grow into new plants.

Ferns

Ferns are generally much larger than mosses and they are more complex in structure. They have real roots, and the leaves are usually divided into numerous leaflets. Some ferns, known as tree ferns, grow to a height of 70 feet, but most of them are less than 5 feet tall. Like the mosses, the ferns have no flowers or seeds. They produce clouds of spores, usually in little brown patches under the leaves. But the spores do not grow directly into new ferns. They first develop into tiny heart-shaped 'plates' and the new ferns grow from these.

Conifers

The *conifers*, such as pines and larches, are nearly all large trees. They form a link between the ferns and the flowering plants because, although they do not have real flowers, they do produce seeds. The seeds are carried in woody cones. Conifers are usually evergreens, and they have narrow, needle-like leaves.

Flowering Plants

The great majority of plants we see around us are *flowering plants*. The bright, scented flowers attract insects, which pollinate the flowers and ensure that the seeds develop. This is much more efficient than scattering pollen to the wind like the conifers do. There are, however, many flowering plants which scatter pollen for the wind to carry. These plants have rather drab flowers and produce large amounts of pollen. Grasses are among the best examples. Flowering plants protect their seeds inside fruits, such as pods or berries, which also help to scatter the seeds when they are ripe.

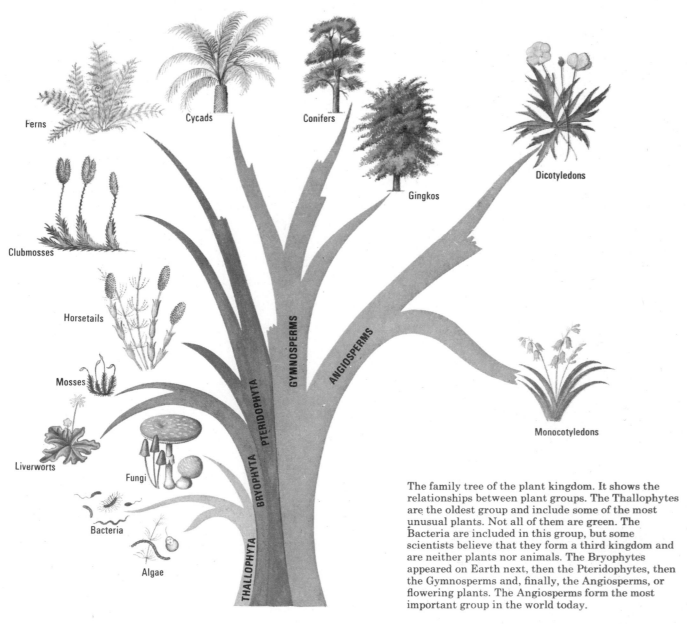

The family tree of the plant kingdom. It shows the relationships between plant groups. The Thallophytes are the oldest group and include some of the most unusual plants. Not all of them are green. The Bacteria are included in this group, but some scientists believe that they form a third kingdom and are neither plants nor animals. The Bryophytes appeared on Earth next, then the Pteridophytes, then the Gymnosperms and, finally, the Angiosperms, or flowering plants. The Angiosperms form the most important group in the world today.

Fungi

One characteristic of plants is that they make their own food with the aid of the green pigment chlorophyll. There are, however, a number of plants which do not contain chlorophyll and cannot make their own food. Many of these *dependent* plants are *parasites,* absorbing food from other living things. The rest are *saprophytes,* existing on dead materials such as twigs, flour and leather.

The largest group of dependent plants are the *fungi.* The smallest of the fungi are the

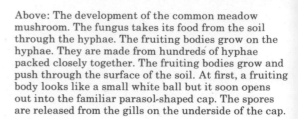

Hyphae   Fruiting Bodies

Above: The development of the common meadow mushroom. The fungus takes its food from the soil through the hyphae. The fruiting bodies grow on the hyphae. They are made from hundreds of hyphae packed closely together. The fruiting bodies grow and push through the surface of the soil. At first, a fruiting body looks like a small white ball but it soon opens out into the familiar parasol-shaped cap. The spores are released from the gills on the underside of the cap.

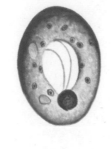

Spirogyra

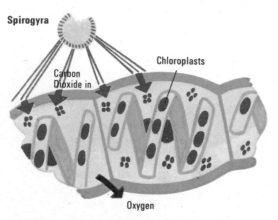

Chloroplasts

Carbon Dioxide in

Oxygen

Spirogyra (above) is a simple plant. But it has an important feature in common with most other plants. It is able to make its own food. In a remarkable process called photosynthesis, food is built up from carbon dioxide and water using the energy of sunlight which is absorbed and converted into chemical energy by the green pigment chlorophyll. Fungi (below) do not contain chlorophyll and are unable to make their own food. They take in food through their cell walls.

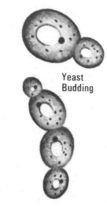

Yeast Budding

Ascospore

yeasts. They are valuable to man. For many years he has used yeasts to make bread, wine and beer. These plants use dissolved sugar for food and produce carbon dioxide and alcohol. They are responsible for the fermentation of liquids.

Among the larger fungi are the *moulds* which may form a lacy pattern over virtually any material derived from plants or animals. Moulds are associated with damp and decay. One of the commonest is Mucor, or pin-mould, which quickly spreads across the surface of damp bread. Like all moulds, it consists of a mass of colourless threads (the *mycelium*) from which small, upright

Below: Most familiar mushrooms, toadstools and bracket fungi belong to the group of fungi called the Basidiomycetes. The parts which can be seen are the fruiting bodies. These show a large variety of shapes, sizes and colours. Many of them are poisonous.

Fungus

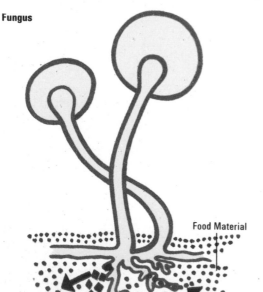

Food Material

Enzymes out

Food in

Above: Yeast is a simple fungus consisting of single, oval cells. It reproduces in two ways. Smaller cells may be budded off from the sides of large cells and may remain together in a long chain. In difficult conditions, yeasts divide to form *ascospores*. These are inside a tough case which will survive until conditions improve. Yeast cells convert sugar into food, and alcohol and carbon dioxide are formed in the process.

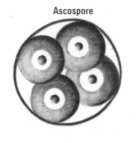

Spotted Fly Agaric

Puff-balls

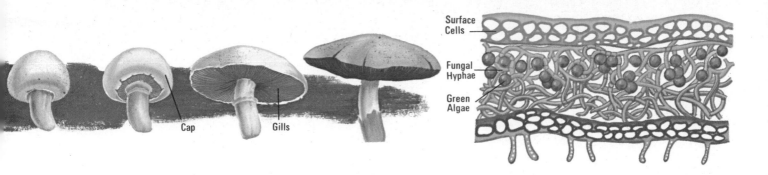

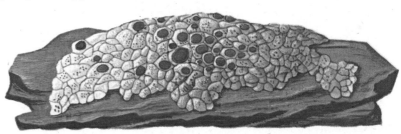

Surface
Cells

Fungal
Hyphae

Green
Algae

branches develop. Each branch ends in a hollow ball containing hundreds of spores from which new plants grow. It is the spore cases which give the mould its colour – usually green, blue or black. Certain moulds are used to produce valuable drugs such as penicillin.

Mushrooms

Probably the best known of all fungi is the common meadow mushroom. This plant is very much like a mould, the chief difference being that the mushroom has only one large spore-bearing stalk. A mushroom begins as a small lump on the underground mycelium. As the lump grows, it pushes its way above ground and first appears as a small white 'button'. Slowly, the button opens out to an umbrella shape, revealing on the underside of the cap a mass of curtain-like folds, called *gills*, covered with spores.

Other edible fungi include champignons, morels, puff-balls, truffles and chanterelles. There are also a number of highly poisonous species, such as the death cap.

Apart from fungi, there are many other dependent plants. One example is the dodder which winds its way around other plants. The dodder is a true parasite, for it is completely dependent upon the juices of the host plant.

Below: A lichen which grows on rocks in upland areas. The red spots are the spore-producing parts.

Above: A cross-section of a lichen scale. A lichen is a combination of a fungus and a small alga. The fungus hyphae make a dense mat of threads and the alga lives within the mat. The alga has chlorophyll and can make its own food, but the fungus needs the alga to make its food.

Only a few flowering plants are parasites. One is mistletoe which feeds on other plants such as the apple and hawthorn, growing high up on their branches. The mistletoe sends out suckers which penetrate the tissues of the host plant and rob it of food materials and water. Mistletoe does, however, possess green leaves and can make some of its own food. It is a *partial parasite*.

The dodder is completely parasitic and climbs up other plants. Once a young seedling has made contact with a host plant, its feeble root withers, and from then on it is completely dependent on its host for food.

The toothwort is parasitic on the roots of elm and hazel trees. Its underground parts put out suckers which penetrate the roots of these plants and obtain nourishment from them.

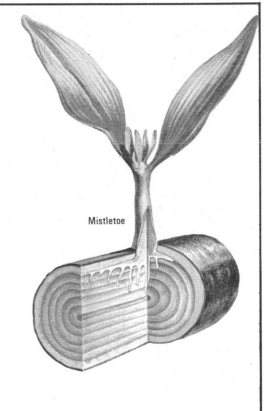

Mistletoe

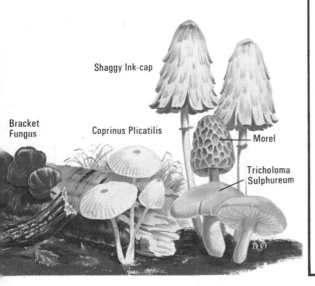

Shaggy Ink-cap

Bracket
Fungus

Coprinus Plicatilis

Morel

Tricholoma
Sulphureum

Diagram of
Dodder Winding
Around Nettle
Stem

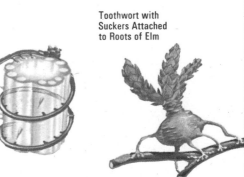

Toothwort with
Suckers Attached
to Roots of Elm

Trees

A tree is a large plant with a thick, woody stem called a trunk. Apart from this, however, trees are not really any different from the other plants we see around us in fields and gardens. They all start life as seeds, they all carry leaves, and most of them eventually bear flowers. Shrubs or bushes are similar to trees in many ways but, instead of having a central trunk, they have several main stems all more or less the same size and all coming from about ground level.

Each kind of tree has its own pattern of branching and, although no two trees are exactly alike, it is possible to recognise some kinds of trees by their shape alone. The English Elm and the Lombardy Poplar are good examples. The shape of a tree, however, depends very much on the conditions under which it grows. A tree growing by itself, in the middle of a park for example, will develop its full shape, with branches quite low down. But trees growing close together in woodland usually lose their lower branches because they are overshadowed.

Wood and Bark

Like all plants, trees make food in their leaves. They need plenty of water for this

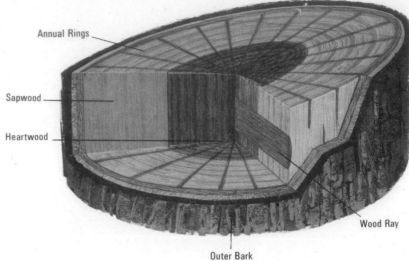

Above: A section of a tree-trunk with a wedge cut from it. The dark wood in the middle is the heartwood. It is made from old water-carrying tubes, squashed together. The paler wood is the sapwood. The medullary rays are living cells through the trunk of the tree.

Below: the largest group of trees is the Flowering Tree group. They are recognised by their broad leaves and branching leaf veins. They produce strong timber, and are called hardwoods.

and the trunk of the tree consists mainly of water-carrying tubes. These are packed densely together and, being very tough, they also give the tree its strength. The branches grow year after year and produce more and more leaves. These require more and more water and so more water-carrying tubes are produced each year. They are added near the outside of the trunk. As autumn approaches and growth slows down, the size of the new tubes gets smaller and then production stops altogether. When spring returns and the sap starts to flow again tube production re-starts. These spring-formed tubes are much larger than the autumn-formed tubes and, if the tree is cut down, one can see distinct lines between the autumn and spring wood. These are called annual rings and, by counting them, one can find out the age of the tree.

As the trunk gets thicker, it gradually buries the bases of the lower branches and, if the tree is used for timber later on, these bases appear again as *knots* in the wood. The earliest water-carrying tubes gradually get squashed in the centre of the trunk and they are then unable to carry water. They form a very dense wood called *heartwood*. Wood which is still carrying water is called *sapwood*.

Around the outside of the trunk there is a layer of bark. It consists largely of cork and it is often quite soft. Its job is to protect the wood underneath. New layers of cork are produced each year as the trunk gets thicker, and the older bark on the outside splits and perhaps flakes off. The bark pattern can often be used to identify the tree. The sweet chestnut bark has spiral ridges, while the plane tree bark flakes off in patches to give a mottled appearance. Beech trees can be recognised by their very smooth grey bark. It is always very thin because the old bark crumbles to dust and never builds up any thickness. The cork oak, which comes from the Mediterranean area, produces extra

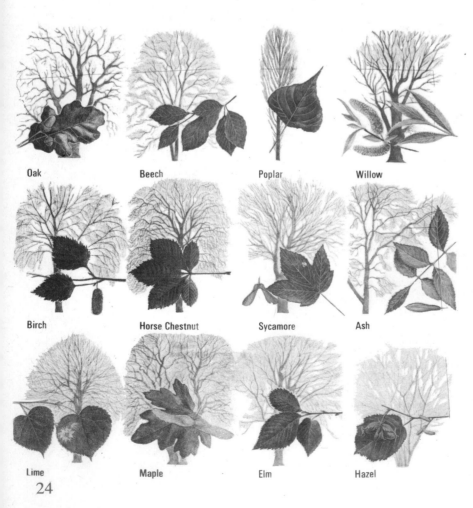

Oak   Beech   Poplar   Willow

Birch   Horse Chestnut   Sycamore   Ash

Lime   Maple   Elm   Hazel

24

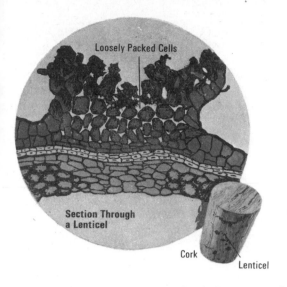

Loosely Packed Cells

Section Through
a Lenticel

Cork

Lenticel

Air enters the tree-trunk through lenticels – groups of loosely packed cells in the bark. It is the lenticels in the cork that allow the air through.

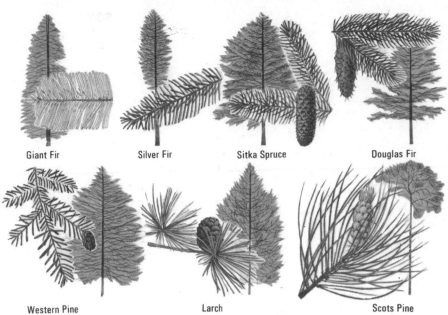

Giant Fir

Silver Fir

Sitka Spruce

Douglas Fir

Western Pine

Larch

Scots Pine

thick cork which can be stripped off every few years without hurting the tree. This is where we get bottle corks and other cork objects from.

Conifers

There are two main groups of trees: those with cones (the conifers), and those with flowers. The conifers include pine, larch, spruce (used for Christmas trees), cedar and yew. The group also includes not only the largest of all trees but the largest of all living things. These are the giant redwood and wellingtonia trees of California. Some of them reach heights of nearly 400 feet and the trunks may be more than 20 feet across at the base. A tree of this size would weigh well over 1000 tons, yet it starts life as a tiny seed little bigger than a pin's head. Conifers have narrow, needle-like leaves and most of them are evergreens. This means that they carry leaves all through the year, although each leaf lives only two or three years. Coniferous trees have no flowers and they generally carry their seeds in woody cones.

The tough leaves of conifers are able to stand up to strong winds and severe cold, and so we find that conifers are the dominant trees in the cooler parts of the world. Huge coniferous forests stretch across Canada and northern Europe. Most of our timber is obtained from conifers today, and so large plantations of spruces and other cone-bearing trees are springing up all over the world to meet the demand.

Flowering Trees

The flowering trees generally have broad, flat leaves and many kinds of trees can be recognised from their leaves alone. The trees that grow in tropical forests are usually *evergreens* – because conditions allow them to grow all the year round – but most of those

Above: The conifers are recognised by their narrow leaves.

Below: Little remains of the thick forests which once covered Britain.

Prehistoric Britain

Britain today

growing in the temperate regions are *deciduous* trees. This means that they drop all their leaves in autumn and stand bare through the winter. The next year's leaves are wrapped up in the winter buds which, like the leaves themselves, can be used to identify the trees. Examples of deciduous trees include elm, beech, maple, ash and many kinds of oak.

Horse chestnut, lilac, apple, and many other garden trees possess large and attractive flowers. These flowers attract insects, which feed on the nectar and then carry pollen to the next flower they visit. This transfer of pollen from flower to flower is called pollination and it is very important because the trees cannot form seeds without it. But not all trees have bright, showy flowers. Many tree flowers are dull green and very hard to see. Because they do not see the flowers, many people do not realise that trees such as oaks and elms have flowers. But they do: the oak carries little strings of greenish flowers, something like the catkins of hazel. These dull flowers are not visited by insects and they simply scatter their pollen in the wind. Some of it will reach another flower and enable it to set seed. Very often the trees flower before their leaves open, thus giving the pollen a better chance of reaching other flowers.

Tree Products

Wood has always been a very important material to man, first of all for making his spears and arrows and for building his fires, and later for building his houses. Even today, with steel and concrete being used in greater and greater amounts, timber is still a most important building material.

The other major commodity that we get from trees is food, usually in the form of fruit.

25

Flower Families

Flowering plants belong to one of two great classes, *monocotyledons* or *dicotyledons,* according to whether their seeds possess one or two seed leaves respectively. There are other differences too. Monocotyledons are almost all herbs (non-woody plants), they have leaves with parallel veins, stem-veins scattered throughout the stem, and flower-parts (stamens, carpels, petals and sepals) in threes or multiples of three. Dicotyledons contain many woody species. Their leaves are generally net-veined, and the stem veins occur in a definite cylinder down the stem. Their flower parts are generally found in fours and fives.

Flower Families

Grasses *(Gramineae)* are monocotyledons with long, strap-shaped leaves and hollow stems. Their flowers are green and not very obvious. When the flowers are ripe, the yellow anthers hang out in the wind so that their pollen will blow away. Cereal grasses are mankind's most important food crops.

The rose family *(Rosaceae)* consists of herbs, shrubs and trees. Their flowers usually have five similarly shaped, separate petals, five sepals, and a large number of stamens and carpels. Cultivated roses have fewer stamens and more petals. Apples, plums, strawberries and blackberries belong to the rose family.

The pea family *(Leguminosae)* usually have compound leaves, with two rows of little leaflets growing from a central leaf stalk. The leaves often have tendrils which help the plants climb. The flowers have five petals and are all of a similar shape, with a large *standard* petal at the back. The fruits are pods.

The parsley family *(Umbelliferae)* is characterized by its *inflorescence,* or flower-head, which is called an *umbel.* The main flowering stem stops growing and a number of smaller flower-bearing stalks grow out from its tip. The flowers are tiny and are generally white or yellow. The stems are hollow.

The daisy family *(Compositae)* have their tiny flowers packed together in dense heads or clusters. What is usually called the flower is really a collection of small flowers, or *florets,* grouped together. The flowers later develop parachutes of hairs.

The cabbage family *(Cruciferae)* is quite easy to recognise because the flowers have four petals. There are six stamens as a rule, four long and two short. As well as all the cabbages, this family includes wallflowers, honesty, watercress and candytuft.

26

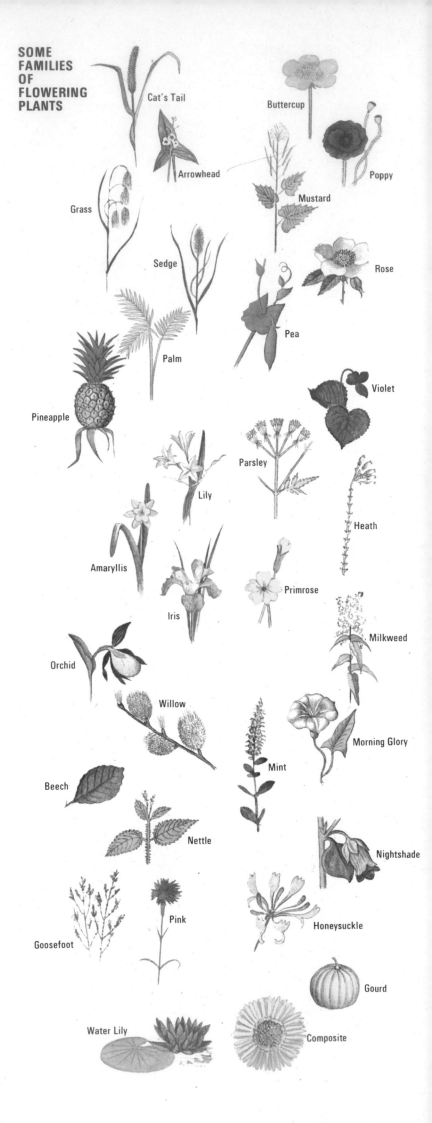

SOME FAMILIES OF FLOWERING PLANTS

Cat's Tail
Buttercup
Arrowhead
Poppy
Grass
Mustard
Sedge
Rose
Pea
Palm
Pineapple
Violet
Parsley
Lily
Amaryllis
Heath
Iris
Primrose
Milkweed
Orchid
Willow
Morning Glory
Beech
Mint
Nettle
Nightshade
Goosefoot
Pink
Honeysuckle
Gourd
Water Lily
Composite

Flowering Plants

The life of a flowering plant begins at the moment of fertilization, that is when a male cell from a pollen grain joins with a tiny egg cell in a flower. The fertilized cell will eventually grow and form a new plant. But the newly fertilized cell cannot begin an independent life right away. It cannot grow without food, and this food must be provided by the parent plant. So the little cell remains inside the ovary of the parent plant. Fed by the parent, it grows and multiplies and forms a little embryo. This is a miniature plant, with root, shoot, and either one or two special leaves called *cotyledons,* or *seed-leaves.* Additional food is laid down around the embryo or in its seed leaves, and while this is going on a tough coat forms around the outside. The embryo, with its surrounding food reserves and its tough coat, is now called a seed. It is ready to leave the parent plant and begin life on its own.

Germination

Protected by the tough coats, seeds can usually remain at rest for quite a long time. They will not grow unless they have both water and warmth, so they will not grow when stored indoors and they will not grow if they are sown in cold weather. But when conditions are right they will spring to life and germinate. The germinating seed absorbs water and swells up. The seed coat bursts and the little root pushes its way out. No matter how the seed is sown, the root will always turn downwards to anchor the plant in the soil and to begin absorbing the water needed for further growth. Shortly after the root appears, the shoot pushes its way out and begins to grow upwards. It will produce the stem and leaves. The seed leaves may grow up with the shoot or they may remain below ground in the seed coat. Growth so far has been at the expense of the food stored up in the seed, but this food is soon exhausted and the young plant begins to make its own food by photosynthesis.

Using the food made in its leaves, the young plant grows larger. Excess food is stored in various parts of the plant and some of it will eventually be used in the production of flowers.

The Flower

The main function of the flower is to reproduce the plant by forming more seeds, and the essential parts of the flower are the *stamens* and the *carpels.* The stamens pro-

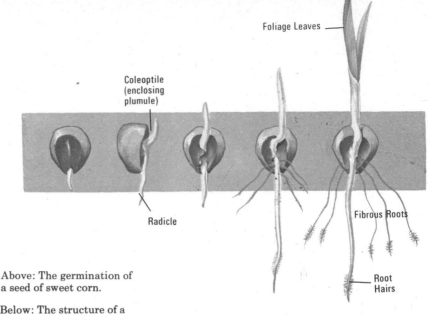

Above: The germination of a seed of sweet corn.

Below: The structure of a flower.

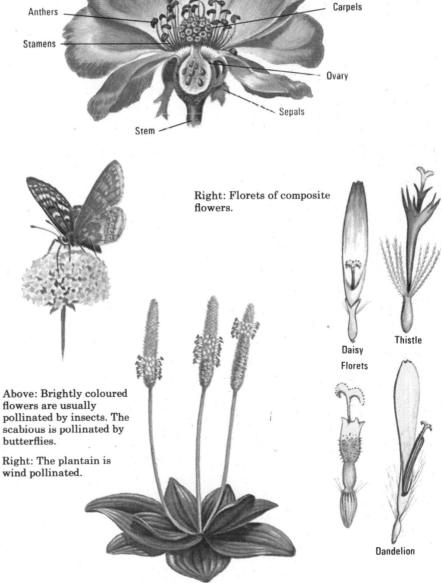

Right: Florets of composite flowers.

Above: Brightly coloured flowers are usually pollinated by insects. The scabious is pollinated by butterflies.

Right: The plantain is wind pollinated.

duce the pollen, while the carpels contain one or more ovules which later become seeds. Most flowers contain both stamens and carpels, but some plants carry their stamens and carpels in separate flowers. The vegetable marrow is a good example. Some species even carry their stamens and carpels on different plants. The holly does this and, as the berries develop from the carpels, it means that some holly trees never carry berries.

Pollination

As well as the stamens and carpels, most flowers have *sepals* and *petals*. The sepals are on the outside and their main job is to protect the young flower before it opens. They fold back or fall off when the flower opens. The petals are generally brightly coloured and their main function is to attract insects to the flowers. They are aided in this job by the flower's scent and nectar. The insects are very important for the flowers because they carry pollen about with them and some of it rubs off on to the carpels. This transfer of pollen from the stamens to the carpels is called *pollination* and it is the first step towards producing seeds. The pollen must reach a special part of the carpel known as the *stigma,* and then it can make its way inside the carpel.

Although most flowers are pollinated by insects, the grasses and a good many trees are pollinated by the wind. Their flowers are not brightly coloured and they have neither scent nor nectar. Very often they do not even have any petals. Wind-pollinated trees frequently have their stamens and carpels on different flowers, and the male (stamen-containing) flowers are often grouped into hanging catkins. The slightest breeze sways the catkins and shakes out the pollen. Grass pollen is scattered when the wind shakes the stamens, which hang from the flowers on slender stalks.

Wind pollination is rather wasteful because large amounts of pollen never reach another flower. The carpels do, however, have large feathery stigmas which increase the chances of their trapping some pollen. Wind-pollinated trees frequently produce their flowers before the leaves appear, thus allowing the pollen a better chance of reaching the carpels. Examples include the hazel, ash, and elm trees.

Fruits and Seeds

When a pollen grain has landed on a stigma of the right kind of flower it sends out a tiny tube which grows down into the carpel. Cells from the pollen grain move down the tube and one of them will join with an egg cell inside one of the ovules to begin seed formation as already described.

While the seed and embryo are developing in the ovule, the surrounding carpel is also changing. It becomes the fruit. There are many kinds of fruits, ranging from hard nuts to soft berries. The job of the fruit is to protect the developing seed or seeds inside it and then to help scatter them when they are ripe. Some fruits have 'wings' or feathery 'parachutes' which help them to float away on the wind. Others have hooks which catch into animal fur. Juicy fruits like cherries and blackberries attract birds, which eat the juicy parts and spit out the hard seeds. All of these methods help the seeds to get away from the parent plant and perhaps find a suitable place to grow into a new plant.

Seeds are dispersed in various ways. Some fruits have 'wings' or feathery parachutes which help them float away on the wind. Some seeds are scattered when the fruits burst open. Others are shaken through holes in the fruits.

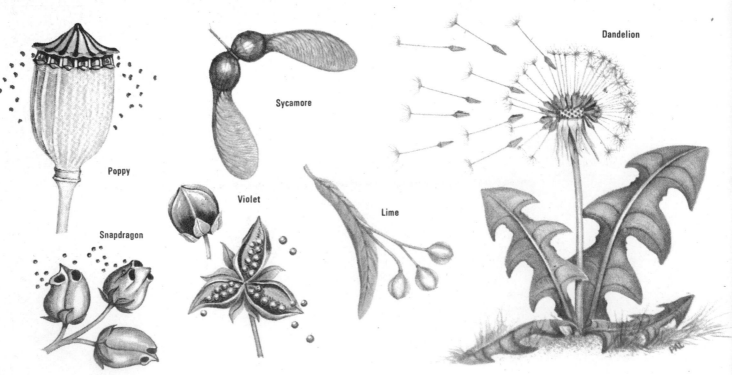

Poppy

Snapdragon

Sycamore

Violet

Lime

Dandelion

Road Transport

After the fall of the Roman Empire, the roads which the Romans had built across Europe were allowed to fall into disrepair. In the Middle Ages, rutted tracks used by horsemen or slow-moving carts covered Europe.

By the eighteenth century, there was a great need to improve roads as more and more goods and people moved about the country. Turnpike trusts were formed to improve roads, and engineers like Metcalf, McAdam and Telford introduced new methods of road-laying. The new, surfaced roads brought about the great coaching era. This reached its peak in the 1820's when fast, passenger-carrying stage-coaches served most of the country's main roads, and the largest inns kept up to 2,500 horses to provide fresh teams.

The stage-coach era was brought to an end by the growth of railways and road transport was reduced to local traffic. Then, at the end of the nineteenth century, a new form of road transport appeared. In 1885, two German engineers, working independently, produced vehicles that can be considered the forerunners of modern automobiles. The engineers, Karl Benz and Gottlieb Daimler, both used internal combustion engines with petrol as fuel. Their cars were slow, open to the weather and bumpy to ride in because the wheels had solid tyres. From then on, however, the development of the automobile was rapid.

Sedan Chair

Eighteenth century Phaeton

Eighteenth century mail coach

Above: The early development of road transport. The early 1800's were the heyday of the coach in Europe. In North America, stage-coaches flourished for some time in the American West until the penetration of the railways made them obsolete.

In 1913, Henry Ford introduced in the U.S.A. a successful method of mass production in which the automobile was assembled part by part as it moved down a line of workers. This method of assembly line production, using conveyer belts, is the one used to produce automobiles today. Ford concentrated on one model, his famous Model T, or 'Tin Lizzie'.

Since that time, trucks have carried more and more goods, buses and coaches have replaced many railway services, and everywhere fast, cheap automobiles crowd the roads.

Automobile Engine Systems
The *engine* of the automobile provides the power to turn the car wheels. The engine power comes from burning a mixture of petrol and air in the *cylinders*. Most engines have four or six cylinders in a straight line. Some are in the shape of a 'V'.

Inside each cylinder is a close-fitting *piston* which can move up and down. The gases produced by burning the fuel push the piston down. The pistons are connected to a *crankshaft* and force it round. At one end of the crankshaft is a heavy *flywheel*, which smoothes out the motion.

Most engines work on what is known as the *four-stroke cycle*. This means that the piston only produces power on one out of four *strokes,* or movements. Some engines work on a *two-stroke* cycle and produce power on every downward stroke.

Fuel for the engine is forced by a pump along a pipe to the *carburettor*. In the

Right: A steam road carriage of the mid-nineteenth century. The steam engine was to prove no rival to the petrol engine in the field of road transport.

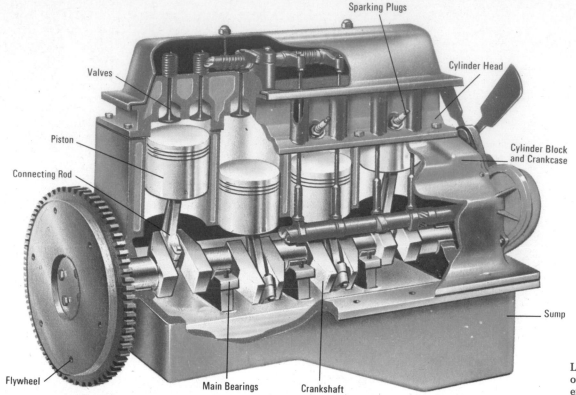

Sparking Plugs

Valves

Piston

Connecting Rod

Cylinder Head

Cylinder Block
and Crankcase

Sump

Flywheel

Main Bearings

Crankshaft

Left: The principal parts
of a four-cylinder petrol
engine.

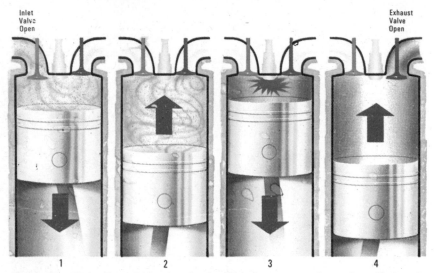

Inlet
Valve
Open

Exhaust
Valve
Open

1 2 3 4

The four-stroke cycle. 1, Induction Stroke. The piston moves down the cylinder, thus creating a partial vacuum above it. A mixture of petrol and air is forced into the cylinder by means of atmospheric pressure. 2, Compression Stroke. The piston moves up the cylinder, compressing the petrol and air mixture. 3, Power stroke. When the piston reaches about the end of the compression stroke, the petrol and air mixture is ignited by an electric spark. The rapid expansion of the hot gases drives the piston downwards on the only working stroke of the cycle. 4, Exhaust Stroke. The piston moves upwards and the spent gases are forced out of the cylinder past the open exhaust valve.

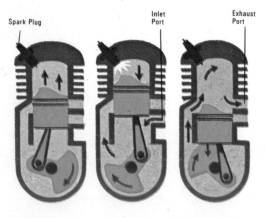

Spark Plug

Inlet
Port

Exhaust
Port

Left: The two-stroke cycle, where power is produced on every downward stroke. 1, Upward compression stroke. 2, Downward power stroke. 3, Lower part of downward stroke where spent gases are expelled and fresh fuel enters the cylinder.

carburettor, the petrol mixes with air drawn in by the engine to form a fine spray that burns easily.

The petrol mixture enters the engine cylinders through valves and is ignited by a spark when electricity 'jumps' across a gap between the metal points of a *sparking plug*. The sparks are needed in the cylinders at different times. A rotating arm in the *distributor* 'distributes' the electricity to each sparking plug in turn.

Diesel engines, used in most heavy trucks, differ from petrol engines because they have no sparking plugs or carburettors. Diesel oil is injected into the engine directly and burnt by the heat of air compressed in the cylinders. It thus works by compression ignition rather than by the spark ignition of petrol engines. Fuel injection is also used in some petrol engines.

The battery is charged continually while the engine is running by the *dynamo*. It provides power not only for ignition but also for the starter motor to start the engine, the lights, the horn, and the windscreen wipers.

When fuel burns inside the engine cylinders, it produces a lot of heat. This heat must be removed if the engine is to work properly. Most engines are cooled by circulating water through them. But some are cooled by blowing air over them.

In a water-cooled engine, water is pumped through passages called *water jackets* surrounding the cylinders. It absorbs heat there and passes into the tiny tubes of the *radiator*. A fan driven by the engine draws

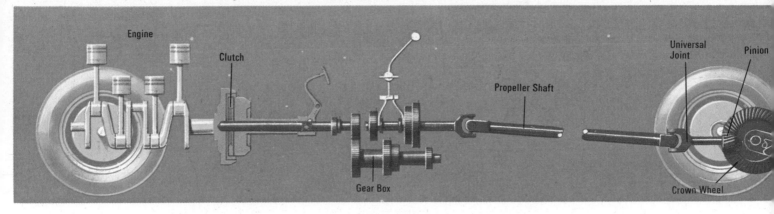

cold air over these tubes to cool the water. The colder water then returns to the engine.

The many moving metal parts in the engine must be continually oiled, or lubricated, to prevent wear. Oil from a trough called a *sump* is pumped through a *filter* to the moving parts. Some parts receive oil directly; others are merely splashed.

Transmission System

The transmission system of the automobile transfers power between the engine and the road wheels. A driver uses the *clutch* to disconnect the engine from the rest of the system when he wishes to change gear or stop.

The *friction* clutch contains sprung metal plates and the *fluid* clutch contains oil to transfer power between the flywheel and the gearbox. The fluid clutch works automatically.

The driver changes gear to make his automobile go faster or slower for the same engine speed and to reverse. The *gearbox* consists of a number of toothed wheels of different sizes which mesh together to turn at different speeds. In cars with *automatic transmission,* the gears change automatically.

The *propeller shaft* takes the power to a *final drive* at the rear axle. This transfers the power to the driving wheels. More cars are now being built with front-wheel drive. In this case, no propeller shaft is needed.

Steering and Braking

The driver steers his automobile by turning the *steering wheel.* This movement travels down the *steering column* into the *steering box,* and from there by a system of rods and arms to one of the road wheels. The two wheels are connected by the *track rod* so that one turns with the other.

Every car has two independent braking systems. The foot brake acts on all four wheels and acts by hydraulic (liquid) pressure. The hand brake acts on the back wheels only and is linked to them by rods or cables.

Each wheel has a brake drum or disc on it. When the driver applies the brakes, a pad of hard material called a *brake lining* is forced against the drum or disc and slows it down.

Suspension Systems

For a comfortable ride, every automobile must have an efficient suspension system. Most suspension units include springs over each wheel to cushion the vehicle from bumpy roads. In *independent suspension,* each wheel can move up and down without affecting the others. *Dampers,* or *shock absorbers,* are included in suspension systems to prevent the vehicle bouncing on the springs too much. In most cars the front and rear suspensions are separate. But in some, they are linked in such a way that when the front of the car goes over a bump, the back of the car rises too.

The bodies of some automobiles are made of fibre-glass, but most are made of steel sheet by *integral,* or *unitary construction.* Huge steel presses shape the body as a strong, rigid shell.

The other body parts and mechanical units are attached to the shell. Some automobiles and heavy vehicles have a separate frame, or *chassis,* on which the body and other units are mounted.

Above: The transmission system of an automobile.

No Pitch

No Bounce

Above: Some cars have hydrolastic suspension which dampens pitching and bouncing by the transfer of fluid between the front and rear wheels. The diagrams show the hydrolastic response to pitch and bounce.

Right: The main braking system of a modern car acts by hydraulic pressure. The hand brake works simply by metal rods or cables. In the diagram, disc brakes are shown on the front wheels and drum brakes on the rear wheels.

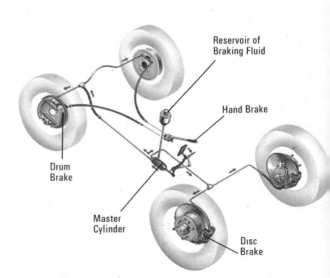

Rail Transport

Until the 1800's, transport by land was desperately slow. Roads were in a terrible condition, and travel by stage-coach was both uncomfortable and unreliable. Then, in 1803, the British engineer Richard Trevithick thought of mounting the newly developed steam carriage on rails to provide a smoother ride. A year later he demonstrated the first rail locomotive. The idea of 'railways' was not new, however. Horse-drawn railways were being used in most large mines at the time.

The first railway line—the Stockton and Darlington colliery line—was opened in 1825. George Stephenson built the 10-mile line and its first engine—*Locomotion*. He built the first passenger line and the engines

Above: On Japan's New Tokkaido line trains travel at an average speed of over 100 m.p.h.

Left: The world's first public railway opened on 25th September, 1825. George Stephenson's locomotive *Locomotion* hauled 12 wagons of coal and 21 wagons containing passengers at a speed of 10 miles an hour between Stockton and Darlington in north-east England.

Below: Railway journeys across the United States became possible in 1869, when railways from east and west met in Utah.

Locomotive Design

The Railway Age was made possible by the steam locomotive. Today, many countries have changed to electric or diesel locomotives which are cheaper and cleaner to run. But the steam locomotive is a much simpler piece of machinery, and it will be some years before it is replaced everywhere.

Modern steam locomotives work on much the same principles as George Stephenson's *Rocket*. Coal or oil is burned in the *firebox* and tubes carry the smoke and hot gases through a boiler where water changes to steam. The steam forces *pistons* back and forth in the *cylinders*. The pistons are linked to the *driving wheels* by *connecting rods*. The fuel and water for the firebox are carried in a towed *tender*.

Electric locomotives are driven by electric

for it, too. This line was the Liverpool and Manchester Railway (1830), and the first locomotive to run on it was the famous *Rocket*.

From then on, development was rapid. As early as the 1850's it was possible to travel by train through several European countries. Soon, lines were opened all over the world, most of them using British locomotives to start with. With the growth of railways, goods and raw materials could be moved speedily between mines and factories, towns and ports. Towns began to spring up in previously uninhabited regions.

Nowhere was the impact of the railways greater than on the vast continent of North America. After the American Civil War, work started from both sides of the continent on the 'Great American Railway' from the Pacific to the Atlantic coasts. In 1869 the two sections met. Today, the United States has a greater track mileage than any other country—almost a quarter of a million miles.

motors connected to the driving wheels. The current to power the motors is picked up either from a conductor rail or an overhead wire. An electric locomotive is a highly efficient machine. It needs no preparation for service. It can accelerate rapidly, haul very heavy loads, and also run at high speed over long distances. So it is an ideal power unit for fast lines where the volume of traffic justifies the cost of electrification. The world speed record is held by two French electric locomotives which reached 205 miles per hour on a test run.

Diesel locomotives are classified according to the way in which the power from the engine is transmitted to the wheels. In the *diesel-electric* type, the engines turn generators which produce electricity. The electricity powers motors to drive the wheels. The *diesel-mechanical* type has the same type of transmission system (clutch and gearbox) as a road vehicle. The *diesel-hydraulic* type has an automatic fluid transmission. The most powerful diesel locomotives yet built are about 4,800 horsepower.

For short- and medium-distance passenger services, diesel or electric power units are often built into train sets consisting of two, three or four coaches permanently coupled together with a driving cab at each end. If a longer train is required, two or more train sets can be coupled together. Multiple-unit electric trains are used on underground railway systems.

Gas-turbine locomotives are now in service in some countries. Fuel is burned in their power unit to produce hot gases which spin the blades of a turbine. The drive from the turbine may be mechanical (gears) or electric (generators and motors).

Modern Railways

Railways are now being modernized throughout the world in order to meet competition from road and air transport. Track-laying and maintenance are now highly mechanized. Rails are being welded together to make continuous lengths for smoother running. Built-in automatic warning systems on the track and in the locomotives help to prevent crashes. Signalling is by swift, push-button control.

At present, railways carry more freight (goods) than passenger traffic. Many goods travel in standard-sized containers, which simplifies handling. There are tanker wagons for bulk liquids, multi-decked transporters for vehicles, and refrigerator vans for foodstuffs.

Speeds approaching 100 miles per hour

Above: The Victoria line, a new underground railway beneath London, opened in 1969. This line has many advanced features. The speed of the trains is regulated automatically to make journeys as quick as possible.

Above: The monorail is a current development in rail transport. This one in Tokyo runs on top of a rail with wheels on either side to steady it. In other designs the train may be suspended from a rail.

Underground Railways

Many cities have electric railways which run below ground in the central area and may come out into the open in the suburbs. In North America they are called *subways*. In some countries they are called *Metros*, after the first Metropolitan Railway.

The tunnels are often close to the surface, and are made by digging a large trench and roofing it. Some systems also have deep-level tunnels which are bored through the ground. In London, deep-level tunnels form a group called the 'tubes'.

Trains are multiple units, with automatic sliding doors. They usually have plenty of standing room because journeys are short and the trains are very crowded at times. An automatic colour-light signalling system is used with only short sections between which enables the trains to follow each other quickly. Moving staircases, or *escalators*, cope with the periodic flood of passengers from the trains. Some stations even have moving platforms to speed the flow.

The world's first underground railway was the 'Metropolitan Railway' opened in London in 1863. In 1890 the first deep-level 'tube' was opened, running beneath the River Thames. London's underground system is still the world's largest, with over 240 miles of route including 70 miles of bored tunnel. The New York system, opened in 1904, is almost as large and even more compact. It carries more than 1,600 million passengers a year. The Paris Métro was opened in 1900. Its trains have rubber tyres which makes it quieter than most other systems. This method has been adopted in Montreal and will also be used in Mexico City.

are becoming a common feature. On Japan's New Tokkaido line the train travels at an *average* speed of over 100 m.p.h. In the future, regular services at 200 m.p.h. may be common. Already, the French *Aérotrain*, which 'hovers' on a single rail, has exceeded 235 m.p.h.

It is probably in 'monorails', 'hover' trains and a new method of electric propulsion called *linear induction* that the future of the railways lies.

.E. —C

North America

The Land

North America is the third largest of the world's continents and occupies nearly a fifth of the Earth's land area. Only Asia and Africa are larger. Its physical limits are Panama in the south, and Alaska and Greenland in the north. The northern four-fifths of the continent are occupied by Canada and the United States, while the remainder is made up of Mexico and Central America. There are also a large number of islands, the most important of which are the Caribbean Islands and Greenland, the world's largest.

North America has an area of 9,635,000 square miles. It is almost as wide as it is long: from north to south it stretches some 4,500 miles, and from east to west about 4,000 miles. It has a population of 295,600,000.

Its land regions are fairly well marked. The Lawrentian region is an area of low-

Above: Pulpwood logs and grain elevators in Ontario, Wheat and wood are two of Canada's major exports.

Left: A panoramic view of the New York skyline.

Below: The Canadian prairies are one of the world's greatest wheat growing regions. The fields sometimes stretch unbroken to the horizon.

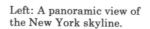

Above: Citrus groves in Florida, the sub-tropical extremity of the U.S.A.

Right: Eskimos inhabit the cold wastes of northern Canada. In recent years, special government schemes have enabled many Eskimos to leave the old tribal life and become skilled workers.

ARCTIC OCEAN

GREENLAND

HUDSON BAY

CANADA

St. Lawrence

Vancouver
Edmonton
Calgary
Winnipeg
Missouri
Quebec
Ottawa
Montreal
Minneapolis
Toronto
Boston
Milwaukee
Hamilton
Buffalo
Detroit
NEW YORK
Chicago
Cleveland
San Francisco
U.S.A.
Philadelphia
Denver
Indianapolis
Pittsburgh
Baltimore
Kansas City
Cincinnati
Los Angeles
St. Louis
Washington

PACIFIC OCEAN

ROCKY MOUNTAINS

Phoenix
Memphis
Atlanta

ATLANTIC OCEAN

Rio Grande
Dallas

New Orleans
Mississippi

Houston

GULF OF MEXICO

Miami

MEXICO

Havana
CUBA
DOMINICAN
REPUBLIC
PUERTO
RICO

Mexico City
HAITI
JAMAICA

CARIBBEAN SEA

GUATEMALA
BRITISH
HONDURAS
HONDURAS

NICARAGUA

COSTA RICA
PANAMA

60°N
20°N
140°W
100°W
60°W

0   200   400   600   800   1000

Scale in Miles

Legend:

Cool Coniferous Forest

Temperate Forest

Tropical Forest

Equatorial Rain Forest

Grassland   Temperate Desert

Savanna   Tundra

Hot Desert   Mountain Vegetation

lying rocky land that stretches round Hudson Bay. It extends from the Arctic Ocean in the north to Labrador in the east. Much of it is unexplored forest, well watered with icy lakes and streams.

The Appalachian region consists of a range of mountains running south-westwards from Quebec in Canada to Alabama in south-eastern United States. The Appalachians include the Allegheny plateau and other mountain ranges.

In the south of the continent, bordering the Gulf of Mexico and the Atlantic Ocean, there are flat coastal plains. Vast areas of these plains are swampy.

To the west lie the great Western Highlands. They are called the Cordilleras in Central America, and the Rocky Mountains in the rest of the continent. They stretch from Alaska to Central America. The highest peak in North America is Mt McKinley (20,320 ft), in Alaska, but in the Colorado Rockies alone there are 55 peaks that reach 14,000 feet or more. Running parallel to the Rockies are the Coast and Cascade ranges, and the Sierra Nevada. They border a narrow, fertile, coastal strip along the shores of the Pacific.

The Great Plains form a 1,500-mile wide belt, including part of central and northern Canada and the interior of the United States. These are great grazing and grain-growing lands.

Rivers flow westwards to the west of the Rockies, and eastwards, southwards, and northwards on the eastern side of the mountains. Westward-flowing rivers, such as the

Above: In winter the Niagara Falls sometimes freeze into a curtain of ice.

Below: Independence Hall, Philadelphia, site of the signing of the Declaration of Independence in 1776.

Yukon, Snake, and Colorado are generally swift torrents. The Missouri-Mississippi river system is 3,700 miles long, one of the longest in the world. The St. Lawrence flows eastwards and connects the Great Lakes with the Atlantic.

The Great Lakes, on the borders of Canada and the United States, are the most important in the world. They are lakes Superior, Michigan, Huron, Erie and Ontario. The best known falls are the Niagara Falls, which are famed for their striking scenery.

The climate in the far south is always warm, and in the far north it is always cold. Most of the continent has warm summers and cold winters. Rainfall is heavy (up to 140 inches a year) on the western slopes of the Rockies; but in the desert regions there may be only about 1½ inches of rain a year.

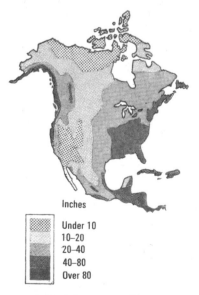

Inches

Under 10
10–20
20–40
40–80
Over 80

The eastern half of North America has an anual rainfall between 20 and 70 inches, the amount generally increasing towards the south-east. The western half of the continent is semi-arid except for the Pacific coast where the rainfall exceeds 100 inches in places.

January

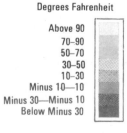

Degrees Fahrenheit

Above 90
70–90
50–70
30–50
10–30
Minus 10—10
Minus 30—Minus 10
Below Minus 30

July

Over much of North America there is a considerable range of seasonal temperatures. There are no east-west mountain barriers to hinder the southward movement of cold polar air in the winter or the northward movement of hot air from the Gulf of Mexico in the summer. The moderating effect of the ocean is confined to a narrow coastal strip in the west.

Above: White House, the official residence at Washington of the President of the U.S.A.

half of its wheat harvest to other countries. But in the Latin American countries of the continent the land is so poor and farming methods and machinery so out-of-date that there is barely enough food produced to feed the population. Coffee, bananas and sugar are the chief crops of most of the Central American countries.

North America has some of the world's richest deposits of minerals. The most important are coal, petroleum, gold, iron, nickel, silver, lead, zinc and copper. Both Canada and the United States are among the leading industrial nations of the world, with large manufacturing centres in many places. But the Latin American countries import a large quantity of their manufactured goods, because local industries cannot supply all the country's needs.

The People

Most of the people in the Latin American countries of the continent speak Spanish, but in the United States and Canada, Eng-

Flora and Fauna

North America is still very rich in animal life, but as the population increases and spreads, the wildlife is rapidly disappearing from the continent. A hundred years ago the plains were filled with enormous herds of bison. Today, only a few herds remain, carefully protected in game preserves. Nevertheless, the woods of central and eastern North America still hold black bears, deer, musquash, porcupines and beavers. The Rockies are the home of eagles, grizzly bears, elk, and moose. In the far north are found some of the most valuable fur-bearing animals, including Arctic foxes, fur seals and polar bears. Tropical creatures such as alligators, monkeys, jaguars, ant-eaters, armadillos and a host of colourful birds inhabit Central America.

North America's plant life varies from the mosses and lichens that survive in the coldest regions of the Arctic, to the desert cactus of the waterless areas of the southwest. Trees include the red-woods and sequoias of California, the largest trees in the world, maples (whose leaf is the emblem of Canada) and tropical palms. Canada has enormous forests of fir, spruce and pine. The vast grasslands of the Great Plains feed herds of sheep and cattle.

Resources

North American agriculture is strikingly uneven. In the United States and Canada there are millions of acres of fertile land, and the yield per acre is constantly increasing because farmers use the latest equipment and methods. Canada exports more than

Right: Sledge dogs are still a necessity in northern Canada and Greenland despite the advent of motorized transportation. They are able to cover more than 75 miles per day.

Below: An onyx offering bowl in the form of an ocelot from Mexico (c. A.D. 600).

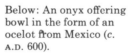

An Aztec sacrificial knife with a chalcedony blade and wooden haft inlaid with turquoise and shell (late 15th century).

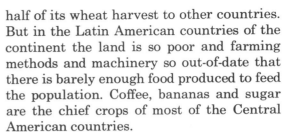

lish (with some French in Canada) is the main language.

Some of the world's greatest cities are located in North America. The largest Canadian cities are Montreal, Toronto and Vancouver. In the United States, New York City, Los Angeles, Chicago, Philadelphia, Detroit and Houston are the main population centres, each with more than a million people. In the Latin American countries Mexico City and Havana, in Cuba, are the largest cities.

The first European explorers reached North America nearly 500 years ago. The wild region they found was inhabited by Indians who are believed to have come originally from Asia. They have certain similarities to the Mongols. The Aztec and Maya Indians of Mexico had developed a high standard of civilization, but the northern Indians lived in primitive conditions.

In the far north the Eskimos arrived from Asia about 2,000 years ago. Most inhabitants of the continent have European ancestors, but about a tenth of the people are Negroes, originally brought from Africa as slaves.

The High Plains east of the Rockies are the great ranching lands of North America. The total cattle population of the U.S.A. is second only to that of India.

The states of the U.S.A. (excluding Alaska and Hawaii). The original Thirteen, the states which signed the Declaration of Independence in 1776, were Delaware, Pennsylvania, New Jersey, Georgia, Connecticut, Massachusetts, Maryland, South Carolina, New Hampshire, Virginia, New York, North Carolina and Rhode Island. The biggest single step in the development of the U.S.A. was the Louisiana Purchase of 1803 which doubled the size of the country.

Fuel for Power

Fossil Fuels

All the common fuels we burn to provide heat and power come from the ground. Coal, petroleum and natural gas were all formed millions of years ago deep down in the Earth from decayed plant and animal matter. These fuels are really 'stored sunlight', because the plants needed the Sun's energy to grow and the animals needed the plants as food. They are often called *fossil fuels*. Wood, too, was once an important fuel.

Petroleum is by far the best of the fossil fuels. Pound for pound, it has one and a half times the heating value of coal, and three times that of wood.

Oil Prospecting

There was a time when oil was discovered almost by accident; a slight seepage of oil on the ground indicating the presence of large

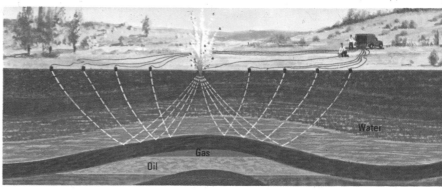

Above: Scientists detect oil beneath the ground by exploding small charges and registering the patterns of shock waves produced. The waves are reflected back by certain underground layers, telling the scientists about the rocks below.

Below: An oil refinery seen through a heat haze caused by burning waste gases.

or small deposits far underground. Today more scientific methods are used, and underground oil can be detected and the size of deposits estimated without having to search for tell-tale patches of surface oil.

The instrument most used is the *seismograph*, which is also used to detect and measure the strengths of distant earthquakes. A seismograph is basically a small pendulum which moves when the ground vibrates. In *seismic oil prospecting* a number of small seismographs are placed in the

ground over a wide area. These instruments contain special devices (similar to a microphone) which transmit a vibrating electric current to a portable control station when the ground vibrates. A charge of dynamite is now set off in the area, and the seismographs measure the resulting vibrations in the ground. Some of these may go deep down into the ground and be reflected back to the surface, where the seismographs can detect and measure this underground 'reflection'. Depending upon the measurements made the geologists can decide whether or not the underground layers reflecting back the vibrations are likely to contain oil deposits.

The oil which is found far underground does not exist as pools of liquid. It is dispersed as tiny droplets. When we drill down to the deposits, however, the pressure of surrounding water and natural gas deposits drives these droplets together to form actual liquid pools.

Oil Wells

The main feature of an oil well is the *derrick,* a tall metal framework supporting a block and tackle holding up the drill pipe. This is a hollow steel rod which carries the *drill bit,* a diamond-studded toothed steel cone which can gnaw its way through solid rock. At ground level the drill rod is clamped to a circular steel *table,* which turns the drill rod, and is itself turned by a petrol engine connected to it by a belt or chain. As the drill gradually moves downwards it is periodically hoisted back to the surface by the block and tackle, and a fresh section of drill rod is connected. In time the drill rod may extend in sections to depths of a thousand feet or more.

The rock powder which is produced by the rotating drill bit is brought to the surface by pumping down a mixture of soft mud and water through the central hole in the drill pipe. This mud and water mixture then returns to the surface in the space between the drill pipe and the hole which has been drilled. The walls of this hole are prevented from caving in by the continual insertion of lengths of steel tubing, or *casings,* which are lowered into the hole and fixed by having concrete poured in around them.

When oil is struck the derrick is removed and the gushing well is plugged with a complicated system of valves called a *christmas tree.* This is connected with the pipelines which will carry the oil to the refinery or to the port where waiting tankers will load for transport.

Oil Refining

The dark brown thick liquid which comes from an oil well must be refined before the wealth of raw materials it contains can be

Above: Laying a pipeline to carry natural gas across the country.

used. The bewildering maze of steel towers and coiling pipes of a modern oil refinery consists of two main types of equipment. The *fractionating columns* are vertical steel cylinders in which the oil is heated so that the various liquids it contains are boiled off. Their vapours are then condensed back again at different temperatures, so that they become separated from one another. These liquids in turn are then placed in *crackers;* large steel tanks where further separation takes place under the influence of heat and pressure and the use of *catalysts.* These are special substances which cause chemical reactions to take place. In the refinery the oil is broken down into various useful fuels such as benzene, paraffin (kerosene), petrol, various oils used for lubricating cars and machinery, diesel fuel and fuel oil for use in heating homes and factories.

Natural Gas

By drilling down into the ground we can not only secure petroleum but *natural gas,* which is a mixture of compounds of carbon and hydrogen such as methane, ethane, propane and butane.

There was a time when natural gas was regarded as waste material escaping from oil wells, but today more and more natural gas is being taken from the ground and under the sea, and in many countries is replacing coal gas as a source of power. The gas can be liquefied under pressure and transported from the gas fields in *tankers.* Arriving at its

Below: Much natural gas is found under the sea bed. Huge drilling rigs are erected in the sea to bore down and tap deposits of natural gas.

port of destination, the gas is vapourized and flows through long pipelines to the towns and cities where it is to be used.

Coal

The coal we use today comes from the trees and plants which were growing in the forests of the world more than two hundred million years ago.

When these trees and plants died they were acted upon by bacteria. Simple chemical compounds were formed which were used by other plants. But in very moist soils this bacterial action was prevented by the production of certain acids, like humic acid. And in the hundreds and thousands of years that followed, these dead plants became buried under layers of sand and loose rock. Increasing pressure and heat caused hydrogen and oxygen to be squeezed out in the form of water, carbon dioxide and other gases. Left behind was a very high proportion of carbon.

Above: When coal-burning steam engines powered industry and rail transport, complex water systems were constructed to facilitate the movement of coal.

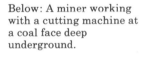

Right: Much coal is carried by railway trucks. The railway may come directly to the pithead, where the trucks are loaded with coal.

Below: A miner working with a cutting machine at a coal face deep underground.

Rank of Coal

The more carbon coal contains, the higher its grade or *rank*. In general, the older a coal deposit is, the higher is its rank. And the higher its rank, the more useful and efficient it is as a fuel.

So-called 'hard coal', or *anthracite,* has the highest rank and contains over 90% of carbon. A much softer coal, called lignite, or brown coal, was formed less than two hundred million years ago, and contains only 70% of carbon or less, along with fragments of plants and wood which we can still see.

Bituminous coal, which contains between 70% and 90% of carbon, is our most important fuel, and was formed during the Carboniferous Period about 250 million years ago. It is very black and shiny and easily breaks up into small pieces.

Coal Mining

Coal occurs underground in layers, or *seams,* which sometimes slope upwards to form *outcrops* at the surface. Here the coal can be quarried out directly by *open cast* mining. Most of the coal we use, however, is obtained by excavating shafts down to the seam.

A modern coal mine, or *colliery,* has at least two shafts to ensure proper ventilation for the miners working below. At the top, or *head,* of one shaft a system of fans ensures a good circulation of air. A derrick, or *head gear,* at the surface lowers a cage down into the shaft. This is used to carry miners to their work and bring up the mined coal.

From the shaft the miners dig along the seam, cutting coal from the *face,* loading it into small cars which run on rails back to the shaft, where they are carried to the surface. Today many mines are equipped with long conveyor belts to carry the coal, and the coal itself can be cut from the face with automatic cutting machines. The roof of rock above the working miners' heads must be continually held up by beams supported by adjustable *pit-props* to prevent cave-ins.

In spite of the modern equipment and safety devices used, mining is still a dangerous business. One of the greatest hazards is the accidental explosion from a pocket of inflammable natural gas. Because of this miners carry special *safety lamps,* or spark-proof electric lights, fixed to their helmets.

Nuclear Fuel

Uranium can be used as a source of power because, under certain conditions, its atoms will split up and release great amounts of energy. One pound of uranium can produce as much heat as 1,500 tons of coal. At present, power from nuclear fuel is dearer than that produced from fossil fuels.

Painting and Sculpture

Painting is a method of depicting scenes, or designs, on a plane surface by means of pigments. The oldest examples, found on the walls of caves, are many thousands of years old. Probably, these paintings were used in connection with rituals celebrating hunting, and were also part of magical ceremonies to ensure further success in the chase. Together with painting went forms of sculpture, which is the representation of objects (also animal and human forms) by means of carvings, or models.

Methods of Painting

Paint consists of colouring matters (pigments) which can be mixed with a medium (water, oil, resin) and applied with a brush (or possibly fingers, sticks, leaves, etc., in earlier times), so that, when dry, they remain fixed to the surface used. For centuries, colours were various earths, woods and bones burnt black and ground smoothly to a powder. Juices of plants were also used, e.g. indigo. In one method of painting, known as *encaustic,* waxes mixed with pigments were applied with a hot iron. This technique was limited and eventually, the main method was that known as *fresco painting.* This was the direct application of colours to wet plaster. Areas of a wall were treated with plaster and the designs or pictures were quickly applied before the base became dry and hard. Although many famous paintings were produced by this method the speed at which the artist had to work did not allow him to paint in great detail, or achieve any great warmth, or realism. A great advance was made when colours were mixed with fast drying oils. Oil painting could be carried out slowly on wood (later, canvas) and many corrections, and additions, made. Many great paintings are in 'oils'. From being a method of wall decoration painting became the art of separate works which could be moved from one place to another. More especially, oil paint enabled artists to depict human scenes and portraits, in a more warm and natural manner. Artists could experiment with rendering detail, and perspective, i.e. a sense of space, and proper dimensions. Other methods of painting are *tempera,* and *water-colour.*

Methods of Sculpture

At first, most sculpture was produced by carving stone, wood, or bone, into the desired form. Sculpture can also be produced by moulding a form from soft clay, usually over a base of wood or metal, known as an *armature.* The finished model is baked, and frequently used to prepare a mould into which hot metal, or cement, is poured to produce a replica of the original. Much sculpture is in the form of relief, i.e. raised figures carved from stone, or wood, leaving a background against which the work can be viewed like a picture. Some of the greatest sculptures have been produced by the carving method, and one of the stones often used was marble. Massive figures were hewn from rocks by the Ancient Egyptians, among others. More recently, modern sculptors have experimented with metal, and plastic materials, glass, wood, and so on, to produce constructions rather than carvings.

Development of Painting

A full history of painting would take many volumes, and still remain incomplete. Little is known, for instance, about Greek painting since no works survived. But, broadly speaking, once artists moved from frescoes to oils a more natural art arose. Towards the end of the 13th century the work of the Italian artist Giotto inspired a new school of painters at Sienna. Fra Angelico carried this movement on, notably with a painting of *The Annunciation.* He was followed by others, especially Botticelli, who, about a century later, produced two great pictures, *Spring* and *The Birth of Venus.* The great revival of learning known as the Renaissance produced many fine artists. One of the world's most famous paintings, the *Mona Lisa,* was produced at this time by Leonardo da Vinci. Michelangelo decorated the Sistine Chapel in Rome, a work which took many years. The great Venetian school arose and again the whole style and approach changed. A fine example of this school is *The Sleeping Beauty* by Gorgione. Painting progressed through the Bolognese school, a 17th century group aiming to revive and emulate the finest of the old masters of the past, to the 18th century when elegant and romantic paintings (especially of landscapes) contrasted with paintings of great realism, often making some pointed comment on the society of the day. Notable developments in England were the works of Constable and Turner. Both strove to render natural scenes, with special emphasis on the observed effects of light. Turner, in particular, aimed to paint sunsets, mists, seas and clouds in a new way. This concern with light and natural colour was carried to the ultimate lengths by the French *Impressionists.* With a new range of recently invented, subtle chemical pigments they explored the whole nature of light and abolished the use of clear line and 'black' shadows. The invention of the photograph eventually turned the attention of

The perfect proportions of classical sculpture inspired the works of the great Renaissance sculptors. Above: Greek marble statue of a youth. 'The Strangford Apollo'. Below: Michelangelo's statue of David.

Right: Madonna, Child and St. John by Raphael.

Portrait of a Woman with a Fan by Hals.

The Shrimp Girl by Hogarth.

The Duke of Wellington by Goya.

artists away from purely representational painting to other effects, i.e. pure line, construction, and, eventually, abstract painting. Two important movements showed how ideas as well as forms were interesting artists. The first was *Cubism,* which aimed to break down an object and reveal many aspects of it at one and the same time. The second was *Surrealism,* which aimed to surprise, or even shock, the viewer by contrasting unlikely objects, or by depicting 'impossible' dream scenes.

Development of Sculpture

Sculpture was always extensively used to decorate buildings, symbolise beliefs and to commemorate and honour gods, kings, and leaders. The art was developed on a grand scale by the Ancient Egyptians, with their huge statues of *The Sphinx,* The Pharaohs and their great triumphal colonnades, some of which survive today. However, their sculpture, like much that went before it, was stylised and conventional, leaving little room for free expression. The Greeks, in about 600 B.C. began to produce wonderfully realistic statues of the human form, though these were greatly idealised in most cases. The Romans followed the Greek tradition, imitating their work but adding nothing to it. During the Romanesque, and Gothic periods, sculpture changed, and there was a return to religious sculpture, and to the use of wood as a basic material. One of the greatest changes in the art was brought about by the French artist Rodin who used sculpture as a form of portraiture, and to capture movement. He was noted for considering even the play of light and shade on a model as a factor in its effect, and appeal. The tendency of modern sculpture is towards the abstract, especially in the works of the British sculptor, Henry Moore.

The Birth of The Earth

The Birth of the Earth

The Earth is one of a family of planets circling the Sun. Some scientists believe that the planets were formed at the same time as the Sun from a great cloud of gases slowly rotating in space. Other scientists believe the Sun was formed first, and that a close approach by another star drew from it a large thread, or filament, of material. This then separated into a number of pieces revolving around the Sun and condensed to form the individual planets.

It is believed that, as the Earth condensed and its surface rocks formed, some of these rocks were later melted by the heat produced by radio-active materials contained in them. This may account for the pockets of molten rock still present in the Earth's crust.

While this was happening, an immense amount of water vapour was being released from the heated interior into the primeval atmosphere, and for many millions of years the planet was masked by a dense pall of cloud. But no water appeared on the surface of the Earth, for raindrops were boiled back to vapour long before they could reach the intensely hot ground. When, at last, the crustal rocks had cooled sufficiently to allow rain to fall, a great deluge must have followed, out of which the young oceans were born.

Below: An impression of the birth and evolution of the Earth covering a span of at least 4,500 million years.

At some point during its early life, the Earth probably passed through a semi-molten phase. This was when the heaviest minerals sank towards the centre while the lightest rose to the surface and the remainder arranged themselves in between.

The Structure of the Earth

The Earth is, roughly speaking, a ball, or sphere, about 8,000 miles in diameter. It is rocky on the outside and is about 5½ times as heavy as a quantity of water the same size would be. Parts of its surface are very rugged, and almost three-quarters of the total surface area is covered by water.

Scientists cannot learn much about the inside of the Earth by studying the surface of it. They learn more by studying earthquake waves. When there is an earthquake, a shock may travel a long way through the Earth, and the scientists can tell from the type of shock wave and the speed at which it travels, what type of substance it is travelling through.

The Earth's *crust* consists of two main types of rock – *sima* and *sial*. Sima is made mainly from silicon and magnesium. Sial is made mainly from silicon and aluminium. Sima is a dense rock similar to that which comes out of volcanoes, and may have been formed when most of the Earth was in a *molten* (liquid) state. Sial occurs as great

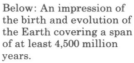

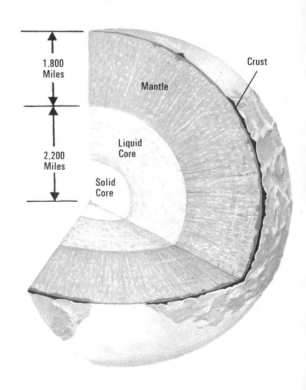

Right: The evidence of earthquake waves suggests that the crustal rocks, rarely more than 30 miles thick, overlie a 'mantle' of very dense rocks extending to a depth of 1,800 miles. Below this lies the Earth's core composed mainly of iron with some nickel and chromium. The outer part of the core may be molten and the inner part solid.

Above: Earthquake waves have helped to prove the existence of a central core of very dense material in the Earth. For every earthquake there is a 'shadow zone' round the Earth where quake waves are not received. Those waves which strike the core are sharply deflected while those which just miss the core travel on as normal. This produces a gap in the waves reaching the surface.

'rafts' floating in the heavier sima. Each of the 'rafts' is a continent.

Beneath the crust there is a layer, called the *mantle,* of very heavy rocks about 1,800 miles deep. The mantle surrounds the *core,* which is in two parts. The outer core, about 1,350 miles deep, is liquid, and probably made from molten iron and nickel. The inner core is also believed to be composed of iron and nickel, but is solid. It is about 1,700 miles across.

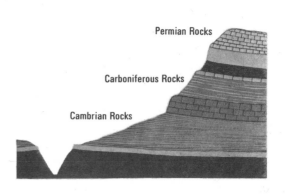

Right: Much can be learned about the history of the Earth from a study of the crustal rocks. In forming the Grand Canyon, the Colorado River has cut through rock strata accumulated over 1,000 million years.

Permian Rocks

Carboniferous Rocks

Cambrian Rocks

The Ages of the Earth

Since the geological history of the Earth covers such a great span of time, it is convenient to divide it up into units. One dividing line can be drawn at the point in the past where fossils start to appear in considerable numbers in rocks and from then on reveal the changing pattern of life up to the present day. The two sections resulting from this division have been named the Cryptozoic Eon (Greek *kryptos* = hidden and *zoon* = life) and the Phanerozoic Eon (Greek *phaneros* = evident and *zoon* = life). The Phanerozoic Eon is in turn divided into three *eras,* a division based upon life forms, namely the Palaeozoic Era (Greek *palaios* = ancient), the Mesozoic Era (Greek *mesos* = middle), and the Cenozoic Era (Greek *kainos* = recent). The Cryptozoic Eon embraces over 80% of geological time. Eras of time correspond to *groups* of rocks, but the rocks of the Cryptozoic Eon are collectively termed Pre-Cambrian.

The eras of the Phanerozoic Eon are further subdivided into *periods* of time, each of which corresponds to a *series* of rocks. Both the system and the period bear the same name, which usually refers to the region where the system was first defined. Thus the Cambrian Period is named after Cambria, the Roman name for Wales where this system of rocks was first recognised. On the other hand, the Cretaceous Period was so named because of the prominence of chalk amongst the rocks of this system (Latin *creta* = chalk).

The periods of the Phanerozoic Eon are as follows: Cambrian Period (began 570 million years ago); Ordovician Period (began 500 million years ago); Silurian Period (began 440 million years ago); Devonian Period (began 395 million years ago); Carboniferous Period (began 345 million years ago); Permian Period (began 280 million years ago); Triassic Period (began 225 million years ago); Jurassic Period (began 195 million years ago); Cretaceous Period (began 136 million years ago); Tertiary Period (began 65 million years ago); Quaternary Period (began 1,500,000 years ago).

200,000 Years Ago

Present Day

Rocks and Minerals

Rocks form the material which makes up the Earth's crust. Rock consists of substances which have a definite chemical make-up, or composition. These substances are called *minerals*. Some rocks, such as chalk, contain only one mineral. Other rocks, such as granite, contain two or more minerals.

Sedimentary Rocks

The gradual, but never-ending action of the weather breaks down even the hardest rocks into tiny particles. Streams carry the particles away and deposit them in another place. Over millions of years, layer upon layer builds up and gradually becomes cemented, or bound together, into a hard mass.

The kind of rock formed in this way is called *sedimentary* rock, because it is made up of layers of deposits, or *sediments*. It is also called *bedded* rock. The layers of rock are called *strata*.

Sedimentary rocks of this kind include sandstone made up of compressed sand, and shale made up of compressed clay. Rock formed when large pebbles and boulders are cemented together is called *conglomerate*.

Another kind of sedimentary rock is formed when minerals in the older rocks are gradually dissolved by water flowing over them. A stage is reached when the water can hold no more minerals, and the minerals begin to be deposited as crystals. They gradually form layers and eventually become rock-like. Rock salt and some limestones are

Above: Conglomerates are sedimentary rocks composed of rounded pebbles cemented by silica or lime.

Below: An unconformity in rock strata. The lower, older rocks were folded and eroded for a long time before the upper ones were laid upon them. The irregular junction represents the passage of many millions of years.

sedimentary rocks of this kind. Some kinds of limestone consist mainly of the chalky remains of tiny sea creatures.

Rock strata are more or less horizontal when they are first formed at the bottom of a river or sea. In some of the limestone cliffs you see today, the strata are still horizontal, but many of the sedimentary rocks have been pushed and twisted by movements of the Earth's crust. The strata show definite slopes, or *dips*. Some strata are even vertical. Many are bent into gentle curves, which are generally called *rock folds*.

Sometimes the strata did not bend but slipped vertically so that they are slightly out of step. This break in the strata is called a *fault*.

Massive Rocks

The two other kinds of rock are *igneous* rock and *metamorphic* rock. They are often known as *massive* rocks because they are the same throughout. They do not have any noticeable layers like the sedimentary rocks. Igneous rocks are formed when molten material from inside the Earth cools at or near the surface. Metamorphic rocks are formed when igneous and sedimentary rocks are remelted due to heat and pressure and crystallize again.

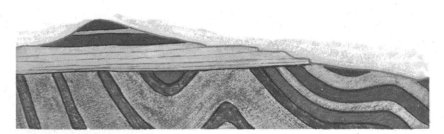

Left: Stalactites and stalagmites develop where water drips out from limestone rocks. The water contains dissolved limestone. This is left behind when the water evaporates. Impurities such as iron or manganese may stain the rocks striking colours.

Below: The Giants' Causeway on the coast of Northern Ireland is part of an old lava flow which, on cooling and contracting, developed into six-sided columns of basalt.

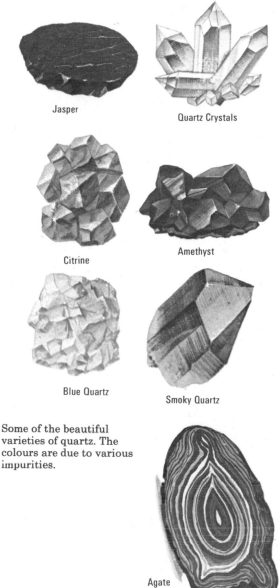

Jasper

Quartz Crystals

Citrine

Amethyst

Blue Quartz

Smoky Quartz

Some of the beautiful
varieties of quartz. The
colours are due to various
impurities.

Agate

Minerals

Rocks themselves are made up of collections of substances called *minerals*.

Minerals, like everything else on Earth, are composed of certain basic chemical units, or *elements*. The common mineral quartz, for example, is made up of a certain amount of the element silicon and a certain amount of the element oxygen. Quartz will always contain the same relative amounts of these elements.

Some minerals consist of only one element. They are often called *native* elements. They include the metals gold, silver, copper and platinum, and the non-metals graphite and diamond, which are both forms of the element carbon.

Most minerals consist of two or more elements. Often a *metallic* element, such as iron, is combined with a *non-metallic* element, such as oxygen or sulphur. Minerals that are compounds of metal and oxygen are very common. They are called *oxides*. Minerals containing metals combined with sul-

Above: Devil's Tower, Wyoming, U.S.A., is a volcanic rock tower almost 300 feet tall.

Below: Diamonds are crystallized pure carbon, the hardest substance known.

phur are called *sulphides*. They are also very common. Iron oxides and sulphides, for example, are found throughout the world.

Metallic elements will also combine with groups of other elements to form minerals. The commonest groups are the *silicates* and the *carbonates*. The silicates contain silicon combined with oxygen. Clays are complicated aluminium silicates. The carbonates contain carbon combined with oxygen. Common chalk and limestone are forms of calcium carbonate.

Precious Stones

A great many of the minerals can be found in beautiful crystals of a variety of shapes and sizes. The hardest and rarest of these crystals are used in jewellery. They are known as precious stones, or *gems*. The diamond, the hardest substance on Earth, is the most precious gem. Diamonds are pure carbon. Rubies, sapphires and emeralds are other popular gems. The first two are forms of corundum; the last is a form of beryl.

Fossils

Fossils are traces of animals and plants which have been naturally preserved in various ways, sometimes for many millions of years. Very occasionally, the actual skeleton may be preserved. This has happened where animals have been trapped in bogs or tar pits and quickly buried. The Californian tar pits, for instance, have yielded a wealth of skeletons. And under very unusual conditions the entire animal may be preserved. Mammoths (relatives of present-day elephants) have been found in Alaska and Siberia preserved almost intact in ice.

More often, however, the buried skeletons are petrified (replaced by stone). This is caused by ground water depositing minerals in the pores of the bones, a process known as *permineralization*. On the other hand, each particle of the substance may be eaten away and *replaced* by a particle of mineral matter.

Above: Soft-bodied worms and jellyfish found in late Pre-Cambrian rocks of Australia. Most Pre-Cambrian life-forms were soft-bodied, and their fossils are consequently rare.

Below: This dinosaur skeleton was found in the southern Gobi Desert. It is estimated to be some 60 million years old.

Petrified bones are usually produced by the first process and petrified wood by the second.

Some buried substances may be completely eaten away by percolating ground water, leaving a space in the rock corresponding to the original form of the object. This is known as a *mould*. Ground water may later fill this cavity with mineral matter to produce a rock *cast* of the object. Interesting moulds have been formed by insects becoming trapped in resin dripping from evergreen trees. This gradually hardens to form amber, and although most of the insect dries and withers away, the outline of its original form can clearly be seen from the hollow in the transparent material. Moulds of extremely thin objects, such as leaves, are generally called *imprints*.

Many plant fossils are simply residues of carbon which give the actual shape of the original object, and fossils of soft-bodied, invertebrate animals are occasionally formed in this way too. Sometimes the petrified

skeleton of an animal may be surrounded by a film of carbon which shows the actual fleshy outline of the creature as it was.

Unusual fossils are the tracks left by animals in mud which later hardened to become rock. Excellent dinosaur footprints, for instance, have been found by the side of an old water-course in the Gobi Desert of Central Asia and in many other places.

The Key to the Past

Fossils are a key to the past. They help to explain the changing pattern of life through the ages. Many years ago it was realized that certain fossils were confined to certain rock formations. This means that it is possible to identify a particular rock formation, wherever it is exposed, by the fossils it contains. The reason why certain fossils appear only in certain rocks is quite simple: life forms have evolved continuously throughout the Earth's long history. Thus, a single species of plant or animal is confined to a certain span of time, and its fossilized re-

Above: A mould of a trilobite, the impression that may remain after the actual animal has disappeared.

Above: A cast of a trilobite, formed by the later deposition of mineral matter in the mould.

mains will only appear in rocks laid down during that time.

Radioactive Dating

In this way fossils have made it possible to build up a record of rocks representing a long span of the Earth's history. The rocks in turn give an indication of the age of the fossils, for it is possible to date some of them by the radio-active minerals they contain. Radio-active elements, such as uranium and thorium, gradually break down or *decay* into more stable elements (in these cases lead). Since the rate at which this happens can be calculated, it is possible, by noting the amount of lead produced at the expense of uranium or thorium in such rocks, to determine their age. The rocks which can be dated in this way act as markers in the *geological time scale*.

Very recent fossils can be dated by the amount of carbon-14 they contain. Carbon-14 is a radioactive isotope of carbon which is present in living things.

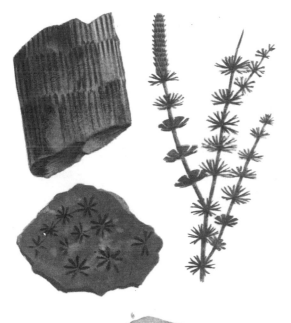

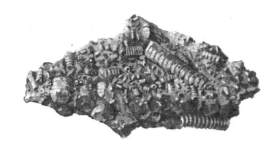

Right: Crinoidal limestone consists almost entirely of the remains of sea-lilies (*crinoids*).

Left: Fossils of Carboniferous horsetails, showing the cast of a stem, some fossil leaves, and one of the plants as it looked when it was alive.

Right: A film of carbon shows the original outline of the body of a Jurassic ichthyosaur.

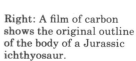

Left: Fossils include the marks left by animals, such as this reptile footprint.

Right: Fossil of archaeopteryx, the first known bird, found in Jurassic rocks. Even the shape of the feathers can be seen.

Left: Fossil ammonites from Jurassic rocks. Some measure eight feet across.

Prehistoric Animals

No one can say when life first appeared on Earth. It must have been many millions of years after the Earth was created before conditions were suitable for living things, but just how long is impossible to tell. And no one can say which was the first living thing. But scientists believe that it must have been some kind of plant, for the Earth's primeval atmosphere consisted mainly of carbon dioxide, water vapour and nitrogen. They are fairly certain that the large amounts of free oxygen which all animals need to live were produced *after* plants appeared on the Earth, for these take in carbon dioxide and produce oxygen in their food-making processes. Only after plants had been on Earth for millions of years, steadily building up the supply of oxygen in the atmosphere, was the way paved for oxygen-breathing animals.

There is another reason why plants must have appeared first. They are the very basis of life – the only living things which can make their own food using the energy of the Sun. Animals must have their food ready-made, so they feed either directly on plants, or upon animals which have already turned plant food into flesh.

The first plants must have been very simple, but whether they were simple green plants or something quite different we shall probably never know. The earliest traces of life on Earth date back some 2,500 million years. They are not very impressive, simply lumps of limy material, very similar to those made by some marine plants today. And for the next 2,000 million years or so, the occasional imprints of jellyfish and other soft-bodied creatures, or the traces of primitive plants, are the only clues to the life forms which lived at that time.

From Cambrian times onwards, the changing pattern of plants and animals becomes a little clearer. Fossils show that for a long time all animals were confined to the sea. Then, about 450 million years ago, the first vertebrates appeared. They were fish-like creatures, the forerunners of a very successful group of animals.

Some 325 million years ago, the first fish-like creatures ventured out of the sea and gave rise to the amphibians. The amphibians never truly broke away from the sea. They still have to return to the water to lay their eggs. But some of the early amphibians began to lay eggs with hard shells and grew large scales on their bodies. These animals gave rise to the reptiles which were better adapted to life on land. Gradually the reptiles

Above: Archaeopteryx was one of the first birds. It had feathers and a long tail. The claws on its wings were probably used for climbing.

came to dominate the world. One group of reptiles – the dinosaurs – included the largest animals that have ever lived on the land.

When the great dinosaurs became extinct, about 70 million years ago, their ruling position was rapidly taken over by a group of animals which had been on Earth almost as long – the mammals. But many millions of years were to pass before Man inherited the Earth. If the complete history of the Earth is represented on a 24-hour clock, then Man appears at a quarter of a minute to midnight. Yet, in this space of time, which is a minute fraction of the Earth's long history, Man has come to dominate the world more surely than any living thing before.

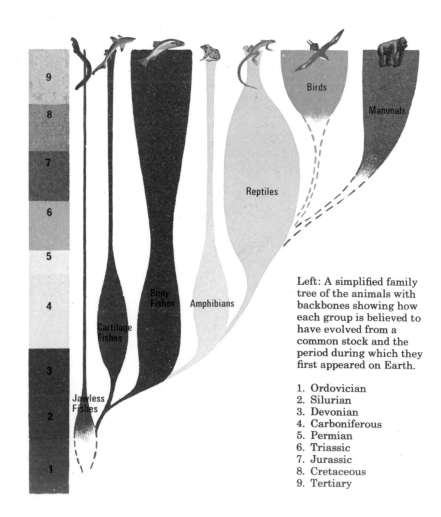

Left: A simplified family tree of the animals with backbones showing how each group is believed to have evolved from a common stock and the period during which they first appeared on Earth.

1. Ordovician
2. Silurian
3. Devonian
4. Carboniferous
5. Permian
6. Triassic
7. Jurassic
8. Cretaceous
9. Tertiary

1. Life in Cambrian times was confined to the sea. There were tiny protozoa, sponges, jellyfish, sea-lilies and starfish. There were sea shells and worms and small creatures called trilobites and graptolites.

2. Eryops, one of the first amphibians.

3. Styracosaurus was a plant-eating dinosaur. It had a frill round its neck and was armed with a powerful horn.

4. Stegosaurus was a plant-eating dinosaur. It was protected by rows of bony plates on its back and spikes on its tail.

5. Tyrannosaurus was the most terrifying of the dinosaurs. It ran with huge strides on its massive hind legs and used its dagger-like teeth to attack its prey.

6. The mammoth, one of the largest land mammals, lived during the Ice Age. It was kept warm by its thick, hairy coat.

7. Diplodocus was about 80 feet long. It has a very long neck and a very long tail. It was one of the largest dinosaurs.

Paper and Printing

In the first century A.D., the Chinese discovered that certain plant materials could be broken down into fibres (of cellulose) and pressed into a sheet which made a good writing material. This was the origin of paper in the form we know today.

Until the mid-1800's most paper was hand-made from rags or from grasses such as hemp and esparto. But then it was discovered how paper could be made from wood-pulp.

Wood-pulp is produced mainly from softwood trees such as fir, pine, and spruce. The felled trees are cut into logs and transported, often by water, to the pulp-mills. There they are first debarked in a revolving drum. Then they are broken down into a pulp either by grinding or by boiling with chemicals in a pressure cooker called a digester. Chemical digestion is used to produce rag and esparto pulp, too.

Groundwood, or mechanical pulp, is used mainly for producing newsprint – the paper on which newspapers are printed.

The pulp may be pressed into sheets for transport to the paper-mill. There, the sheets are converted back into a wet pulp in a big tub (the hydropulper). The wet pulp then passes to a beating machine, which frays the fibres.

From Pulp to Paper

At the 'wet end' of the paper-making machine, the watery pulp is spread over a wire-mesh belt. Most water drains or is sucked away to leave a damp paper web.

The web is then pressed into a firm sheet by heavy rollers and dried by being passed over a series of heated cylinders. Finally, *calender presses* (heavy, heated rollers) give the paper a smooth finish.

Different grades of paper are made by blending various pulps and by varying the amount of beating in the beating machines – the more beating, the denser the paper. High-quality printing papers are coated with materials such as clay to give them a glossy surface. Some papers are *sized* (treated with glue) to make them take writing better. Tissue papers are given their texture by being scraped off the drying cylinders.

Above: The 'wet end' of a paper-making machine where the watery pulp flows onto a wire-mesh belt.

Below: The web of paper is pressed into a firm sheet by heavy rollers and dried by heated cylinders. Huge reels take the paper from the 'dry end' of the machine.

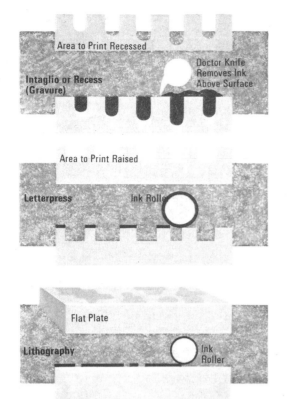

Area to Print Recessed

Intaglio or Recess (Gravure)

Doctor Knife Removes Ink Above Surface

Area to Print Raised

Letterpress   Ink Roller

Flat Plate

Lithography   Ink Roller

Right: Newspapers being delivered in a constant stream from the press.

Left: The three basic printing processes. In intaglio or recess (gravure) printing, the design is cut into the plate. In the letterpress process, it is the raised parts of the plate which deposit ink on the paper. Lithographic plates are chemically treated so that they attract greasy ink only on the parts where the image is.

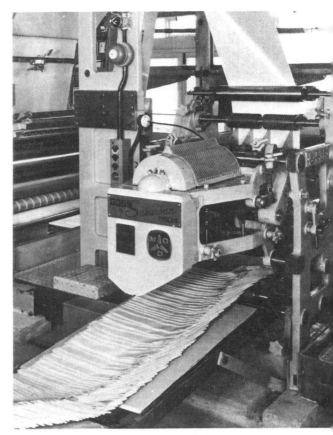

Printing

Before the 1400's, books were written or copied by hand in Europe. They were rare and expensive and far beyond the reach of the ordinary man. In about 1456, Johannes Gutenberg published copies of the Bible printed from movable metal type on a printing press. So began a revolution in communications that has brought knowledge within the reach of everyone who can read.

The first job of the printer is to set the copy in even lines of *type*. The type is set in the *composing room*, generally by machines. In the most common processes, the letters are cast in hot metal in tiny moulds.

A more recent method of setting is *film setting*, in which type is set on a sheet of photographic film or paper.

After setting, the type is made up into the form of pages. Subsequent processes depend upon which method of printing is to be used. *Letterpress* printing is the most common method. Printing is done by inking the raised surface of the type and pressing it against the paper *(relief printing)*. On a *cylinder press*, the made-up type is placed flat on a bed, which moves back and forth. The paper is pressed against it by a revolving cylinder. On the *rotary press*, printing is done from a rotating cylinder. Curved metal plates made from the type form the printing surface. Rotary presses can be fed with continuous reels of paper and can therefore work much faster than flat-bed presses.

Offset-lithography, or *litho*, is a method of

Below: Lifting a heavy photogravure cylinder onto the machine.

printing from a flat surface (*planographic* printing). The flat printing plate is made photographically from a printed copy of the made-up type. It is treated chemically so that it attracts greasy ink only on the parts where the image is.

Printing takes place on a rotary press with three cylinders, one above the other. The printing plate transfers, or offsets, an inked image to the middle roller, which in turn transfers it to the paper pressed against it by the third roller.

Sometimes the printing plates are made directly by photographing the original typescript copy, without setting it in type. This is called *facsimile* printing.

Photogravure, or *gravure*, is used mainly for illustrations. It is a method of printing from a pitted, or recessed plate (*intaglio* printing). It is thus the reverse of relief, letterpress printing.

Illustrations

So far we have considered only the reproduction of words. Now let us see how pictures are reproduced. It is quite simple really. The picture is itself photographed but through a special screen, which reduces it to a series of dots. The film produced can be used to make the plates for printing.

Colour pictures, too, can be reproduced in a similar way, only the colours are first split into different shades of red, yellow and blue. Separate printing plates corresponding to these colours are then made.

Languages

There are about 2,800 different languages, not including *dialects* (local variations in a language). The language spoken by the greatest number of people is Chinese, with about 600 million speakers. English comes next, with 400 million, then Hindi (over 200 million) and Spanish (about 150 million).

Some languages die as people stop using them. Sanskrit and Latin are now dead languages. But many words in living languages come from Latin and Sanskrit words. All languages change gradually. People invent new words and new words come into the language from other languages.

There are several families of languages. The largest is the *Indo-European* family, spoken by half the world's people. This family contains eight branches: the *Germanic* branch, with German, English, Dutch and the Scandinavian languages: the *Romance* branch, with French, Italian and Spanish; the *Balto-Slavic* branch, with Russian; and the *Indo-Iranian, Greek, Celtic, Armenian* and *Albanian* branches. The only other large family is the *Sino-Tibetan* family, spoken by a quarter of the world's population. Chinese is a Sino-Tibetan language.

Languages are written down in alphabets – groups of characters or symbols. English is written in the *Roman* alphabet with 26 letters. Most other European languages are written in this alphabet, but the actual characters or letters may be pronounced in different ways. The 26-letter alphabet is not large enough for some of these languages, so accent marks are added to the letters to show differences in pronunciation.

There are several other alphabets in common use. The *Greek* alphabet has 24 letters. It is used only in Greece, although scientists use the letters as symbols in their work. The word 'alphabet' comes from its first two letters: α (alpha) and β (beta). Russians and other Slavs use the *Cyrillic* alphabet, which developed from Greek about 1,100 years ago. Gaelic is written with an alphabet of 18 letters derived from the Roman alphabet.

All these alphabets contain symbols for vowels and consonants. The Arabic and Hebrew alphabets have symbols for consonants only. Vowels are indicated only by accent marks and often never used at all.

Some languages can be written in two alphabets. Serbo-Croat is written in the Roman alphabet in one part of Yugoslavia and in the Cyrillic in another.

Recently, new phonetic alphabets have been designed to help children learn to read.

Above: The ancient Egyptians used picture signs, or hieroglyphics, for writing.

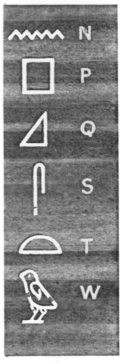

Left: The Rosetta Stone was discovered in 1799. It was a royal decree written in the three scripts of Egypt – hieroglyphics, demonic (a shorthand version of hieroglyphics), and Greek.

Right: A comparison of the characters of five different alphabets. They are (left to right) Arabic, Hebrew, Greek, Cyrillic and Roman.

Arabic	Hebrew	Greek	Cyrillic	Roman
١	א	α	а	A
ب	ב	β	б	B
ج,ك	כ,ס	κ,σ	к, с	C
د	ד	δ	д	D
ۀ	ה	ε,η	е, э	E
ف	פ	φ	ф, θ	F
ج،ه،غ	ג,ח	γ	г	G
ه،ح	ה,ח	ʿ	г	H
ی	י	ι	и, й	I
ج		—	дж	J
ك	כ	κ	к	K
ل	ל	λ	л	L
م	מ	μ	м	M
ن	נ	ν	н	N
و	ו	ο,ω	о	O
پ	פ	π	п	P
ق	ק	ϙ	—	Q
ر	ר	ρ	р	R
س,ث	ש,ס	σ,ς	с	S
ط,ت	ט,ת	τ	т	T
و	ו	υ	ы, ю	U
و	ו	υ	в	V
و	ו	ϝ	—	VV
—	—	ξ	кс	X
ی	י	ι,υ	я	Y
ظ,ز	ز,ء	ζ	з	Z

Education

Education is the process of development a child passes through in order to become an adult. In this process he gradually learns about the world he lives in. Going to school is only a part of this process of learning.

All animals educate their young. A mother cat teaches her kittens how to wash themselves. In the same way the cave men taught their children how to hunt and to light fires. As civilization has become more complex, so has the process of learning.

The first schools were those in Ancient Greece. These schools taught only three subjects: dialetic (speech, writing and grammar), gymnastics and music. In the Roman civilization that followed the Greek civilization, more subjects were taught, but they were still classed in the same three groups: reading, writing and arithmetic; singing and music; and boxing, wrestling, running and gymnastics.

With the rise of Christianity, the Church founded schools to teach people intending to become Christians. By the Middle Ages, all the schools in Europe were attached to monasteries. These schools taught the 'Seven Liberal Subjects' – grammar, rhetoric (including the study of law), logic, geometry (which was really geography), arithmetic, music and astronomy.

During the Renaissance, there was a renewed interest in the civilizations of Ancient Greece and Rome. The study of Greek and Latin literature became the basis of all education for over 200 years. Since then, there have been many new theories about education. Jan Amos Comenius (1592–1670) was the first great theorist. He believed that things, not words, were the basis of learning. John Locke (1632–1704) believed that children only learn how to live by living. The Frenchman Jean-Jaques Rousseau (1712–1778) believed that children should be allowed to grow up naturally, learning only what they want to. More recently, Froebel founded a school in which he tried to put some of these ideas into practice. All these men and their ideas have helped to make education today as good as it is.

Because of the 'population explosion', there are more children at school now than ever before. There has also been a 'knowledge explosion', and there are more facts for teachers to teach. Classes are often so big that teachers have to use teaching aids. Television may be a teaching aid, and some schools also have 'teaching machines' of various types.

Above: A Buddhist monk teaches his pupils the ancient art of calligraphy.

Right: The Lomonosov University, the State University of Moscow, is the largest higher educational establishment in Russia. The vast building, on the Lenin Hills, was opened in 1953.

Literature

Literature is a broad term which covers almost any composition which has a permanent record in writing, or print. It includes stories, ballads, poems, novels, plays, essays, philosophy, history, and accounts of people's lives, or great events, and so on. It is usually used, however, to describe works which have some lasting interest, or artistic merit, and value, though it may also mean anything that is compiled, and printed, for purposes of information, or even to persuade people to accept certain ideas, (such as advertising pamphlets, or religious, and political tracts). Literature began, in a sense, as soon as man learned how to make a permanent record of his ideas by means of writing, and left accounts of his thoughts, feelings, and actions, in the form of manuscripts, or books.

Records of Literature

Literary records have existed for many thousands of years in the form of books. But, the earliest books were long scrolls of papyrus, or parchment, fastened to two sticks. In order to read the contents it was necessary to unroll the papyrus sheet, winding it from one stick to the other, and then re-rolling it again into the right position. Such books had no general circulation, but were kept in libraries, usually maintained by rulers who employed scholars to look after the records, and study them. There were libraries in Alexandria, also

Above: An ancient bust of the poet Homer.

Ancient Babylon, Egypt, and Baghdad. One of the most famous caliphs, or rulers, in the East, Harun-al-Rashid, had many thousands of books, during his reign in the latter part of the 8th century A.D. Wealthy people often pursued learning, or patronised scholars, and accumulated many private collections of books, and manuscripts. The first public library was established in Greece in 330 B.C. Possibly the greatest ancient library was that founded at Alexandria in the 4th century B.C. by Ptolemy I, which is believed to have consisted of nearly half a million volumes. It lasted for hundreds of years, but was finally destroyed by fire. The Romans plundered many of the Greek libraries at various times, hence a great number of the

PERFORMANCE OF A DRAMATIC MYSTERY AT COVENTRY.

Right: The earliest drama in Europe developed from Church ritual. The picture shows the performance of a Mystery play on a cart in Coventry.

Left: Part of *The Prologue* from an early illuminated edition of Chaucer's *Canterbury Tales*.

books were gradually destroyed. Many were lost and dispersed throughout the world during the Dark and Middle Ages, which followed the collapse of the Roman Empire. The monasteries set up by the Roman Catholic Church preserved and copied many ancient manuscripts. The monks were extremely skilful at producing finely illustrated books, which, by this time, were taking on the more familiar form of many leaves of paper secured between two covers. Many of the ancient and medieval books were works of devotion, copies of the Bible, and, in the East, of the Koran, or holy book of the Muslims. Many were books of hymns and psalms, but early texts of plays, philosophical works, astronomical studies, and so on, were also preserved, as well as treatises on mathematics, and early scientific ideas. It was not until the middle of the 15th century that the invention of printing made it possible to

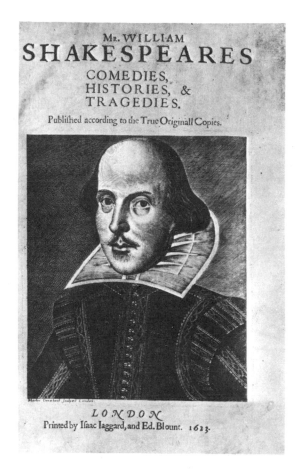

Above: The 17th century French dramatist, Racine is famed for his classical tragedies

had many collections of poetic tales. The epic poems of ancient Greece, attributed to the blind poet Homer, still survive, though they may have been written down by others, after the death of the originator – or, more likely, they were added to, and embellished, by story-tellers, and minstrels, over many years. These tell of the adventures of Ulysses, a sailor and adventurer, and also of the Greek wars with the Trojans. Later came the classical plays, both dramas and comedies, which were written to be performed in open-air theatres. After the collapse of the Roman Empire the drama declined until revived by the medieval Church as a form of mystery play, teaching religious truths, and pointing moral lessons. Ultimately, the theatre became more secular, and many great plays were written, and published in book form. These works were intended to be acted out by players, but they form an important part of recorded literature, nevertheless. Histories were also important early forms of literature, as well as biographies (the life stories of notable people). Side by side with these works went the composition and publication of poems, which were written in rhythmic and rhyming forms, often very elaborate and precisely defined (such as sonnets, lays, ballads, etc.) Poems were often records of stories, but more often than not they were written to express feelings, and reflections on life. Apart from plays, such as those of Shakespeare in English, Racine, Molière, and others in French, and the classic plays, much of literature was factual, not fictional. Towards the middle of the 17th century, however, many romances were written, and novels began to appear. The novel was a longer form of story dealing with the lives and characters of several people, in a more serious and realistic way than the ballads, and romantic stories. In time, it became one of the most popular forms of writing, and many of the great books which we regard as literature are in the novel form.

Above: Tolstoy, the most distinguished Russian novelist of modern times. His greatest works include *War and Peace* and *Anna Karenina*.

produce many copies of the same book comparatively quickly and cheaply. There followed a great change in learning, and a renewed interest in, and distribution of, books. The various translations of the Bible, especially, paved the way for a revolution in thinking that led to many basic changes throughout Europe. The terrific power of the written word, widely distributed, became a major factor in life from then onwards. Universities began to set up libraries, new works were written, broadsheets – the forerunners of modern newspapers – appeared. Pamphlets, and printed matter, of all kinds began to circulate. There was an enormous impetus to the study of language. In time, most people learned to read, in the more civilized areas of the world. Popular education became easier, and eventually compulsory. Public libraries were set up, often by philanthropists such as Andrew Carnegie, on a large scale. A huge publishing industry developed to manufacture, and market books, magazines, and newspapers, of all kinds.

Forms of Literature

Some of the earliest forms of literature, were ballads, stories, and narrative poems. Many of these were sagas, or poetic histories, of various peoples, or the myths which they invented to explain their origins, and extol the virtues of their great heroes. The Norsemen, and the people of Iceland, for example,

Right: Like Homer, the great English poet Milton lost his sight before writing his greatest works. Here, the poet dictates *Samson Agonistes* to his daughter.

War on Land

The first organized permanent army was established by the Romans. They relied almost entirely on heavy infantry. The Roman soldier was tough, could march twenty miles in a day without difficulty, and was expert in constructing fortifications. Cavalry was little used except for scouting and pursuing a beaten enemy. The success of Hannibal during the wars between Rome and Carthage can be largely attributed to his superior cavalry. The Romans, however, developed powerful catapults for attacking strongly defended positions.

The Roman Empire was finally destroyed by hordes of barbarian horsemen, and for hundreds of years cavalry was superior to infantry, for the mounted soldier could now fight effectively because of the invention of the stirrup.

Knights and Castles

During the Middle Ages, war became less and less a matter of pitched battles and more concerned with seiges. A strategically placed castle could dominate large areas of the surrounding countryside, and an invader had to subdue the castles in his way or risk having his lines of communication cut. Seiges tended to be length, since often the only effective method of overcoming a castle lay in starving the defenders into submission. It was the invention of gunpowder which reduced the impregnability of castles, and even then it took hundreds of years before seige artillery became really efficient.

In the thirteenth centry, the longbow became the chief English weapon, and it was used with great effect on cavalry, not so much because it could pierce armour as because the rider's horse could not be properly protected. After the introduction of the longbow, the importance of the medieval knight declined.

Arms and Artillery

The longbow in turn gave way to the arquebus, the primitive ancestor of the musket. It could fire only forty rounds an hour (though the musket was even slower) but it was officially adopted in the reign of Elizabeth I.

In the seventeenth century, armies became larger and more permanent, bringing with them problems of supply. The formation of the New Model Army during the English Civil War laid the foundation of a regular army. It consisted of cavalry, dragoons (mounted troops who generally dismounted to fight), musketeers, pikemen to protect

Knights fighting, from a thirteenth century manuscript. The importance of the medieval knights declined with the invention of the longbow and disappeared with the invention of gunpowder.

Above: An Assyrian relief depicting the siege of a castle.

Below: Cavalrymen were long the elite of the army, but were made obsolescent by mechanized and armoured transport.

58

Above: Air transport has made ground forces extremely mobile.

Below: A Titan II missile in its underground silo. This missile has six times the power of all bombs dropped during World War II.

them from cavalry charges, and field artillery. With the introduction of the bayonet in 1678, the functions of the musketeer and pikemen were merged.

The careful organization and discipline of a regular army was further improved by Marlborough, who made the British army one of the best in Europe. His campaign to curb the spread of France under Louis XIV which culminated in the decisive battle of Blenheim was a triumph of organization. Marlborough also fully recognized the value of military intelligence.

Generally, however, armies in the eighteenth century were slow-moving and handicapped by ponderous baggage trains. Napoleon recognized the value of mobility, and many of his battles were won because he managed, by rapid marches, to concentrate his strength where it would do most good. But he over-extended his resources, and by attacking Russia without completely subduing Spain he invited his own destruction.

At the beginning of the nineteenth century, great advances were made in both small arms and artillery. Rifles gave greater range and accuracy than muskets, and, with the invention of breach loading, a more rapid rate of fire. A commander could now make use of railways to transfer large bodies of troops. Bright uniforms made easy targets for rifle fire and so camouflage was gradually adopted. In order to survive, men had to dig themselves into systems of trenches.

Two World Wars

Infantry was now extremely vulnerable, since hundreds of men could be cut down by a single machine gun. The vast loss of life in the First World War was due to generals still making use of massed infantry in frontal attacks. It was only the introduction of the tank that broke the stalemate, but little intelligent use of this new weapon was made until the Second World War.

The Second World War was as flexible as the First was static. The German army developed *blitzkrieg* (lightning war) which involved a rapid advance under close air support. Tanks to a large extent replaced infantry, thus lowering the casualty rate. But Hitler made the mistake of attacking Russia, just as Napoleon had done, and depleted his forces in the terrible warfare of the Eastern Front. The worst features of this war were the enormous civilian casualties.

Apart from limited wars, the 'precarious peace', or Cold War, that has lasted since 1945, is largely due to nuclear weapons being used as deterrents. It is now virtually impossible for a major power to win a war against another major power.

War at Sea

In recent history, the object of sea warfare has been to destroy ships rather than men. This has not always been the case. In earlier times, sea battles tended to be regarded simply as land battles that took place onboard ship.

The first major naval engagement took place at Salamis. In 480 B.C., the Persians sent a huge army across the Bosporus, and Themistocles, the Athenian commander, realized that the only way to defeat the enemy was to cut his supply lines, which meant destroying his fleet. Themistocles therefore managed to entice the Persian galleys into a bottleneck, where they could not manoeuvre, and inflicted a decisive defeat on them.

Naval tactics did not greatly change until the battle of Lepanto, fought not far from Salamis between the combined fleets of the Holy League and the Turks in 1571. The only sure way to sink an enemy vessel was by ramming, and the main tactics were still grappling and boarding, although cannon was used at Lepanto to some effect.

During the Middle Ages, ships began to rely increasingly on sail rather than oars. This meant that the position of a fleet in relation to the wind was all-important, and ships would try to 'gain the weather-gauge' – to get between the wind and the enemy. Adverse weather conditions could contribute to a defeat as much as enemy guns, as

Left: A Roman galley from a bas-relief. The Romans used hooks for grappling and carried bridges for boarding other vessels.

the ill-fated Spanish Armada found in 1588, when trying to land an invasion force in England. After a series of running battles, the Spanish ships lost their formation and ran out of ammunition, and were forced to sail around Scotland and the west coast of Ireland, where many of them were driven on to the rocks.

The Spanish fleet suffered from their attempts to operate in a rigid military formation, and until the end of the eighteenth century, opposing fleets still formed parallel lines in attack. But at Trafalgar, Nelson formed up his fleet in two columns and sailed at the enemy line from the side, thus concentrating his fire on a small number of the enemy ships, whose fellows were too far away to be of help.

Modern Naval Warfare

The first stage in the development of modern naval warfare was the introduction of ex-

Below: An engraving of the Spanish Armada as first seen sailing up the English Channel opposite the Lizard. After a series of running battles, the Spanish ships were forced to sail around the coasts of Scotland and Ireland, where many foundered on rocks.

Above: The flight deck of an aircraft carrier. During World War II, aircraft carriers became the most important capital ships. The Pacific sea battles were fought largely between carrier-based aircraft.

Above: The open hatches of a missile-carrying nuclear submarine. Such submarines can remain submerged for months at a time, immune from detection. Their powerful guided missiles can be fired from beneath the water at targets more than two thousand miles away.

Above: The drawn battle between the early ironclads *Monitor* and *Merrimac* during the American Civil War was a turning point in naval history.

Below: The Battle of Trafalgar. The British fleet under Nelson met the combined French and Spanish fleets off Cape Trafalgar. Nelson attacked in two columns and punched two holes in the crescent-shaped Franco-Spanish line. The battle destroyed Napoleon's hopes of invading England.

Above: The *Victory*, Nelson's flagship at the Battle of Trafalgar, is now preserved in dry-dock.

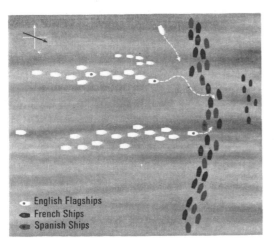

- English Flagships
- French Ships
- Spanish Ships

plosive shells in the 1830's. Ships could now put shore batteries out of action, and could make short work of unprotected wooden vessels. Eventually, armoured ships were introduced as a defence against more powerful gunnery. The first of these ships were known as 'ironclads' and were powered entirely by steam.

Before the First World War, the major powers became involved in a ship-building race. Ships could now be made of relatively thin steel, rather than iron. The torpedo had already been introduced, and submarines were developed during the course of the war. In the event, the sea played only a subsidiary part in the struggle. The one major battle, Jutland, was indecisive, both sides claiming victory.

The innumerable sea battles of the Second World War were fought on three levels, on and under the sea, and in the air. Through the development of the aircraft carrier, ships were able to fight without being able to see each other. The Germans concentrated their attacks on convoys, often with devastating results, while the submarine added a new dimension to naval warfare. Since the War, the nuclear submarine, capable of staying below the surface for months, has become a major factor in naval warfare.

61

War in the Air

The first application of flight to warfare was purely a matter of reconnaissance. Generals wanted a means of looking at 'the other side of the hill', and balloons were used for this purpose in the seige of Paris in 1870. The first controlled flight was made by the Wright Brothers in 1903, but few people at the time grasped the military implications of this event. The U.S. Army Air Arm, did, however, come into being in 1907. In the British Army, the Air Battalion was organized in 1911, though most senior officers preferred the idea of reconnaissance by cavalry. The following year it became the Royal Flying Corps.

The Germans put more faith in the airship, a development of the balloon. It had a much greater range than the aircraft of the time, but it was never a success because of its vulnerability to artillery fire.

The First World War
During the first months of the First World War, the pilots and their observers merely carried small arms. Later, the British machines began to carry the Lewis machine gun. At first this was mounted on top of the wings, and the pilot had to manoeuvre his plane in order to hold his opponent in the gunner's field of fire.

The greatest advance in air gunnery during the First War was the invention by a Dutchman, Anthony Fokker, of a device which enabled the pilot to shoot between the revolving blades of his propellor. This meant that a pilot could now aim simply by altering course.

The best known fighter pilots of the First War were individual aces, but it soon became obvious that a single pilot could not adequately guard his rear. The 'scouts' began to fly in pairs and later in groups of four or more. Tactics became more complex; the pilots learned the advantage of height superiority and the desirability of attacking 'out of the sun'. Nevertheless, aircraft did not greatly affect the course of the war, if only because not enough were built and they were not properly used by the army commanders who could not see that a single aircraft was more valuable than a whole squadron of cavalry.

Both sides built up their defences in the years between the wars, the Germans in secret, as they were officially forbidden to have an Air Force. Planes such as the Heinkel and Messerschmitt fighters and the Stuka dive-bomber were developed, and the Spanish Civil War gave Germany a chance to

Above: A jet fighter aircraft of the United States Air Force. This aircraft has a rocket engine mounted in its tail to give it extra power. It can fly to an altitude of 36 kilometres (120,000 feet).

Bombing of civilian targets has been a feature of warfare since the Spanish Civil War (1936). Right: Coventry Cathedral was destroyed by German bombs in 1940, during World War II.

try them out. The Royal Air Force retaliated with the Hurricane and the Spitfire. Radio enabled commanders to keep in closer touch with their units, and the British also had the immeasurable advantage of radar.

The Second World War

When Nazi Germany started to push out its frontiers at the expense of its neighbours, it developed a technique known as *blitzkrieg* (lightning war). The essence of this was speed coupled with close co-operation between air and ground forces. From this point onwards, neither side could win a land or sea battle without first obtaining command of the air.

A feature of the Second World War was the intensive bombing of airfields, since it is easier to destroy aircraft on the ground than in the air. The Germans prepared for the invasion of England by attacking the R.A.F. bases with bombers heavily escorted by fighter formations. Some people were in favour of the 'big wing', a massed squadron

Above: A surprise raid by 360 Japanese aircraft on Pearl Harbor, Hawaii, in 1941 brought the United States into World War II.

Left: A bombing formation of British biplanes of World War I.

of fighter aircraft. This could be effective against bomber attacks, but took longer to assemble and left some areas undefended. In practice, fighters nearly always operated in smaller, more flexible formations, usually groups of four aircraft.

The next problem facing the Allies was how to carry the war into enemy territory. The most satisfactory way of doing this was to attack factories and war production centres. Cologne was attacked by a force of over 1,000 bombers, and the resulting destruction was on an unprecedented scale. The newly-developed incendiary bombs were capable of causing raging fires over huge areas. The gradual development of radar navigational aids made night bombing more accurate. The Americans, however, after heavy initial losses, proved that day-time high-altitude bombing could also be effective.

Left: A Supermarine Spitfire, a famous British fighter aircraft of World War II. This model had clipped wings to increase the rate of roll at low altitude.

The Germans continued trying out new forms of air combat right up until the end of the war. The 'flying bombs' and V2 rockets might have had far more effect had they been introduced earlier, and jet aircraft were operating by 1944, though never in great numbers.

Jet aircraft were developed after the Second World War, and were later armed with homing missiles. Their very high speeds made it almost impossible for a squadron to keep together, and planes reverted to operating singly or in pairs. The techniques of refuelling in flight have been perfected and this development has greatly increased the range of fighter aircraft.

Left: A Consolidated Liberator, an American Bomber aircraft of World War II, flying over Montreal. This model was used by the Royal Air Force as a transport between Britain and Canada.

Famous Battles

Actium (31 BC) Octavian, who later became the Emperor Augustus, led the Roman fleet to victory over the Egyptian fleet of Cleopatra and Mark Anthony. The battle, which took place off the west coast of Greece, ended the influence of Egypt in Roman affairs and, in some ways, signalled the end of the Republic.

Agincourt (1415) Henry V of England, with a superbly trained fighting force of about 6,000 archers and men-at-arms, routed a French army 25,000 strong. This battle of the Hundred Years' War enabled the British to reconquer Normandy.

Alamein (1942) The British Eighth Army, under General Montgomery, defeated the German and Italian forces of General Rommel ("the Desert Fox"). El Alamein lies about 70 miles West of Alexandria, in Egypt. The battle was a decisive turning point in World War II.

Armada (1588) The English fleet under Lord Howard of Effingham, defeated the 130-ship "Invincible Armada" of Spain sent by Philip II to invade England. Drake, Frobisher, and Hawkins played prominent roles in the victory. It was the first great gun battle at sea.

Austerlitz (1805) Napoleon and the French army defeated the combined Austrian and Russian armies. This resulted in the break-up of the Holy Roman Empire and left Napoleon a dominant force in Europe.

Balaclava (1854) This battle in the Crimean War included the famous charge of the Light Brigade (September 26), in which the Light Cavalry was sent against Russian artillery. The effect was disastrous. Almost 250 officers and men were killed or wounded from a force of about 670.

Bannockburn (1314) The Scots under Robert Bruce defeated the English troops of Edward II and saved their country from English rule. They were greatly outnumbered, but fought from a better position.

Blenheim (1704) Austrian and English troops under the Duke of Marlborough and Prince Eugène of Savoy heavily defeated a Bavarian and French army under Marshal de Tallard. This battle saved Vienna from invasion and profoundly influenced the course of European history.

Britain (1940) Planes of the Luftwaffe, the German Air Force, tried to bomb Britain into submission, but fighters of the Royal Air Force beat them off. The British were heavily outnumbered but had superior planes — "Hurricanes" and "Spitfires". The use of radar for early warnings of attacks also played a vital role in the Battle of Britain.

Bull Run (1861) The First Battle of Bull Run was the first major clash of the American Civil War. Federal troops attacked Confederate troops but met with resistance "like a stone wall" and were defeated. The Second Battle of Bull Run also resulted in a victory for the Confederates.

Cannae (216 BC) Hannibal commanded the Carthaginian army of 50,000 men which defeated 90,000 Roman troops at this ancient town in south-western Italy.

Châlons-sur-Marne (AD 451) Roman troops under Flavius Aetius and Visigoths under Theodoric defeated Attila and his Huns and this saved Europe from Hun domination.

Coral Sea (1942) An American fleet intercepted a Japanese invasion fleet making for Port Moresby in New Guinea. Most of the fighting was done by carrier-based planes. The battle blocked Japan's push towards Australia.

Crecy (1346) Edward III led English soldiers to victory against the French under Philip VI in this, the first battle of the Hundred Years' War. The English used cannon for the first time in this battle.

Culloden (1746) The Scots under Prince Charles Edward Stuart, "Bonny Prince Charlie", were defeated by the English under the Duke of Cumberland on Culloden moor, near Inverness.

Below: Nelson was hit fatally by a French sniper as he walked the decks of *Victory* at the height of the Battle of Trafalgar.

Dunkirk (1940) The Germans relentlessly attacked retreating Allied troops who were evacuated to England in one of the best-ordered withdrawals ever carried out. All kinds of vessels from destroyers to rowing-boats took part in the evacuation.

Gettysburg (1863) General George Meade's Union army defeated the Confederate army of General Robert E. Lee when they met accidentally. It was a turning point in the American Civil War which heralded defeat for the South.

Hastings (1066) William, Duke of Normandy defeated the Saxon king Harold in one of the most important battles in history. It gave the Normans control of England.

Iwo Jima (1945) American Marines captured this tiny, but strategically important island in the Pacific from the Japanese in some of the bloodiest fighting of World War II.

Jutland (1916) This was the only major sea battle between the main fleets of Britain and Germany in World War I, and left Britain undisputed master of the seas. The British Grand Fleet was under Admiral Jellicoe, the German High Seas Fleet under Admiral von Scheer. The engagement took place in the channel between Norway and Jutland called the Skaggerak.

Leipzig (1813) A combined force of Austrians, Prussians, Russians, and Swedes crushed Napoleon's army in what is often referred to as "The Battle of the Nations"

Lepanto (1571) Don John of Austria led the fleet of the Holy League (the Papal States, Spain, and Venice) against the Turks under Ali Pasha in the eastern Mediterranean. This, the last great battle between galleys, ended Turkish domination of the Mediterranean.

Marathon (490 BC) Miltiades led a badly outnumbered force of Athenians and Plataeans to victory against Darius's Persian army and saved Greece from invasion

Marne (1914) French troops under General Joffe successfully counter-attacked the German invasion forces, who had to retreat beyond the Marne, losing the chance for the quick victory in World War I they had hoped for.

Midway (1942) The Pacific fleet of American Admiral Nimitz defeated the Japanese fleet under Admiral Yamamoto, who was aiming to capture Midway Island to be within striking distance of Hawaii and the United States in World War II.

Orleans (1429) Joan of Arc led the French army which forced the English to give up the seige of Orleans during this decisive battle of the Hundred Years' War.

Poltava (1709) Peter the Great's Russian army routed the invading Swedish forces of Charles XII. This battle marked the beginning of the decline of Sweden as a great European power, and the rise of Russia.

Quebec (1759) General Wolfe made a successful surprise attack on the besieged French in Quebec from the St. Lawrence River. Both Wolfe and the French commander, the Marquis de Montcalm, were killed in the battle, which marked the end of French control in North America.

Salamis (480) The Greek fleet under Themistocles lured the Persian fleet into the straits of Salamis, where the large Persian ships could not manoeuvre. The smaller, faster Greek vessels destroyed more than half the Persian fleet.

Saratoga (1777) General Bourgoyne's English troops were defeated by the American forces of Horatio Gates during the American War of Independence. This prompted the French to enter the war on the American side, the decisive factor which ensured eventual American victory.

Stalingrad (1942-3) The German Sixth Army under General von Paulus captured Stalingrad (now Volgograd) from the Russians after prolonged heavy fighting in World War II. Russian forces under Marshal Zhukov counter-attacked and encircled the Germans in the city. After a long siege, von Paulus surrendered. It was the first major defeat of the Germans in Russia.

Thermopylae (480 BC) At this mountain pass in ancient Greece took place one of the most celebrated battles in Greek history. Leonidas, King of Sparta, headed a small Greek force which fought to the death to stem the invasion of their lands by Xerxes and the Persians.

Trafalgar (1805) Admiral Lord Nelson led the British fleet to victory over a combined French and Spanish fleet under Admiral Villeneuve off Cape Trafalgar on the southern coast of Spain.

Above: The Battle of Waterloo. Wellington's army held its lines all day under terrific assaults by the French. The outcome of the battle was decided by the arrival of Blücher's Prussian army towards evening.

Right: In the Pacific the Americans conducted an island-hopping war. Many islands, such as Iwo Jima, were bitterly defended by the Japanese.

Nelson, on HMS *Victory*, lost his life in the battle, which established Britain's command of the seas.

Waterloo (1815) An outnumbered allied force under the Duke of Wellington ("The Iron Duke") held off Napoleon's French forces until the arrival of Prussian reinforcements under Marshal Blücher. Napoleon suffered a crushing defeat which brought about his final downfall and exile to St. Helena.

Flags of the Nations

A flag is a piece of material, usually an oblong of cloth, which stands for a particular thing, such as a nation, group, person or idea. A national flag, for example, represents the entire nation – not only its ideals, but also its prestige and power, its government and its people.

The ancient Egyptians were the first people to fly flaglike streamers. These were attached to long poles or *standards,* and were used in battle – a practice that continued throughout history. Each side had its *stand-ard-bearer,* who held the standard high for all to see. This helped soldiers to find their

Below: A selection of the world's flags. The oldest national flag is that of Denmark which has had the same design for over 700 years. The cross as a Christian symbol is found on many flags. Other re-

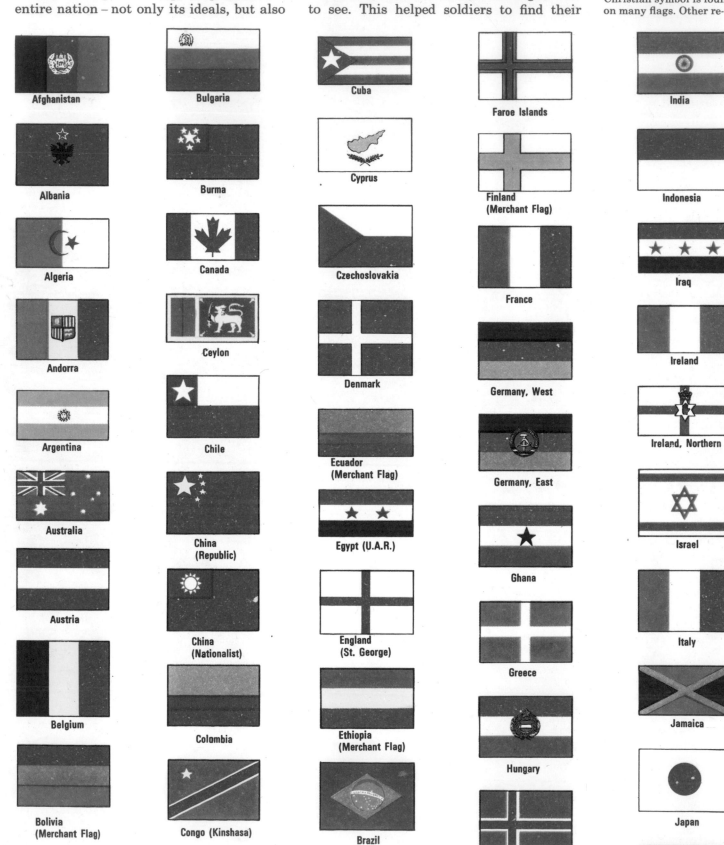

Afghanistan
Albania
Algeria
Andorra
Argentina
Australia
Austria
Belgium
Bolivia (Merchant Flag)

Bulgaria
Burma
Canada
Ceylon
Chile
China (Republic)
China (Nationalist)
Colombia
Congo (Kinshasa)

Cuba
Cyprus
Czechoslovakia
Denmark
Ecuador (Merchant Flag)
Egypt (U.A.R.)
England (St. George)
Ethiopia (Merchant Flag)
Brazil

Faroe Islands
Finland (Merchant Flag)
France
Germany, West
Germany, East
Ghana
Greece
Hungary
Iceland

India
Indonesia
Iraq
Ireland
Ireland, Northern
Israel
Italy
Jamaica
Japan
Jordan

ligious symbols include the crescent moon, a sacred Muslim sign which appears on the flags of some Arab nations; the rising sun, found on several Asian flags; and the six-pointed Star of David, featured on Israel's flag.

comrades quickly in the heat of battle.

Flags have always been important as a means of identifying ships. Particularly in wartime, it may be necessary to know under what country's flag a ship is sailing, before coming too close. Sailors also use flags for sending messages in the International Flag Code.

The most familiar flags in the modern world are those of nations and of international organizations such as the United Nations and the Red Cross. Most of these are oblong in shape. The section of the flag nearest the staff is called the *hoist,* while the part which hangs free is called the *fly.* Each national flag has its own distinctive design, which is repeated on both sides of the material.

Korea, North

Korea, South

Lebanon

Liberia

Liechtenstein

Luxemburg
(Standard of the
Grand Duchess)

Malaysia

Malta

Mexico

Morocco

Netherlands

New Zealand
(Government Flag)

Nigeria

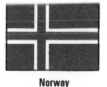

Norway

Pakistan

Persia (Iran)

Peru
(Merchant Flag)

Philippines

Poland

Portugal

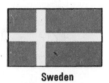

Rhodesia

Rumania

Saudi Arabia

Scotland

Thailand (Siam)

Sierra Leone

Singapore

South Africa

Spain
(Merchant Flag)

Sweden

Switzerland

Tibet
(Former Flag)

Tohga

Trinidad &
Tobago

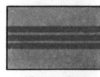

Tunisia

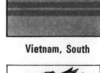

Turkey

United Kingdom

United States

U.S.S.R.

Vatican City

Venezuela
(Merchant Flag)

Vietnam, North

Vietnam, South

Wales

Yugoslavia
(Merchant Flag)

United Nations

The Divided World

Since the end of the Second World War, in 1945, Europe has been divided into two zones, each with fundamentally different political systems. One zone is dominated by Russia, and the various 'satellite' countries which adopted the communist form of government. The other consists of part of Germany, and countries liberated from Nazi domination, supported by Britain and America.

At first, the division was only apparent in Europe but it gradually extended to the Far East, and even the Caribbean Sea. This division gave rise to the expression 'The Iron Curtain' in Europe, and 'The Bamboo Curtain' in the Far East. The reasons for this great split must be sought in world history from the year 1917 onwards. It turns upon two fundamentally opposed theories of government, the communist and the democratic.

The First Communist Revolution
In 1917 revolution broke out in Russia. The party which captured power was called 'communist'. It was led by Lenin who preached the views of a German philosopher, Karl Marx. Marx predicted that the workers in all societies would eventually revolt and found states in which private ownership of all means of production and distribution of wealth would be abolished. This system was adopted by Russia, and other countries feared that communist ideas might bring about revolutions in their own lands. For a time, in fact, Russia seemed likely to incite and support world revolution. But, on Lenin's death, his successor, Stalin, devoted himself to establishing Russia as a modern state. All opposition to his rule was crushed, and he kept Russia in isolation from the rest of the world.

The Rise of German Nationalism
In the uneasy peace between the First and Second World Wars (1918-1939) a new movement gained power in Germany under a fanatical leader, Adolf Hitler. Hitler believed in dictatorship, and in nationalizing a country's resources. He swept away the democratic republic set up in Germany after the war, abolished free elections and all political parties other than his own, and enforced his ideas through secret police forces. He aimed to conquer Europe, and dominate the world. His movement was called National

Above: Adolf Hitler was dictator of Germany from 1933-45.

Below: Karl Marx, whose Communist philosophy led to the Bolshevik Revolution in 1917. The revolution was led by Vladimir Lenin (bottom) who founded and developed the first Communist state.

Socialism (Nazism) but he was opposed to Marxist communism. Hitler eventually began a series of attacks (on Austria, Czechoslovakia, Poland) which finally forced Britain and France to declare war on him. German forces quickly overran Europe, and were only prevented from invading Britain by the great victory of the Royal Air Force over the German Air Force, in the Battle of Britain. After this defeat, Hitler turned to attack Russia.

After terribly costly struggles the Germans were prevented from overwhelming Russia, and the Allies made a joint effort to defeat Germany. Russia launched attacks in the east, and Anglo-American forces invaded France. The allied forces met in the centre of Germany, and the problems of occupation and restoration of order began.

It soon became clear that Russia was determined to maintain communist satellite states (Poland, Hungary, Rumania, East Germany) in her sphere of influence, as protection against invasion in the future. Thus Germany, and Europe, split into East and West zones, one communist, the other democratic and capitalist.

The Berlin Wall
One outcome of the joint invasion and occupation of Germany was the fact that the former capital, Berlin, was isolated in the East German, or communist, zone, and neither the Anglo-American authorities nor the Russians could agree on its future. Berlin thus became symbolic of the struggle between the two systems. In 1948, the Russians refused to allow road, or rail, transport to pass through East Germany to the city, hoping to force it to surrender. The Western Allies organized a massive system of supplies by air, known as the Berlin Air Lift, to keep the city from collapse. Faced with this determined resistance, and unwilling to risk a 'shooting war', the communist blockade was abandoned. But, from then onwards, a silent war, called the 'cold war' began, and, in 1961, the East Germans, with Russian support, began to erect a great wall between the two halves of the city. Old houses were re-inforced with concrete, walls erected, obstacles and minefields set up.

In time, some of the satellite countries attempted to loosen their ties with Russia. There was a revolt in Hungary, which Russian tanks soon suppressed. Later, in Czechoslovakia, Russia again invaded to prevent a more liberal socialist regime from emerging. Poland, Rumania, and Bulgaria, remained communist. Yugoslavia eventually broke away from direct Russian domination, remaining communist, but on its own terms.

The Far East

While the great struggle was taking place in Europe the Americans were confronted with the fact that Japan had invaded China, bombed American naval bases, and swept through the East, taking country after country. Bitter battles by air, land and sea ensued and Japan finally surrendered when atomic bombs were dropped on Hiroshima and Nagasaki. China, long divided by various war lords, was partly under the rule of a nationalist leader, General Chiang-kai-shek. Americans supported his regime, but, in the north, a determined communist movement under Mao Tse-tung was preparing to take over from Chiang. Mao's movement succeeded, and Chiang retreated to the island of Formosa, off the Chinese mainland.

Communist Wars in the Far East

Strong communist movements persist in the Far East. The country of Korea was partitioned into North and South areas after the Japanese defeat. But, with Chinese backing, the northern (communist) part tried to take over the southern half. The United Nations Organization, largely with American Forces, fought a war to prevent the destruction of the South Korean republic. This war lasted from 1950-1953, and became a bitter issue for Americans.

Meanwhile, another communist movement was brewing in Viet-nam, formerly known as Indo-China. This area was once part of the French colonial empire, but under the leadership of a dedicated communist, Ho-chi-minh, French forces were defeated in 1954 and driven from the country. As a result of a conference of several nations, the country was divided, like Korea, into North and South Viet-nam. But the communist North eventually invaded the South and the Americans again found themselves involved in a costly and bitter war.

NATO – North Atlantic Treaty Organization

In 1949, European and North American countries signed a pact of mutual support and protection. Belgium, France, Luxemburg, the Netherlands, United Kingdom, Canada, Denmark, Iceland, Italy, Norway, Portugal and the U.S.A. were finally joined by Greece, Turkey, and the West German Republic, in this treaty. It provided for joint forces in Europe, and was based on the fear that the Security Council of the United Nations Organization would be unable to prevent Russian attacks, because of the power of veto in the General Assembly (see United Nations Organization). France eventually withdrew from the pact, resenting American influence in Europe.

Warsaw Pact

This pact was a treaty signed in Warsaw in 1955 by Albania, Bulgaria, Czechoslovakia, Hungary, Poland, Rumania, the East German Republic and the U.S.S.R. It was an agreement of mutual assistance for a period of 20 years, and was virtually the communist response to the NATO pact signed by the Western democracies in 1949.

European Economic Community

In 1957, France, Italy, West Germany, Belgium, Holland and Luxembourg, signed the Treaty of Rome. This basic agreement forms the basis of what has come to be known as The Common Market. It provides for a plan gradually to eliminate internal customs tariffs, to unify economic plans, and to eliminate restrictions on the free movement of workers and capital between the various national areas. It was a step towards the unification of democratic Europe, and is important because it introduces the idea of a limitation of national sovereignty in the cause of promoting the general good of all.

United Nations Organization

At the San Francisco Conference of 1945, 50 nations founded the United Nations Organization, as a step towards the establishment of world government, and international co-operation. It succeeded the League of Nations, set up after the First World War with similar aims.

It has several councils, but the most important of the Organization is the General Assembly. There are now over 110 nations with representatives in this Assembly. It has been effective, in some cases, in limiting the spread of war, but is hampered by the fact that, if any nation vetoes a decision, it has no effect and cannot be enforced. It was as a result of this power of veto that the North Atlantic Treaty Organization was formed (see NATO). Thus, despite much good work done by the Organization, the basic world division is apparent even at the highest levels.

Above: Barbed wire in front of the Brandenburg Gate in Berlin bears witness to the ideological and actual barrier between East and West.

Below: Mao Tse-tung, the Chairman of the Chinese Communist party. As a result of his policies, the Communist movement has been split into two factions – one supporting Russia, the other, China.

Atoms

Inside the Atom

Everything in the universe is made of incredibly tiny particles called atoms. Atoms are so small that if ten thousand million could be placed end to end they would measure half an inch.

The idea of atoms is not new. The Ancient Greeks suggested that tiny particles which they called atoms might exist and we still use their word for these minute particles.

In the past atoms were thought to be solid particles of stuff like miniature billiard balls or ball-bearings, and although it is often convenient to consider atoms in this way, modern science indicates that atoms consist largely of empty space!

At the centre of every atom lies its core or nucleus, which is very small compared with the size of the atom as a whole. Despite its small size it is in the nucleus that most of the mass of the atom is concentrated. Furthermore, the nucleus is always positively charged. At some distance from the nucleus, circling around it like planets around the Sun, are tiny, very light particles called *electrons*. These electrons are negatively charged and are held in orbit by the attraction between their own negative charge and the positive charge of the nucleus in much the same way as the opposite poles of magnets will attract one another.

What is the nucleus made of? The nucleus contains small heavy particles called *protons*, which possess the positive charge, and other small particles called *neutrons* which have the same mass as the protons but have no charge at all.

Atomic Number

The electrons have just as much negative charge as the protons have positive charge, although the protons are almost 2,000 times heavier. Because the negative charge of one electron will exactly cancel the positive charge of one proton, the number of protons in the nucleus must be equal to the number of electrons in orbit for the atom as a whole to remain neutral. The number of protons possessed by any atom is called its *atomic number* and there are usually at least as many neutrons as there are protons in the nucleus of an atom. Hydrogen is the only atom which possesses no neutrons. Atomic structure can perhaps be more clearly understood by considering the kinds of atoms in order of rank from the simplest to the more complicated.

Above: A hydrogen atom consists of a single electron moving round a single proton. The orbit of the electron changes so rapidly that it seems to weave a solid shell round the nucleus.

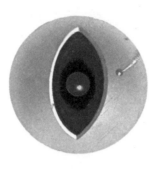

Above: The orbit of the electron is shown as a solid shell, cut-away to reveal the proton at the centre.

Below: An oxygen atom has eight protons and eight neutrons in its nucleus. Eight electrons circle the nucleus, two in the inner shell and six in the outer shell.

Atomic Weight

We might expect an atom of helium (atomic number 2) to be twice as heavy as an atom of hydrogen (atomic number 1) but it is in fact four times as heavy. This extra heaviness (mass) is of course due to the presence of two neutrons in the nucleus of helium. Since the proton is very small and the electron even smaller, it can be seen that the atom consists largely of space with most of its mass concentrated at the centre. (Although atoms are shown as a billiard ball type of sphere, it must be remembered that there is really no solid shell like this around them.)

In atom number 3, lithium (symbol Li), three electrons orbit around a nucleus containing three protons and four neutrons. By adding up the total numbers of protons and neutrons we see that an atom of lithium is seven times as heavy as an atom of hydrogen. In other words, the *atomic weight* of lithium is seven. Atom number 6 is carbon (symbol C). Its nucleus is made up of six protons and six neutrons, giving it an atomic weight of twelve. The six positive charges on the protons are balanced by six negatively charged electrons circling the nucleus.

Electron Shells

The electron orbits in every atom are arranged in a series of shells. The innermost shell can hold no more than two electrons

Far right: Below 1080°C., copper is a solid. Its atoms are closely packed and vibrate together while remaining in their fixed pattern. This is why it is difficult to press a solid into a new shape.

Right: Between 1080°C. and 2580°C., copper is a liquid. The atoms are still tightly packed but they slip against each other in all directions. The hotter the liquid is, the faster the atoms will be moving. Because the atoms slide so easily, a liquid has no shape.

and the second shell can hold no more than eight. The heavier atoms have more shells.

Very few varieties of atoms have been considered so far, but if we so wished we could go on building up the atoms in the same way and eventually show how all of the atoms were made up, provided that we strictly follow certain rules. These rules govern the number of electrons permissible in each electron shell.

Elements

If we could separate all the atoms in the Universe we should find there are over 92 different kinds. A substance whose atoms are all of one kind is called an *element*.

In an element atoms are held together by mutual attraction. In a *solid* this attraction is strong. In a *liquid* it is weak. In a *gas* the atoms move freely. Heating can weaken the attraction between atoms, thus changing an element from a solid to a liquid, and then to a gas.

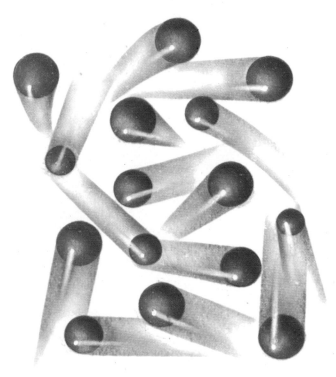

Right: Above 2580°C., copper is a gas. The atoms are moving so fast that they have broken free of each other. They take up much more room than as a solid or a liquid. Like a liquid, a gas has no shape, but, unlike a liquid, it will spread out to fill completely any container.

Radioactivity

Radioactivity was first discovered by Henri Becquerel in Paris in 1896. He had noticed that some undeveloped photographic plates had been fogged by being left in contact with a bottle of uranium ore. Becquerel concluded after some experiments that the uranium was giving off radiations. Today we know that the atoms of radioactive elements such as uranium and radium are continually disintegrating, and can give off three kinds of radiation. In two of these *alpha particles* (written α particles) and *beta particles* (written β particles) are given off. An alpha particle consists of a group of two protons and two neutrons, while a beta particle is identical to an electron. Both types of particle come from the atom's nucleus. A third kind of radiation, called *gamma rays,* does not consist of particles. Gamma rays are like very penetrating X-rays.

Radioactive Isotopes

There can be several kinds of the same atom, called *isotopes,* and many of these are also radioactive. Atoms of carbon, for example, have a number of isotopes which differ only in the number of neutrons contained in their nuclei (plural of nucleus). Some radioactive isotopes give off only alpha particles. Others give off beta particles. Still others give off both. Today radioactive isotopes can be made artificially for use in industry and medicine. Such isotopes are made by exposing carbon, iodine and other elements found in nature to strong radioactivity in special 'ovens' or *reactors* using uranium.

Detection of Radioactivity

Scientists working in plants where radioactive isotopes are being made and used must be protected by special clothing. They also carry small badges or *dosimeters* containing strips of photographic film. At the end of a day's work the film is developed to see if a dangerous 'dose' of radiation has fogged it.

Radioactivity can be detected by *geiger counters.* A small tube contains two metal electrodes connected with an amplifier and a voltmeter, and sometimes a loudspeaker. Radioactive particles passing through the tube cause an electric current to flow, which gives a reading on the voltmeter. The presence of radiation can also be heard as a series of clicks from the loudspeaker.

Uses of Radioactive Isotopes

In medical research scientists can tell what is happening in the brain and other organs of the body using radioactive isotopes. Radioactive iodine, for example, can be injected in very small quantities into the bloodstream. From there the isotope is absorbed by the thyroid glands. By placing a geiger counter near the throat, the isotope can be detected as it is being absorbed by the thyroid. In this way more can be learned about the thyroid, which influences our rate of growth.

One of the many interesting uses of radioactive isotopes in industry is in the detecting of blocks in oil pipelines. A small plug called a 'go-devil' is put into one end of the pipeline. The flow of oil carries the go-devil to the block, where it stops. In the go-devil a tube of radioactive isotope has been placed. All that has to be done is to move along the length of the pipeline with a geiger counter, which will start clicking at the exact spot where the go-devil has come to a stop.

Above: Disposing of radioactive waste materials. While the materials are being buried in a special container, the radiation is monitored to protect workers.

Below: The half-life period of a radioactive isotope is the time taken for half of the atoms in any given sample to decay to atoms of another element. For sodium-24 this is 15 hours. For uranium-238 the half-life period is nearly 5,000 million years.

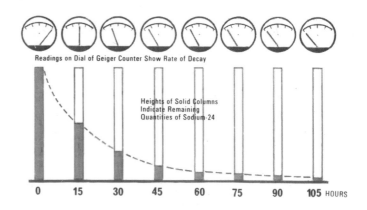

Readings on Dial of Geiger Counter Show Rate of Decay

Heights of Solid Columns Indicate Remaining Quantities of Sodium-24

0   15   30   45   60   75   90   105 HOURS

Half-Life Period

As atoms of a radioactive element disintegrate they change or *decay* to atoms of another element. Atoms of uranium decay eventually to atoms of lead. The time that it takes for half of the atoms to change or *decay* to atoms of another element is called the *half-life period*. This ranges from a fraction of a second for some radioactive elements to many many millions of years for others. The artificial radioactive isotope sodium-24 has a half-life period of 15 hours. During this time half of the atoms in one gram of sodium-24 would decay to atoms of magnesium, leaving half a gram of the radioactive isotope. During the next 15 hours half of the remaining atoms of sodium-24 would decay, leaving one-quarter of a gram of the radioactive isotope, and so on.

Archaeologists are sometimes able to use the half-life period to measure the age of historic objects made of once-living materials, such as wood. Carbon-14 is a naturally occurring radioactive isotope of carbon found in living things. By measuring the carbon-14 content in an old wooden object and comparing it with the content in a piece of new wood, the age of the wooden object can be calculated. *Radio-carbon dating,* as this process is called, was used in studying the Dead Sea Scrolls.

Right: Atoms of uranium 235 decay into atoms of another element by emitting charged particles from their nuclei. But these atoms, too, are unstable and decay into other atoms. The process continues until a stable isotope is reached, in this case lead-207. This is called a radioactive series.

Below: Aided by a mirror, and protected by a shield of lead bricks, a scientist works with radioactive materials.

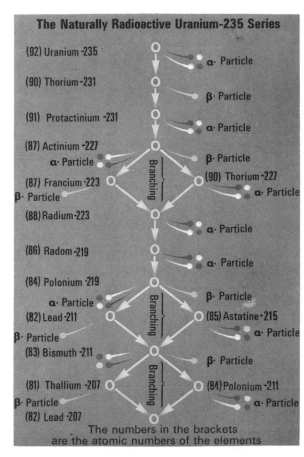

The Naturally Radioactive Uranium-235 Series

(92) Uranium -235
α- Particle

(90) Thorium -231
β- Particle

(91) Protactinium -231
α- Particle

(87) Actinium -227
α- Particle
β- Particle

(87) Francium -223
(90) Thorium -227
β- Particle
α- Particle

(88) Radium -223

(86) Radom -219
α- Particle

(84) Polonium -219
α- Particle
β- Particle

(82) Lead -211
α- Particle
(85) Astatine -215
α- Particle

(83) Bismuth -211
β- Particle
β- Particle

(81) Thallium -207
(84) Polonium -211
β- Particle
α- Particle

(82) Lead -207

Branching

The numbers in the brackets are the atomic numbers of the elements

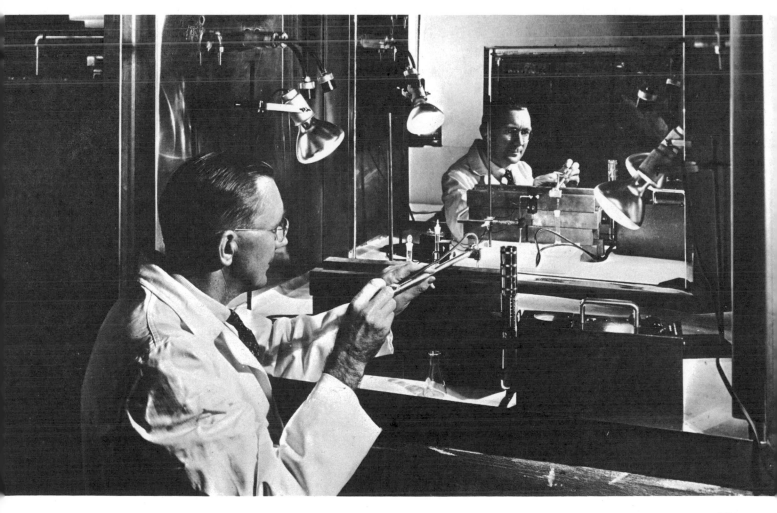

Nuclear Power

Splitting the Atom

The nucleus of the atom consists of particles called protons and neutrons, held together by powerful attractive forces. When the nucleus is broken to pieces, these forces are released as energy in the form of heat and radiation. In 1932 Sir John Cockcroft and E. T. S. Walton 'split' atoms of lithium by 'bombarding' them with protons. The protons, being positive electrically, were speeded up by being attracted down metal tubes which were charged negatively. At the bottom of the tubes was placed a piece of lithium metal. This apparatus was one of the first *particle accelerators* or 'atom smashers'.

Atom-smashing Machines

A more powerful type of accelerator for splitting atoms and studying the energy produced was invented by E. O. Lawrence during the 1930's. His apparatus, called the *cyclotron,* used two hollow metal electrodes, each shaped like the letter D. These *dees,* as they were called, were given alternate positive and negative charges by an alternating current. This exerted a 'push and pull' effect on the particles, which whirled around and around in the dees at ever increasing speeds, finally 'bombarding' the specimen placed at the exit from the dees.

One of the most modern types of atom smashers is the *synchrotron.* The walls of a circular tube (which can have a diameter of

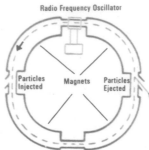
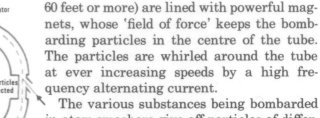

Above: The synchrotron is the most modern type of atom-smashing machine. Protons are fed into the synchrotron from a high-energy source such as a Van der Graaff generator or a linear accelerator. The protons are accelerated in the synchrotron by a radio frequency accelerator and kept in a circular path by the action of the ring of magnets.

Below: In the AGR (advanced gas cooled reactor) the reactor is cooled by carbon dioxide gas. The hot gas goes to heat exchangers where the heat turns water into steam to drive turbines connected to electrical generators. The concrete biological shield protects workers from dangerous radiation.

60 feet or more) are lined with powerful magnets, whose 'field of force' keeps the bombarding particles in the centre of the tube. The particles are whirled around the tube at ever increasing speeds by a high frequency alternating current.

The various substances being bombarded in atom smashers give off particles of different kinds, including alpha particles and beta particles.

The Chain Reaction

When an atomic bomb explodes, a vast amount of energy is released in a tiny fraction of a second. In the bomb, the energy that was locked up in the nuclei of uranium atoms is released when these nuclei are split up. This *fission reaction* is triggered off by the capture of a neutron by a single uranium nucleus. The nucleus breaks up, throwing out a number of fragments, neutrons among them. These neutrons are captured by more uranium nuclei which then split up producing another generation containing still more neutrons. The process keeps on repeating itself until the whole mass of uranium is consumed. In this *chain reaction* a vast amount of energy is created using quite a small mass of uranium.

Nuclear Power

The atomic explosion is an example of an *uncontrolled fission reaction,* with all the energy released in as short a time as possible. To drive power stations, a steady source of energy is needed, and this may be obtained from a *controlled* fission reaction. In this, the uranium 'fuel' must be consumed slowly and steadily. The energy of the exploding nuclear fragments is then converted into heat energy, which is carried away and used to turn water into steam to drive the turbines. This process is carried out in a nuclear *reactor,* or *pile.*

Nuclear Reactors

Every pile uses nuclear fuel – a material that will support the controlled chain reaction. The fuel most commonly used in nuclear reactors is uranium. Naturally occurring uranium is a mixture of different isotopes (atoms of the same element but of different masses). Over 99% of the naturally found element is uranium-238, and less than 1% is the lighter isotope, uranium-235. It is the uranium-235 that is most useful in promoting a chain reaction, and to make atomic bombs, great expense and trouble was incurred in extracting the lighter isotope.

For use in nuclear reactors it would be obviously easier and cheaper to be able to use uranium in its naturally occurring form.

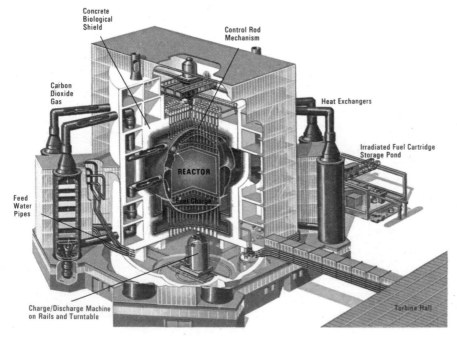

Concrete Biological Shield

Control Rod Mechanism

Carbon Dioxide Gas

Heat Exchangers

Irradiated Fuel Cartridge Storage Pond

REACTOR

Fuel Charge

Feed Water Pipes

Turbine Hall

Charge/Discharge Machine on Rails and Turntable

To do this, the pile has to be constructed so that fission of the uranium-235 occurs, while the uranium-238 is not allowed to interfere with the process. A large block of graphite (the kind of carbon found in pencil 'lead') has holes drilled in it. In these holes are placed a number of *fuel rods* which are made of uranium-238 which also contains a small proportion of the 'explosive' atoms of uranium-235. These keep on splitting and giving off energy within the uranium-238 and heat is produced in the graphite block. As the uranium-235 atoms split, very fast-moving neutrons are produced. Uranium-238, unfortunately, absorbs fast neutrons, but not slow-moving neutrons. So to keep the 're-action' going the fast neutrons are slowed down when they pass through the graphite block, which for rather obvious reasons is called a *moderator*. Now the uranium-238 will not absorb the neutrons, which can freely move about among the uranium-235 atoms, bombarding them so that they will

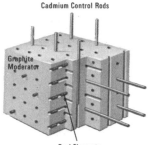

Above: In the core of a uranium-graphite pile, uranium fuel elements are placed in loading tubes separated by blocks of graphite moderator. Cadmium control rods may be pushed in or out of the pile.

Below: C-Stellarator, the largest U.S. device used for thermonuclear research.

keep on splitting as a 'controlled' chain reaction.

The heat energy produced by this type of reactor can be harnessed in a nuclear power station. Air or carbon dioxide is pumped around the moderator block, is heated, and then passes into a boiler, where the hot gas changes water into steam. The steam is then piped off to drive steam turbines, which in turn drive generators producing electricity. To stop the reactor working the fuel rods are withdrawn from the moderator.

Thermonuclear Power

Just as the *fission* of heavy atomic nuclei releases energy, so does the *fusion* of light atomic nuclei. The fusion of hydrogen is the Sun's chief source of energy. Fusion, or *thermonuclear*, reactions are a promising source of power. Deuterium, an isotope of hydrogen, is used as the starting point for man-made nuclear fusions since it is easier to fuse than ordinary hydrogen.

Africa

Africa is the world's second largest continent. With its area of 11,671,000 square miles, it is three and a half times as large as the United States. But Africa has only 320,000,000 people. The United States has about twice as many people to every square mile.

Large parts of Africa are almost empty wastelands. Great, burning-hot deserts, including the Sahara in the north and the Namib and Kalahari in the south, cover about two-fifths of Africa. Life is only possible where water is available. For example, nearly all Egyptians live in the valley of the River Nile. Either side of this valley is empty desert.

Near the Equator, especially in western and west-central Africa, the rainfall is very heavy, sometimes more than 150 inches a year. This hot, rain-drenched region is covered by thick, luxuriant forests. The trees grow so close together that their leaves blot out the sun.

Although most of Africa lies within the tropics, more than a third of the continent is a great *plateau* (high plain). Because they are so high, many parts of Africa close to the Equator have a pleasant climate. Travellers going inland from the steaming-hot seaports of Mombasa and Dar-es-Salaam in eastern Africa climb steeply to the plateau. Average temperatures fall at a rate of about 1°F for every 330 feet. In eastern Africa are the continent's two highest mountains, Kilimanjaro in Tanzania (19,340 feet above sea level) and Mount Kenya (17,058 feet). Snow and ice cap the peaks of these mountains.

Grassland called *savanna* covers much of

Above: The trunk of the giant baobab tree can reach 30 feet in diameter.

Below: The ruined stone city of Zimbabwe in Rhodesia is believed to date from the 10th century A.D. or earlier.

Below: Above Kinshasa the Congo is navigable by river boats for more than 1,000 miles.

the high plains of Africa. Great herds of animals still roam over Africa's grasslands and forests. In the past, thousands of animals were killed by hunters and poachers. To save the animals, many African governments have set up special parks and game reserves.

Throughout the eastern African plateau runs the deep African rift valley. This colossal valley stretches from Syria in Asia through the Red Sea and eastern Africa to Mozambique. It contains many lakes, including Lake Tanganyika, the world's longest freshwater lake.

Africa's largest lake is Lake Victoria, which lies between Kenya and Tanzania. Africa's greatest rivers are the Nile, the Congo, the Niger and the Zambesi.

People and Products

North of the Sahara, most of the people are Arabs or Berbers. They follow the Muslim religion. Negroid Africans, who make up three-quarters of Africa's population, live south of the Sahara. Some of them follow tribal religions. More than five million people of European ancestry live in Africa, many of them in South Africa. Their ancestors were the pioneers who introduced western ideas of farming, mining and industry. About half a million people of Asian origin also live in Africa. About 35,000,000 people, including most of the Europeans, are Christians.

Most Africans are farmers. They either rear cattle or grow crops to feed their families. The wealth of many African countries is based on one or two crops which are grown on plantations. For example, Ghana's most important export is cocoa. Eastern Africa's main products are coffee and sisal. Africa produces nearly three-quarters of the world's palm oil and

Above: Catching fish in bamboo traps at rapids on a tributary of the Congo (Zaïre) River.

Key to Independent Countries

1, Algeria; 2, Botswana; 3, Burundi; 4, Cameroon; 5, Central African Republic; 6, Chad, 7, Congo (Brazzaville); 8, Zaire; 9, Dahomey; 10, Egypt; 11, Equatorial Guinea; 12, Ethiopia; 13, Gabon; 14, Gambia; 15, Ghana; 16, Guinea; 17, Ivory Coast; 18, Kenya; 19, Lesotho; 20, Liberia; 21, Libya; 22, Madagascar (Malagasy Republic); 23, Malawi; 24, Mali; 25, Mauritania; 26, Mauritius; 27, Morocco; 28, Niger; 29, Nigeria; 30, Rwanda; 31, Senegal; 32, Sierra Leone; 33, Somalia; 34, South Africa; 35, Sudan; 36, Swaziland; 37, Tanzania; 38, Togo; 39, Tunisia; 40, Uganda; 41, Upper Volta; 42, Zambia.

Key to Colonies and Territories

43, Afars and Issas; 44, Angola; 45, Canary Islands; 46, Cape Verde Islands; 47, Comoro Islands; 48, Madeira Islands; 49, Mozambique; 50, Portuguese Guinea; 51, Réunion; 52, Rhodesia; 53, St. Helena; 54, São Tomé and Principe; 55, Seychelles Islands; 56, South West Africa; 57, Spanish Sahara.

palm kernels. Other crops include cotton, fruits, tea and tobacco.

Africa produces almost all the world's diamonds and a large quantity of gold. Other important minerals are copper, cobalt, petroleum and uranium. Africa has little coal, but hydro-electric power is used by the few manufacturing industries.

History

Northern Africa was important in the early growth of civilizations around the Mediterranean Sea. The Nile valley was the centre of one of the greatest early civilizations.

But little was known of Africa south of the Sahara. Arab traders visited the area and found great empires in western Africa. But to Europeans, Africa was a 'dark continent'. After Vasco da Gama had sailed to Asia around the southern tip of Africa in 1497, many ships used this route. Soon the African coastline was charted. But few people were interested in exploring the interior.

From the 1400's, European sailors began to ship slaves from Africa. The slave trade continued until the 1800's. An estimated 14 million African slaves were shipped to the Americas. Usually the slave traders bought

Right: Berber woman from Morocco. The peoples north of the Sahara belong to the Caucasoid race.

Right: Washing clothes at an oasis. The Sahara contains many oases, ranging from mere water-holes to large fertile areas where many people live.

Below: Gold mining in South Africa, the world's leading gold producing country.

Below: Negroid peoples inhabit most of Africa south of the Sahara. The Negroes of eastern and southern Africa have a lighter skin colour than the 'true' Negroes of western Africa.

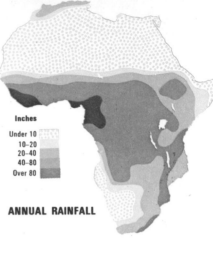

Inches

Under 10
10–20
20–40
40–80
Over 80

ANNUAL RAINFALL

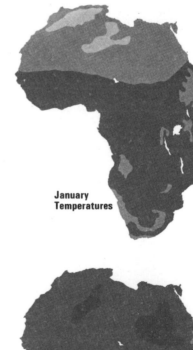

°F.

Over 90
70–90
50–70
Under 50

January Temperatures

July Temperatures

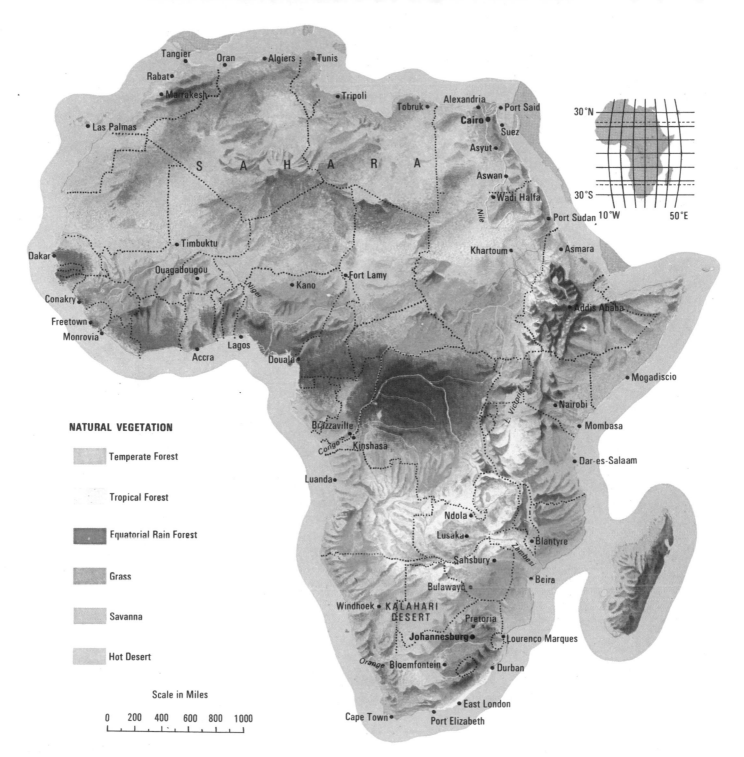

NATURAL VEGETATION

Temperate Forest

Tropical Forest

Equatorial Rain Forest

Grass

Savanna

Hot Desert

Scale in Miles

0 200 400 600 800 1000

slaves from African coastal chiefs whose people raided inland tribes. European traders seldom travelled inland.

An early and important settlement at the Cape of Good Hope was established in 1652. This settlement developed to form part of present-day South Africa.

The great period of European exploration of the interior came during the 1800's. Many explorers were missionaries who helped to stamp out the terrible slave trade. Bold men, such as David Livingstone in southern Africa, Mungo Park in western Africa and Henry Morton Stanley in the Congo region, braved many hardships to discover the secrets of Africa.

Information brought back by explorers interested European governments, who

Below: Huge herds of animals once roamed Africa's grasslands. Now they are protected in game rserves.

began to establish settlements and colonies. By the 1890's, almost all of Africa was divided up between the European powers.

From the 1890's to the 1950's, most African countries were European colonies. The Europeans introduced new ways of life and developed Africa. But many Africans resented foreign rule. In the late 1950's and early 1960's nearly all African countries achieved independence.

Most of the countries are poor. Partly as a result of their poverty, many countries were unsettled during the 1960's. Army leaders overthrew several elected governments. Some countries adopted one-party rule. In Congo (Kinshasa) and in Nigeria, terrible civil wars led to many deaths and much suffering.

The Living Cell

In 1667, a famous scientist called Robert Hooke looked at some thin pieces of cork through a primitive kind of microscope. He saw that the cork was made of tiny box-like units, and he called these units *cells*. Cork comes from the bark of a tree and was once living material. We know now that all living things are composed of cells. Some of the simplest creatures, such as the Amoeba, consist of only one cell. On the other hand, a human body is composed of millions of tiny cells. It is within these cells that the vital processes of life are carried out.

In a simple one-celled organism, all the processes go on in the one cell, but in the more complicated organisms there are many different kinds of cells, each shaped and designed to do a particular job. There are, for example, muscle cells that enable us to move, bone cells that support us, and nerve cells that carry signals from one part of the body to another. Plants also contain several different kinds of cells. Plant cells differ from animal cells mainly in being surrounded by rigid walls of cellulose.

In spite of the great variety of cell shapes, all living cells have certain features in common. The basis of all living cells is *protoplasm,* often called 'living jelly'. The main component of protoplasm is water, but it also contains a very complicated mixture of proteins, sugars, fatty materials, and salts. Chemical changes are going on in it all the time. There seems to be a very fine network of fibres and channels running through the protoplasm, and these same fibres form an extremely thin membrane which separates each cell from the next.

Inside the cell there is the nucleus. The microscope may also reveal a number of fluid-filled spaces called *vacuoles*. These are usually small in animal cells, but plant cells normally have one or more large vacuoles

Below: Diagram showing simple cell division. The nucleus divides first by mitosis.

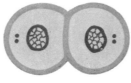

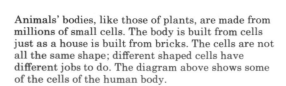

Animals' bodies, like those of plants, are made from millions of small cells. The body is built from cells just as a house is built from bricks. The cells are not all the same shape; different shaped cells have different jobs to do. The diagram above shows some of the cells of the human body.

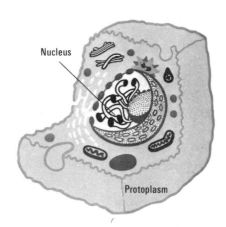

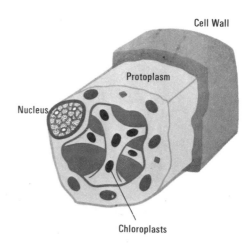

The biggest difference between a plant cell and an animal cell is in the cell wall. The plant cell has a rigid cellulose cell wall. The second difference is that most plant cells have green chloroplasts containing chlorophyll in them. Apart from these differences, plant and animal cells are similar. Both have nuclei and water vacuoles, and protoplasm in which these parts are enclosed. Inside the nuclei there are chromosomes carrying genes.

and the fluid is called cell sap. Plant cells also normally contain *chloroplasts*. Very high magnification, using electron microscopes, will reveal other very small objects in the protoplasm. Among them are the rod-like *mitochondria,* which are believed to be concerned with releasing energy for the cell's activities.

Genes and Chromosomes

The nucleus of the cell is the 'brain', where all of the cell's activities are controlled and guided. The nuclei also carry the 'instructions' which ensure that a parrot egg becomes a parrot, an acorn becomes an oak tree, and so on. These 'instructions', or *genes* as they are properly called, are carried on slender threads called *chromosomes,* which can sometimes be seen through powerful microscopes. The number of chromosomes varies from species to species, but it is almost always an even number. Human cells, for example, contain 46 chromosomes. Cells from pea plants contain 14 chromosomes. The genes are made up of a substance known as deoxyribonucleic acid – DNA for short. The genes are extremely small and there are probably about 250,000 of them in a single human cell.

The genes control the cells and make sure that they are the right sort by ensuring that the right proteins are made in the cell protoplasm. In this way, parrot egg cells will always build parrot proteins and will always grow into parrots, not cuckoos.

When plants and animals reproduce, the behaviour of the chromosomes ensures that the offspring receive the correct instructions. In single-celled organisms, which usually reproduce simply by splitting into two halves, the chromosomes duplicate themselves before the division takes place. Each half of the nucleus then receives a set of chromosomes to take to its new cell. The same thing happens during the growth of many-celled creatures, ensuring that new cells are just like the old ones.

Reproduction in many-celled organisms usually involves two parents and revolves around the joining of two cells—one from each parent. The new creature receives half of its instructions from each parent and it will not be exactly like either of them. A human child, for example, may get instructions for blue eyes from his mother and for brown hair from his father. The way in which genes and characteristics are handed on from parents to their offspring is called *genetics,* or *heredity.*

From time to time, a chromosome or a gene may be damaged or altered when its

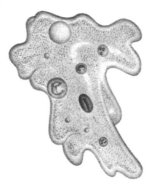

The Amoeba is a one-celled animal. It belongs to the Protozoa group, all the members of which are one-celled. The Amoeba is one of the simplest animals. It can do most of the things that multi-cellular animals do. It breathes, eats, moves and reproduces. It reproduces simply by dividing itself in two.

Parents each give some genes to their children. The genes decide what the child will look like. If both parents are fair haired, the children will also be fair. If one parent is fair and the other is dark then the children will be dark, but will have one fair gene and one dark gene. If one of these children later marries a fair person, then some of their children will be fair and others dark. If they marry another dark haired person like themselves they may have a fair child but will have more dark ones. In the diagrams D indicates dark-hair genes and f fair-hair genes. If both dark-hair and fair-hair genes are present, the former overrides the latter and produces dark hair

cell divides. Such a change is called a *mutation.* If it occurs in an ordinary body cell it is not likely to have much effect, but if it occurs in a reproductive cell – an egg, for example – it can result in a very unusual animal or plant. Mutations are usually harmful and the creature dies, but some mutations are useful, and the altered gene can be passed on to the next generation. This is one of the ways in which living things change, or *evolve,* as time goes by.

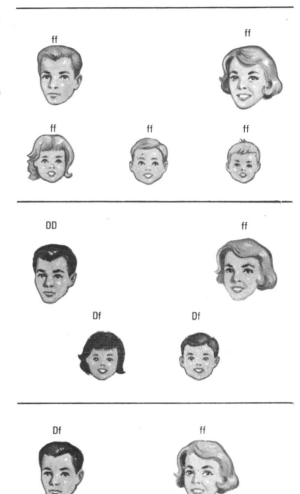

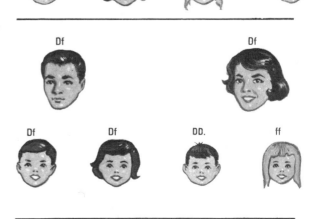

—F

The Animal Kingdom

Biologists know of about a million different species (kinds) of animals, but only about a third as many plants. Animals vary from the tiny one-celled amoeba – so small that it can be seen only under a microscope – to the huge blue whale, which may reach a length of 100 feet and a weight of 150 tons.

One important difference between plants and animals is that most animals have far more accurate and sensitive senses. They can learn more precisely what is happening in their surroundings, and react quickly to it. This is because they have some kind of nervous system. As a result, they can avoid danger and search for food and shelter. Animals can also *adapt* (change) to varying conditions more quickly. It is this great ability to adapt that has led to the great variety of animals. This has occurred through the process of evolution.

But, in spite of this variety, most animals have similar features to some other animals.

Above: Female *Anopheles* mosquito, the carrier of malaria. Man wages a continual battle against insect pests. Insects are one of the most successful groups of animals. There are about one million known kinds, more than all other species of animals added together.

Below: A family tree of the Animal Kingdom.

Biologists use such similarities as the basis on which to classify animals into groups. The closer they are related – the more similar they are – the closer is the grouping. In this way, a number of species may be grouped into a single *genus,* several of which make up a *family.* Families are themselves grouped into *orders.* A number of orders make a *class,* and several classes comprise a *phylum.* The 20-odd phyla are the principal groups that make up the animal kingdom.

Perhaps the most varied and most important phylum is the *Chordata,* the chordates. What distinguishes them from all other animals is the hollow nerve cord that extends the length of their backs. They also have some kind of supporting rod of elastic material. In the more primitive chordates, this is a simple *notochord,* but the *vertebrates* – the most important group of chordates – all have backbones.

The vertebrates are the most advanced and most successful of all the animals. They include the fishes, amphibians, reptiles, birds and mammals. The mammals are the most advanced of the vertebrates, and the most advanced mammal is man himself.

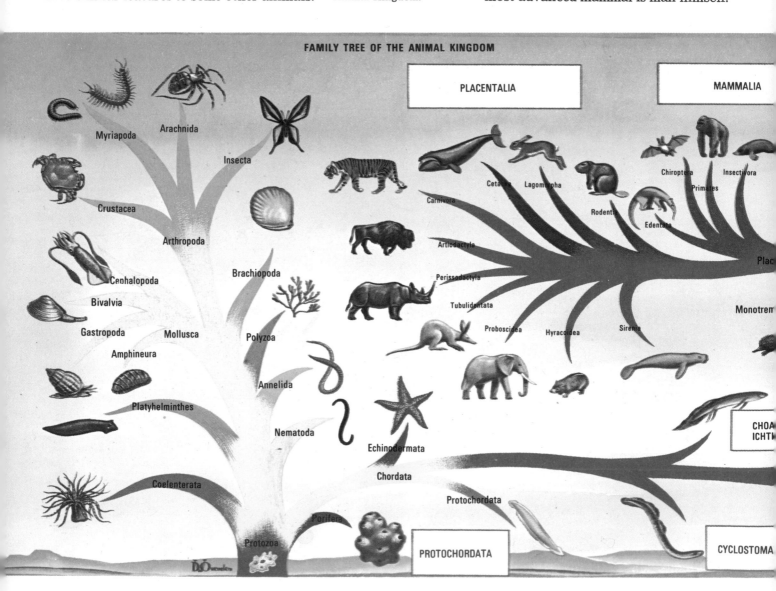

FAMILY TREE OF THE ANIMAL KINGDOM

PLACENTALIA

MAMMALIA

Myriapoda

Arachnida

Insecta

Crustacea

Arthropoda

Cephalopoda

Bivalvia

Gastropoda

Mollusca

Amphineura

Brachiopoda

Polyzoa

Annelida

Platyhelminthes

Nematoda

Echinodermata

Chordata

Protochordata

Coelenterata

Porifera

Protozoa

Cetacea

Lagomorpha

Carnivora

Chiroptera

Insectivora

Primates

Rodentia

Edentata

Artiodactyla

Perissodactyla

Tubulidentata

Proboscidea

Hyracoidea

Sirenia

Plac

Monotrem

CHOA ICHTY

PROTOCHORDATA

CYCLOSTOMA

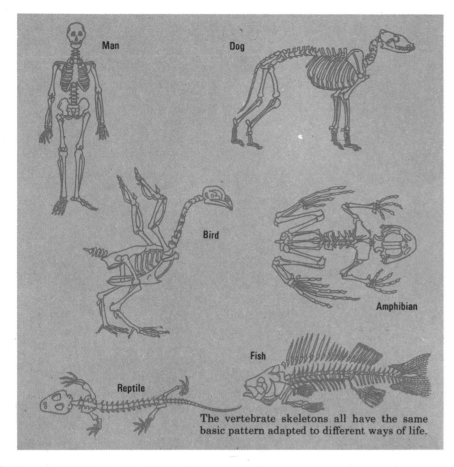

The vertebrate skeletons all have the same basic pattern adapted to different ways of life.

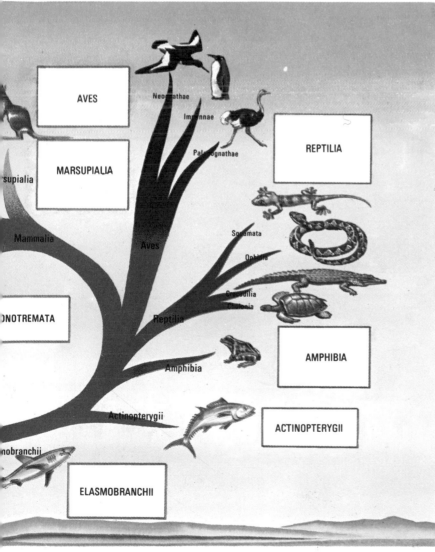

Chordata

Protochordata: Chordates that have no true brain and no braincase or backbone. They lack a heart and the type of kidney typical of vertebrates. Examples are the sea-squirts, lancelets and acorn worms.

Cyclostomata: Vertebrate chordates with an endoskeleton of cartilage. They have no jaws and lack scales and bones. Examples are the lampreys, hag fishes and slime hags.

Elasmobranchii: Fishes with well-developed jaws. They have an endoskeleton made of cartilage; bone is entirely lacking. The skin is covered with horny, teeth-like scales.

Choanichthyes: Fishes with internal nostrils. Their paired fins have fleshy lobes. Examples are the coelacanth and lung fishes.

Actinopterygii: Ray-finned fishes with well-developed jaws. They have an endoskeleton made almost entirely of bone.

Amphibia: Cold-blooded vertebrate animals that usually need to return to the water to breed. Except in some limbless forms, they lack scales. They usually have lungs and a moist skin through which they can breathe. Examples are frogs, toads, newts and salamanders.

Reptilia: Cold-blooded vertebrates fitted for life on land. The skin is dry and covered in scales. They have lungs and show an advance on amphibians in laying shelled eggs which hatch on land. Examples are crocodiles, snakes, turtles and lizards.

Aves: Warm-blooded vertebrates that have feathers like most reptiles they lay shelled eggs. Another reptilian characteristic is the presence of scales on the legs and feet. The fore-limbs are modified as wings.

Mammalia: Warm-blooded vertebrates that have hair. The young are nourished by milk which is provided by milk or mammary glands. Except for the monotremes which lay eggs, mammals bear their young alive.

Monotremata: The egg-laying mammals. Examples are the platypus and spiny ant-eater. Neither animal has teeth.

Marsupialia: The pouched mammals. These bear their young alive but in a small, relatively unformed state. The female has a pouch on the lower part of the abdomen in which the young are carried and suckled until they are able to fend for themselves. Examples are the kangaroos, wallabies, koalas and opossums.

Placentalia: Mammals in which the young during their early development are connected to the mother by a 'plate' of tissue – the placenta. This passes on food, oxygen and chemicals to the embryo. The young are born at a more advanced state than in other mammals. Examples are the rodents, cats, dogs, horses, sheep, monkeys, apes and man.

Insectivora: Primitive insect-eating placentals.

Primates: Mostly tree-dwelling placentals; big toe and thumb often well developed and can be moved to other digits in order to grasp objects.

Chiroptera: The only mammals capable of flapping flight. The wing is membrane supported by the elongated fingers and stretched between each arm and leg.

Edentata: Placental mammals that have teeth very reduced or absent.

Rodentia: Placental mammals with one pair of gnawing teeth in each jaw.

Lagomorpha: Placental mammals with two pairs of gnawing teeth in the upper jaw and one pair in the lower jaw.

Cetacea: Placental mammals that spend all their life in water. They have paddle-like forelimbs and no hind-limbs.

Carnivora: Mostly flesh-eating placentals.

Artiodactyla: Even-toed ungulates or hoofed mammals.

Perissodactyla: Odd-toed ungulates.

Tubulidentata: Placental mammals with peg-like teeth. The aardvark is the only living example.

Proboscidea: Placentals with a trunk, long incisors forming tusks, and immense grinding molars.

Hyracoidea: 'Rabbit-like' placentals with hoof-like nails or claws, one pair of continually growing incisors in the upper jaw and two pairs in the lower jaw.

Sirenia: Plant-eating placentals highly adapted for life in water. The hindlimbs are not visible externally, fore-limbs paddle-like.

Architecture

In prehistoric days, man was a hunter. He wandered from place to place in search of food, resting when he could in caves or forests. The story of architecture and building begins when he discovered how to grow crops and tend cattle. Only then did man begin to build crude shelters for his comfort and protection.

A very long time passed before these primitive shelters could be called architecture. As far back as 3,500 B.C., however, long before people in Northern Europe had left their caves, a kingdom existed in Egypt. Out of this kingdom grew some of the finest architecture – the temples, the tombs, the statues of Ancient Egypt.

Classical Architecture

It was the Greeks who brought architecture to Europe. Their simple and balanced methods of building have become known as the *Classical* style in architecture. Beginning about 700 B.C. this style had a great influence on architecture in Europe. The Greek design of the columns which supported buildings became known as the *Doric, Ionic,* and *Corinthian Orders*. These are the styles that have influenced architecture to this day.

Later, the Romans went ahead of the Greeks with their invention of the arch and the vault. A vault is a roof that is supported by a number of arches. The contribution of the Romans to architecture was no less than that of the earlier Greeks. Architecture has always reflected the people and the ways of life of its time.

Medieval and Modern

In the tenth to twelfth centuries *Romanesque* was the main style of architecture in Europe. 'Romanesque' literally means 'the style of the Romans'. At first this was simple and sturdy, but buildings became larger and more elaborate as time went on. Next came the *Gothic* style, with its lighter and more graceful buildings. Then, in Italy in the fifteenth century, there was a revival of the Classical style in art and architecture. This was the beginning of the *Renaissance* period, which literally means 'rebirth'. It lasted until about the 19th century, when people began to return to a kind of Gothic and Romanesque revival, and to styles based on modern structural inventions. Today architecture is more functional and elaborate decoration is not as important as the practical use of the space available.

Above: Saint Paul's Cathedral, London, designed by Sir Christopher Wren.

Right: Part of the U.N.E.S.C.O. building in Paris, an example of modernistic design.

Below: The Doric, Ionic and Corinthian orders of architecture. The Tuscan order, established in Italy in the 16th century, is a simplified form of Doric.

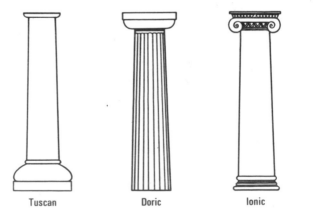

Tuscan   Doric   Ionic   Corinthian

GLOSSARY OF ARCHITECTURAL TERMS

Abacus A slab forming the upper part of a column capital. The Greeks used the abacus in their Doric capitals, where it took the form of a square block. It also appears in the Ionic, Corinthian, and Roman Composite Orders.

Alcove A recess in the wall of a room.

Ambulatory An aisle, often with chapels off it, surrounding an apse.

Apse A vaulted semicircular or polygonal (many-sided) termination, usually to a chancel or chapel.

Aqueduct The Roman system for conveying water to cities. Ruins of aqueducts can still be seen in most regions that were once part of the Roman Empire.

Baluster A short post or column.

Balustrade A row of balusters, usually supporting a handrail on staircases or around roofs of buildings.

Boss An ornamental knob or projection covering the intersection of ribs of a vault.

Canopy A small sculptured covering over a statue, tomb, altar, etc.

Clerestory The upper part of the main walls of a church, pierced by windows.

Cloisters A quadrangle surrounded by roofed or vaulted passages which connect the monastic church with the domestic part of the monastery.

Corfers Sunken squares, formed in ceilings, domes and vaults.

Corbel A block of stone projecting from a wall to support a beam or other horizontal member.

Cosmati Work Decorative work in marble with inlays of coloured stones, mosaic, and so on.

Crypt An underground chamber usually below the east end of a church.

Dormer Window A window placed vertically in a sloping roof.

Façade The front of a building.

Facing The finish applied to the outer surface of a building.

Festoon A carved garland of fruit and flowers, tied with ribbons and suspended at both ends in a loop.

Frieze The middle division of an entablature, between the architrave and the cornice. It is usually decorated. The term also applies to any decorative band around a wall.

Gable The triangular upper portion of a wall to carry a sloping roof.

Grille An openwork screen.

Jamb The straight side of an archway, doorway, or window.

Mezzanine A low intermediate storey between the ground floor and the first storey.

Mosaic Ornamental surface of small cubes of coloured stone, glass, marble, or tile embedded in cement.

Piazza An open space surrounded by buildings.

Relief Carving or modelling in which the forms stand out from a flat surface.

Rib A projecting band on a ceiling or vault.

Rotunda A building or room that is circular in plan and usually domed.

Shaft The trunk of a column between the base and the capital.

Spandrel The wall space beyond the outer curve of an arch or between two arches.

Stucco Plasterwork.

Transom A horizontal bar of stone or wood in a window.

Wainscot The timber lining to walls. The word also applies to the wooden panelling of pews.

Egyptian: Temple of Amenhotep III (Luxor)

Greek Doric: Temple of Neptune, Paestum

Roman: Arch of Constantine, Rome

Byzantine: Santa Sophia, Constantinople

Romanesque: Pisa Cathedral

French Late Gothic: St. Ouen, Rouen

Italian Gothic: Milan Cathedral

English Decorated: York Minster

Roman Renaissance: St. Peter's, Rome

Baroque: Santiago de Compostela

Anglo-Classic: St. Paul's Cathedral

Modern: Empire State Building, New York

THE DEVELOPMENT OF ARCHITECTURE

B.C.

3200 Rise of Ancient Egyptian Kingdoms. Egyptian Period begins. Great Pyramid of Cheops; Great Sphinx.

3000 Early Greek civilization.

1800 Stonehenge begun.

700 Greek Doric.

525 Egypt becomes a Persian province.

400 Greek Ionic and Corinthian.

147 Roman Period begins.

30 Egypt conquered by Rome.

A.D.

300 Byzantine Period begins (Eastern Roman Empire).

400 Early Christian Period begins.

500 Roman Empire begins to collapse.

800 Crowning of Charlemagne. Romanesque Period begins (in Northern Europe).

1066 Norman Period begins (in England).

1140 Gothic Period begins (in France. First Gothic building, Choir of St. Denis, near Paris).

1175 Norman Period ends (in England). Canterbury Cathedral is rebuilt bringing Gothic architecture to England. Early English Period begins.

1200 Romanesque Period ends (in Northern Europe). High Gothic Period begins (in France).

1245 Building starts on Westminster Abbey.

1250 Late Gothic and Flamboyant Period begins (in France).

1299 Decorated Period begins (in England).

1330 Perpendicular Period begins (in England).

1400 Early Renaissance Period begins (in Italy).

1485 Tudor Period begins.

1500 High Renaissance Period begins (in Italy Michelangelo).

1530 French Renaissance Period begins.

1558 Elizabethan Period begins.

1600 Baroque Period begins (in Italy).

1603 Jacobean Period begins.

1650 Baroque Period begins (in France).

1666 Fire of London. Rebuilding of London by Christopher Wren. Baroque Period begins (in England).

1715 Georgian Period begins.

1750 Rococo Period begins (in France).

1811 Regency Period begins.

1837 Victorian Period begins.

1920 Modern Architecture.

N.B. Since the styles of architecture changed quite slowly, the dates given above are, in most cases, only approximate.

Headline History

B.C.
5000 Earliest settlements in Egypt and Mesopotamia.
3500 Sumerian civilization flourishes.
3000 Menes unites the Lower and Upper kingdoms of Egypt into one nation and founds his capital at Memphis.
2870 Great Pyramid Age begins in Egypt. First settlements at Troy.
2450 Sargon founds the first Semitic dynasty in Sumer.
2100 Thebes becomes new capital of Egypt.

1900 First Babylonian Dynasty.
1860 Building of Stonehenge begins in Britain.
1800 Code of Hammurabi.
1700 Delta and lower Egypt overrun by the Hyksos (wandering raiders from the Syrian plateau). Palaces at Cnossus and Phaestus in Crete destroyed and rebuilt.
1580 The Hyksos driven out by the Egyptians.
1500 Founding of the sixth (Homeric) city of Troy.
1450 Zenith of Minoan (Cretan) civilization.
1400 Palaces at Cnossus and Phaestus destroyed a second time. Cretan civilization rapidly declines.
1375 Amenhotep IV introduces monotheism to Egypt in the form of sun worship.
1358 Tutankhamen, Pharaoh of Egypt.
1300 Sidon, Phoenician city-state, attains height of its maritime power.
1292 Rameses II, Pharaoh of Egypt; great military figure and builder.
1280 Egyptian treaty with the Hittites.
1230 Moses leads the Hebrews out of Egypt.
1200 The Hebrews under Joshua enter their 'Promised Land'.
1193–1184 The Greeks at war with the Trojans.
1180 Traditional date of the fall of Troy.
1125 Tiglath Pileser I extends the Assyrian Empire in north-east and north-west.
1122 Chou Dynasty begins in China.
1100 Tyre, under King Hiram, rivals the supremacy of Sidon.
1080 Hebrews subjugated by Philistines.
1025 Saul anointed by Samuel as King of Hebrews.
1000 David leads Hebrews to victory against Jebusites and retakes Jerusalem.

960 Solomon builds a temple to Jehovah at Jerusalem.
933 The kingdom of the Hebrews splits into two: Judah and Israel.
876 The first Assyrian Empire comes to an end.
845 Founding of Carthage.
776 The first Olympiad. The beginning of the Greek calendar.
753 Traditional date of the founding of Rome.
745 Tiglath Pileser III conquers Babylon and founds new Assyrian Empire.
735 The Greeks invade Sicily.
722 Samaria overrun by Sargon II, King of the Assyrians, who destroys the kingdom of Israel and leads away the Israelites into captivity.
712 Egypt conquered by the Ethiopians.
700 Naukratis, the first Greek outpost in Egypt, founded.
674 Esarhaddon overthrows the power of the Ethiopians in Egypt and takes Thebes.
663 Psamtik overthrows the Assyrians and founds a new Egyptian dynasty.

612 Nineveh captured by Cyaxares, King of the Medes, who destroys forever the power of the Assyrians.
608 Battle of Megiddo. Necho, the Pharaoh of Egypt, defeats Josiah, King of Judah.
604 Necho defeated by Nebuchadnezzar II.
594 Solon introduces constitutional reforms in Athens.
586 Nebuchadnezzar captures Jerusalem and leads the children of Judah into captivity to Babylon.
578 A wall is built round Rome by Servius Tullius.
558 Cyrus founds the Persian Empire.
546 Cyrus defeats the King of Lydia.
538 Babylon falls to Cyrus, who allows Jews to return to Palestine.
536 The Jews commence rebuilding of the Temple.
529 Cyrus is succeeded by Cambyses.
525 Cambyses conquers Egypt, which becomes a satrapy of Persia. Both Buddha and Confucius lived about this time.
521 Darius succeeds Cambyses.
519 Darius invades Indus valley.
510 Tarquin expelled from Rome. Athenian democracy established by Cleisthenes.

508 The first treaty between Carthage and Rome.
499 The Plebeians in Rome demand political rights from the Patricians.
492 Coriolanus banished. First Persian expedition against Greece.
490 Second Persian expedition. Greeks defeat Persians at the Battle of Marathon.
488 Buddha dies.
485 Darius succeeded by Xerxes, who continues the war against Greeks.
480 Xerxes invades Greece and defeats Greeks at Battle of Thermopylae. Later, Persians defeated at Battle of Salamis.
479 The Persians led by Mardonius are defeated at Platae and Mycale.
478 Delian league is formed under the leadership of Athens.
471 Recognition of Plebeian assemblies in Rome.
461 Pericles comes to power in Athens.

451 Decemviri in Rome appointed. The twelve tables.
449 Decemviri deposed. Consuls and tribunals restored in Rome.
447 Building of Parthenon begins.
431–404 The Peloponnesian War between Athens and Sparta.
430 Plague in Athens.
429 Battle of Chalcis. Death of Pericles and Herodotus.
425 Athenians defeated at Delium.
421 Temporary peace between Athens and Sparta.
415–413 Athenian expedition against Syracuse.
411 Revolt of the Four Hundred in Athens.
409 Alcibiades captures Byzantium.
408 Rhodes founded.
405 The Egyptians under Amyrtalis overthrow the Persians.
404 Athens captured by Lysander.
403 Thrasybulus restores democratic government to Athens.
400 Athenians defeated by Persians. Retreat of the ten thousand under Xenophon.
399 Death of Socrates.
394–391 The walls of Athens are rebuilt.
390 The Gauls under Brennus sack Rome.
387 Spartans make temporary peace with Persia.
382 Spartans capture Thebes.
377 New Confederacy of Athens.
372 Athenians and Spartans make peace.
367 Aristotle joins Plato in Athens.
364 The Praetors are instituted in Rome.
359 Philip, King of Macedonia.
356 Birth of Alexander the Great
340 First Samnite War.
338 Philip of Macedonia defeats Greeks at Chæronea.
336 Macedonian troops enter Asia. Murder of Philip.
335 Alexander the Great destroys Thebes.
334 Battle of Granicus.

Left: Restored painting at the ruins of Cnossus, Crete.

Below: The ruins of Tyre, one of the leading Phoenician cities.

Hadrian

161 Marcus Aurelius and Lucius Verus joint Emperors.	**361** Emperor Julian reverts to paganism but issues edict of universal religious tolerance.	**655** Moslems defeat Byzantine fleet.

161 Marcus Aurelius and Lucius Verus joint Emperors.

166 A great plague carried back to Italy by the Roman army from Macedonia spreads throughout the Empire.

180 Death of Marcus Aurelius.

193 Emperor Pertinax assassinated. From now till 284 Emperors are elected by the army.

208 Emperor Severus in Britain; supervises repairs to Hadrian's Wall.

211 Severus dies at York; succeeded by Caracalla and Geta.

212 Geta murdered. Roman citizenship bestowed on all freemen in the Empire.

226 Artaxerxes founds new Persian Empire.

231 Romans at war with Persians.

247 Goths cross over the Danube and raid central Europe.

248 Celebrations of supposed thousandth anniversary of founding of Rome.

249 Decius, Emperor. Persecution of Christians. Pope Fabian martyred.

251 Decius killed. Goths defeat Romans.

260 The Emperor Valerian is captured by Sapor I, who in turn is set upon by Odenathus of Palmyra.

261 Romans defeat Scythian and Goth invaders.

266 Odenathus declares himself Emperor of eastern provinces; his wife Zenobia, leads a revolt of Palmyra, Asia Minor and Egypt against the power of Rome.

269 Goths defeated by Emperor Claudius at Nish.

273 Zenobia taken captive to Rome. End of Palmyrian Empire.

284 Diocletian, Emperor.

300 Christianity becomes the recognised religion in Britain.

303 Persecution of Christians under Diocletian.

305 St Alban martyred.

306 Constantine proclaimed Emperor at York.

313–323 Empire shared by Constantine in the west and Licinius in the east. Edict of Milan; Christianity tolerated in the Roman Empire.

325 Constantine presides at the Council of Nicæa. Nicene Creed adopted.

330 Constantinople founded on site of Byzantium.

337 Constantine receives baptism on his death-bed; succeeded by Constantine II. Constantius and Constans as joint Emperors.

350 Huns invade Europe.

360–367 Pict, Irish and Saxon invasion of Britain.

361 Emperor Julian reverts to paganism but issues edict of universal religious tolerance.

375 Huns invade Rome.

379 Theodosius, Emperor.

382 Alaric, King of Goths.

392 Eastern and western Empires unite under Theodosius.

395 Death of Theodosius, last Roman ruler of a united Empire. Honorius and Arcadius, joint Emperors, redivide the Empire, this time permanently.

410 The Goths take Rome under Alaric.

411 Romans withdraw from Britain.

425 English invade Britain. Barbarians over-run Roman Empire.

432 St Patrick preaches in Ireland.

433 Attila, King of Huns.

434 Parthenon becomes a Christian church.

449 Landing of Hengist and Horsa in Britain.

451 Attila raids Gaul but is repelled by Romans, aided by Franks and Alemanni, at Châlons.

453 Death of Attila.

455 Vandals from Africa sack Rome.

457 Hengist establishes kingdom of Kent.

470 Huns disappear from Europe.

476 End of the Roman Empire in the west.

477 Saxons invade Britain.

481 Clovis, King of the Franks.

489 Theodoric becomes King of Italy.

517 King Arthur of England may have lived at this time.

527 Justinian, Emperor.

543 Plague in Constantinople.

546 Totila takes Rome.

553 Justinian drives Goths out of Italy. St Columba lands on Iona.

565 Death of Justinian. Lombards invade northern Italy. Ethelbert, King of Kent. Christianity preached to Picts.

570 Birth of Mohammed at Mecca.

588 Ethelfrith founds kingdom of Northumbria.

590 Rome ravaged by plague.

597 Death of St Columba. St Augustine lands in Britain and reintroduces Christianity.

602 Archbishopric of Canterbury founded.

611 Islamism is proclaimed by Mohammed.

617 Edwin rules all England except Kent.

618 T'ang Dynasty in China.

622 The Hegira. Flight of Mohammed from Mecca to Medina. Founding of Mohammedan religion.

629 Mohammed returns to Mecca.

632 Death of Mohammed.

638 Jerusalem surrenders to Caliph Omar.

655 Moslems defeat Byzantine fleet.

664 Synod of Whitby; England turns to the Roman Church.

668 Moslems attack Constantinople.

670 Moslems conquer North Africa.

711 Moslems invade Spain.

714 Charles Martel ruler of France.

715 Moslem Empire stretches from Pyrenees to China.

717–718 Constantinople withstands Moslem attacks.

720 Moslems invade France.

732 Charles Martel defeats the Moslems at Tours.

735 Death of Venerable Bede.

741 Death of Charles Martel.

749 Moslem Empire begins to crumble.

751 Pepin, King of France.

757–796 Offa, King of Mercia.

768 Death of Pepin. Charlemagne and Carloman, Kings of Franks.

772 Charlemagne becomes sole King of Franks.

779 Offa's dyke marks boundary between England and Wales.

786 Haroun-al-Rashid in Baghdad.

787 Danes invade England.

789 Northmen invade Britain.

800 Pope Leo crowns Charlemagne Holy Roman Emperor.

802 Egbert becomes King of Wessex. Vikings dominate Ireland.

814 Death of Charlemagne; succeeded by Louis the Pious.

827 Egbert becomes first King of all England.

836 Danes sack London.

844 MacAlpine unites Picts and Scots.

846 Moslems pillage Rome.

851 Ethelwulf defeats Danes at Battle of Oakley.

860 Danes sack Winchester.

865 Norsemen under Rurik threaten Constantinople.

866 Ethelred I, King of England.

871 Alfred the Great defeats Danes at Ashdown.

874 Iceland settled by Norsemen.

878 Danes defeated by Alfred at Ethandune. Wessex overrun by Danes.

885 Alfred takes London. Viking attack on Paris.

886 Alfred signs treaty with Danes establishing them in the Danelaw (northern England).

896 Arnolph of Germany takes Rome and is crowned Emperor.

897 Alfred builds his navy.

900 Death of Alfred.

910 Abbey of Cluny founded.

Part of the Bayeux Tapestry, which in 72 scenes depicts the whole story of the conquest of England by William the Conqueror. The tapestry is embroidered on a linen band 230 feet long and 20 inches wide.

919 Henry Fowler elected King of Germany.
928 Pope John X imprisoned by Marozia.
936 Otto, King of Germany.
940 Edmund, King of Wessex.
942 Malcolm I, King of Scotland.
953 Rebellions in Germany against Otto.
958 Edgar, King of England.
960 Sung Dynasty in China.
962 Pope John XII crowns Otto of Germany Emperor.
963 Otto deposes John XII.
973 Edgar crowned at Bath.
975 Edward the Martyr, King of England.
979 Edward murdered; succeeded by Ethelred the Unready.
982 Norsemen discover Greenland.
987 Hugh Capet becomes King of France.
991 Battle of Maldon. Ethelred buys off Vikings.

1000 Lief Ericsson discovers Nova Scotia.
1005 Malcolm II, King of Scotland.
1008 Ethelred II builds a fleet.
1009 Danes attack London. Mohammedans profane the Holy Sepulchre in Jerusalem.
1016 Death of Ethelred. Canute, King of England, Denmark and Norway.
1017 Canute divides England into four earldoms.
1035 Death of Canute.
1040 Duncan, King of Scotland, murdered by Macbeth, who takes title.
1042 Restoration of English accession with crowning of Edward the Confessor.
1052 Edward founds Westminster Abbey.
1066 Death of Edward. Harold elected King. Battle of Hastings; death of Harold. William, Duke of Normandy crowned King.
1072 William the Conqueror invades Scotland.
1074 Revolt of Norman barons against William.
1084 Rome sacked by Robert Guiscard.
1086 The Domesday Book completed.
1093 Malcolm III of Scotland killed at Alnwick.
1095–1099 Urban summons the First Crusade.
1096 The People's Crusade, led by Peter the Hermit, is massacred in Asia Minor.

Above: The taking of Constantinople by the Crusaders.

Left: The murder of Thomas à Becket in Canterbury Cathedral.

1098 Edgar, King of Scotland. The Crusaders take Antioch.
1099 Jerusalem taken by Godfrey de Bouillon.
1100 William II (Rufus) killed in the New Forest. Henry I, King of England.
1118 Founding of Order of Knights Templar.
1135 Stephen elected King of England. Henry II heir to throne. Period of civil war.
1147 The Second Crusade. Founding of kingdom of Portugal.
1154 Peace restored when Henry II ascends English throne. Nicholas Breakspeare, an Englishman, becomes Pope Adrian IV.
1162 Thomas à Becket, Archbishop of Canterbury.
1169 Saladin, Sultan of Egypt.
1170 Murder of Thomas à Becket in Canterbury Cathedral.
1171 Norman conquest of Ireland.
1173 Becket canonized.
1189 Jerusalem falls to Saladin. The Third Crusade.
1190 Richard I of England joins the Third Crusade.
1191 Siege and fall of Acre.
1192 Richard I held a prisoner by Leopold of Austria.
1194 Richard returns to England.
1198 Pope Innocent III. Richard defeats French at Gisors.
1199 John, King of England.

1200–1450 Hanseatic League of German cities promotes trade.
1202 The Fourth Crusade.
1204 The Crusaders take Constantinople.
1206 Genghis Khan founds the Mongol Empire.
1207 John refuses to recognize Langton as Archbishop. England placed under papal interdict.
1209 John excommunicated. Founding of the Franciscan Order.
1212 The Children's Crusade.
1215 John signs Magna Carta at Runnymede.

1216 Henry III, King of England. The first English Parliament.
1217 The Fifth Crusade. The French invasion of Britain fails.
1221 Failure and return of Fifth Crusade.
1227 Death of Genghis Khan whose Empire stretched from the Caspian to the Pacific.
1228 The Sixth Crusade.
1229 Jerusalem ceded to the Christians.
1244 Sultan of Egypt retakes Jerusalem.
1248 The Seventh Crusade.
1260 Kublai Khan becomes the Great Khan.
1264 Battle of Lewes. Henry defeated by Simon de Montfort.
1265 De Montfort's Parliament. Commons meet for first time. Battle of Evesham; de Montfort killed.
1271 Marco Polo begins his travels.
1282 Edward I subdues Wales.
1290 Expulsion of Jews from England.
1291 Fall of Acre; end of Crusading in the Holy Land.
1292 Death of Kublai Khan.
1295 Marco Polo returns to Venice after 20 years' travel in the East. The Model Parliament—the first truly representative English Parliament.
1296 Annexation of Scotland.
1297 William Wallace uprising. Battle of Stirling. Scots victorious.
1298 Battle of Falkirk. Wallace defeated by Edward I.

1304 Stirling taken by Edward.
1306 Pope Clement V. Papal court moves to Avignon. Wallace executed at Smithfield. Robert Bruce rebellion in Scotland.
1307 Edward II.
1314 Battle of Bannockburn. Scotland wins her independence.
1327 Edward II murdered by Queen Isabella.
1332 English Parliament divided into Lords and Commons.
1337 Start of Hundred Years War between England and France. Edward claims French crown.
1339 Edward invades France.
1340 British naval victory at Sluys.
1346 Edward III defeats French at Battle of Crécy.
1347 Calais taken by the English.

1348 The Black Death.	**1455** The start of the Wars of the Roses. Battle of St Albans.	**1520** Henry VIII of England and Francis I of France meet at the Field of the Cloth of Gold. Charles V, Emperor.
1350 Order of the Garter established.		
1356 English defeat French at Poitiers.	**1460** Henry VI taken prisoner at Battle of Northampton. Duke of York killed at Battle of Wakefield.	**1521** Henry VIII writes a pamphlet denouncing Luther. In recognition Pope bestows on him title of 'Defender of the Faith'. Luther excommunicated. Diet of Worms; Luther refuses to abandon his doctrines.
1367 Tamerlane takes title of Great Khan.		
1368 Ming Dynasty in China.		
1369 French war renewed.	**1461** Lancastrian cause suffers defeat at Battle of Towton Field. Edward IV proclaimed King.	
1375 Sole remaining English possessions in France include Calais, Bordeaux, Bayonne and Brest. Truce.		
	1466 Henry VI kept a prisoner in the Tower.	**1524–25** Peasant's War in Germany.
1376 Death of Black Prince.	**1471** Battles of Barnet and Tewkesbury. Death of Henry VI. Earl of Warwick (the Kingmaker) dies at Barnet.	**1526** Tyndale's New Testament published.
1378 The Great Schism. The papacy splits.		**1527** Germans take and pillage Rome. The Pope imprisoned.
1381 Peasant revolt in England. Wat Tyler murdered before Richard II. Lollards spread Wycliffe's preaching.		**1528** Peru subdued by Pizarro.
	1475 Edward IV invades France.	**1529** Fall of Wolsey. He fails to arrange annulment of Henry's marriage. Siege of Vienna by the Turks.
	1476 Caxton sets up his press at Westminster.	
1397 Union of Kalmar; Denmark, Norway and Sweden under one crown.	**1478** Spain introduces the Inquisition.	
	1483 Edward V murdered by Richard III after only two months' reign. Henry Tudor proclaimed Henry VII.	**1530** Death of Wolsey. Henry's quarrel with the papacy begins.
1398 Henry of Lancaster (Bolingbroke) banished.		
		1533 Henry marries Anne Boleyn. Ivan IV (the Terrible), Czar of Russia.
1399 Richard II deposed. Henry Bolingbroke becomes Henry IV.	**1485** Richard III killed at Bosworth. Henry VII, King of England.	
		1534 Act of Supremacy. End of papal power in England.
1400 Owen Glendower leads a revolt in Wales. Death of Chaucer.	**1486** Diaz sails round the Cape of Good Hope.	
	1487 Lambert Simnel revolt.	**1535** Loyola founds Jesuits. Fisher and More executed. The first English printed Bible (Coverdale's).
1403 Percy defeated at Battle of Shrewsbury	**1492** Columbus discovers the New World. Ferdinand takes Granada and drives Moors from Spain.	
1405 Capture of Harflour.		

A tapestry depicting the arrival of Joan of Arc at the Chateau du Chinon in 1428 where she presented herself to the king, Charles VII. Joan was allowed to lead an army to the relief of Orléans. The success of this expedition, followed by Charles' coronation at Reims, was the turning point in the war with England. Joan was captured by the Burgundians in 1430 and ransomed by the English. She was tried for witchcraft by the English and burned in 1431.

1406 James I of Scotland kept a prisoner in the Tower.	**1493** Maximilian becomes Emperor.	**1536** Thomas Cromwell put in charge of dissolution of monasteries. Death of Catherine of Aragon. Anne Boleyn executed. Henry marries his third wife. The Pilgrimage of Grace.
	1497 Vasco da Gama reaches India by the sea route.	
1407 The Great Schism ends.		
1410 Battle of Tannenberg; Teutonic knights defeated by Poles and Lithuanians under Ladislaus II.	**1502** Fourth voyage by Columbus to the New World.	
		1537 Death of Jane Seymour.
	1503 Margaret, daughter of Henry, marries James IV of Scotland.	**1538** Henry excommunicated.
1415 John Huss burnt as a heretic. English defeat French at Agincourt.		**1540** In January Henry marries Anne of Cleves, whom he divorces. In July Henry marries Catherine Howard.
	1506 Death of Columbus. St Peter's, Rome, founded.	
1417 Urban VI in Rome. Clement VII at Avignon.		
	1509 Henry VIII marries Catherine of Aragon.	**1542** James IV of Scotland defeated at Solway Moss. Execution of Catherine Howard. Henry marries Catherine Parr.
1420 Treaty of Troyes. Henry V takes Caen.	**1511** Henry joins Holy League.	
1429 Joan of Arc raises the siege of Orleans.	**1513** Pope Leo X. James IV defeated and killed at Battle of Flodden.	
1430 Joan of Arc taken prisoner.		**1544** Henry invades France.
1431 Joan of Arc martyred.	**1514** Wolsey becomes Archbishop of York. Peace with Scotland and France.	**1545** Council of Trent marks the beginning of the Counter-Reformation.
1437 James I of Scotland murdered.		
1439 Council of Basle creates a new religious schism.	**1515** French under Francis I invade Italy.	**1547** Death of Henry VIII. Somerset Protector in the name of the boy king Edward VI.
	1517 Luther expounds his doctrine at Wittenberg; beginning of the Reformation.	
1450 Jack Cade's rebellion against the government of Henry VI of England.		
	1519 Cortez takes Mexico. Magellan sails round the world. Death of Leonardo da Vinci.	**1549** Act of Uniformity authorizing First Prayer Book.
1453 Turks take Constantinople; end of Eastern Empire. All English posessions in France lost except Calais.		

1552 Second Prayer Book.
1553 Death of Edward. Mary proclaimed Queen of England. Catholic Church restored. Lady Jane Grey makes unsuccessful bid for the throne.
1554 Mary marries Philip of Spain. Execution of Lady Jane Grey.
1556 Cranmer, Latimer and Ridley burnt at stake.
1558 Loss of Calais. Elizabeth, Queen of England. Protestantism restored. Marriage of Mary Queen of Scots to French Dauphin.
1561 Mary Queen of Scots returns to Scotland.
1562 Huguenot wars.
1563 The Thirty-Nine Articles. Council of Trent ends.
1564 Peace of Troyes ends war between England and France.
1567 Revolt in Netherlands against Spain. Mary Queen of Scots marries Bothwell. Mary imprisoned.
1568 Mary escapes to England.
1570 Elizabeth excommunicated.

Richard III
1452-85

Henry VII
1457-1509

1571 Battle of Lepanto; Turkish sea-power defeated by Don John of Austria.
1572 Massacre of St Batholomew in France.
1580 Drake completes his circumnavigation of the world.
1582 Gregorian Calendar introduced by Pope Gregory XIII.
1586 English defeat Spaniards at Zutphen.
1587 Execution of Mary. Expedition against Cadiz.
1588 Defeat of the Spanish Armada.
1598 Edict of Nantes grants religious toleration to Protestants in France.

1600 East India Company granted charter by Elizabeth.
1601 Poor Law established.
1603 James I of England and Scotland. Act of Union.
1604 Hampton Court Conference.
1605 Gunpowder Plot.

1607 Colony of Virginia founded.
1609 Holland becomes sovereign country.
1610 Henry IV of France murdered. Hudson trying to find the N.W. Passage, discovers Hudson's Bay.
1611 Authorized Version of the Bible. Plantation of Ulster with English and Scottish settlers.
1616 Death of Shakespeare.
1618 Thirty Years War begins.
1620 The *Mayflower* sails for America.
1624 England at war with Spain.
1625 Charles I dissolves Parliament.
1628 The Petition of Right.
1629 Charles reigns without Parliament until 1640.
1634 Charles demands ship money.
1638 No Europeans allowed to enter Japan (till 1865).
1640 Charles dissolves the Short Parliament and summons the Long Parliament.
1641 Massacre of the English in Ireland. Court of Star Chamber abolished.
1642 New Zealand and Tasmania discovered. Charles tries to arrest five Members of Parliament. Civil war begins.
1643 Louis XIV of France. (He ruled for 70 years.)
1645 Cromwell's New 'Model Army'.
1647 Charles surrenders to Parliament.
1648 The Treaty of Westphalia brings Thirty Years War to a close. Second Civil War in England. New Model Army defeats Scots and Royalists.
1649 Trial and execution of Charles. England becomes a republic under Cromwell.
1651 Charles II defeated at Battle of Worcester. Flees to France.
1652 First Dutch War. Cape Colony founded by Dutch.
1653 Cromwell becomes Protector.
1656 England at war with Spain.
1657 Cromwell declines crown.
1658 Death of Cromwell: his son Richard becomes Protector.
1659 Resignation of Richard Cromwell.
1660 General Monk brings back Charles II.
1662 Act of Uniformity.
1664 Second Dutch War. English capture New Amsterdam (New York).
1665 The Plague.
1666 The Great Fire of London.
1667 Dutch fleet sails up the Medway.
1668 The Triple Alliance. England, Sweden and Holland line up against France.
1670 The Hudson's Bay Company formed. The secret Treaty of Dover between England and France. If successful it would have restored Catholicism to England.
1672 Third Dutch War.
1674 Peace with Holland.
1677 Princess Mary of England (daughter of Duke of York, later James II) marries William of Orange.
1678 Popish Plot.
1679 Act of Habeas Corpus.
1685 Death of Charles II. James II, King of England. The Monmouth rebellion. Edict of Nantes revoked.
1688 Trial of the Seven Bishops. Flight of James II. William of Orange and Mary offered throne. Protestant succession restored.
1689 William and Mary. Bill of Rights.
1690 William defeats James II at Battle of the Boyne.
1692 The Massacre at Glencoe.
1694 Bank of England founded. Death of Queen Mary.
1696 Peter the Great, Czar of Russia.
1697 Treaty of Ryswick between Louis XIV and William III.

1700–21 Great Northern War between Sweden and other Baltic Powers. Swedes, led by Charles XII, gained remarkable initial successes but were utterly defeated by Russians at Poltava (1709). Russia emerged as a major European Power.
1701 Frederick I of Prussia. Act of Settlement establishes Protestant Hanoverian Succession in England.
1701–1713 War of Spanish Succession.
1702 Queen Anne. England joins war of Spanish Succession.
1704 British capture Gibraltar. Battle of Blenheim. Marlborough defeats French and Bavarians.
1708 First combined English and Scottish Parliament.
1713 Treaty of Utrecht.
1714 George I of Britain.
1715 Louis XV of France. Jacobite rising in Scotland. Battle of Preston. Riot Act passed.
1717 Triple alliance between England, Holland and France.
1718 The Emperor joins the Triple Alliance. England at war with Spain.
1719 France declares war on Spain.
1720 The South Sea Bubble.
1727 George II of Britain.
1729 Peace with Spain.
1736 Porteous riots in Scotland.
1739 England at war with Spain.
1740 Frederick II (the Great) becomes King of Prussia.
1741 Sweden at war with Russia. War of Austrian Succession.
1743 George II defeats France at Battle of Dettingen.
1745 French victorious at Battle of Fontenoy. Charles Edward (Bonnie Prince Charlie) lands in Scotland. Battle of Prestonpans; Jacobite victory. They reach Derby but return again to Scotland.
1746 Battle of Culloden; Jacobites routed.
1747 Admiral Hawke defeats French Fleet off Belle Isle.
1748 Peace of Aix-la-Chapelle.
1751 Clive takes Arcot.
1752 Reformed Gregorian calendar adopted in Britain.
1756 Seven Years War begins: The 'Black Hole' of Calcutta. Britain at war with France. Loss of Minorca.
1758 Prussia invaded by Russians.
1759 Wolfe captures Quebec for Britain.
1760 George III of Britain. Russians in Berlin. British conquest of Canada completed.
1762 England at war with Spain.
1763 Peace of Paris ends Seven Years War. Britain keeps Canada.
1764 The Industrial Revolution begins. Hargreaves invents the spinning jenny.
1770 Captain Cook discovers New South Wales.
1773 'Boston Tea Party'.
1774 Louis XVI of France.
1775 Lexington: first action in American War of Independence. Washington assumes command of American army.
1776 American Declaration of Independence. British evacuate Boston.
1777 Burgoyne capitulates at Saratoga.
1778 France recognizes the U.S.A., declares war against Great Britain.
1779 Spain at war with Great Britain.
1780 The Gordon riots in London.
1781 Surrender of British under Cornwallis to American and French forces at Yorktown.
1782 Britain acknowledges the independence of the American States.
1783 Treaty of Versailles between Britain and U.S.A.

1786	Impeachment of Warren Hastings.
1788	First Congress of U.S.A. at New York. Colonization of Australia begins.
1789	Fall of the Bastille and outbreak of French revolution.
1791	Jacobin Revolution.
1792	France becomes a republic—royalty abolished. France declares war on Austria.
1793	Louis XVI beheaded. Reign of Terror begins. Britain at war with France.
1794	The execution of Robespierre brings Jacobin republic to an end.
1795	Acquittal of Warren Hastings. Directory established in France. Napoleon invades Italy as Commander-in-Chief.
1796	Spain at war with England.
1797	Peace of Campo Formio brings the republic of Venice to an end. Battle of Cape St Vincent.
1798	Napoleon in Egypt. Battle of the Nile; Nelson victorious.
1799	Siege of Acre. French Directory overthrown and Napoleon made First Consul. Pitt introduces income-tax in Britain.
1800	Legislative Union of Ireland and England. Napoleon in Austria. Austrians are defeated at Battle of Marengo.
1801	Treaty between France, England and Austria signed. Battle of Copenhagen. First Parliament of United Kingdom.
1802	Peace of Amiens between England and France.
1803	France sells Louisiana to U.S.A. Napoleon invades Switzerland. War with France renewed.
1804	Napoleon made Emperor.
1805	Nelson defeats French navy at Battle of Trafalgar. Battles of Ulm and Austerlitz; Napoleon victorious.
1806	Napoleon overthrows Prussia at Battle of Jena. Holy Roman Empire dissolved.
1807	Slave trade abolished throughout British Empire. Treaty of Tilsit; Alexander of Russia becomes Napoleon's Ally.
1808	Napoleon's brother, Joseph Bonaparte, King of Spain. Peninsular War begins in Spain.
1809	Napoleon excommunicated. Pope arrested. Napoleon divorces the Empress Josephine.
1810	Marriage of Bonaparte to Marie-Louise. Holland annexed by France.
1811	The Prince of Wales becomes Regent owing to permanent insanity of George III. Luddite riots.
1812	U.S.A. declares war on Great Britain. France at war with Russia. Napoleon burns Moscow.
1813	Wellington invades France. Napoleon defeated at Battle of Leipzig.
1814	Abdication of Napoleon. Restoration of Bourbons. Napoleon confined to Elba. Peace of Paris. Peace between Great Britain and U.S.A. Louis XVIII of France.
1815	Napoleon escapes from Elba. Battle of Waterloo. Napoleon, finally overthrown, surrenders to British. Exiled to St Helena. Treaty of Vienna brings peace to Europe.
1819	Spain cedes Florida to U.S.A. Singapore founded.
1820	George IV of Britain.
1822	Declaration of Greek Independence.
1823	'Monroe Doctrine' announced by U.S.A.
1824	Bolivar dictator of Peru.
1825	First railway, Stockton to Darlington, opened.
1827	Egyptian and Turkish fleets destroyed at Battle of Navarino by British fleet.
1829	Metropolitan Police established in Britain. Catholic Emmancipation Act in Britain.

1830	William IV of Britain. Louis Philippe proclaimed King of France.
1832	The First Reform Bill.
1833	Slavery abolished in British Empire.
1836	Great Trek of Boers from British South Africa. Texas gains independence from Mexico.
1837	Queen Victoria of Britain.
1839	Chartist riots.
1840	Marriage of Queen Victoria and Prince Albert. Penny post introduced.
1846	Repeal of the Corn Laws. Free trade established.
1848	Louis Philippe abdicates. French Republic proclaimed.
1848–1852	Second French Republic. Communist Manifesto produced by Marx and Engels.
1849	Italian Republic proclaimed.
1851	The Great Exhibition in Hyde Park. *Coup d'état* by Louis Napoleon.
1852	Louis Napoleon proclaimed Emperor in France.
1854	Outbreak of Crimean War.
1856	Peace treaty with Russia signed at Paris.
1857	The Indian Mutiny. Relief of Lucknow.
1859	Franco-Austrian War.
1860	Garibaldi takes Naples and proclaims Victor Emmanuel first King of Italy.
1861	Abraham Lincoln, President of the U.S.A. Death of Prince Consort. American Civil War breaks out.
1862	Bismarck chief minister in Germany.
1863	Lincoln abolishes slavery in the U.S. Battle of Gettysburg.
1864	Red Cross organization formed.
1865	General Lee surrenders to General Grant.

The surrender of General Lee at Appomattox, April 9, 1865.

	Lincoln murdered. End of American Civil War.
1866	Prussia and Italy at war with Austria.
1867	Emperor Maximilian of Mexico shot. Dominion of Canada established. Russia sells Alaska to U.S.A. for $7 million.
1869	Opening of Suez Canal.
1870	France declares war against Prussia. French defeated at Battle of Sedan. Germans besiege Paris. Third French Republic. Rome made part of Italian kingdom.
1871	Paris surrenders. William I of Prussia proclaimed Emperor of Germany. Peace treaty signed between France and Germany. Riots in Paris. Trade Unions in Britain legalized.
1872	Election balloting system introduced in England.
1873	Death of Napoleon III.
1877	Queen Victoria proclaimed Empress of India.
1877–1878	Russo-Turkish War.
1878	Afghan War. Paris Exhibition.

1879	Zulu Wars. Tay Bridge disaster.
1880	First Boer War.
1881	Transvaal becomes a republic. British defeat at the Battle of Majuba Hill. Peace with Boers.
1882	Germany joins Triple Alliance (Austria, Germany, Italy). British forces occupy Egypt.
1884	Germany founds her African Empire.
1885	General Gordon killed at Khartoum.
1887	Queen Victoria's Jubilee.
1890	Lord Salisbury cedes Heligoland to Germany.
1891	Education Act, granting free education, passed. France and Russia sign an alliance.
1893	Home Rule for Ireland Bill passed in Commons but rejected by Lords.
1894	Japan declares war on China.
1895	Jameson raid.
1896	Cecil Rhodes resigns as Premier of Cape Colony.
1897	Turko-Greek War. Queen Victoria's Diamond Jubilee.
1898	U.S.A. at war with Spain.
1899	Second Boer War.
1900	Attack on Ladysmith. Relief of Ladysmith and Mafeking. Boxer rising in China.
1901	Death of Queen Victoria. Founding of Commonwealth of Australia.
1902	End of Boer War.
1903	Pope Pius X.
1904	*Entente Cordiale* between France and Great Britain.
1904–1905	Russo-Japanese War.
1906	San Francisco fire and earthquake.
1908	King and Crown Prince of Portugal assassinated.
1909	Blériot flies the English Channel. Union of South Africa. Peary reaches North Pole.
1910	King George V of Britain.
1911	Italy declares war on Turkey. Amundsen reaches South Pole. Revolution in China.
1912	China declared a republic. *Titanic* disaster.
1913	War in the Balkans.
1914	Irish Home Rule Bill Passed. Panama Canal opened to traffic. Outbreak of World War I. First British Expeditionary Force lands in France. Germans defeat Russians at Tannenberg (Aug. 26–30).
1915	Dardanelles campaign by Allies against Turks fails.
1916	Unrestricted submarine warfare begins (Feb. 1). Battle of Jutland (May 31). German offensive at Verdun (Feb.–July). Battle of the Somme (July–Nov.). Tanks first used by British (Sept. 15).
1917	Revolution in Russia (Mar. 12). Germans retreat to Hindenburg Line (Mar.). U.S.A. declares war against Germany (Apr. 6). Italians defeated by Austrians in Caporetto Campaign (Oct.–Dec.). Bolshevik Revolution in Russia (Nov. 7). Passchendaele won by Canadians (Nov. 6). Hindenburg Line breached by British in first great tank raid (Nov. 20–Dec. 3).
1918	Treaty of Brest–Litovsk between Russia and Central Powers. German offensive begins in West (Mar. 21). Germans stopped just short of Paris in Second Battle of the Marne (July–Aug.). General Allied offensive begins in West (Sept. 26). Italian victory at Battle of Vittorio Veneto (Oct. 24–Nov. 4). Turkey surrenders (Oct. 30). Kaiser abdicates (Nov. 9). Armistice signed (Nov. 11).
1919	First aeroplane crossing of the Atlantic (June 15). Peace of Versailles.

1920 Joan of Arc canonized. First meeting of the League of Nations.

1921 Greece at war with Turkey. Irish Free State set up by Peace Treaty with Britain (Dec. 6).

1922 Tutankhamen's tomb discovered in Egypt. Fascists march on Rome.

1923 Rhine Republic. Turkish Republic.

1924 Death of Lenin. Wembley Exhibition. First Labour Government.

1926 General Strike in Britain.

1928 Lindbergh makes the first solo flight across the Atlantic (May 21).

1929 Byrd flies over South Pole (Nov. 30). Wall Street crash.

1931 Britain abandons Gold Standard.

1933 Hitler appointed Chancellor of Germany by Hindenburg. Burning of the Reichstag (Feb. 27).

1934 Death of Hindenburg; Hitler becomes dictator.

1935 Silver Jubilee of George V. Saar returned to Germany. Italy invades Abyssinia.

1936 Death of George V. Civil War begins in Spain (July 18). Edward VIII abdicates (December 10). George VI succeeds to throne.

1938 Austria annexed by Germany (March 13). Munich Agreement between Chamberlain, Hitler, Daladier and Mussolini (Sept. 29).

1939 Bohemia and Moravia annexed by Germany (Mar. 16). Germany invades Poland (Sept. 1). Britain and France declare war on Germany (Sept. 3).

1940 German invasion of Denmark and Norway (Apr. 2). Invasion of Holland, Belgium and Luxembourg (Apr. 10). Evacuation of British army from Dunkirk (May 27–June 4). Italy enters war (June 10). Fall of France (June 25). Air Battle of Britain begins (Aug. 15). British drive against Italians begins in North Africa (Dec. 8).

1941 Tobruk captured by Australians (Jan. 22). Rommel begins attack in North Africa (Apr. 3). Air-borne invasion of Crete (May 20). German battleship *Bismarck* sunk (May 27). Germany attacks Russia (June 22). Japan attacks Pearl Harbor (Dec. 7) and U.S.A. enters war. Tobruk relieved (Dec. 9).

1942 Singapore surrenders to Japanese (Feb. 15). U.S. naval victory in Battle of Midway marks turning point in Pacific War (June 3–7). Tobruk falls to Germans (June 21). German advance halted at Stalingrad (Sept. 6). Battle of El Alamein opens Allied offensive in Egypt (Oct. 23). Allied landings in North Africa (Nov. 8).

1943 Russian victory at Stalingrad (Jan. 31). Allied landings in Sicily (July 10). Allied invasion of Italian mainland (Sept. 3). Italy surrenders (Sept. 8).

1944 Allied landings at Anzio (Jan. 23). 'D-Day': Allies invade Normandy (June 6). Japanese defeated at Imphal (June 7). First V-1 falls on England (June 12). Allies invade southern France (Aug. 15). Paris liberated (Aug. 23). First V-2 falls on England (Sept. 8). Air-borne landings at Arnhem (Sept. 17). Japanese sea-power crushed at Battle of Leyte Gulf (Oct. 25). The Battle of the Bulge: last German offensive (Dec. 16–25).

1945 U.S. forces battle for Iwo Jima (Feb. 19–Mar. 17). U.S. invasion of Okinawa (Apr. 1). American and Russian forces meet on the Elbe (Apr. 25). Death of Hitler announced (May 1). End of war in Europe (May 8). Atomic bombs dropped on Japan (Aug. 6 and Aug. 9). Japan surrenders (Aug. 14). Nuremburg trial of war criminals opens (Nov. 20).

1946 General Assembly of United Nations opens in New York (Oct. 23).

Left: Unemployment was the major social problem between the two World Wars, especially in industrial areas such as Lancashire. It became worse after the Great Depression of 1929.

Below: The signing of the U.S.–U.K. Marshall Aid pact.

1947 Marshall's offer of aid to Europe. India and Pakistan gain independence. U.N. votes in favour of partition of Palestine.

1948 British Railways nationalized. Gandhi assassinated in New Delhi (Jan. 30). Burma becomes independent republic. State of Israel proclaimed (May 14). Berlin airlift begins (Apr. 1).

1949 North Atlantic Treaty signed (Apr. 4). People's Republic of China established by Communists.

1950 Korean War begins (June 25).

1951 Festival of Britain opens (May 3).

1952 Death of George VI (Feb. 6). Elizabeth II succeeds.

1953 Death of Stalin (Mar. 6). Mount Everest climbed (May 29). Coronation of H.M. Elizabeth II (June 2). Korean armistice signed (July 27).

1954 French defeat at Dien Bien Phu (May 7). Food rationing finally ends in Britain (July 3).

1956 Krushchev denounces Stalin. Col. Nasser elected President of Egypt (June 24). Nationalization of Suez Canal Company (July 26). Israel invades Egypt (Oct. 28). Anglo-French Suez Expedition (Oct. 31). Russian forces enter Budapest to crush Hungarian uprising (Oct. 4).

1957 Ghanaian independence. European Common Market Treaty signed (Mar. 25). Suez Canal opened to shipping (Apr. 9). First satellite launched by Russia (Oct. 4).

1958 First American satellite launched (Jan. 31). First crossing of Antarctica completed by Commonwealth Trans-Antarctic Expedition. General de Gaulle Prime Minister of France (June 1). General de Gaulle elected President of France.

1959 Castro comes to power in Cuba. Alaska becomes a state of the American Union. Opening of the St Lawrence Seaway (June 26).

1960 Belgian Congo gains independence. M. Tshombe declares independence of break-away Katanga. Cyprus becomes independent republic. Federation of Nigeria gains independence. John Kennedy elected President of U.S.A. (Nov. 9).

1961 Yuri Gagarin (U.S.S.R.) becomes first man in space (Apr. 12). South Africa becomes a republic and leaves the British Commonwealth.

1962 *Telstar*, communications satellite launched (July 10); first live television between U.S.A. and Europe. Cuba crisis; U.S.S.R. agrees to dismantle missile bases on Cuba (Oct. 28).

1963 Tereshkova (U.S.S.R.) becomes first woman in space (June). Assassination of President Kennedy (Nov. 22).

1964 U.S. Civil Rights Bill enacted (July 2).

1965 Death of Sir Winston Churchill (Jan. 24). U.S.A. begins retaliatory raids against North Vietnam (Feb.). Leonov (U.S.S.R.) makes first 'walk' in space (Mar. 18). Border war between India and Pakistan begins (Sept. 6); U.N. ceasefire accepted Oct. 22. Unilateral declaration of independence by Ian Smith's Rhodesian government.

1966 Assassination of Dr Verwoerd, South African Prime Minister (Sept. 6). Aberfan colliery-tip disaster (Oct. 21); 144 people die including 116 children. Extensive floods in Italy (Nov.).

1967 Chichester completes solo round-the-world voyage (May). Six-day Arab–Israeli war begins (June 5).

1968 Senator Robert Kennedy assassinated (dies June 6). Soviet invasion of Czechoslovakia (Aug. 20).

1969 U.S. astronauts step on Moon (July 21).

1970 Brazil's third World Cup win (June 21). General de Gaulle dies (Nov. 9).

1971 China admitted to U.N. and Taiwan expelled (Oct.). Indo-Pakistan war.

1972 President Nixon visits China (Feb.). Israeli athletes killed by terrorists during Munich Olympic Games.

1973 U.K., Ireland and Denmark join E.E.C. (Jan. 1). Agreement to withdraw U.S. forces from Vietnam signed (Jan. 28). East and West Germany admitted to U.N. (Sept.). Arab-Israeli war (Oct.).

1974 346 people perish in worst ever air disaster near Paris (March). Portugal's dictatorship overthrown (April). President Nixon resigns over Watergate affair (Aug).

1975 Apollo-Soyuz space link-up (July). European Security Conference held in Helsinki (Aug).

Civil Engineering

Dams and bridges are among the most spectacular structures built by man. Massive dams up to a thousand feet high block deep river gorges and store water for producing electricity. Slender bridges suspended from cables carry traffic hundreds of feet over wide river estuaries. Many bridges form part of a network of motorways that carry high-speed traffic the length and breadth of the country.

Designing and building dams, bridges, and roads forms an important part of a branch of engineering called *civil engineering*.

Bridge-Building

The simplest kind of bridge consists of a long piece, or *beam,* of timber or steel, supported at the ends by piers. This is called a *beam bridge.* But the span – the distance between the piers – cannot be too great, otherwise the weight of the beam will make the bridge collapse in the middle. One way of increasing the strength, and therefore the span, of a beam bridge is by building a truss on it. A *truss* is a simple framework of jointed pieces of metal.

The disadvantage of a simple beam bridge is that it can be built with only short spans. For greater spans, an *arch bridge* can be used. In an arch bridge, the weight of the bridge is transmitted at an angle down both sides of an arch to the supporting *abutments*.

Above: Spinning the wire cables of the suspension bridge over the River Forth, in Scotland. The bridge was completed in 1964. In the background is the Forth rail bridge, a cantilever bridge built in 1890 to carry the mainline railway to northern Scotland.

Right: This spectacular viaduct carries a railway across a steep valley in Switzerland. The shape of the arches gives the bridge its strength. The load is carried down the arches to the supporting piers and to the sides of the valley.

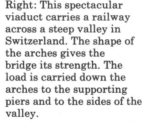

Left: The busy Los Angeles Freeway. Multi-lane highways are needed to cope with the ever increasing volume of traffic. Today, there are well over 100 million road vehicles in the world – over half of them in the U.S.A.

Arch bridges can be built of stone, brick, concrete, and steel. The Romans built large numbers of stone-arch bridges two thousand years ago, and many are still standing. The largest spans were about 100 feet. Modern steel-arch bridges have spans many times greater. One of the longest is the Sydney Harbour Bridge in Australia, which has a span of 1,650 feet.

The suspension bridge is one of the most spectacular examples of civil engineering. The road literally hangs in the air from a pair of cables carried by two towers, one on or near each bank.

The *suspension cables* supporting the bridge are made up of thousands of strong steel wires, bundled tightly together. Some bridges have cables more than three feet thick. The cables are anchored firmly behind the high suspension towers. The road deck hangs from the cables by steel rods called *suspenders*.

Most kinds of bridges are supported evenly along their length by arches, piers, or cables. But the *cantilever bridge* is somewhat different. It consists really of two identical but separate parts, which may meet in the middle or be joined by another part.

Each main part consists of a beam that is supported by a pier about half way along its length. One end of the beam is anchored to the bank. The other end merely projects outwards towards the identical projecting beam from the other bank.

Road Construction

Today there are well over 100 million motor cars in the world, and the number is increasing rapidly. As a result, many new roads must be built and existing roads reconstructed to carry the increasing volumes of traffic.

Below: A combined excavator and tunnel shield. The tunnel shield was invented by Marc Brunel for boring tunnels through clay or soft rock. In the 140 years since the shield was invented, many modifications have been made but the principles remain the same. Under the protection of the shield the clay is dug out. This may be done by men using pneumatic spades, or by digging equipment in the shield itself. As the *spoil* is removed the shield is jacked forward.

The first stage in road building is to map out, or *survey,* the countryside to find the best possible route to take. When the route has been chosen, preparation of the road bed can begin. Many kinds of earth-moving machines are used for levelling and digging the ground. They include bulldozers, scrapers, and excavators.

The properties of the soil beneath the road – the *subgrade* – are very important. They are found by testing samples of the soil in a laboratory. If the soil is found to be weak, materials such as sand and gravel must be mixed with it to strengthen it. The subgrade can also be improved by heavy rolling or ramming.

The final stage of road building is to lay the top surface, or *pavement*. There are two basic kinds of pavement – rigid and flexible. A rigid pavement is made of concrete and will not give even if the soil beneath it sinks a little. The concrete is laid on a base of crushed stone or gravel between parallel

metal plates, or *forms*. Spreading and finishing machines smooth and compact the concrete. They travel on rails alongside the forms.

A flexible pavement consists of small broken stones, usually held together by tar. The mixture of stones and tar is called *tarmacadam,* or *tarmac.* It is spread hot by finishing machines that squeeze it evenly over the road and compact it. Heavy rollers then compact it further into a hard-wearing surface.

Tunnelling

It is often necessary when building roads or railways to drive tunnels through hillsides and mountains in order to avoid a steep, winding route. The Mont Blanc Tunnel between France and Italy carries a road for seven miles through solid rock, thousands of feet below the mountain-top.

In hard rock, tunnels are driven by blasting with explosives. Powerful rock drills, driven by compressed air, bore holes into the rock face. Explosives placed in the holes blast away the rock. The shattered rock is loaded into trucks and removed. Then the process is repeated until the tunnel is completed.

In soft ground, a *tunnelling shield* is used to prevent the tunnel from collapsing during construction. The shield is like an open-ended tin, with a cutting edge at the open end. Powerful pushing devices called *jacks* force the shield forwards into the ground. Workmen then remove the earth from inside the shield, and the process is repeated. Tunnel linings are put into place behind the shield as it moves forward.

If there is danger of water seeping through during tunnelling, compressed air is fed to the shield to keep the water out. The workmen and materials enter and leave the shield through an air-lock to maintain the pressure.

Dam Construction

Dams are among the most massive man-made structures in the world. The biggest ones are giant mounds of earth and rock packed tightly together. They are called *earthen,* or *embankment* dams.

An earthen dam has a very wide base and gradually curves inwards on both sides to become fairly narrow at the top. It has a clay or concrete core, or a steel or concrete facing to make it watertight. *Hydraulic-fill* dams are built from a water-borne mixture of sand, clay, and gravel. The mixture is pumped into position through pipelines.

Other dams are built of concrete or stone blocks. *Arch* dams are suitable for blocking

Above: The foundations chosen to support high buildings depend on the strength of the underlying soil. On clay, a hollow concrete raft may be used to spread the load evenly (top), or concrete piles may be sunk to firmer soil (middle). In soft soil many piles may have to be used.

Right: Steel and prestressed concrete have enabled engineers to plan and build multi-storey buildings using a framework of girders and beams. The outer (curtain) walls do not carry the weight of the building.

narrow gorges. They are curved towards the water in the shape of an arch. It is their shape which makes them strong. The weight of the water is transmitted down the arch to the sides of the gorge. *Gravity* dams, on the other hand, rely on weight alone for strength. *Gravity-arch* dams are combinations of both types.

Skyscrapers

Building construction is one example of civil engineering with which we are all familiar. Tall skyscrapers and large blocks of flats and offices are being built in towns throughout the world. It is on these building sites that most of us see civil engineering in action.

The first stages of building are to survey the site and to drill holes at various points to find out how firm the soil is. If there is firm soil near the surface, excavators remove the upper layers of earth. Concrete foundations can then be laid on a firm base. Sometimes, however, the firm soil is a long way down, and excavating would not be practical. Then *piles* are driven down from the surface to firm soil or rock to support the foundations.

When the foundations have set, work can begin on the upper part of the building. The first job is to build the frame that will support it. The frame may consist of reinforced concrete or steel beams, which are lifted into position by cranes and bolted together. Or it may consist of reinforced concrete cast in position in *shuttering,* or wooden moulds.

The walls and floors, too, may be cast in

position or they may be precast in a factory and lifted into position by cranes.

More modern and quicker methods of construction include the lift-slab and jack-block methods. In the *lift-slab* method, all the floors are cast at ground level and jacked into position. In the *jackblock* method, the whole building is constructed floor by floor near the ground and jacked up into place.

Concrete

Millions of tons of concrete are used every year in building roads, bridges and dams. It is cheap, easy to make, and is waterproof and fireproof. It can also be used under water. When concrete is first mixed, it forms a pasty mass that can be moulded, or *cast,* into any shape. But it quickly sets rock-hard.

Concrete is made by adding water to a mixture of cement, sand, and gravel or stone. The sand is called *fine aggregate* and the stones are called *coarse aggregate*. The sand fills in the gaps between the larger stones so

that there will be no air trapped between them. The presence of air would weaken the concrete.

Ordinary concrete is strong when it is squeezed, or under *compression*. But it is weak when it is stretched, or under *tension*. If, say, a concrete beam is supported only at its ends, this weakness may cause it to crack and collapse.

To prevent this weakness, steel wires or rods are cast into the concrete. It is then known as *reinforced* concrete. The strength can be further increased by stretching, or *tensioning,* the steel wires or rods in the concrete. There are two methods of doing this – pretensioning and post-tensioning.

In *pretensioning,* the concrete is cast around rods that are being stretched. When the concrete sets, the rods 'squeeze' the concrete and make it stronger. In *post-tensioning,* the concrete is cast with holes along its length. Steel wires are inserted in the holes, pulled taut, and then anchored. This again helps to strengthen the concrete.

Above: A large dam under construction in Iran. Cable cars travel to and fro carrying the construction materials.

Below: An arch dam. The weight of the water behind the dam is transmitted down the arch to the sides of the gorge.

-G

The Polar Regions

The polar regions are those parts of the world which lie within the Arctic and Antarctic Circles (these correspond to latitudes 66½° North and South). Everywhere within the Arctic Circle there is at least one day during the northern hemisphere's summer when the sun does not set (i.e. when the whole region is never carried out of the sun's rays by the spin of the Earth). Conversely, there is at least one day during the northern hemisphere's winter when the sun does not rise (i.e. when none of the region is carried *into* the sun's rays by the spin of the Earth). The number of such days increases towards the North Pole where there are six months of continual day and six months of continual night. Exactly the same is true of the southern polar region at reverse times of the year.

The long polar 'night' is not as dark as it sounds, for the reflected moonlight is often bright enough to read by and there are frequent auroral displays in the sky. An aurora, one of the most awe-inspiring weather phenomena, is a magnificent display of changing colours in the sky which can take the form of rays, bands, arcs, draperies or diffused lights. In the northern hemisphere it is called the *Aurora Borealis,* or *Northern Lights,* and in the southern hemisphere the *Aurora Australis.*

The Arctic

The northern polar region includes the Arctic Ocean, which has an area of about 5,444,000 square miles. During the winter, pack-ice covers most of the Arctic Ocean. The ice is continually in motion, and as it grinds together large pressure ridges form. In the spring the ice begins to melt. Stretches of open water *(leads)* appear between the floes, and lakes form on the surface of the ice.

Considerable areas of Asia and North America and a small part of Europe lie farther north than latitude 66½°. Some parts are covered with snow and ice the whole year round (e.g. most of Greenland) but there are other areas which are only covered with snow for two-thirds of the year. These form the *tundra,* the name given to the tree-less plains of northern-most Eurasia and North America. The tundra changes completely from winter bleakness to summer splendour, the ground being gaily carpeted with mosses, lichens, sedges, small bright flowers and even dwarf shrubs.

Reindeer and caribou graze in the Arctic in summer, but travel south in winter. Other animals include bears, ermine and foxes.

The Eskimos are perhaps the most famous of all Arctic dwellers. They inhabit a broad region from the Bering Strait to Baffin Island and along the south-eastern and south-western coasts of Greenland. They are remarkable in the way in which they have skilfully adapted their lives to such adverse conditions.

The Antarctic

The only land within the Antarctic Circle is Antarctica, the coldest, windiest, loneliest and most desolate continent of all. This is a land mass about twice the size of Australia

Above: Protected from the cold by a thick shaggy coat, the musk-ox winters on the high, windswept plateaux of northern Greenland. The musk-ox lives nearer the North Pole than any other land animal.

Below: A group of Lapps stand in front of their tent in northern Sweden, their gaily coloured clothes contrasting sharply with the bleak Arctic landscape.

which is almost entirely shrouded in snow and ice the whole year round. A great ice sheet, well over a mile thick in places, weighs the land down and forms an ice plateau averaging 7,000 feet in height.

There are no flowering plants anywhere in Antarctica, but simply mosses and lichens which cling to patches of bare rock along the coast. The animal life consists of wingless insects, sea birds and seals, but in the summer millions of noisy penguins come to Antarctica and gather in large 'rookeries'. They all leave again in the autumn for the open sea – except for the Emperor penguin which stays to brave out the icy winter and rear its solitary chick.

There is no native population, the only inhabitants being groups of scientists manning scientific stations. The conditions they have to endure in this inhospitable land are harsh. The lowest temperature ever recorded, –127°F. (–88°C.), was near the South Pole and even during the summer temperatures rarely rise above freezing point. It can be so cold that rubber becomes brittle and exhaled breath freezes with an audible crackling sound.

To survive in such a land members of expeditions must be well protected against the weather. The buildings used as living quarters are specially constructed to withstand the intense cold.

Above: Modern Antarctic expeditions use powerful, tracked vehicles.

Top left: Breaking camp in the misty Antarctic dawn.

Middle left: A supply ship forces a path through the polar ice.

Bottom left: Crevasses are one of many hazards to Antarctic travellers.

Below: In winter, when other penguins leave for the open sea, the Emperor penguin stays to rear its solitary chick.

The Microscopic World

The microscope is one of the biologist's most important pieces of equipment because it enables him to study tiny organisms which are invisible to the naked eye. The first microscope was probably made somewhere around 1600 A.D., and, compared with today's models, it was a strange-looking object. It worked, however, and it opened up a whole new world of plants and animals – the microscopic world.

Protozoa

With the aid of a microscope, even an inexpensive one, a drop of apparently lifeless pond water can become a living wonderland full of fascinating animals and plants. One very common microscopic animal, found in nearly every pond and ditch, is the Amoeba. The largest Amoeba is about the size of a full stop on this page, but most of them are much

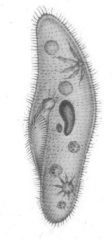

Paramecium moves through the water by waving the tiny hairs (cilia) which grow along its body.

smaller and virtually invisible to the naked eye. It might be thought that such a tiny speck of jelly would have no internal structure, but the microscope shows that it has a 'brain', or nucleus, and several other internal features which enable it to move and feed. Amoeba is always changing its shape by pushing out 'arms' in various directions, and it can move in any direction simply by flowing into one of these arms. It eats smaller creatures and other particles which it engulfs as it flows along.

The nucleus is the 'brain' of the Amoeba, but it does not grow at the same rate as the rest of the body. There comes a time when the body is too big for its nucleus, and this is the time for the Amoeba to reproduce. The nucleus splits into two halves and then the rest of the body divides, each half taking a nucleus and becoming a new Amoeba.

Paramecium is another common microscopic animal which lives in the same sort of places as Amoeba. It is shaped rather like a minute slipper and it is covered with tiny hairs called *cilia*. These cilia beat in and out like thousands of tiny oars and they propel the animal through the water. Special cilia near the mouth are used for drawing food-carrying currents of water into the mouth itself.

Amoeba, Paramecium, and the thousands of other minute animals like them, are probably something like the earliest animals that ever existed, and they are therefore called *Protozoa*, which means 'first animals'. The majority of them live in the water, but many live in the soil.

Animals can live only if they have plants to feed on, and we find that pond water also contains numerous microscopic plants. Unlike the larger plants, these microscopic ones can move about in the water by waving whip-like hairs called *flagella*. They look very much like some of the tiny animals, except that they are green. Chlamydomonas and Euglena are common examples.

Bacteria

Even smaller than the Protozoa and the little green plants are the bacteria. These are found everywhere – in the soil, in the air, and in the water – and they exist in enormous numbers. One of the major activities of the bacteria is to break down plant and animal material and·cause it to decay. This is a nuisance if the bacteria attack our food, but the process is very important in nature.

If it were not for bacteria, most of the fallen leaves would remain on the surface of the land instead of returning their goodness to the soil to feed the next year's plants.

Many bacteria cause illness or disease

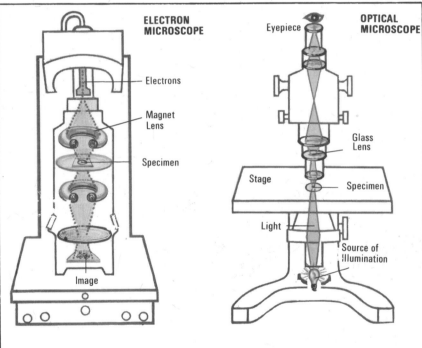

ELECTRON MICROSCOPE	OPTICAL MICROSCOPE
Electrons	Eyepiece
Magnet Lens	
Specimen	Glass Lens
	Stage
	Specimen
	Light
Image	Source of Illumination

The simplest type of microscope is the magnifying glass. The standard optical, or light, microscope is a series of magnifying glasses in a tube. The other parts of the microscope are the supporting foot and the stage where the specimens are put. The light microscope works with light waves. Light waves jump over extremely small objects such as viruses. Consequently, these cannot be seen under a microscope. They can be seen, however, under an electron microscope. Electrons do not jump over these small objects and their image is registered on a photographic plate in the microscope. It is not possible to look directly into an electron microscope, only to look at a photograph of the object under examination.

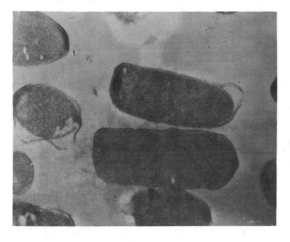

Above: An electron micrograph of bacteria, magnified 120,000 times.

Right: Some disease-causing bacteria and viruses.

Below: The three different types of bacterium.

Bacillus   Coccus   Spirillum

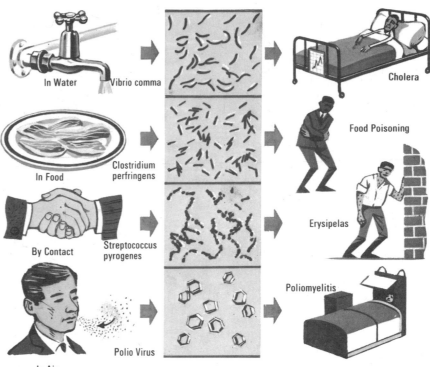

In Water   Vibrio comma   Cholera

In Food   Clostridium   Food Poisoning
            perfringens

By Contact Streptococcus   Erysipelas
            pyrogenes

In Air   Polio Virus   Poliomyelitis

when they get inside our bodies. Examples of these bacterial diseases include typhoid fever, tuberculosis, tetanus, and whooping cough. Only a few bacteria, or germs, may get into the body at first, but they reproduce so rapidly (by splitting into halves like Amoeba) that there are soon millions of them and they make us ill.

People knew nothing about bacteria until microscopes had been invented, and it was not until the 19th century that scientists like Robert Koch and Louis Pasteur proved that many diseases are caused by these minute germs. In earlier days, people used to think that illness was brought on by the Devil.

As well as revealing the existence of all these minute organisms, the microscope has enabled biologists to look at larger plants and animals in more detail and to find out what makes them 'tick'. In 1667, Robert Hooke examined some thin slices of cork with his microscope and he saw that it was made up of many tiny rectangular units. He called these units *cells*. We now know that all living things are made of cells, although there are many different types. There may be only one cell in the body, as in the Protozoa, or there may be millions of them all working together. By examining the cells under the microscope and observing their behaviour, biologists have been able to find out a great deal about how the whole body works. None of this would have been possible without the microscope.

Viruses

Diseases are not only caused by bacteria. They are also caused by *viruses*. Viruses are even smaller than bacteria. They are so small that they cannot be seen under an ordinary light microscope, but only under an electron microscope. Viruses are an extremely simple form of life; a link between the animate and the inanimate worlds. They crystallize, just as salt solutions do, when life conditions become difficult. They can remain as crystals for long periods of time, then become active again when the circumstances are favourable.

Viruses are so simple that they have no systems for digestion or reproduction. They invade other cells and take over their life mechanisms. This causes the other cells to die, and so causes diseases in both plants and animals. The common cold and poliomyelitis are two viral diseases which affect humans. Tobacco mosaic is a viral disease in plants. Some of the viruses shown here eat bacteria; they are called *bacteriophages*.

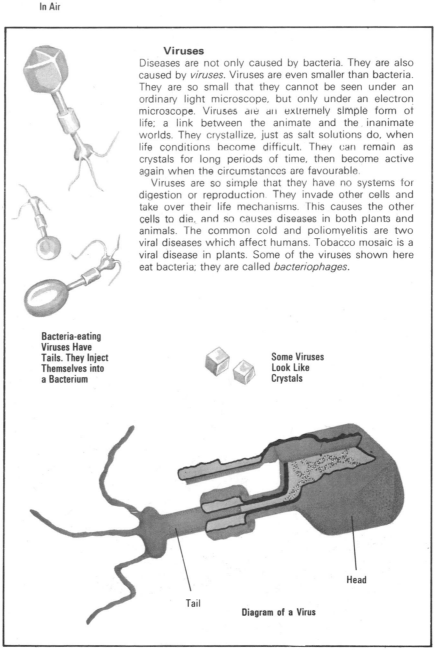

Bacteria-eating Viruses Have Tails. They Inject Themselves into a Bacterium

Some Viruses Look Like Crystals

Tail   Head

Diagram of a Virus

Food and Farming

Farming is the world's greatest industry. Farmers grow many kinds of crops, both as food and to provide raw materials such as fibres and rubber. The most important food crops are cereals such as wheat, rice and maize. Wheat is the leading bread grain and is one of the most widely grown crops. Rice is even more important in that it forms the staple diet of two-thirds of the world's population. Nine-tenths of the world's rice is grown and eaten in Asia. Potatoes rival wheat and rice as a source of food. They yield more food per acre than any of the cereals.

During the present century, mechanization has brought great changes to farming. The number of people working on the land has decreased but their productivity has soared. The main item of machinery used on the farm is the tractor which is used to pull many kinds of implements over the land – to prepare it for seeds, to plant the seeds, and to help cultivate the crops. When the crops are ready to harvest, a great variety of machines can be used to gather them safely in. The combine harvester is a complex machine which gathers wheat and similar crops. It cuts the wheat, threshes it, and deposits the cut stalks back on the ground in a single operation. When cotton is ready for harvesting, rows of machines move through the cotton fields, taking the bolls from the plants. Even fruit can be gathered by machine. The machine is situated under the tree which it shakes thoroughly and the

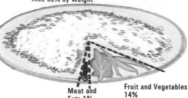

Milk Products 33% by Weight

Meat 10%

Sugar 5%

Potatoes 7%

Cereals 9%

Eggs and Fats 5%

Fruit and Vegetables 31%

Rice 85% by Weight

Meat and Fats 1%

Fruit and Vegetables 14%

Above: A typical daily diet in the U.S.A. compared with the daily diet of an Indian worker. The weight of food eaten by an American is nearly three times that eaten by the Indian, and the protein content is far greater. The aim of the Freedom from Hunger Campaign is to provide a sufficient and balanced diet for everyone.

Right: The combine harvester has done much to increase the world's food output. It has made possible the great wheat fields of North America which sometimes stretch unbroken to the horizon.

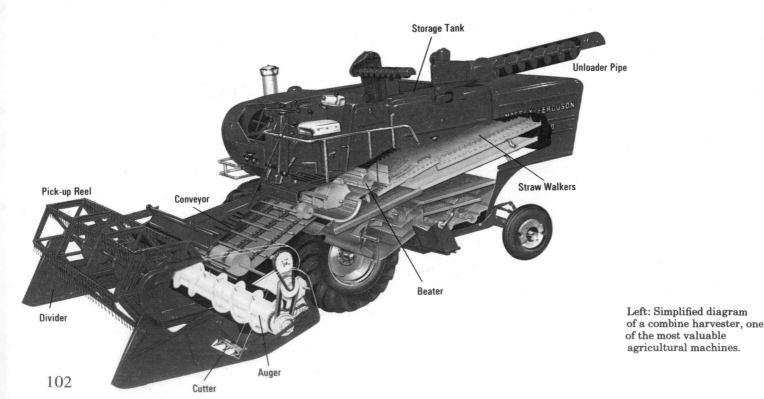

Storage Tank

Unloader Pipe

Pick-up Reel

Conveyor

Straw Walkers

Beater

Divider

Auger

Cutter

Left: Simplified diagram of a combine harvester, one of the most valuable agricultural machines.

102

fruit drops into a catching frame. Farm machinery is also used to help raise livestock. Many cows are milked by electric milking machines and other animals may be fed by conveyors.

Although farming has become highly scientific and mechanized in some parts of the world, in other parts it has remained unchanged for centuries, and the traditional methods can no longer produce enough food for a rapidly increasing population.

Feeding the World Population

In 1840 the world's population was about 1,000 million. It rose to 2,000 million by 1930. By 1960 about 3,000 million inhabited the Earth and it is estimated that the population will reach 6,000 million by the year 2000 A.D. These extra people will need food and homes, both of which make heavy demands upon the land. Hunger and malnutrition are already serious problems in Africa and Asia. They will become even more serious unless the production of food is dramatically increased.

At present, there are about four acres of cultivatable land per head of population. The rest is too dry, too cold, or too mountainous. Of each four acres only about one is cultivated, and that often inefficiently. If the whole acreage were farmed and forested properly, the Earth could support three or four times its present population.

Above: Ploughing the rice paddies with buffaloes in South East Asia. Part of Asia's food problem is due to the lack of mechanization.

Left: Plantation crops such as tea are grown commercially in tropical lands but they are destined mainly for export. The basic foodstuffs are often grown by each family which can produce barely enough for its own needs.

Below: The intensive rearing of animals has played a large part in meeting the growing food demands of Europe and North America.

The present food problems in Asia and Africa are due largely to a lack of technical knowledge and financial resources in the countries concerned. The primitive agricultural methods result in low crop yields; animals are not reared efficiently; and the lack of protein in the human diet results in malnutrition. The aim of the Freedom From Hunger Campaign is to help these countries financially, and to teach the people to farm their lands properly and to eat a balanced diet.

Agricultural Science

Increasing production from existing farmlands involves several aspects of science. Crops take minerals from the soil to build up their tissues. These minerals must be replaced adequately if cropping is to continue without declining yields. The efficient use of fertilizers is therefore of great importance. Not only mineral fertilizers but organic material must be added to the land to keep the soil in good condition. The composting of town refuse for use on the land is likely to play an important role in the future. The

present systems of tipping or burning are wasteful of precious organic material.

Breeding new strains of animal and plant species is now an important aspect of agricultural research. A variety of wheat which gives only a 1% increase in yield would, if grown everywhere that wheat is now grown, produce more than 2,500,000 metric tons additionally each year, enough to feed some 15,000,000 people.

Increasing the production of the land is of no avail unless steps are taken to combat the ravages of pests and disease. Insect pests are the most destructive of crops both in the field and in the warehouse. Millions of pounds worth of food is destroyed by them every year. Efficient control methods must be devised. The dangers of using very large quantities of insecticides have become ap-

parent. New control methods may rely on releasing sterile males into the insect populations. This technique has virtually wiped out the screw-worm fly – a cattle pest – in some regions of the U.S.A. Biological control by using parasites is also gaining in importance.

Land Reclamation

Though much can be done to increase the yield of the present farmlands, more land will have to be brought under cultivation to feed the ever-increasing population. Re-

Above: The first wave of a locust swarm. Locusts cause tremendous damage in Africa and Asia. When a swarm settles, the insects devour every green leaf and blade of grass in sight, devastating crops and pastures.

Left: Spraying crops from the air. Pest control is a vital factor in increasing the world's food. Without pests, the world's harvest would be one-third larger.

clamation of wet ground involves drainage and protection to avoid future waterlogging. Land that has been under the sea must also be treated for the removal of salt before it can be used for agriculture. Land reclamation has been practised extensively in the Netherlands and is still actively in progress in the region of the Zuider Zee. When complete, the reclamation of this area will have added some half-million acres to the agricultural land of the Netherlands.

Irrigation

Farmlands in many parts of the world are supplied artificially with water so that crops can be grown. Irrigation is usually necessary in tropical and sub-tropical regions where the rainfall is less than 20 inches per year. In

cooler regions, the rainfall does not evaporate so swiftly and irrigation is not usually necessary. In some regions, irrigation may only be needed during part of the year whilst in other areas, such as Egypt, crops depend almost entirely upon artificially supplied water. Irrigation is also necessary in places where the rainfall, though normally sufficient, is unreliable. Fully half of the world's cultivated land is irrigated to some extent.

The idea of irrigation is not new. In Egypt, crops have always depended upon the River Nile. The Ancient Egyptians utilised the fact that the Nile flooded once each year. They developed a system of canals to carry the floodwaters through the fields. For the rest of the year they relied upon primitive devices to raise water from the level of the river to the canals. Large-scale efficient irrigation schemes can only be carried out with perennial canals (those which carry water the whole year round). But perennial canals are costly, for they entail the damming of rivers to control floodwaters and to create artificial reservoirs which can be drawn upon at all times of the year.

One of the boldest irrigation schemes of modern times is the Snowy Mountains project in south-eastern Australia. The aim is to impound water from the Snowy River, which flows through a region of adequate rainfall, and lead it back through the mountains to augment the waters of the Murray and Murrumbidgee Rivers for inland irrigation. The plan calls for the construction of nine big dams, more than 100 miles of aqueducts, and at least 10 big power stations; some of them underground.

Fishing

The increasing need for food, especially protein food, in the world today is making ever-increasing demands upon the resources of the sea. Herring, sardines, cod, halibut and plaice are some of the most important commercial fish. They are a rich source of protein and could become a valuable addition to the diet of many undernourished peoples. But already some fishing grounds are seriously over-fished. Experiments are now being carried out with fertilizers added to the sea, just as is done on the land.

Top Left: A modern grain store on the Great Lakes capable of storing 100,000 tons of grain. North America is the world's great grain exporter. Much of it goes to Europe, especially to the U.K.

Middle Left: Irrigated citrus groves. In recent years irrigation schemes have converted large areas of arid land into fertile farmland.

Bottom Left: Over much of Asia irrigation is still carried out by primitive methods.

Australia

The Land

Australia is a country that is also a continent. It lies in the southern hemisphere. It is about three-quarters of the size of Europe, but Europe has 56 times as many people. Australia is a member of the Commonwealth of Nations.

Several islands lie around the coast. The largest and most important of these is Tasmania, which is south of the mainland of Australia. The Great Barrier Reef on the north-eastern coast is a 1,200-mile chain of coral reefs and islets.

Most of the western and central part of Australia is a high, flat plateau. Few people live there. The eastern third of the continent is more varied. Close to the east coast is a long range of mountains, called the Great Dividing Range. The highest mountain is Mount Kosciusko (7,316 feet).

The northern part of Australia lies in the tropics, just north of the Tropic of Capricorn. Along the coast, it is hot and wet, with heavy rains every year. South-eastern and south-

Right: An aerial view of Sydney, the capital of New South Wales and Australia's largest city.

Right: The koala, a small, furry, pouched mammal of eastern Australia feeds almost exclusively on the leaves of the eucalyptus tree.

Left: Australia has over 164,000,000 sheep – 13 for every inhabitant – and produces one-third of the world's wool. Much of it is high quality Merino from sheep kept in the sub-arid interior with less than 15 inches of rain per year. Australia is also the second largest exporter of mutton and lamb.

106

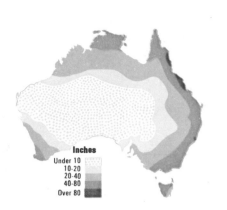

Inches
Under 10
10-20
20-40
40-80
Over 80

Left: Annual rainfall map of Australia. More than one-third of the entire continent receives less than ten inches of rain each year.

Right: Tuna fishing off the coast of New South Wales.

January Temperatures

July Temperatures

°F

Below 30 30-50 50-70 70-90 Over 90

STATES AND TERRITORIES OF AUSTRALIA

State or Territory	Area (sq. mi.)	Pop.	Capital
Australian Capital Territory	939	103,573	Canberra
New South Wales	309,433	4,300,083	Sydney
Northern Territory	520,280	39,556	Darwin
Queensland	667,000	1,688,529	Brisbane
South Australia	380,070	1,107,178	Adelaide
Tasmania	26,383	376,212	Hobart
Victoria	87,884	3,271,993	Melbourne
Western Australia	975,920	863,744	Perth

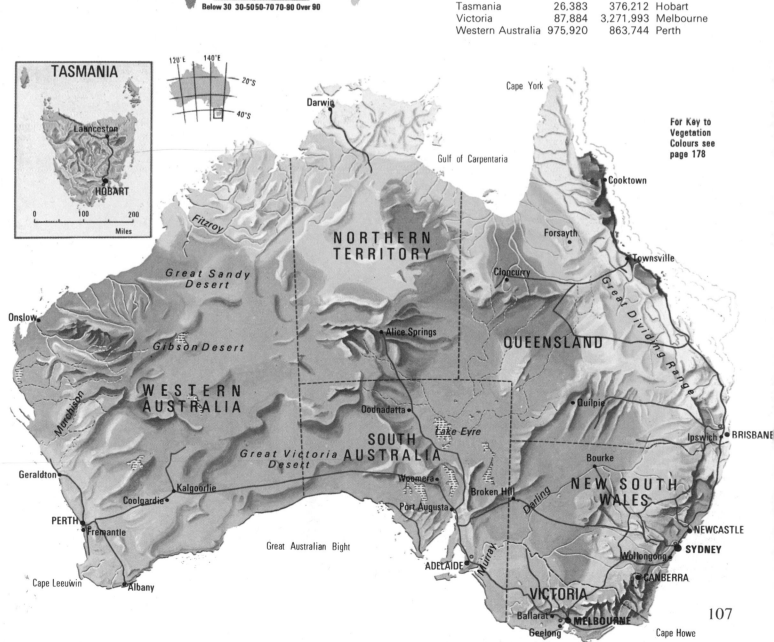

TASMANIA

Launceston

HOBART

0   100   200

Miles

120°E   140°E

20°S

40°S

For Key to Vegetation Colours see page 178

Cape York

Darwin

Gulf of Carpentaria

Cooktown

NORTHERN TERRITORY

Forsayth

Townsville

Cloncurry

Fitzroy

Great Sandy Desert

Onslow

Alice Springs

QUEENSLAND

Gibson Desert

Great Dividing Range

WESTERN AUSTRALIA

Oodnadatta

Quilpie

Murchison

Lake Eyre

SOUTH AUSTRALIA

Ipswich   BRISBANE

Great Victoria Desert

Bourke

Geraldton

Woomera

NEW SOUTH WALES

Kalgoorlie

Broken Hill

Darling

Coolgardie

Port Augusta

PERTH

NEWCASTLE

Fremantle

Wollongong   SYDNEY

Great Australian Bight

Murray

Cape Leeuwin

ADELAIDE   CANBERRA

Albany

VICTORIA

Ballarat   MELBOURNE

Geelong   Cape Howe

107

Bass Strait

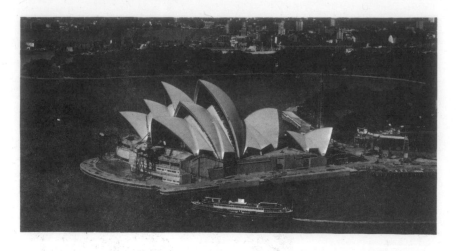

Above: The sail-shaped roof of the Sydney Opera House is as dominant a harbour feature as the famous bridge.

Below: The kookaburra, or laughing jackass, found in southern and eastern Australia, is famed for its unusual call. This takes the form of a full-throated laugh ending in a short, unbelievably human chuckle.

Below: Intricate coral formations make up the Great Barrier Reef which stretches for 1,200 miles down the north-east coast of Australia between 30 and 90 miles offshore.

western Australia have climates similar to those of California and the French Mediterranean coast, with hot, dry summers and warm, moist winters. The east coast also has sufficient rainfall for farming.

Most of the centre of the country has very unreliable rainfall. In some years, rain may fall, but several years of drought may follow.

Australia is rich in minerals, including bauxite, coal, copper, gold, iron, lead, nickel, silver, tin, uranium and zinc. Petroleum and natural gas have been found off the coasts. Huge underground stores of water lie under parts of the country called Artesian Basins.

Forests, particularly in the south and east, contain eucalyptus trees, which provide timber and oils. Australians call them gum trees.

Australia has only a few kinds of animals of its own. They include *marsupials*, which are animals with pouches. The biggest are the kangaroos. Others are koalas, wallabies and wombats. The duck-billed platypus, a mammal which lays eggs, is another Australian animal.

The People

Most of the people of Australia are of British origin. Since World War II more than two million people from Europe have emigrated to Australia. In addition, there are about 40,000 Aborigines, a dark-skinned people whose ancestors were the first inhabitants of Australia.

More than half the people of Australia live in cities. The rest live in small towns or villages, or in lonely farms called *stations*. Some stations are many miles from other farms, and the people use radios and aircraft to keep in touch.

Mining and manufacturing provide more than two-thirds of Australia's wealth. The rest is provided by farming. The country exports great quantities of wool and wheat. It

also has many cattle and produces much butter and cheese.

Australia has a federal form of government. This means that it is a *federation* or group of separate states, with a central government linking them together. Australia has six states: New South Wales, Queensland, South Australia, Tasmania, Victoria and Western Australia. Each state has its own parliament.

Two areas called territories come under the direct rule of the central government. They are the Northern Territory, much of which is desert, and the Australian Capital Territory, a small area around Canberra, the federal capital.

History

The first people to occupy Australia were the Aborigines. They arrived in the continent about 20,000 years ago.

Australia was visited by Dutch explorers such as Tasman in the early 17th century, and at first it was called New Holland. Then, in 1770 the British explorer Captain James Cook landed in Botany Bay, on the south-eastern coast, and claimed the great unknown land for Britain.

The British decided to use the new territory as a *penal settlement* – a kind of open prison where criminals could be sent, guarded by a few soldiers. In 1788, 750 convicts and their escort arrived to set up a colony at Sydney, in the south-eastern part of Australia. During the next 70 years, a steady stream of people arrived in Australia to settle.

Gold was discovered in New South Wales and Victoria in 1851. During the next ten years about 700,000 people flocked to Australia to look for gold. The transportation of convicts had ceased by 1852, except to Western Australia, where it continued until 1867. Australia became an independent country in 1901 as the *Commonwealth of Australia*.

During World War I, Australian troops fought in Europe against the Germans as part of the Australian and New Zealand Army Corps (the Anzacs). Their bravery in attacking Germany's allies, the Turks, at Gallipoli in 1915 won them undying fame. During World War II, Australian forces fought in northern Africa and against the Japanese in New Guinea.

Before and after World War II, Australia grew both in population and wealth. More and more gold, wool and other Australian products were sold to other countries, and more people came to settle there. In 1965, Australian troops went to fight in the Vietnam war.

New Zealand

The Land

New Zealand is a country over 1,000 miles south-east of Australia. Most of New Zealand is made up of two large islands, called North Island and South Island. It contains several other islands, but they are very small. New Zealand is almost as big as the British Isles. More than nine-tenths of all New Zealanders were born in the British Isles, or are descended from British and Irish people who settled in New Zealand.

North Island, where two-thirds of all New Zealanders live, extends about 500 miles from north to south. Its low mountains and hills include two active volcanoes. South Island is separated from North Island by the 16-mile-wide Cook Strait. From the Strait, the Southern Alps stretch south-westwards for more than 500 miles throughout the island. New Zealand's highest mountain, Mount Cook, rises from this range.

In addition to active volcanoes, New Zealand has other natural features associated with volcanic activity. On North Island is a region where hot springs and boiling mud pools are found. Some of the hot springs are *geysers*, which periodically shoot up a tall column of hot water and steam.

New Zealand has a mild climate. In January the country's mid-summer temperature averages about 68°F (20°C). In July, temperatures drop to about 42°F.

Above: A sheep-shearer at work. New Zealand ranks second in the export of wool and first in the export of lamb.

Right: Cattle are important in New Zealand and butter is a major export. Mount Egmont, a volcanic peak, rises in the background.

Below: The city and harbour of Wellington, North Island.

(6°C). Rainfall is very varied, averaging between 20 and 200 inches in various parts of the islands.

New Zealand has several species of rare birds. The tail-less kiwi is often used as a symbol for the country.

The People

About 7 people out of every 100 are *Maoris*, who are descendants of the Polynesian people who sailed to the islands about 700 years ago. Many marriages have occurred between Maoris and Europeans. The official language of New Zealand is English, but the Maoris also have their own language.

Resources

New Zealand is one of the most prosperous countries in the world. It was one of the earliest countries to introduce social reforms and a social security system, including old age pensions.

Half of New Zealand's area is farmland, and the country exports butter, lamb, fruit

History

The earliest-known people in New Zealand were Moriois — a Polynesian people. They were conquered in about the 1300's by another Polynesian people, Maoris, who settled mainly on the coastal parts of North Island.

Abel Tasman, commander of a ship sailing for the Dutch East India Company, sighted New Zealand in 1642. The Dutch named the islands after Zeeland, a province in the Netherlands. The Dutch kept their discovery secret. James Cook, a British sea captain, found and charted the island in 1769. But the British took little interest in the country for the next 70 years.

In 1839, Edward Gibbon Wakefield, a British statesman, who had formed a New Zealand Company, sent a group of British colonists to settle on the islands. The first colonists settled at Wellington. To protect them, the British government incorporated New Zealand into their Australian colony of New South Wales.

In 1840, Maori chiefs signed a treaty accepting British rule; and in 1841 New Zealand became a colony independent of Australia. Disputes about land led to war between the Maoris and the settlers in 1845-1848. Fighting occurred again in the 1860's and 1870's.

In 1907, New Zealand became an independent dominion within the British empire. Its troops fought in Europe in both World Wars. More recently New Zealand has sent troops into Vietnam to support the Australian and United States troops.

and other food products, especially to Britain. New Zealand has fertile soil. Farmers grow cereals for consumption in New Zealand. Because the most modern methods of farming are used, only a sixth of the country's people work on the land. Two-thirds of the people work in manufacturing and processing industries of various kinds. Much electrical power comes from hydro-electric plants, which harness the power of New Zealand's rushing rivers.

Forests cover about a fifth of New Zealand. Most of the forests were planted in the 1920's. The country's mineral wealth includes coal, iron ore, gold, limestone, natural gas, silver and tungsten.

Government

New Zealand is a monarchy. It has the same queen, Elizabeth II, as Britain. In New Zealand, the Queen is represented by a governor-general. The government is headed by a prime minister. He and his cabinet are members of the elected House of Representatives, the nation's parliament.

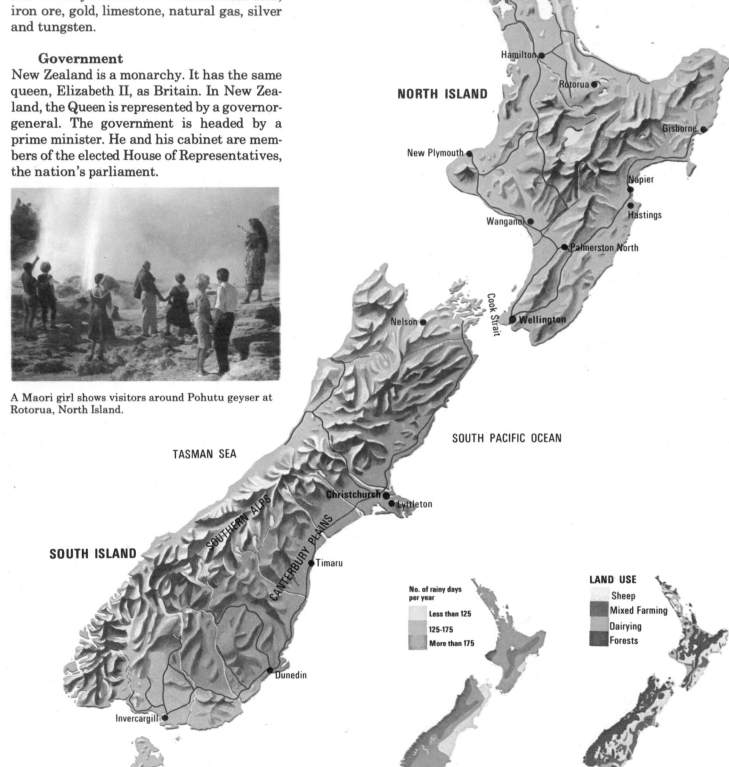

A Maori girl shows visitors around Pohutu geyser at Rotorua, North Island.

NEW ZEALAND

North Cape

NORTH ISLAND

Auckland
Hamilton
Rotorua
Gisborne
New Plymouth
Napier
Hastings
Wanganui
Palmerston North
Wellington

Temperate Forest
Grass
Railways

Cook Strait

Nelson

SOUTH PACIFIC OCEAN

TASMAN SEA

SOUTHERN ALPS

CANTERBURY PLAINS

Christchurch
Lyttleton

SOUTH ISLAND

Timaru

No. of rainy days per year
Less than 125
125-175
More than 175

LAND USE
Sheep
Mixed Farming
Dairying
Forests

Dunedin

Invercargill

Stewart Island

110

The Insect World

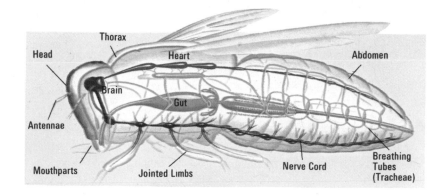

Insects include animals such as butterflies, bees, beetles, grasshoppers, dragonflies, and earwigs. They all belong to a large group of creatures called *arthropods,* in which the whole body is encased in a tough coat. This coat is an external skeleton, rather like a suit of armour, with joints to allow movement. If you look carefully at an insect you will see that it has three parts to the body, three pairs of jointed legs, and one pair of feelers or antennae. Most insects also have two pairs of wings.

Many people lump spiders, woodlice, centipedes, and other 'creepy-crawlies' with the

Above: The generalized body-plan of an insect. The body consists of three main regions: the head, thorax and abdomen. The thorax usually bears wings and three pairs of walking legs. The head bears a single pair of feelers (antennae) and jointed mouthparts.

Left: The body of a typical insect (a bee) viewed from above.

Right: The common housefly is a dangerous insect pest. It spreads disease by transferring to fresh food germs picked up on previous visits to animal dung and rotting vegetation.

and successful? The ability to fly obviously helps because it enables the insects to spread themselves rapidly from place to place. A rapid breeding rate also helps them to spread quickly. But one of the most important reasons for their success is their small size. The heaviest insect weighs only about four ounces, while most of them are very much smaller and some cannot be seen without a magnifying glass. The largest insects are certain stick insects with bodies about 12 inches long, or moths with 12-inch wingspans, but even then the bodies are quite slender.

insects but, although they are arthropods, none of these creatures fits the description of an insect. None of these other arthropods has wings, and so any winged arthropod must be an insect. But not all insects have wings: many simple soil-living insects are wingless, and so are silverfish and fleas.

A Million Kinds of Insects

Nobody knows just how many different kinds of insects there are. About a million different kinds have already been found and more are being discovered every day. There are more kinds of insects than all the other kinds of animals put together. Insects also exist in enormous numbers. If we could collect up all the insects in the world we would find that they weighed more than all the other land animals put together.

Very few insects have managed to invade the sea, but they manage to live almost everywhere on the land and in fresh water. They are certainly a very successful group of animals. But what makes them so numerous

Right: A selection of insects showing the wide variety of forms which is to be found amongst this group of animals. There are more kinds of insects than all the other kinds of animals put together.

Breathing in Insects

The small size of insect bodies is controlled partly by their method of breathing. We breathe by taking air into our lungs and then carrying the oxygen around our bodies in our blood. Insects have no lungs, however, and they breathe in a very different way. Along the sides of the insect there are a number of small holes called *spiracles,* most easily seen in large caterpillars. The spiracles lead to tiny tubes called *tracheae* which spread through the body. Air has to seep along these tubes to supply the insect with oxygen, and this seepage is rather slow – too slow to supply the needs of a large animal. Even in the bulkiest insects there are rarely any parts more than about half an inch from the surface.

Above: A scarab beetle rolling a ball of dung with its hind legs. An egg laid in the dung develops into a grub which feeds inside the ball (shown cut open).The scarab beetle is one of many scavenging insects.

Feeding in Insects

The small size of insects enables them to inhabit places and use food supplies which could not possibly support larger animals. Many insects spend their lives tunnelling between the upper and lower surfaces of leaves, and we notice their presence only through the brown blotches that appear on the leaf surface. One group of insects spend most of their lives inside the eggs of other insects.

There can be very few materials that are not eaten by one kind of insect or another. Wood, blood, hair, wax, dung and mould are some of the unusual things eaten by insects in addition to the more usual diets of plants and other animals. The ability to use so many different foods is another reason why the insects are such a successful group of animals.

Above: The male (top left), queen (top right), soldier (bottom left), and worker (bottom right) of the harvesting ant.

The mouths of insects are well designed for their various diets. Beetles and grasshoppers feed on solid materials and they possess strong jaws for cutting and chewing their food. Butterflies and moths suck nectar from flowers and their mouths are drawn out into long 'tongues' which they push into the flowers. When the 'tongue' is not being used it is rolled up under the head. Blood-sucking insects, such as fleas and mosquitos, have needle-like jaws which puncture the skin and form a channel for blood to flow into the mouth. Sap-sucking insects, such as greenfly, have similar mouths. Houseflies and bluebottles pour saliva and other juices over their food and then mop it up with spongy pads.

Insect Life Histories

The tough outer skeleton of an insect does not grow with the animal and it has to be replaced by a larger one at intervals. This coat-changing is called *moulting* and it takes place between two and fifty times during the insect's life. Four or five moults are most common and the moult takes place in the following way. When the young insect's coat has become too tight, the insect rests for a short while and then puffs itself up with air (or water if it lives in water). This action splits the old coat but a new and larger one has already grown underneath. The insect wriggles out of the old skin and, when the new one has hardened, it gets rid of the air or water, thus leaving room for the next growth stage.

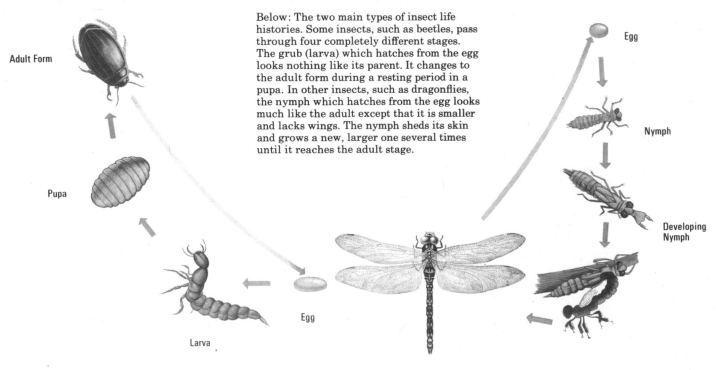

Below: The two main types of insect life histories. Some insects, such as beetles, pass through four completely different stages. The grub (larva) which hatches from the egg looks nothing like its parent. It changes to the adult form during a resting period in a pupa. In other insects, such as dragonflies, the nymph which hatches from the egg looks much like the adult except that it is smaller and lacks wings. The nymph sheds its skin and grows a new, larger one several times until it reaches the adult stage.

Adult Form

Pupa

Larva

Egg

Adult Form

Egg

Nymph

Developing Nymph

There are two main types of life history among insects, one in which the young looks something like the adult and one in which the young does not look anything like the adult. The grasshopper has the first type of life history. The young grasshopper looks like the adult except that it is smaller and has no wings. At each moult the grasshopper gets larger and so do its wings, which grow from little 'buds' on the back. After the final moult the wings are fully formed.

The second type of life history is followed by butterflies. The young butterfly looks nothing like a butterfly at all and is called a caterpillar. It has biting jaws and it eats leaves instead of drinking nectar. When it moults it gets bigger, but there is no sign of wings. The creature remains a caterpillar until it reaches full size. Then it changes into a *pupa* or *chrysalis*. The pupa does not move about, and inside it the caterpillar's body is converted into a butterfly. The adult butterfly then breaks out of the pupa skin and, after its wings have hardened, it flies away. The change from young to adult therefore takes place at one particular stage in the butterfly, instead of taking place gradually as it does in the grasshopper. Once the insect has its fully developed wings, it will not grow or moult any more. Little flies do not therefore grow into bigger flies.

Social Insects

Most insects lead solitary lives, and even if they live close together they do not usually help each other. A few insects, however, live in large family groups, with each member of the colony doing a certain job for the good of the whole community. These are the *social* insects, which include the termites, ants, and some bees and wasps.

Camouflage and Mimicry

The insects are masters of camouflage and many of them are hard to find when they are resting. Many moths, for example, are just the same colour as the tree trunks on which they rest and they become almost invisible when they settle. Some insects go a stage further and actually resemble objects in their surroundings. Examples include a moth that looks like a bird dropping, plant hoppers that look like prickles, and many stick insects and leaf insects. The resemblance to twigs and leaves is clearly an advantage because birds and other enemies would not think to attack twigs and leaves.

Not all insects are camouflaged, however. Some are brightly coloured and stand out clearly. Insects like this are usually poisonous or unpleasant in some other way, and the bright colours or bold patterns warn their

Above: Some wasps make nests of clay (top). Others make nests of paper (middle). A section through a paper nest (bottom) shows the cells in which the eggs are laid and the grubs live until they change into the adult form.

enemies to keep away. Once a young bird has tried one of these unpleasant insects it remembers the pattern and avoids it in the future.

With so many different kinds of insects in the world, it is not surprising that some of them resemble each other. Quite often a harmless species looks like a poisonous one with warning colours. The harmless one will benefit from this resemblance, or *mimicry* as it is called, because birds will think it is poisonous and will therefore avoid it. Some of the best examples of mimicry are found among the hover flies which look so much like bees and wasps.

Insects and Man

Many insects are a great nuisance to us because they eat our food, our clothes, and even our houses. They also carry diseases which affect us, our animals, and our crops. But not all insects are harmful, and some of them are extremely useful to us. One of the most useful is the honey bee which provides us with honey and also pollinates many of our plants. Without the bees' aid, the plants could not produce fruits and seeds. Wasps are useful, too. Young wasps are fed on small insects and a single wasp nest will account for thousands of garden pests. The silkworm is another very useful insect. It is really the caterpillar of a moth and it wraps itself in a silken cocoon before turning into a pupa. Many caterpillars do this, but they do not make such good silk as the silkworm and nearly all the world's silk comes from this insect.

Below: A bush cricket, one of the long-horned grasshoppers which chirp by rubbing their wing covers. Short-horned grasshoppers chirp by rubbing the inside of their back legs on a hard ridge on their wing covers.

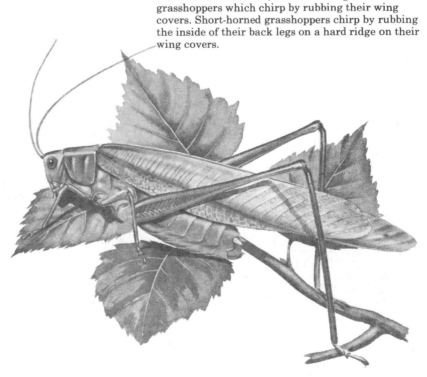

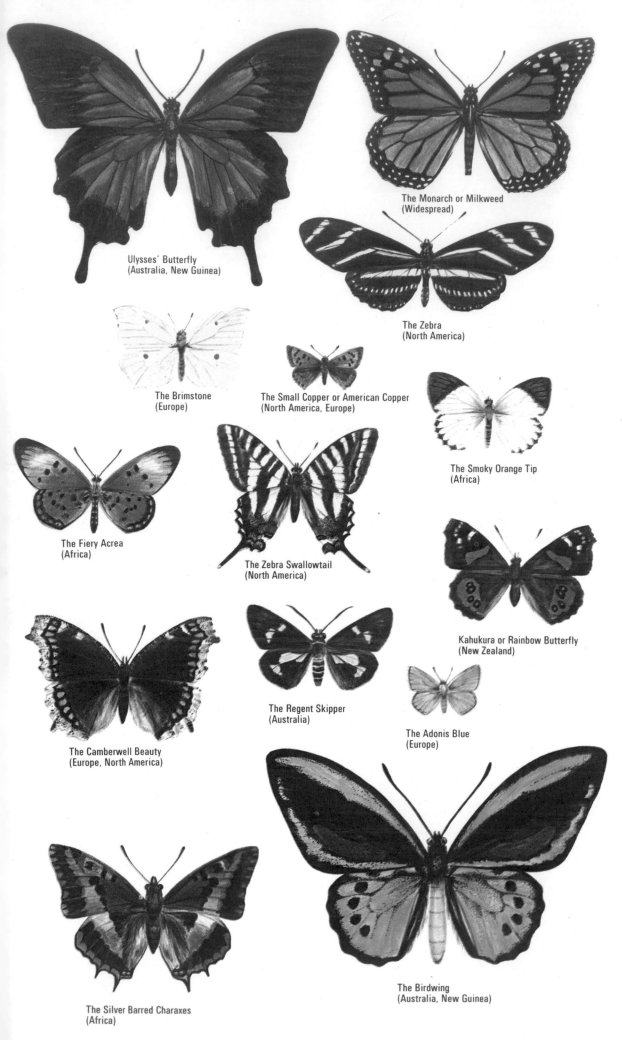

Ulysses' Butterfly
(Australia, New Guinea)

The Monarch or Milkweed
(Widespread)

The Zebra
(North America)

The Brimstone
(Europe)

The Small Copper or American Copper
(North America, Europe)

The Smoky Orange Tip
(Africa)

The Fiery Acrea
(Africa)

The Zebra Swallowtail
(North America)

Kahukura or Rainbow Butterfly
(New Zealand)

The Camberwell Beauty
(Europe, North America)

The Regent Skipper
(Australia)

The Adonis Blue
(Europe)

The Silver Barred Charaxes
(Africa)

The Birdwing
(Australia, New Guinea)

Left: Butterflies are the most beautiful of insects. Like moths, butterflies have large wings, often with brilliant colours and striking patterns. The colours come from minute scales which cover the wings. Adult butterflies feed on nectar from flowers, sucking up the liquid through a long tongue, or proboscis, which, when not in use, is coiled up under the head. It is not always easy to tell butterflies and moths apart, but, as a general rule, moths fly at night and butterflies during the day. Also, a butterfly usually holds its wings upright when it alights on a flower, whereas a moth usually spreads its wings out flat.

These butterflies are all drawn two-thirds natural size.

Spiders

Spiders are not insects; they have only two parts to their body instead of three; four pairs of legs instead of three; and no antennae. They are, in fact, the most important members of the *Arachnida,* a class of animals which also includes scorpions, mites and harvestmen.

Apart from a similar body plan, another feature all spiders have in common is the ability to produce strands of silk from their bodies. But not all spiders use the silk to spin webs, and those which do, differ in their skill. Webs range from crude, bluish, tangled masses of threads to delicate symmetrical designs.

Web-spinning

Perfectionists in the art of web-spinning are the members of the *Argiopidae* family such as the garden spiders. Their cartwheel webs, composed of radiating strands connected by cross-threads, form a delicate drape over windows and hedges. When its web is complete, the spider rests in the centre, or hides among the leaves at the edge. But it remains in contact with the web by means of a thread, and quickly senses vibrations caused by a trapped insect. Then the spider rushes out and wraps its victim in fresh silk, biting it once or twice in the process (all spiders have poison fangs with which to paralyse their prey).

If the web is damaged by the victim's struggles, the spider rarely bothers to repair it. New ones are made almost daily. The commonest house spider of all, *Tegenaria domestica,* spins webs so often that it eventually wears out its spinning apparatus, and has to invade the web of another, younger house spider.

By no means all spiders spin webs. The crab spider, so called because of its curved legs, lurks on a flower, changing its colour to suit its surroundings, ready to bite an unsuspecting insect. The wolf spider runs down its prey with a tremendous burst of speed. Some wolf spiders are inconspicuous, scurrying creatures, but one is probably the most famous spider of all – the tarantula. Despite all the legends, the bite of a tarantula is not deadly to human beings; the worst effect is likely to be a slight irritation. Spiders which really are dangerous to human beings are those of the genus *Latrodectus,* such as the famous black widow of America. The bite of this notorious spider is by no means always fatal, but it is extremely painful.

Above: Spiders belong to the Arachnid group which also includes scorpions. Arachnids have four pairs of walking legs. The scorpion also has a large pair of jaws (chelicerae); the jaws of spiders are much smaller. Many spiders build webs in which to catch their prey. When a 'cartwheel' web is touched, the spider rushes out of hiding and moves to the centre of the web. From there it can feel which part of the web is vibrating.

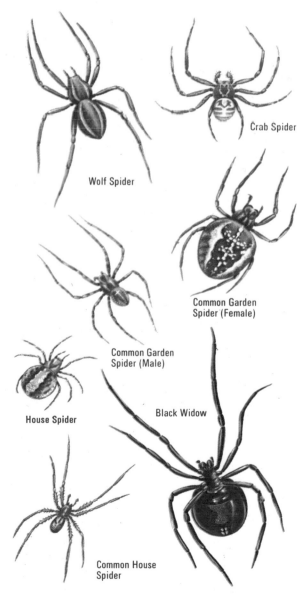

Crab Spider

Wolf Spider

Common Garden Spider (Female)

Common Garden Spider (Male)

House Spider

Black Widow

Right: Some members of the spider family. The Black Widow can inflict an extremely painful bite.

Common House Spider

The Story of Flight

Birth of the Aeroplane

In 1903, two American brothers, Wilbur and Orville Wright, built a flimsy machine of wood, cloth, and wire which was powered by a petrol engine. On December 17, Orville made the first-ever powered flight on a deserted stretch of sand at Kitty Hawk, in North Carolina. The first flight was for only 120 feet, but it demonstrated at last that heavier-than-air flight was a practical proposition.

Lighter-than-Air Craft

The Wright brothers' flight marked the beginning of the aeroplane as we know it. But a long time before that man had been flying, first in *balloons* and then in *airships*. These craft are lighter than air and this is why they can fly. Being lighter than air, they rise upwards through it just like a cork, which is lighter than water, rises through water.

The first balloons (1780s) were *hot-air balloons*. Hot air rises because it is lighter than the cold air surrounding it. Fill a bag with hot air and it will rise. And that was the basis of the hot-air balloons. The air was kept warm by a brazier of hot coals slung beneath the open base of the balloon. This, of course, was not very desirable, and the balloons often caught fire.

The *hydrogen balloon* was a great improvement on the hot-air balloon. Hydrogen is the

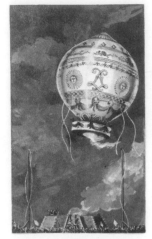

Above: The first manned balloon flight was made in 1783 with a hot-air balloon designed by the Montgolfier Brothers. A hydrogen-filled balloon designed by the French scientist J. A. C. Charles flew later in the same year.

Below: Count Ferdinand Zeppelin launched his first rigid, hydrogen-filled airship in 1900. His airships were soon in regular use carrying passengers and mail. On May 6, 1937, the Zeppelin *Hindenburg* exploded at Lakehurst, N.J., U.S.A. with the loss of 36 lives. This was one of a series of disasters which foreshadowed the end of passenger-carrying airships.

lightest of all gases and is fourteen times lighter than air. It is therefore an excellent gas for filling lighter-than-air balloons. It gives a much greater upward 'lift' than hot air. The dangerous disadvantage is that hydrogen burns extremely readily.

The design of hydrogen balloons has remained more or less the same from the beginning. The passenger car, or *gondola*, is suspended from a net thrown over the balloon to distribute the weight evenly. There is a hand-operated valve in the balloon to let the gas out when passengers wish to descend. Bags of sand are taken in the car to be used as *ballast*. The loose sand can be thrown out to make the balloon rise higher.

Ballooning was a popular sport right up until the 1930's, and even today there are many keen balloonists. But the greatest present-day uses of balloons are in weather-forecasting and scientific research. Most of today's balloons contain helium, which is heavier than hydrogen but is not inflammable.

Airships

The disadvantage with balloons is that they can only go where the wind blows them. In 1900, Count Ferdinand Zeppelin launched the first really successful *dirigible* (steerable) balloon, or *airship*, powered by the recently developed petrol engine. Soon Zeppelin's airships were carrying passengers and mail. Britain, America, and Russia built similar, cigar-shaped craft. They were still filled with hydrogen. A series of disasters in the 1930's throughout the world

showed how dangerous airships were. And, in any case, by that time heavier-than-air transport in the shape of the aeroplane had become well established.

Heavier-than-air Craft

Aeroplanes are heavier than air. Their ability to fly lies in the shape of their wings. These have what is called an *aerofoil* cross-section. When the plane travels forwards, the flow of air over the wings produces an upward force on them called *lift*. As the plane goes faster and faster, the lift increases until it is greater than the plane's *weight* – that is, the downward force on the plane. When this happens, the plane will rise into the air and fly.

Aircraft Engines

The force to make the plane travel forwards, the *thrust,* may be provided by the powerful jet from a jet engine or by a propeller. But, as the plane is thrust forwards, the air pushes against it and tends to slow it down. This air resistance is called *drag*. To travel through the air, the plane must produce enough thrust to overcome the drag.

The majority of today's large aeroplanes, both military and civil, are propelled by jet engines. The high-pitched whine of a jet is a familiar noise at an airport. The whine changes to an ear-splitting roar as the aeroplane accelerates along the runway during take-off.

Some engines are pure jets, or *turbojets*. Their power comes entirely from the thrust

Above: The wing of a plane is sharply curved at the top and fairly flat at the bottom. Air passing over the top surface travels faster than the air passing beneath because it has further to go. This means that the air pressure above the wing is less than that below it. The suction produced in this way provides the 'lift' necessary to keep a plane in the air. The lift is increased by angling the wing upwards slightly.

of a stream, or jet of gases. This is called *jet propulsion*. Other engines obtain their power partly from the jet but mainly from a propeller. They are called *turboprops*. Turboprops are more economical to run than turbojets but are not suitable for very high-speed flight as turbojets are.

Jet engines burn vast amounts of fuel. The huge, four-jet airliners used across the Atlantic have to carry 20,000 gallons or more of fuel for the 3,600-mile flight. The fuel used in jet engines is kerosene (paraffin) which is similar to that used in paraffin heaters at home. Kerosene is a lot cheaper than petrol and is also safer to handle.

Many light aeroplanes still have *piston,* or *petrol engines* which drive propellers, as did all aircraft before the development of jet propulsion.

Jet engines have several advantages over piston engines. They use a cheaper and more easily manageable fuel. They are much lighter and smaller than piston engines of equivalent power. Their action is simpler and smoother than the rhythmic action of the piston engine. This results in much less vibration.

Some military aircraft are fitted with *rocket engines* in addition to their normal jet engines. These engines supply extra power for short periods – during take-off and in combat, for example.

The Fuselage

The main body of an aeroplane, called the *fuselage,* houses the crew, the passengers, and the cargo. It is made up of a thin 'skin'

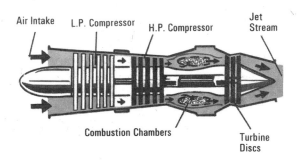

Above: In a jet engine, compressed air from the compressor is fed into the combustion chambers with a jet of fuel and the mixture is ignited. Before the hot gases escape from the jet pipe at the rear, they are directed onto the blades of a turbine rotor which they cause to revolve at high speed. The turbine drives the compressor. In the supercharged jet, two compressors are used instead of one. This increases the pressure ratio and gives a lower fuel consumption.

Left: Practical knowledge gained from early glider flights helped to pave the way for powered aircraft.

of lightweight metal on top of a supporting structure, or 'skeleton'. The circular, crosswise supports are called *frames,* or *formers.* The lengthwise stiffeners are called *stringers.* The plane's two wings and the tail are attached to the fuselage.

The pilot and other members of the crew sit in a cockpit right in the nose of the plane. The cockpit houses all the controls and instruments needed for flying. Airliners usually have a larger *flight deck.* Vision to the front and side is provided by a windshield. This is made of alternate layers of toughened glass and plastic and may be more than an inch thick. Many planes have a dome called a *radome* on the nose, which contains radar equipment for aiding navigation and detecting thunderstorms in their flight path.

The passenger section in an airliner may be divided into two or more cabins, maybe a first-class cabin and a tourist-class cabin. It also houses pantries, where the meals served during a long flight are prepared, and toilets.

The fuselage of airliners and other large planes are *pressurized* so that passengers and crew can breathe easily at the high altitudes at which the planes fly. The pilots of smaller high-flying aircraft have to wear special suits supplied with oxygen.

The planes must also have an efficient air-conditioning system. This keeps the passengers and crew cool when the plane is on the ground during hot weather. It also keeps them warm when the plane is cruising at 30–40,000 feet. This is very necessary be-

Pitching

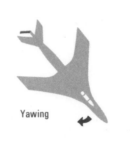
Yawing

Rolling

Above: Pitching, yawing and rolling are natural motions of a plane. A plane is so designed that it tends to correct itself and remain stable in flight. Pitching is corrected by the tailplane. Yawing is corrected by the tailfin. Rolling is corrected by inclining the wings up slightly from the fuselage.

cause at that height the temperature is about minus 60°C., or about minus 80°F. – more than 110 degrees of frost!

Manoeuvring
A pilot controls his plane with his hands and feet, just as a driver steers and controls his car with his hands and feet. Some planes do, in fact, have a *steering wheel* which operates the control surfaces. Others have a simpler *control column,* or *joystick.* The other essential control is the throttle.

The wheel or column is connected by cables, rods, or more complicated systems to hinged after-sections of the tail and wings. Pushing and pulling the column operates the tail *elevators.* Pushing the column forwards tilts the nose of the plane downwards. Pulling the column back tilts the nose upwards. The action of the elevators alone will not make the plane dive or climb. All it does is to change the position, or *attitude,* of the plane relative to the direction of travel.

Vertical movement of the plane in normal flight is, in fact, controlled simply by opening and closing the engine throttle. All the pilot has to do to climb is to open the throttle and increase his speed. Increasing the speed increases the lift on the wings, and the plane moves upwards. Conversely, decreasing the speed decreases the lift, and the plane drops. Often a combination of engine and elevator control is used for climbing and diving.

Moving the column from side to side operates the wing *ailerons.* Moving it to the

Above: Concorde, a supersonic jetliner, at the point of touch-down. The pronounced nose-up position gives the wings greater lift at lower speeds. The pointed nose is in its lowered position to give the pilot better visibility for landing.

Left: Flying displays by highly skilled pilots have been popular with the public ever since the daring American 'barnstormers' performed spectacular stunts in the post-World War I years. Modern formation aerobatics performed by groups of jet planes require intense concentration and split-second timing.

left causes the left-hand aileron to go up and the right-hand one to go down. This has the effect of making the left wing dip. Moving the column to the right makes the right wing dip. This is called *banking*.

To turn the plane, the pilot operates the *rudder* on the vertical part of the tail. He moves the rudder by depressing foot pedals. Pressing the left pedal deflects the rudder to the left and swings the nose round to the left. Pressing the right pedal brings the nose round to the right.

However, the pilot seldom, if ever, uses the rudder by itself to turn. If he did, the plane would tend to 'skid', or slip sideways, just as a racing car tends to skid on a corner. In fact the pilot uses the ailerons as well as the rudder so that the plane banks and turns at the same time. In this way the pilot can keep the plane firmly under control without any *side-slip*.

Supersonic Flight
Aircraft which can travel at speeds greater than the speed of sound are called *supersonic*. At sea-level, the speed of sound is about 760 m.p.h. At 40,000 feet, it is about 660 m.p.h. The fastest fighter aircraft of the world's air forces can travel at speeds of 1,700 miles and hour or more, which is about

Below: One of the many roles of the helicopter is in air-sea rescue operations. It can hover and winch up a person in the sea on a life-line.

Helicopters
The helicopter is our most versatile flying machine. It can fly straight up or down, hover like a fly, and go forwards, backwards, or sideways. It therefore needs no long, prepared runway like a normal aeroplane does. It can operate from a flat roof in the city or from a clearing in the jungle with equal ease.

Helicopters, which have a top speed of about 200 miles an hour, are nowhere near as fast as normal fixed-wing aeroplanes. But their manoeuvrability has made them invaluable for inter-city transport, sea rescue, spraying crops, fighting forest fires, moving troops, and hundreds of other uses.

The helicopter has often been called the 'flying windmill' because of the long, rotating blades, or *rotor*, on top of its body. This *main rotor* serves as both the propeller and the wings of a fixed-wing aeroplane. It provides both the thrust to drive the helicopter along and the lift to raise it off the ground. The rotor blades have the same aerofoil shape as wings and propellers to generate the required lift and thrust.

When the main rotor rotates, the body of the helicopter tends to spin in the opposite direction. This is called *reaction*. To counteract the spinning reaction in a helicopter, a small rotor is mounted vertically on the tail. The thrust produced by this *tail rotor* just balances the turning tendency of the helicopter body, which therefore remains still. Both the main and the tail rotors are driven by the helicopter engine through the same gearbox.

Movement of the helicopter in any direction — forwards, backwards, sideways, up or down — is achieved simply by varying the pitch of the rotor blades. The *pitch* is the angle at which the blades slice through, or 'bite' the air.

Left: Model of the Wright brothers' plane in which the first controlled heavier-than-air flight was made.

2½ times the speed of sound, or Mach 2·5. The Anglo-French supersonic airliner *Concorde* is designed to travel at Mach 2, about 1,300–1,400 miles an hour. At this speed, the 3,600 mile London to New York flight would take only about 3 hours.

Supersonic aircraft have to be carefully designed in order to pass safely through what is known as the 'sound barrier' – the severe buffeting caused by shock waves when an aircraft travels near the speed of sound.

Aircraft designers have found that they can delay the formation of shock waves by building aircraft with sharply swept back wings of thin section. All the supersonic jet fighters and airliners have such wings. As for all aircraft, tests on models in wind tunnels play an essential part in perfecting the shape.

Modern supersonic aircraft are so well designed that they can fly through the 'sound barrier' with little or no noticeable change in handling qualities. Once they are

travelling at supersonic speeds, the buffeting ceases and the flight is smooth once more. Shock waves are still formed, but they do not adversely affect the aircraft.

Sonic Booms

Shock waves do, however, affect people and buildings on the ground. They cause what is known as a *sonic bang*, which sounds exactly like an explosion. And, like the shock waves, or blast from an explosion, they can cause damage. Low-level sonic bangs can shake buildings and shatter windows over quite a wide area.

Another problem becomes increasingly important as speeds rise above Mach 2. At these speeds the friction, or rubbing, of the air against the metal skin of the aircraft produces quite a lot of heat. Above Mach 2·5 the heat produced is sufficient to weaken seriously the aluminium alloys which are normally used in aircraft construction. This point is often called the 'heat barrier'. It can be overcome by using such metals as stainless steel and titanium, which retain their strength at high temperatures.

Airports

A large, modern airport is a scene of intense activity both by day and by night. At peak periods, huge jet airliners weighing over 200 tons and carrying 150 or more passengers take off and land every minute or so. More than 150 million passengers fly on scheduled services every year.

To deal with such vast amounts of traffic, every activity at the airport must be carefully co-ordinated. As soon as an aircraft has

Below: The giant Boeing 747, capable of carrying almost 500 passengers, has heralded a new era in international travel.

landed on the runway, it moves along a 'side road' called a *taxiway* to an area called an *apron*. Immediately, trucks to carry baggage and buses to carry passengers hurry towards it. Then fuel tankers move in to refill the airliner's fuel tanks, which may hold 20,000 gallons or more.

Air Traffic Control

The most important people at the airport are the air-traffic controllers in the *control tower,* who supervise the landing and take-off of each aircraft. They bring down an aircraft from a height of 5 or 6 miles onto a runway about 2 miles long and 200 feet wide. This is an extremely precise task. Any slight error could mean disaster.

Aircraft contact the control tower as they approach the airport. If the runways are full, the controller tells the aircraft to circle one above the other, at intervals of 1,000 feet, until the runway is free. This is called *stacking.* As the runway becomes clear, the controller calls in the aircraft at the bottom of the 'stack'. And he instructs the aircraft above to descend to the next level.

The ground controller uses a variety of instruments to bring the aircraft down safely in all kinds of weather. His main ones are radio and radar. His radar screen indicates the direction and distance of the aircraft. The controller can therefore tell the pilot what adjustments to make to his height, direction, and speed to bring him safely down along the correct glide path.

Instrument Landing Systems

Many airliners are now equipped with what is called the *Instrument Landing System* to help the pilots line up their aircraft onto the correct glide path. Certain electronic devices in the aircraft 'lock' onto radio beams coming from the runway along the correct glide path. But the pilot still has to make the actual landing himself.

In thick fog and bad visibility, when the pilot cannot see the runway on the final approach, conventional landing systems are too risky. But so-called *blind-landing systems* have been developed that bring down an aircraft automatically without the pilot touching the controls at all. Eventually this kind of system will be a standard feature of airliners. And they will then be able to fly in all weather conditions. Already, of course, planes are flown for much of the time by the so-called automatic pilot.

When the aircraft has touched down, the controller tells the pilot which taxiway to use to take him towards the airport terminal. In a similar way the controller guides the aircraft from the apron, along the taxiways, to the main runway, and gives the pilot the 'go-ahead' for take-off.

Most airports have several runways and numerous taxiways. And at any one time there may be scores of aircraft moving along them, taxiing into position for take-off, taking off, landing, and taxiing after landing. Control of aircraft on the ground is therefore as vital as control in the air.

The Seashore

The seashore is the stretch of land which borders the sea. It is a very difficult place for plants and animals to live. On most shores the tide comes up twice a day, so that sometimes the shore is underwater and sometimes it is exposed to the air. It is battered by the waves during storms and the hot sun shines down on it in the summer. The plants and animals living on the seashore must be able to withstand all these conditions. Since there are so many difficulties to overcome, it would not be surprising to find that nothing lived on the shore. In fact, it is teeming with life.

The tides affect the life on the shore a great deal. The tides do not always cover the same amount of shore. They are affected by the Moon. When the Moon is new or full, both the Sun and the Moon are pulling at the tides. The water comes far up the beach and goes down very low. These are the spring tides. In between the water only comes up and goes down a little way. These are the neap tides. Between these two extremes is the mean tide level – the normal tides.

Above: Each month there are some large tides, called spring tides, and some small tides, called neap tides. High water mark and low water mark are far apart during the spring tides and close together during the neap tides.

The plants on the seashore are all algae. They are all seaweeds. There are a few flowering plants found on the cliffs, but only seaweeds can survive in the salt water. There are three kinds of seaweed – the green, the red and the brown.

There are five zones on the seashore. These show best on the rocky shore. The first zone is the splash zone. The sea never covers this zone, but it is splashed by salt water. Lichens and channelled wrack grow in this zone and periwinkles and sea-slaters are found there.

The next zone is the upper shore zone. This zone is above the normal high tide line. It is only covered by the sea during the spring tides. It is dry for much of the time and only a few animals live there. It usually has sand-hoppers and dead seaweed in it.

Above: A selection of plants and animals characteristic of the various zones of the sea-shore.

Below: the body of the hermit crab is not protected by a hard shell. Instead, the crab finds an empty sea-shell in which to live. As the crab moves around, it carries the shell with it. As the hermit crab grows, it must find larger shells in which to live.

The third zone is the middle shore zone. This is a very wide zone. It is the part of the shore which is always covered and uncovered by the normal tides. It has a great many plants and animals living in it. The flat wrack usually grows at the top of the middle shore zone and bladder wrack and saw wrack grow farther down. The flat periwinkle and the edible periwinkle live in the middle shore zone.

The lower shore zone is below the level of the lowest normal tide and above the level of the low spring tides. It is not often exposed to the air. The tangleweeds grow in this zone and the grey topshell lives there.

The fifth zone is the sublittoral zone. This part of the shore is never exposed to the air and it is the beginning of the true sea dwellers' homes. The oarweeds grow in this zone and the fishes usually live there. The animals that live in this zone may be trapped in rock pools when the tide goes out.

Types of Seashore

There are basically four types of seashore. There is the rocky shore, the shingle shore, the sandy shore and the muddy shore.

The rocky shore is the most interesting to investigate, because it is easy to see the animals and plants on it. The animals may hide in pools or under the seaweed, but they cannot bury themselves in the rock. The rocks have wracks and other seaweeds growing on them. There are limpets, barnacles, whelks, sea-anemones, topshells, sea-mats, tube worms, sponges and sea-squirts to be found on rocky shores. Ribbon worms hide in crevices and sea-urchins, starfishes, crabs, shrimps and fishes may be found in rock pools.

The shingle beaches have very little living on them. They do, however, have beautiful pebbles, shaped by the sea.

Sandy shores look lifeless, but there are a great many animals buried in the sand. They come to the surface of the sand to feed when the tide is in. Cockles, tellins, razor shells, shrimps, crabs, sea-urchins, starfishes and even fishes may be buried under the surface of the sand. The coiled mounds of the lugworm are the only sign that there is anything alive on the beach.

Muddy shores have animals and seaweeds on the surface as well as buried in the mud. There are often large stones and boulders on the surface. These may have seaweeds growing on them. Shore-crabs, periwinkles, shrimps and bristle worms may be sheltering in the hollows round boulders. Peacock worms come out of their tubes when the tide comes in. Cockles and clams burrow in the mud.

Animals on the Seashore

Most of the large groups of animals are represented on the seashore, but the crustaceans and the molluscs are the major groups. The crustaceans are the crabs, lobsters, shrimps, barnacles and sandhoppers. All the crustaceans except for one small group live in the water, and most of them live in the sea. They are often called the 'insects of the sea'.

The molluscs are the cockles, winkles, razor shells, sea-slugs, sea-hares, cuttle fishes and octopuses. Most of this group live in the sea. In warm seas the beautiful conch shells and cowries add to the beauties of the beach.

There are a great many worms living on the shore. Apart from the lugworms there are the ragworms, paddleworms, ribbonworms, tube worms and keelworms. The beautiful sea-mouse, with its rainbow coloured hairs, is a worm.

The echinoderms are all sea animals. These are the starfishes, sea-urchins, brittle-

Sting Winkle

Dog Whelk

Cockle

Venus Shells

stars and sea-cucumbers.

Apart from these there are the coelenterates, the sea-anemones and jellyfishes. Most of these are marine animals. The other major group of animals on the seashore is the fishes. There are many smaller groups, like the sea-mats and the sea-squirts.

The main groups of plants on the shore are the green, brown and red algae. They are found on the sea and as far into the sea as the light will penetrate. Green seaweeds tend to grow in the shallower water. Brown seaweeds can grow in deeper water and red seaweeds grow deepest of all.

Life on the Seashore

A sea-shore is a rich hunting ground for the naturalist. All forms of marine life are to be found on the seashore, as well as the many birds that get their food there. They include the seagulls and other flying hunters that often nest in cliffs, and the long-legged wading birds that walk in calm shallows picking up their prey.

Above: The common cormorant is about 36 inches long. It swims well and may dive as deep as 100 feet to catch fish.

Above: A great variety of shells are to be found on the sea-shore.

Right: Despite its plant-like appearance, the sea-anemone is an animal. The tentacles around its mouth contain stinging cells which can paralyse very small creatures. These are then dragged into the mouth by the tentacles and slowly digested.

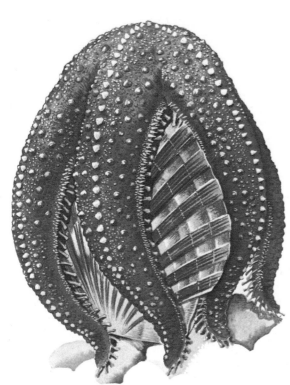

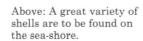

Above: Green seaweeds are found only on the upper shore. Brown seaweeds grow in the middle, lower and sublittoral zones. Red seaweeds live deeper in the sea than brown seaweeds.

Left: Starfishes eat bivalves. They use their tube feet as suckers to pull the shells of bivalves apart.

Below: Ragworms can be found in muddy sand, under boulders and in seaweed. They are usually covered with bristles.

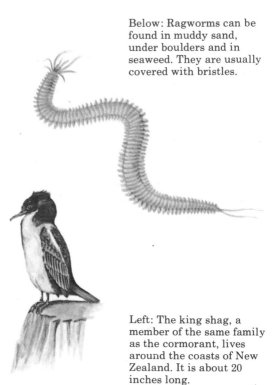

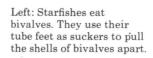

Left: The king shag, a member of the same family as the cormorant, lives around the coasts of New Zealand. It is about 20 inches long.

123

The World of Sound

Sound is energy in the form of *vibrations* which can be detected by the ears. These vibrations, which are movements to and fro of air, are called *sound waves*. They travel through the air and make the eardrums vibrate also. Nerves sense the eardrums' vibrations and send messages to the brain, and so we hear the sound. We need two ears to determine the direction the sound is coming from.

When an object such as a guitar string or door bell vibrates, we pick up the sound waves almost immediately. But if we watch a man chopping wood in the distance, we see the axe hit the wood before we hear the sound of the blow. This is because light travels faster than sound. Sound waves in air travel at about 1,120 feet per second. Sound travels faster through *denser* materials such as

Sound waves are waves of pressure produced in the air when objects vibrate. As a guitar string (black) is plucked it vibrates at a constant rate in the air (grey). As it moves, it produces a wave of high pressure ahead (dark grey) and a wave of low pressure (light grey) behind. These waves are produced every time the string vibrates, and they move outwards away from the string through the air.

Below: A modern stereophonic tape recorder.

Tape Recording

Sound recordings on tape are used extensively in place of ordinary records. They can be made on portable equipment and the recording can be played back immediately.

In making a recording, sound waves are converted into a varying electric current by a microphone. This current is fed into the tape recorder where it is amplified and passed on to the recording 'head'. The head is really an electromagnet with a narrow gap cut into it. The magnetic field in the gap varies with the microphone current. Plastic tape coated with iron oxide is drawn across the gap at a steady speed and is magnetized by the varying field. Each particle of iron oxide becomes a permanent magnet with a strength proportional to the size of current flowing in the head at the instant when that particle was in the magnetic field. To play back the recording, the tape is rewound onto its reel and then drawn past the same head at the same steady speed. In effect we have a series of tiny magnets (the tape) moving near to a coil (the head) — a situation which always produces a current of electricity in the coil. This current varies with the strength of the 'magnets' and is therefore a replica of the original microphone current. After amplification it goes through a loudspeaker to reproduce the original sound. If the recording is no longer required the tape can be 'wiped clean' by passing it over an erase head. The erase head is similar to the recording head but produces a rapidly alternating magnetic field which demagnetizes the tape.

Right: Compass needles are deflected near a magnet.

Far right: In a magnetic tape, the particles of iron oxide act as tiny compass needles. As the tape passes the magnets in a tape recorder, the particles are magnetized; their magnetic poles are deflected in the same way forming a magnetic pattern in the tape. This pattern corresponds to the sound being recorded.

water and metal. Sound cannot travel at all in a vacuum because there is no *medium* (substance) to carry the vibrations.

Pitch, Loudness and Quality

We can tell one sound from another by its *pitch, loudness* and *quality*. The vibrations of a low pitched note are slower than those of a high note. The speed of the vibrations is called the *frequency*.

Loudness is the apparent intensity of sound which we hear. Noises may not sound equally loud to different people because people's ears are not equally sensitive. Sound *intensity* is measured in *decibels*. A sound of 0 decibels can scarcely be heard by a normal human ear. A sound of 140 decibels is so intense that it is painful.

The further away from the sound source you are, the quieter the sound will seem, because the energy decreases as it travels outwards. Sound waves produced by great energy will have a large *amplitude* – that is, the vibration to and fro will be greater than if the sound were produced with little energy – and sound loud.

The quality of sounds differs because almost all noises are made up of more than one frequency. When an object vibrates, its parts vibrate at the same time, producing a mixture of sounds. Each half, third or quarter of a cello string, for instance, may vibrate separately, giving notes at a higher pitch, though with less energy. It is those additional vibrations, called *harmonics*, which add to the interest of the sound and give it its characteristic tone quality. Noise is produced by an irregular mixture of vibrations; musical notes are regular, ordered vibrations.

The pitch of a sound depends on its wavelength (the distance between one high-pressure wave and the next) and the rapidity or frequency at which the pressure waves arrive. The deep sound of a double bass has a long wavelength and a low frequency (1). The high-pitched sound of a flute has a short wavelength and a high frequency (2). In soft sounds, such as a violin makes, the pressure of the sound waves is low (3). A jet engine produces high-pressure waves, and a loud sound (4).

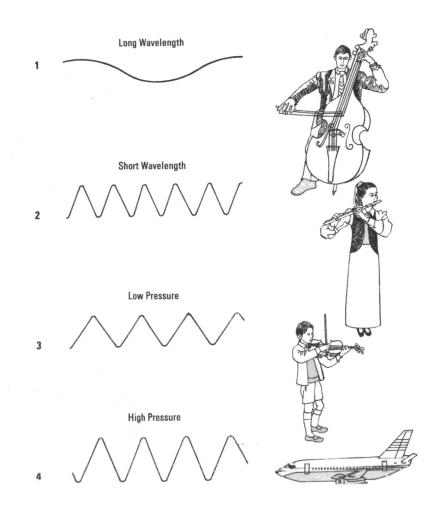

1 — Long Wavelength

2 — Short Wavelength

3 — Low Pressure

4 — High Pressure

The Telephone

The telephone has both a microphone and an earpiece. A voice speaking into the microphone causes the diaphragm to vibrate. As it does so, carbon granules behind it are in turn compressed and released. An electric current passing through them is affected by this, and its variation corresponds to the vibrations of the diaphragm. The current is passed through cables to the exchange.

The earpiece consists of an electromagnet and a metallic diaphragm. The current energises the magnet, which pulls the diaphragm towards it. Variations in the current make the diaphragm move to and fro, the vibrations setting up sound waves reproducing the sounds at the other end of the line.

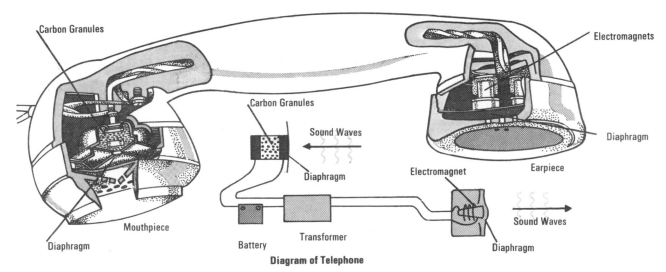

Diagram of Telephone

Light

Light is a form of energy, as heat and sound are. Our eyes are sensitive to light, and we see things because light is reflected from them. If there is no light, we cannot see. Light is produced whenever an object gets extremely hot. For instance, if we heat a poker in a fire, it first gets red hot and gives off a feeble red light. Then it gets yellow, and finally it glows white hot. A white-hot object giving off light is said to be *incandescent*. The wire filament inside an electric lamp becomes incandescent and gives off light when an electric current passes through it. A candle flame contains particles of burning wax which become incandescent and give off light. The Sun is a fiery ball of incandescent gas.

Light travels in straight lines. It will not go round corners and for this reason objects exposed to a single strong source of light cast shadows. Light travels by radiation. To a scientist, it is a form of radiant energy and is closely related to heat rays, X-rays, and even radio waves.

The Nature of Light
Early scientists believed that light is made up of millions of tiny particles called *corpuscles* travelling at enormous speeds. Reflection of a ray of light by a mirror seemed to support this theory; they thought that each corpuscle 'bounced' off the surface of the mirror in much the same way that a rubber ball bounces off a wall. The angle at which a ray of light strikes a mirror (the angle of *incidence*) is exactly the same as the angle at which it is reflected back (the angle of *reflection*).

The British scientist Sir Isaac Newton supported the corpuscular theory of light, and because of his influence the theory

Above: An oil refinery by night. Light is produced on a massive scale in the modern world.

Below: The rival theories of the nature of light: the corpuscular theory and the wave theory. Both are now believed to be in part correct. Light consists of 'packets' of energy called quanta which travel as waves.

held sway during the 1700's. But in the 1800's, most scientists returned to the earlier theory of the Dutch astronomer Christian Huygens who suggested that light consists of waves. For a while, the whole world of science argued over who was right. The supporters of the wave theory finally won, because they could satisfactorily explain certain properties of light which the corpuscular theory could not.

According to the wave theory, light radiates out from its source as a series of waves – rather like the ripples in the surface of a pond spread out from a stone's splash. Like water waves, light waves consist of a succession of crests and troughs. The distance between any two successive crests (or troughs) is called the *wavelength* of the light. These wavelengths are so small (about a few millionths of an inch) that they are measured in special units. The number of waves passing a point in space every second is the *frequency* of the light.

The Speed of Light
Light travels at an enormously high speed – in fact at the fastest speed known to man. In a vacuum or in outer space, light travels at about 186,000 miles a second. In air or water or glass, light travels very slightly slower.

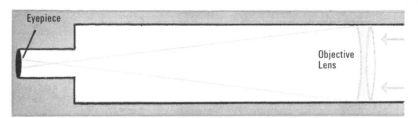

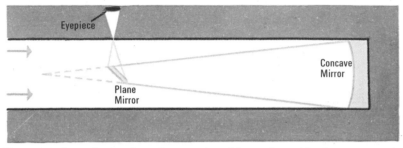

In a refracting telescope, the objective lens forms a real image which is observed through the magnifying eyepiece.

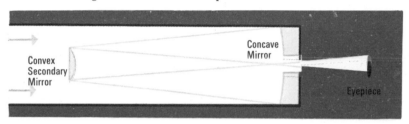

Newtonian form of reflecting telescope. A real image formed by the concave mirror is observed through the side of the telescope.

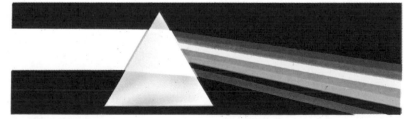

Cassegrain form of reflecting telescope. A real image formed by the concave mirror is observed through the end of the telescope.

Telescopes

There are two chief kinds of telescopes, *refracting telescopes* and *reflecting telescopes*. Refracting telescopes consist of a tube with a convex lens at one end, and a concave lens at the other. The convex lens is called the *objective lens*. The concave lens is called the *eyepiece*. The objective lens collects light from the object, and forms a small image of the object inside the tube. The eyepiece then magnifies the image. The distance between the objective lens and the eyepiece can be adjusted to make the image sharp.

In the refracting telescope, a concave mirror collects light from the object being studied, and reflects it onto the plane (flat) mirror. The plane mirror then reflects the light and the image through the side of the tube to the eyepiece, which magnifies it. Today, most large telescopes in observatories are reflecting telescopes.

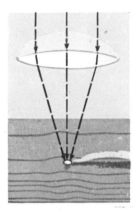

Right: A double concave lens spreads out light rays which pass through it. A double convex lens brings together light rays which pass through it so that they meet at the focus. A burning glass is a double convex lens. It concentrates a beam of sunlight to a point.

The denser the medium, the slower it travels. This slowing down bends the light waves slightly, and so a light ray passing into water or glass is bent. This bending is called *refraction* and it is how lenses focus beams of light.

The Colours of Light

The wavelength of light also determines its colour. For example, red light has a longer wavelength than has blue light. When white light from the Sun, which consists of a mixture of all wavelengths, passes through a glass prism, each wavelength is refracted to a slightly different extent. As a result, a prism can split white light into its component colours or *spectrum*. A rainbow consists of the Sun's spectrum formed when light is reflected round the inside of millions of raindrops.

The Quantum Theory

According to modern quantum theory, all kinds of radiation consist of tiny 'packets' of energy called *quanta* which travel as waves. A quantum of light is called a *photon*, and it corresponds in many ways to one of Newton's corpuscles. Photons travel as waves – and so Huygens' wave theory was also basically correct.

Above: Refraction can be demonstrated by the 'cup and coin' trick. A coin is placed at the bottom of a cup so that it is just out of sight of a viewer. If the cup is then filled with water, the viewer will be able to see the coin. This is because light rays from the coin have been bent at the surface of the water so that they do enter the viewer's eye.

Above: When 'white' light passes through a prism it is split into its component colours: violet, indigo, blue, green, yellow, orange and red.

Below: Objects appear coloured because they absorb a portion of the light falling upon them and reflect the remainder.

127

Heat

If you put a pan on a fire or a stove, it soon gets hot. It does not look any different, but something has obviously happened to it. If you could see the molecules, the small particles that make up the pan, you would find that they were moving about more vigorously than when the pan was cold. In this way, you would see that heat is a form of energy, and that it takes the form of molecular motion.

We get most of our heat from the Sun, and there is also heat deep inside the Earth, which comes to the surface in volcanoes and hot springs. Men produce heat by burning fuels such as coal or oil. These fuels contain carbon, which combines with oxygen from the air to produce heat when the fuels are burned. Nuclear reactions also produce heat.

Temperature

The hotness or coldness of things is called their *temperature*. Instruments called *thermometers* measure temperature. People measure temperature in units called *degrees*:

Above: All substances contain a certain amount of heat, even ice. If a container of liquid oxygen is placed on a block of ice, the oxygen will boil back to a gas. Liquid oxygen has a boiling point of $-183°C$, whereas ice has a temperature around $0°C$. Heat flows from the ice into the liquid oxygen.

the more degrees, the higher the temperature. For most scientific purposes the temperature at which water turns to ice is called 0 degrees, and the normal temperature at which water boils is 100 degrees. This is the *Centigrade* scale, from two latin words meaning a *hundred steps*. It is sometimes called the Celsius scale, after its inventor, Anders Celsius, a Swedish scientist.

Some people use another scale, called the Fahrenheit scale, after its inventor, Daniel Fahrenheit. On this scale water freezes at 32 degrees and normally boils at 212 degrees. Fahrenheit thought that he had found the lowest possible temperature, which he called 0 degrees in his scale. Scientists now believe the lowest temperature, which they call Absolute Zero, is minus 460 degrees on the Fahrenheit scale, or about minus 273 degrees on the Centigrade scale.

Movement of Heat

Heat can travel in three ways: by *radiation*, by *convection*, and by *conduction*. In radiation, heat travels through space, as it does from the Sun or a fire. In convection, it travels through moving water – as in a central heating system – or moving air, as from a convector heater. In conduction, heat

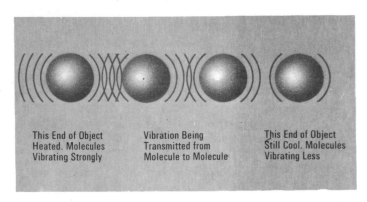

| This End of Object Heated. Molecules Vibrating Strongly | Vibration Being Transmitted from Molecule to Molecule | This End of Object Still Cool. Molecules Vibrating Less |

Above: Diagram showing how heat travels by conduction. As one end of an object is heated, the molecules at that point vibrate strongly, and this vibration is transmitted from molecule to molecule throughout the object.

Right: A water-heating system. Cold water, heated in a boiler, rises through convection and is stored in the hot water tank. Cool water from the bottom of the hot water tank returns to the boiler to be reheated. When hot water is drawn off, more water enters the system from the cold water tank.

Left: Black bodies absorb and therefore radiate more heat than white bodies. This is the reason for the white clothes worn in the Tropics.

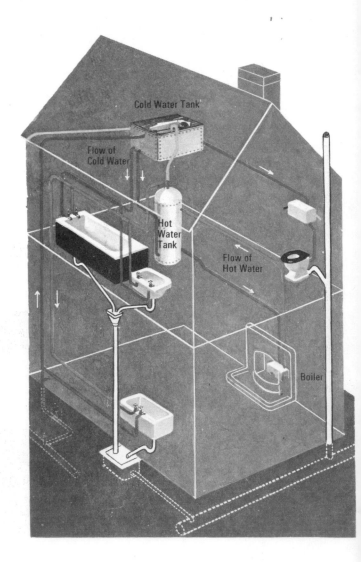

travels through a substance, as it does along a metal rod when one end of it is held in a flame.

Heat travels very slowly through some substances. These substances are said to be *insulators*. Examples of good insulators include wood, bricks and paper.

Many things change when they are heated. Metals *expand*, that is, they grow slightly larger in size. Railway engineers often leave gaps between the ends of rails, so that if they expand in the heat of the Sun they do not buckle but have room to 'grow'. Air also expands when it is heated. Early fliers used hot air to fill their balloons, because the expanded hot air in the balloon was less dense than the cold air around it. Water expands when heated. For example, a full kettle overflows when the water in it gets hot. Very hot water becomes steam, which expands very greatly.

Solids, Liquids and Gases

Many solids turn to liquid when they are heated – for example, ice turns to water, and metals finally melt. When heat is applied to a solid, it can either go to raising its temperature or to melting it. Heat which raises the temperature does so by making the solid molecules *vibrate*, or move faster. This kind of energy is called *kinetic* energy, which means energy of motion. If heat is continually supplied to a solid, its molecules vibrate more and more until eventually they 'fall apart' and the solid melts. In a similar

way, heated liquid eventually boils and becomes a gas or vapour. Heat which changes the state of a substance from a solid to a liquid, or from a liquid to a gas, is called *latent heat*.

Man uses heat for many purposes. The most important is for keeping himself warm. He also uses it to change the nature of things, for example in cooking food and firing pottery.

Measuring Temperature

Thermometers are instruments that measure the hotness or temperature of an object. Temperature is measured in degrees. Every change brought about by heating can be used to measure temperature. An obvious change is the *expansion* or increase in size, which most objects undergo when they get hotter.

The *mercury thermometer* makes use of expansion. It consists of a fine glass tube connected to a bulb containing mercury. As the temperature rises, the mercury expands and rises along the tube. The position of the mercury against a scale of degrees marked on the glass tube indicates the temperature. Doctors use a *clinical thermometer*, which is a special mercury thermometer. The tube is kinked just above the bulb, so that the mercury does not fall immediately the thermometer is removed from a patient's mouth. Some thermometers contain alcohol, which is generally dyed red or blue to make it easier to see.

Alcohol is used with mercury in the *maximum and minimum thermometer*. This U-shaped thermometer contains two metal markers, which mark the highest and lowest temperatures recorded.

One kind of electrical thermometer uses the principle of the *thermocouple*, a device that generates electricity when it is heated. Temperatures are indicated by the voltage generated. Another electrical thermometer, the *platinum resistance thermometer*, indicates temperatures in terms of the resistance of a piece of platinum wire. The *optical pyrometer*, for high temperatures, makes use of a material that changes colour as it becomes hotter.

Electricity

An Electric Current

An electric current is a movement, or flow, of minute particles called *electrons*. Normally, electrons are attached to an atom and circle round its central nucleus in orbits – just like artificial satellites orbiting the Earth. Each electron has the same charge or 'packet' of electricity described as a *negative* charge. Usually the nucleus has exactly enough *positive* electrical charges to balance the negative charges on the electrons, so that the atom as a whole is neutral.

In some materials, however, a few of the electrons in each atom are only loosely held.

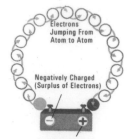

Above: An electric current is a flow of electrons which jump from atom to atom when there is a difference of electrical 'pressure' (voltage) between the ends of a wire.

These *free electrons* can jump from atom to atom, and it is a steady drift of free electrons that carries electricity through a wire.

Why should electrons move about between atoms? The basic law of electricity is that two similar charges (either both positive or both negative) repel each other and two opposite charges (one positive and the other negative) attract each other. Since electrons carry negative charges they are repelled by negatively charged atoms and attracted by positively charged atoms. As a result, the electrons are pushed around from atom to atom until they find one with a shortage of electrons. Alternatively, an electron may join a neutral atom if it pushes another electron out.

When some kind of 'driving force' is applied to the wire, the wandering electrons

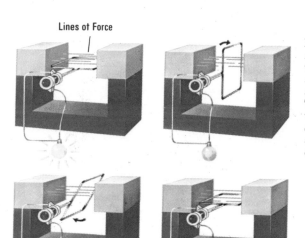

Left: A simple generator. As the wire loop is moved through a magnetic field, a voltage is set up in it and a current flows through it. The current is greatest when the loop is cutting *across* the lines of force and least when it is moving *along* the lines of force.

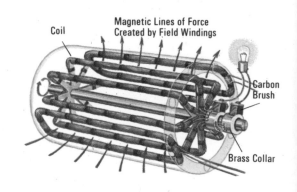

Above: A practical generator has a number of coils of wire to minimise the current fluctuations. They are wound on an iron core (not shown) which helps to concentrate the magnetic lines of force. The magnetic field is produced by electromagnets. Carbon brushes collect the electric current generated.

Below: In a power station, heat energy is converted to electrical energy. The heat may be derived from burning fuel or from nuclear reactions. In both cases the heat is used to turn water to steam. The steam drives a turbine which turns the armature of a generator.

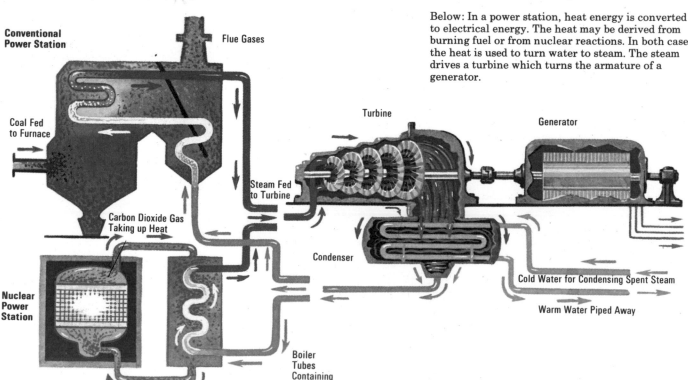

Opposite: A huge generator being lowered into position in a modern power station.

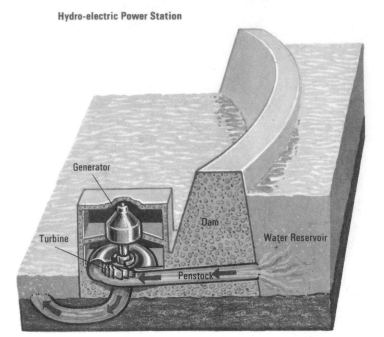
Hydro-electric Power Station

Generator

Turbine

Dam

Water Reservoir

Penstock

are organized into a steady one-way drift. The driving force is simply a difference of electrical 'pressure' (voltage) between the ends of the wire. It is provided by either a battery or generator. Electrical 'pressure' starts the drift of electrons by pushing the loosely held electrons from the first atom in the line to the next, and so on.

A current of electricity must have a completely unbroken path, or *circuit*. If we could follow a current as it flowed along a wire we should eventually arrive back at our starting point.

Wires which carry an electric current are often made of copper. Copper, like most metals, is a good *conductor* of electricity. It has plenty of free electrons, so a current has little difficulty in travelling through copper. Materials such as rubber and plastics are good *insulators* (bad conductors). Their atoms do not have any loosely held electrons. When an electric current flows through a conductor that offers resistance to its flow it heats the conductor up. If the conductor is made of suitable *resistance* wire it will glow red and give off a good heat. This is the principle used in electric fires.

If conditions are suitable and the right type of resistance is chosen it will glow white hot and can be used to illuminate a room and light up the road ahead of an automobile.

Generating Electricity
Electricity for lighting, heating, etc., is generated by what are called *alternators*. These machines make use of the fact that

Above: In a hydro-electric power station, water rushing out from the base of a dam is directed onto the blades of a turbine, causing it to revolve at high speed. The turbine drives the armature of a generator.

Above: When an electric current flows through a conductor which offers resistance to its flow, the conductor becomes hot. This is the principle used in the electric light bulb. A coil of fine wire with a high resistance glows white-hot as an electric current passes through it. The wire is made from a metal such as tungsten which has a high melting point.

when a wire moves through a magnetic field a current is set up, or *induced*, in the wire. In an alternator the wires are arranged in a circle around a rotating shaft called the *armature*. The current is taken from the wires through metal rings on the shaft which make contact with two fixed *carbon brushes*. As the wires rotate they move downwards through the magnetic field and then upwards. This means that the direction of the induced current keeps changing – it is an alternating current. In the United Kingdom the power supply mains use current that alternates fifty times a second: it is said to be a 50 cycles per second supply. In the United States, 60 cycles per second are used.

Direct current can be obtained by fitting a *commutator* instead of slip rings. This device keeps reversing the current to automatically compensate for the natural reversals. Machines of this type are called *dynamos*.

Electric Motors
Direct current electric motors are constructed in the same way as dynamos. When they are switched on the electric current flows through the wires around the armature setting up a magnetic field around them. This field interacts with the main field of the rotor causing the wires on one side to be forced down and those on the other side to be forced up. This causes the armature to rotate and drive anything connected to the motor. Alternating current motors are constructed in a slightly different way, but work on the same principle.

Batteries
Batteries generate electric current through chemical action. A popular type, the *dry cell*, which is widely used to power electric torches, transistor radios, etc., uses a zinc case filled with sal ammoniac in the centre of which is a carbon rod. Chemical action in the battery leaves the carbon rod positively charged and the zinc case negatively charged.

Static Electricity
The familiar *static electricity* effects occur when an object such as a comb or a pith ball is given an excess of electrons, or if a number of them are removed. It then becomes either negatively or positively charged. Positively and negatively charged pieces of material will attract each other. Two positively or two negatively charged objects will repel each other. On a much larger scale, clouds charged with static electricity lose their charge by means of an electric spark which we call lightning.

Magnetism

Magnetism owes its name to the fact that the early Greeks found the natural magnetic material called lodestone in an area called Magnesia. Lodestone, like the man-made magnets we are familiar with today, has several very interesting properties. For one thing it will attract pieces of iron. For another, the lodestone always points towards the North Pole of the Earth and so can be used by ships to find their way about when they are out of sight of land.

The first recorded reference to the use of the magnet as a means of finding direction seems to have been made by the Chinese mathematician and instrument-maker, Shen Kua, who lived about the time of the Norman Conquest of Britain.

Nature of Magnetism
Materials owe their magnetism to the way in which the electrons of their atoms are arranged. In some materials, such as lodestone, iron and steel, the arrangements of the electrons are such that the individual molecules of the material are each a tiny magnet. At one end of each molecule there is what is known as a north-seeking pole; at the other end there is a south-seeking pole. If it were possible to pivot the molecule so that it could revolve, it would be found that the

Above: One property of a magnet is that it will attract pieces of iron to it.

Above: A compass needle is a small bar magnet which is allowed to swing freely. It always comes to rest with one particular end pointing towards the Earth's magnetic north pole.

molecule would come to rest with its north-seeking (or north) pole pointing towards the North Pole of the Earth.

In a natural piece of iron, the individual molecules lie in many different directions and the bar of iron itself does not point in any particular direction, because some of its molecules are trying to pull in one direction and some in another.

To convert the bar of iron into a compass needle we need only stroke the south pole of an existing magnet along its length. As it moves along, the south pole will cause the north poles of all the molecules to swing round and point towards it. By the time it reaches the far end of the bar, all the molecules will be pointing in the same direction. The whole bar will now act as the individual molecules do, only in a much more powerful manner. The bar of iron has become a magnet.

From this behaviour we can see that a south pole will attract a north pole. Similarly, a north pole will attract a south pole. However, if we place two south poles or two north poles together we find that they repel each other.

We can also make a piece of iron or steel into a magnet by wrapping a coil of wire round it and connecting the coil to a direct current supply. When the current flows through the coil it will set up a magnetic field, just like that of a real magnet, and this will pull the molecules into line. This is called electromagnetism.

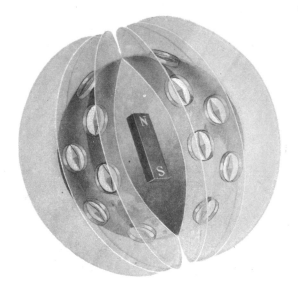

Above: The Earth acts as though it contained a vast bar magnet. One end of a compass needle will always come to rest pointing to the Earth's magnetic north pole. The magnetic north and south poles do not correspond to the geographic north and south poles, a fact which must be taken into account with compass readings. Moreover, the position of the magnetic poles changes over the years.

Right: Every magnet has two poles, a north and a south. The unlike poles of two magnets attract each other.

Right: The like poles of two magnets repel each other.

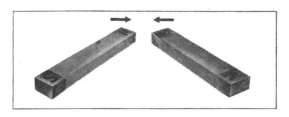

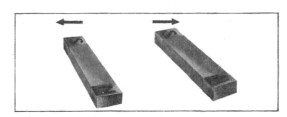

Right: When an electric current is passed through a coil of wire, the coil behaves like a bar magnet. The strength of the magnetic field can be increased by placing a soft iron core inside the coil. Coil and core are together known as an electromagnet.

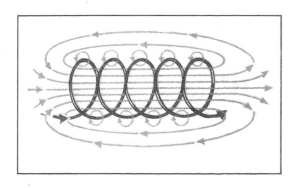

Music

Music is made up of three things: *melody, harmony* and *rhythm.*

A melody is a tune. Nearly all pieces of music contain tunes. Some are very easy to follow, such as the tune of a folk-song, or the latest recording of a 'pop' group. Others, such as the many little bits of tune in a *symphony* (piece for orchestra), may be harder.

Harmony is what we call the combined sound when several notes are played at once. A group of such notes is called a *chord.* Sometimes musicians produce a form of harmony by playing two or more tunes at once, called *counterpoint.*

Rhythm is the regular 'beat' of music. It is the simplest kind of music known.

The Story of Music

How old is music? Nobody can really say. But we do know, for instance, that six thousand years ago people called Sumerians, who lived in and around the region that is now Iraq, were highly musical and were already influencing other tribes in Asia and North Africa with their musical ideas. The Ancient Egyptians, Hebrews, and Greeks received some of their inspiration and knowledge of music from the Sumerians.

The Ancient Egyptians carved pictures on the walls of their tombs which show that they used orchestras of five or six hundred people playing flutes, harps, and drums. The Hebrews believed that music came from heaven, and they used it as part of their worship. They were particularly fond of flutes, harps, trumpets, and cymbals. The Ancient Greeks used music in their plays and religious ceremonies. Their favourite instruments were the flute and the *lyre* (an instrument like their harp, but with a large sound chest).

Influence of the Church

After the Romans had been converted to Christianity, the Church leaders developed music from Jewish temple worship into forms suitable for Christian worship. Their choice was influenced by their love for the music of their own native countries. Gradually they developed a style of chanting sung without musical accompaniment. It was called *plainsong.*

Until about 1600, music was heard mainly in church, in the courts of the noblemen, at folk dances and singsongs. Most noblemen kept a small group of musicians to play for them privately, or publicly on such special occasions as festivals or parties. The noblemen of those days were also entertained by wandering minstrels who travelled through the country from castle to castle, singing their romantic or humorous songs to a lute or vièle accompaniment. The *lute* looked like a round-backed guitar, and the vièle was the ancestor of the violin. The Germans called these minstrels *minnesingers,* and the French called them *troubadours.*

Musical Plays

In the 1600's, music took on a new look. Two different kinds of musical plays were developed. One kind, called *oratorio,* was religious and the other, called *opera,* dealt with non-religious subjects. The first public concert was an opera. It was performed in Italy, and this form of entertainment became popular in many parts of Europe. Of course, there had always been some music to be heard outside the church, which was sung and danced to by the ordinary people of the countryside and villages. This was folk music, which is still very much alive today.

New Instruments and New Forms

As new musical instruments were invented, and old ones improved, composers gradually began to experiment with new forms of music and try out fresh ideas. Instrumental music, as distinct from music mainly for voices, was played more and more. Antonio Stradivari was making his wonderful violins in the late 1600's and early 1700's. The piano was invented in 1709. Before this, the clavichord and the harpsichord, two earlier keyboard instruments, were the most important instruments.

The 1700's were the years in which the *symphony* developed. This is a long piece of music made up of three or more *movements* (sections), usually with a pause between each. The movements are carefully designed as part of the overall plan of the symphony. *Chamber music* (music for a small group of musicians) was also greatly developed at that time. Josef Haydn, Wolfgang Mozart, and Ludwig van Beethoven excelled at both these forms.

The early 1800's saw the rise of *romanticism* in music. This led composers, with larger orchestras and new instruments at their disposal, to write more for effects and emotion than earlier musicians. Beethoven in his nine symphonies showed that he was a master of both the romantic and the earlier style of writing called *classical.* Other German composers continued with the romantic style. Among these were Franz Schubert, who wrote over 600 glorious songs, Robert Schumann, and Felix Mendelssohn.

Guitar

Scottish Bagpipes

Harp

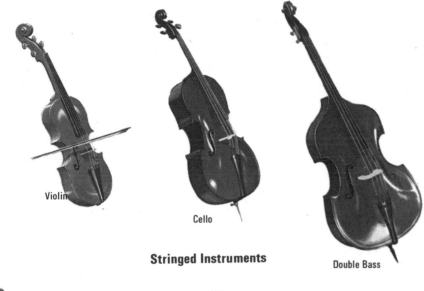

Violin

Cello

Double Bass

Stringed Instruments

Clarinet

Flute

Oboe

Piccolo

Woodwind Instruments

Brass Instruments

French Horn

Flugel Horn

Trumpet

Percussion Instruments

Timpani (kettledrums)

In the later 1800's, several composers began to emphasize national characteristics in their music. The Italians concentrated on opera, in which Giuseppe Verdi was the leading composer. German opera was dominated by Richard Wagner, who wrote the words as well as the music of his masterpieces, and called them *music dramas*. The French composer, Hector Berlioz, used new instruments and demanded huge orchestras for his romantic symphonies.

The 1900's have been years of searching for new forms of expression in music. Composers have experimented with strange harmonies, unusual scales, and unfamiliar rhythms. Electronic music, composed with the aid of sounds from tape recorders, has appeared. There are many outstanding composers today in Europe and the Americas who have contributed to various aspects of the new music. Some people find this music strange and difficult to listen to. But despite the critics, their music will, no doubt, be accepted without surprise by future generations.

Above right: The classical ballet is a complex and beautiful combination of music and movement.

Below right: Many ancient civilizations developed highly stylised ritualistic dances in which every movement of the body has a special significance.

The Restless Earth

The crust of the Earth is a thin, wrinkled 'skin', rarely more than 20 miles thick. At various times in the past, movements within the Earth have folded, twisted, and fractured the crustal rocks. In some places these *earth movements* have created great mountain chains.

Mountain Building

Earth movements give rise to three kinds of mountains – fold, block, and volcanic. *Fold mountains* form when two ancient land masses move towards each other and compress the land in between. The compression forces the land into great, wave-like folds. The Swiss Alps in Europe are examples of fairly young folds – about 15 million years old.

Sometimes earth movements may produce lines of weakness in the Earth's crust called

Above: Diagram showing how rock layers fracture and move against each other. The vibrations set up spread outwards in all directions. Those which reach the surface cause an earthquake. The quake is strongest directly above the centre, or *focus*, of the disturbance.

faults. As the movements continue, great block-like masses of the crust move along the line of the faults. They may subside below, or be raised above, the general land level to form *block mountains,* such as the Sierra Nevada in the United States.

Earthquakes

Stresses and strains in the Earth's crust may fracture rock layers, and as the broken ends move against each other, vibrations are set up. These spread outwards in all directions, their strength depending on the type of rock through which they pass. They are much stronger in granite than in loose sand and gravel. The area of the Earth's surface directly above the centre of the disturbance is called the *epicentre,* and it is here that the earthquake can cause severe damage. The vibrations get weaker as they travel away from the epicentre and cause less damage.

Earthquakes can occur anywhere. There are, however, two main areas which between them account for more than 80% of the

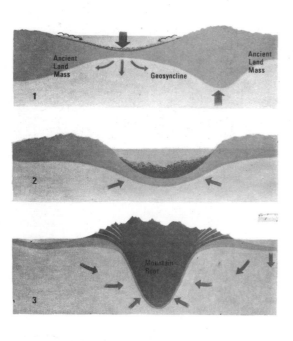

Left: Fold mountains are born under the sea as sediments collect in a slowly subsiding trough between two adjacent land masses called a geosyncline (1).
As the geosyncline fills with sediment the land masses on either side move towards each other (2). The mass of rock in the geosyncline is folded and buckled. The lower rocks are squeezed downwards to form a deep 'root' while the upper rocks are lifted out of the water. The main uplift of the new mountain range comes at a later stage as the mass of rock rises slowly from the dense sub-crustal rocks to float like an iceberg in water (3). The mountain building process is a very gradual one which takes place over millions of years.

Left: Despite the height and grandeur of mountain ranges such as the Alps, they are merely temporary wrinkles in the Earth's crust which will be eventually smoothed away by erosion. Many great ranges have been created and destroyed during the Earth's long history.

earthquakes in modern times. The *Circum-Pacific belt,* which runs from Chile, north to Alaska and then down through Japan to New Guinea, is the larger of the two. The *Mediterranean belt* extends from Spain and North Africa, through Italy and the Middle East, and joins the Circum-Pacific belt in the East Indies.

Seismology is the study of earthquakes, and seismographs are the instruments used to detect their occurrence and the size of vibrations. If seismographs had been invented at the time, it is possible that the greatest earthquake ever recorded would have been in Lisbon, Portugal, in 1755. Lakes in places as far away as Norway were disturbed. The energy of an earthquake of such an intensity is equal to an explosion of over a million tons of T.N.T.

The earthquake which caused the greatest damage was recorded in Japan in 1923. In the cities of Tokyo and Yokohama some half a million buildings were completely destroyed and the sea-bed in one place sank over 1,000 feet.

Volcanoes

There are many types of volcanic activity, but the term *volcano* is usually used for those cone-shaped mountains which periodically shoot out *lava* and hot ashes.

Lava is molten rock (*magma*) which was previously situated in pockets in the solid rock beneath the Earth's surface. Almost all active volcanoes are found in places which are undergoing earth movements, probably connected with the formation of mountain ranges. It is possible that friction between the moving rock masses heats and melts the rock, which then proceeds towards the surface through fissures and lines of weakness in the crust.

The explosive force of an eruption is due mainly to the violent expansion of steam and other gases released from the magma as it nears the surface. When a volcano is first formed, the exploding gases may form a crater of considerable size. The broken rocks and cinders usually fall around the mouth, forming the typical mound (*ash cone*).

Below: The aftermath of an earthquake in Caracas, Venezuela. The collapse of a modern six-storey building has left the floors piled one upon each other. The construction of quake-resistant buildings in recent years has done much to reduce the toll of life in such disasters, but there is no safeguard against the strongest quakes which can destroy entire cities.

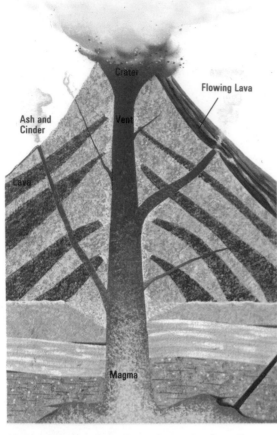

If the lava contains a lot of silica, iron and magnesium, it is 'mobile' and flows freely. Continuous eruption of this type of lava forms volcanic cones with shallow slopes.

Between eruptions, a volcano is said to be *dormant*. When an eruption ceases, the lava solidifies in the central *vent*. When the magma begins to rise again, enormous pressures are built up. There is a violent explosion which expels the *plug* of solidified lava and scatters rock fragments, dust and ashes into the air.

Another important type of volcano is the *fissure eruption,* in which lava wells up along cracks in the Earth's surface and may cover vast areas of land. Such lava flows contract on cooling and may form characteristic six-sided columns of basalt.

Below: The distribution of the main earthquake regions corresponds closely with that of volcanic regions. Both are associated with recent mountain building. The most recent of the great mountain systems is that which stretches across Europe and Asia to the Java Sea.

Above: A section through a volcano showing alternating beds of lava and ashes. Many volcanoes, including Vesuvius, are of this type. The ash layers are produced at the start of a new eruption when the vent is blocked by solidified lava. The rising magma causes an explosion which scatters rock fragments and ashes into the air.

Below: A volcanic eruption on an island off the coast of Iceland.

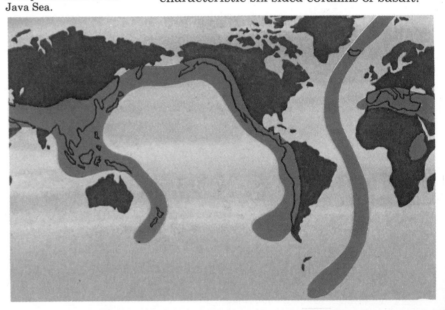

The Face of the Land

The surface of the Earth is constantly being worn away by natural forces such as running water, waves, ice, and the wind. This process is called *erosion*. It takes place slowly, but surely. Even the hardest of rocks are gradually reduced to pebbles and sand. Over the past millions of years, many mountain ranges have been created and then slowly worn away. Even the greatest mountain ranges are merely temporary wrinkles in the Earth's crust. Though we shall not be here to see it, the mighty Himalayas will eventually be smoothed away by erosion.

River Erosion
In most regions, running water has the greatest erosive effect on a landscape. Water moving along a stream bed continually picks up and deposits rock fragments. The scraping action of these fragments deepens and enlarges the stream. The faster the flow, the greater is the action. A stream in flood can easily move massive boulders a great distance. Throughout the course of a river, particles are being worn away, transported, and deposited. The finer particles are transported to the lower reaches of the river where they are deposited as *silt*.

Marine Erosion
On the coast, waves carrying sand and pebbles pound ceaselessly against the shore,

Above: A canyon on the Rio Grande. The high, vertical rock walls show the erosive power of a river. Perhaps the most spectacular example of river erosion is Grand Canyon in Arizona, U.S.A., a gorge cut by the Colorado River which is over 5,000 feet deep in places.

Left: Sand deserts are produced by wind erosion in arid climates. Rock particles are reduced to sand and dust as they are dashed against solid rocks by the wind. This process also sculptures the solid rocks, sometimes producing fantastic shapes.

Below: There is a constant battle between the land and the sea, but the material eroded by the waves from one stretch of the coast will be deposited later along another stretch.

cutting into and weakening the rock. Cliffs result from the under-cutting action of the waves which carve a notch back into the base of the rock until the material above collapses, exposing a bare rock face.

Glaciation

Moving ice plays a considerable role in the sculpturing of the land. *Striated* (scratched) rocks, U-shaped valleys with truncated spurs, gouged rock basins and fiords – the unmistakable signs of glacial erosion – are to be found in many parts of the world.

In the past there have been times when large areas of the land were covered by sheets of ice. These periods are known as the Ice Ages. During the most recent Ice Age, which began nearly a million years ago, much of Europe, Asia and North America lay beneath ice. As the ice advanced, it scraped the land clear of soil, levelling the surface, smoothing the mountain peaks, and carrying large quantities of rock for hundreds of miles.

It may seem strange that moving ice can erode rock which is much harder than itself. Part of the answer lies in the boulders and pebbles which, gripped firmly by the ice, turn a moving glacier into a giant piece of 'sandpaper', with the ability to smooth and deepen the valleys through which it passes. But even pure ice can erode. Frozen into the ice, and thus held in a firm grip, whole blocks may be torn from a rock face as a glacier moves along.

Wind Erosion

In dry regions, the wind picks up particles of dust and sand and hurls them against the rock. This natural 'sand-blasting' gradually breaks down the rock into sand and dust. Wind erosion can sculpture rocks into quite fantastic shapes.

Deposition

The debris removed by the tools of erosion is deposited elsewhere sooner or later. Most of the material transported by rivers is dropped nearer the sea, where they wind lazily in great loops, called *meanders,* across plains.

Sometimes a large amount of material is dumped by a river where it enters the sea and its flow is checked. This material builds up

to form a *delta* through which the river filters to the sea. Many of the world's largest rivers, including the Nile, Mississippi and Ganges, have deltas.

The rest of the rock debris is dumped in the sea where it is slowly cemented into solid rock again. Earth movements may later raise these new rocks above the sea to form land.

Deposition takes place along the coast, too. The sand and gravel removed from one part of the coast will be deposited at another part to form sand bars.

The debris scraped from the land by glaciers is deposited as they melt. Large areas of North America and Europe are 'plastered' with boulder clay stripped from lands farther north.

Below: In the final stages of river erosion, a river winds lazily in great loops (*meanders*) across a nearly flat plain (*peneplain*). The sluggish water has little erosive power and instead tends to drop the rock debris transported downstream along its banks and on its bed.

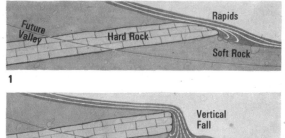

Left: An outcrop of hard rock in a river valley can lead to rapids as the river wears away the softer rock on either side (1). The under cutting action of the water may turn the rapids into a vertical waterfall (2). The waterfall recedes upstream as the falling water undercuts the hard rock ledge which falls away piece by piece. In this way the waterfall is gradually smoothed away (3).

Below: The Appalachians are the stumps of mountains once the height of the Alps which have been worn away by erosion.

NEWER APPALACHIANS   OLDER APPALACHIANS

Appalachian Plateau   Ridge and Valley Belt   Great Valley   Blue Ridge   Piedmont   Fall Line   Coastal Plain

North West

South East

Fishes

Fishes are cold-blooded animals – their bodies take on the temperature of the water surrounding them. They are found all over the world.

Fishes can be grouped into *fresh-water* and *salt-water* fishes. But as some fishes can live in both kinds of water, scientists prefer to classify fishes by their body structure into three classes. The majority of fishes are *bony* fishes – they have skeletons made of bone. The *cartilaginous* fishes – sharks, skates, and rays – have skeletons of cartilage, a gristly substance. The lampreys and hagfish are jawless fishes with cartilaginous skeletons.

Fins and Scales

A fish moves through the water by bending its body to and fro, and by moving its tail. The *dorsal* fins, along the topside of the body, and the *anal* fin, on the underside just in front of the tail, help to keep the fish on an even keel. The two *pelvic* fins in the middle of the underside and the pair of *pectoral* fins just behind the head control vertical movement and also act as brakes. Turning movements are controlled by the tail and the pectoral fins.

Most fishes are covered with scales, although they are always born without them. In most bony fishes, there is a line of special scales along the middle of the body. This line is called the *lateral line,* and through these scales a fish can sense vibrations in the water.

Internal Organs

The fish's internal organs are similar to those of other backboned animals. The kidney has an additional function of maintaining the correct proportion of salt in the blood, depending on whether the fish lives in salt water or fresh water. Bony fishes have an additional body organ to those of other animals: the *swim-bladder*. This is a small bladder of gas that gives the fish the *buoyancy* required at whatever depth it is swimming.

Fishes obtain oxygen from the water by means of *gills*. These are feathery structures behind the head which, except in the cartilaginous fishes, are covered by a flap called the *operculum*. The gills are fed with blood from the heart. In the gills, oxygen passes from the water into the blood.

Senses of Fish

Most fishes have eyes situated at the sides of the head so that they have vision over a

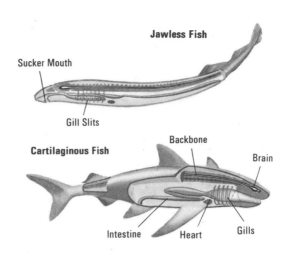

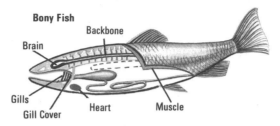

wide field. They can see in colour. Hearing is not well developed in fishes, although they sense vibrations with the lateral line. The sense of smell can be very acute, and many fishes, such as sharks, hunt only by smell.

Feeding in Fishes

Fishes feed in two ways. They either hunt and capture other fish, or large invertebrates, or they filter the minute plants and animals from the plankton through their gills. The first group of fishes have sharp teeth. The second group eat and breathe at the same time.

Life of Fishes

Almost all fishes hatch from eggs, but the ways in which the parents care for them vary enormously. Many produce millions of eggs at a single spawning, leaving the eggs and newly-hatched fish unprotected. Few of these millions survive. If all did, the world's oceans would soon become full of fish. Other fishes are more involved with their young. Some sticklebacks build nests for their eggs, and the male keeps guard over the eggs and young fish. The male pipefish and the male sea-horse carry the eggs in a brood pouch on the underside of the body, in which the eggs hatch. Some catfishes and mouthbreeders, both male and female, carry the fertilized eggs in their mouths.

A few fishes bear living young. These include several popular aquarium fishes such as the guppy, and some sharks. Some fishes, such as skates and dogfish, lay their eggs in horny cases popularly called 'mermaids' purses', which can be found on the seashore.

Left: The jawless fish group is the smallest of the three fish groups alive today. Jawless fishes have skeletons made of cartilage, not bone. They do not have proper jaws: the mouth is circular with teeth all round the lips. They do not have scales. The lamprey is an example. The cartilaginous fish group includes the sharks and rays. These fishes have skeletons made of cartilage and tooth-like scales. The bony fish group is the largest of the three groups. These fishes have skeletons made of bone and their bodies are covered by flat scales. They have a swim-bladder which helps them float.

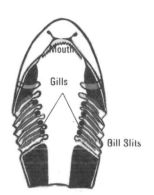

Cartilaginous Fish

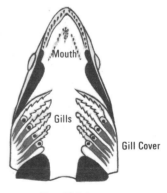

Bony Fish

Above: Fishes breathe with their gills. The water, which contains dissolved oxygen, goes into their mouths and out through their gills. In the gills, oxygen passes into the blood and carbon dioxide passes out, into the water.

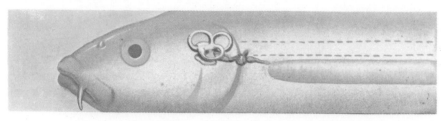

Fishes' ears are inside their bodies at the back of the skull. They have no external ears and nothing shows on the outside of the body. The ears help the fish with its balance as well as with its hearing.

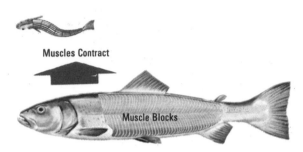

Muscles Contract

Muscle Blocks

Left: Fishes move through the water by bending their bodies in S-shaped curves. Their muscles are arranged in blocks on each side of their bodies. When one set of blocks contracts, the fish's body bends sideways.

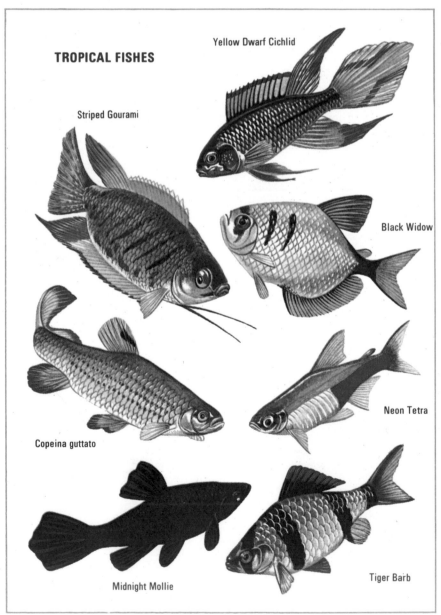

TROPICAL FISHES

Yellow Dwarf Cichlid

Striped Gourami

Black Widow

Copeina guttato

Neon Tetra

Midnight Mollie

Tiger Barb

Ways of Life

Many fishes have strange habits fitted to their mode of life. The flying fish can glide for up to 150 yards over the waves, using its pectoral fins as wings. The archer fish can catch insects by squirting water at them. The mudskipper can crawl about the land and even up trees, staying alive by retaining water in its gills.

Deep-sea fishes live at depths of 2,000 to 20,000 feet in the ocean. At these depths, it is completely dark to the human eye, the temperature is just above freezing, and the ocean currents are very slow. The animals of this dark, cold, still world have developed strange forms and habits which enable them to survive.

Deep-sea fishes have sensitive eyes and nearly all of them produce their own light. The light organs are arranged in patterns along the body, and as each species has its own pattern, they serve as recognition signals, helping the fishes to find mates and food. Some lantern fishes have a large light organ above or below the eye which illuminates their surroundings.

Food is scarce at great depths. Plant life does not exist below a depth of about 500 feet, where the light becomes too weak for plants to survive. Deep-sea fishes are therefore *carnivorous* animals with efficient ways of feeding. Their mouths are often gigantic, with rows of razor-sharp teeth. But the fishes themselves are rarely more than a foot long.

Electric Fishes

Some fishes produce shocks of electricity to stun their prey and to defend themselves from attacks. The shocks are produced by special muscles that may take up a large part of the fish's body. Instead of producing movement, like ordinary muscles, these muscles produce electric impulses. The impulses are strong enough to paralyse prey such as fishes, frogs and crustaceans, and to keep enemies at bay.

The electric eel is the most powerful electric fish. It lives in rivers in South America, and grows to a length of about seven feet. It cannot see very well and sends out weak electric impulses to help locate objects. When attacking its prey, it produces shocks of 200 to 300 volts at a current of a half to one ampere – enough to stun a man, though not to kill him.

Other electric fishes are not quite so powerful. The gymnotus is an eel-like fish also of South American rivers. The electric catfish lives in African rivers and the electric ray in the eastern Atlantic Ocean and the Mediterranean Sea.

FRESHWATER FISHES

Common Carp

Dace

Barbel

Climbing Perch

Pike

Bleak

SALT-WATER FISHES

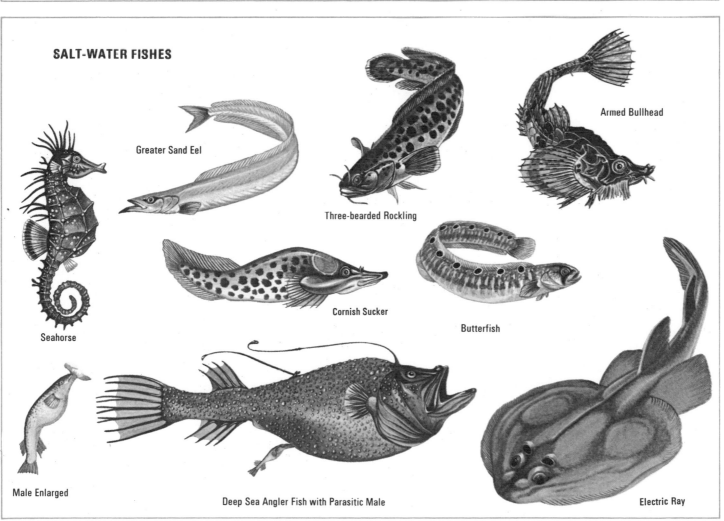

Greater Sand Eel

Armed Bullhead

Three-bearded Rockling

Seahorse

Cornish Sucker

Butterfish

Male Enlarged

Deep Sea Angler Fish with Parasitic Male

Electric Ray

143

Famous People

Famous Men and Women

Aeschylus (525–456 B.C.) was the first great Greek dramatist, and is regarded as the 'father of tragedy'. He wrote more than 70 plays, but only seven have survived. Among them is the famous *Oresteia* trilogy.

Akbar the Great (1542–1605) was the greatest of the Mogul emperors. He restored and strengthened the empire throughout northern India, and ruled wisely and humanely.

Procession led by Akbar the Great.

Alexander the Great (356–323 B.C.), the famous Macedonian king, carried out a series of brilliant invasions, including those of Asia Minor and India. He conquered the Thebans, the Persians and the Egyptians and founded the great city of Alexandria.

Alexander the Great

Alfred (849–899?), King of Wessex, was a great soldier and administrator. He was the only king to defeat the Danes, who threatened to overrun the whole of England. He enforced laws, organized a local militia, founded schools and built a small fleet—the first English Navy.

Amundsen, Captain Roald (1872–1928), the famous Norwegian explorer, was the first to sail through the North-West Passage. In 1911 he reached the South Pole, a short time before Captain Scott's party.

Amundsen

Archimedes (287–212 B.C.), the mathematician and philosopher, was born at Syracuse in Italy. He studied at Alexandria and made many discoveries, including the principle of specific gravity.

Aristotle (383–322 B.C.) was a Greek philosopher who studied under Plato. He wrote on a wide range of subjects including metaphysics, politics, ethics, logic and literature.

Armstrong, Neil (b. 1931), was the first man to set foot on the Moon. He stepped on to the surface on July 21, 1969 during the United States' Apollo 11 spaceshot. His fellow astronaut, Edward Aldrin, joined him there.

Arthur (500's B.C.), King of the Ancient Britons, is the subject of many famous legends concerning his court at Camelot and the Knights of the Round Table. But it is not certain that such a person existed.

Atatürk, Kemal (1881–1938), founded modern Turkey and completely revolutionised the Turkish way of life.

Attila (406–453) This ferocious man led the barbarian tribes, the Huns, against the Roman Empire. As he attacked and devastated cities throughout Europe, he earned himself the title of 'Scourge of God'.

Austen, Jane (1775–1817), was an outstanding British novelist. Her six novels are all humorous, realistic and unsentimental. Her most famous work is *Pride and Prejudice*.

Bach, Johann Sebastian (1685–1750), was one of the most gifted composers of all time. In his day he worked as an organist and choirmaster. He composed many choral and instrumental works.

Bacon, Francis (1561–1626), was an English philosopher and statesman. His *Essays* and *Novum Organum* are among his most celebrated works.

Bacon, Roger (1214–1294), a Franciscan friar, was one of the first experimental scientists. Although he was imprisoned on suspicion of heresy, he was commissioned by the Pope to write works on grammar, logic, mathematics, physics and philosophy—*Opus Maius.*

Baden-Powell, Lord Robert (1857–1941), founded the Boy Scout Movement in 1908, and in 1910, with his sister, Agnes, the Girl Guides. He is renowned as a soldier for his brilliant defence of Mafeking during the South African War.

Baird, John Logie (1888–1946), a Scottish engineer, was one of the pioneers of television. He gave the first practical demonstration in 1925.

Becket, St Thomas à (1118-1170), was Chancellor of England from 1155 to 1162, when he was made Archbishop of Canterbury against his will. He upheld the authority of the Church against his former close friend Henry II. After fleeing to France, he returned to England where he was murdered by the King's knights at the altar of Canterbury Cathedral.

Beethoven, Ludwig van (1770–1827) This great German composer wrote some of the finest orchestral, choral and chamber-music of all time. Among his most celebrated works are his nine symphonies and his violin concerto.

Beethoven

Bell, Alexander Graham (1847–1922), a Scottish-born American scientist, invented the telephone in 1876.

Alexander Bell at the opening of the New York to Chicago line, in 1892.

Bismark, Prince Otto von (1815–1898), was Chancellor of Prussia under Kaiser William. He dominated Prussia and European affairs. He did much to unite the German people and was known as 'The Iron Chancellor'.

Boadicea (Boudicca) (A.D. ?–62) was Queen of the Iceni tribe. She united the eastern Britons in revolt against the Romans. She led them to victory against Colchester, London and St. Albans. When finally defeated, she poisoned herself.

Bolivar, Simon (1783–1830), was the first president of Venezuela. He led a revolt against the Spaniards, liberating Venezuela, Colombia, Ecuador, Peru and Bolivia. The latter is named after him.

Borgia, Caesar (1476–1507), was a notoriously unscrupulous and clever nobleman who murdered every rival who stood in the way of his ambitions. Both he and his sister, Lucrezia, loved luxury and were great patrons of the arts.

Brahms, Johannes (1833–1897). This German composer worked in the shadow of Beethoven. Though not an innovator his work was still original. His works include the *German Requiem,* four symphonies, and much chamber-music.

Brontë, Charlotte (1816–1855) and **Emily** (1818–1848). These two sisters were remarkable novelists. They wrote two of the greatest novels in English literature. Charlotte wrote *Jane Eyre* and Emily *Wuthering Heights.*

Brown, John (1800–1859), was an American who tried to abolish slavery by force. He formed an army to raid the southern States but was defeated and later hanged. He is the subject of the Civil War marching song 'John Brown's Body'.

Bruce, Robert (1274–1329), was a courageous Scots noble who was crowned king at Scone in 1306. He raided England (1312–13) and defeated Edward II in 1314. A famous story tells that Bruce was encouraged to persevere in his struggle by watching the persistent attempts of a spider to reach its web —an apt comparison.

Brunel, Isambard Kingdom (1806–1859), the famous British engineer was largely responsible for building the Great Western Railway. He designed a number of famous bridges and played a great part in the development of ocean steam navigation.

Buddha (565?–488? B.C.), born Siddhartha Gautama, was the great spiritual teacher who founded Buddhism. He renounced the luxurious life to which he was born and preached a simple doctrine of upright living, unselfishness and generosity to others.

Cabot, John (1450?–1498), and his son **Sebastian** were Italian-born navigators who discovered the mainland of North America and paved the way for English colonization of America.

Caesar, see **Julius.**

Calvin, John (1509–1564), was a leading Protestant reformer, who established the Calvinist religion. He was born Jean Cauvin, in France.

Caxton, William (1422–1491), set up the first printing press in England.

Cervantes Saavedra, Miguel de (1547–1616), the great Spanish novelist, dramatist and poet, is renowned for his novel *Don Quixote.*

Charlemagne (742–814) Charles the Great, King of the Franks, was one of the greatest European rulers. He conquered the Gauls, the Lombards, the Saxons and the Avares. In A.D. 800 the Pope crowned him Emperor of the Holy Roman Empire.

Chaucer, Geoffrey (1340–1400), was the father of English poetry and the English language. Amongst his many great works is the *Canterbury Tales* which presents us with an unrivalled picture of life in Medieval England.

Chekhov, Anton (1860–1904), was a great Russian dramatist and short-story writer. Amongst his many brilliant plays are *Uncle Vanya, The Three Sisters* and *The Cherry Orchard.*

Chopin, Frédéric (1810–1849), the celebrated Polish composer, wrote brilliantly for the piano and was himself a superb pianist. His work was greatly influenced by Slavonik folk music and rhythms.

Churchill, Sir Winston Spencer (1874–1965), was the great British Statesman who led Britain through World War II. A brilliant leader, he was also a notable author. His works include *A History of The English-Speaking Peoples.*

Cicero, Marcus Tullius (106–43 B.C.), was probably the finest Roman orator. He was made Consul in 63 B.C. but his orations against Mark Antony, although renowned for their style, caused his downfall. He was made an outlaw and was murdered.

Cid, El (1043–1099) This was the name given to the Spanish soldier and adventurer, Rodrigo Diaz.

Cleopatra (69–30 B.C.) was the beautiful queen of Egypt. She captivated first Julius Caesar, whom she accompanied to Rome, and then Mark Antony. When she failed to charm Octavian, who defeated Mark Antony, she is said to have killed herself by allowing an asp, a poisonous snake, to bite her.

Clive, Robert (1725–1774), started his career as a clerk in the East India Company. He distinguished himself in the war with the French in India and after defeating the Nawab of Bengal, he established British rule in Calcutta. When he returned to England a rich man he was given a peerage, but was later accused of corruption. In the end he took his own life.

Coleridge, Samuel Taylor (1772–1834), was an outstanding poet, philosopher and literary critic. His *Ancient Mariner* and *Kubla Khan* are poetic masterpieces.

Columbus, Christopher (1451–1506), was an Italian-born seaman who went to sea at the age of 14. His great aim was to find India by

Columbus

sailing westwards. In 1492, Columbus sighted land—one of the outer islands of the Bahamas. Thinking that India lay beyond them he named them the West Indies. After three more voyages, he landed in 1498 on the mainland of South America.

Confucius (550–479 B.C.) was one of China's greatest teachers and social reformers. His sayings were written down by his followers and after his death he was venerated. The religion of Confucianism is based on his teachings.

Constable, John (1776–1837), was a great English landscape painter, noted for his naturalistic views of the English countryside. The *Hay Wain* and *Salisbury Cathedral from the Meadow* are two of his most admired works.

Cook, Captain James (1728–1779), the distinguished English navigator, made three voyages of discovery to the Pacific and Antarctic oceans. He kept remarkably accurate charts and looked after the health of his seamen. He met his death in a dispute with some natives of Hawaii.

Copernicus, Nicholas (1473–1543), a Polish astronomer, is regarded as the founder of modern astronomy. He derided Ptolemy's theory that the Earth is the centre of the Universe and demonstrated in his celebrated book *Concerning the Revolutions of the Celestial Spheres* that the Earth is simply a planet circling around the Sun.

Cortés, Hernando (1485–1547), was a Spanish soldier who defeated the Aztecs and conquered Mexico for Spain in 1520.

Cromwell, Oliver (1599–1658), headed the only republican government in Britain as Lord Protector of the Commonwealth of England. He achieved prominence in the Civil War when with his troops (the Ironsides) he defeated the Royalists at Marston Moor (1644) and at Naseby (1645). He then took command as ruler of England. Charles I was executed and his son defeated. Cromwell was made Lord Protector in 1653 and it was not until after his death that the republic collapsed.

Oliver Cromwell

Curie, Marie (1867–1934), with her husband, Pierre discovered the rare radioactive element radium. In 1904 Marie, Pierre and their friend Becquerel were awarded the Nobel Prize for their work. In 1906 Pierre was killed but Marie continued with their work until she died from leukaemia, doubtless caused by the radiation from the radium.

Dalton, John (1766–1844), was an English chemist whose discovery of the atomic theory in chemistry formed the basis of modern theoretical chemistry. He also formulated important chemical laws, including his Law of Partial Pressures. Another important discovery he made was that of colour-blindness. Both he and his brother were colour-blind.

Dante (1265–1321) Dante Alighieri is regarded as one of the greatest of all poets. His life and his personality are fascinating and his works are outstanding. His *Divine Comedy*, which tells the story of the poet's visit to hell, purgatory and paradise with the Roman poet Virgil as his guide, is a masterpiece.

Dante glimpses Beatrice, the woman who inspired his great poem *Vita Nuova*.

Darwin, Charles Robert (1809–1882), the English naturalist and scientist, put forward a revolutionary theory that shook the world. His book *The Origin of Species*, published in 1859, set forth his theory of evolution which he had begun developing after studying the animals of the Galapagos Islands.

De Gaulle, Charles (1890–1970), became President of the Fifth Republic of France in 1959. His personal prestige helped him to weather many a political storm. During World War II, he began a Free French movement, based in London, to continue the struggle against Nazi Germany. After the war, under his guidance, France began to pursue a more independent course in world affairs.

De Lesseps, Ferdinand (1805–1894), was a French diplomat and engineer who conceived and built the Suez Canal, completed in 1869. His plan for the Panama Canal ended in disastrous failure.

Descartes, René (1596–1650), the French philosopher and mathematician made important contributions to the study of mathematics. His system of philosophy, called the Cartesian philosophy, is summed up in his own phrase *'Cogito, ergo sum'* which means 'I think, therefore I am'.

Dickens, Charles (1812–1870), is often considered England's most popular novelist. His works vividly portray life in 19th century England with its great social evils. He created some of the most unforgettable characters in fiction, such as Oliver Twist, Scrooge, Mr Pickwick and David Copperfield.

Diogenes (412–322 B.C.). This celebrated Greek philosopher is reputed to have scorned material comfort and pleasure so much that he lived in a tub for years.

Dostoevsky, Fyodor (1821–1881), the Russian author of such penetrating novels as *The Idiot, Crime and Punishment* and *The Brothers Karamazov* ranks among the world's greatest and most influential writers.

Drake, Sir Francis (1540–1596). This great Elizabethan seaman made many voyages, some piratical and some for exploration. He made many daring raids on the Spanish Main. In 1577 he set off in the *Golden Hind* to circumnavigate the world. After this triumph he further distinguished himself by his brilliant defeat of the Spanish Armada in 1588.

Sir Francis Drake

Edison, Thomas Alva (1847–1931), the celebrated American inventor, perfected the electric light and invented the phonograph, or gramophone. In all he patented well over a thousand inventions.

Einstein, Albert (1879–1955), gained world-wide renown from his researches and discoveries in the field of mathematical physics His *General Theory of Relativity* caused a fundamental change in established scientific views of gravitation. Einstein became an American citizen after fleeing from Nazi Germany.

Eisenhower, Dwight David (1890–1969), became Supreme Allied Commander in Europe in World War II. He directed Operation Overlord, the invasion of Normandy on D-Day, June 6, 1944. He later became a popular Republican President of the United States (1953–1961).

Erasmus, Desiderius (1466–1536), the Dutch humanist and intellectual, was one of the greatest Renaissance scholars. His own writings and his version of the New Testament paved the way for the Reformation.

Euclid (300's B.C.) was a Greek mathematician who founded a school for the study of mathematics at Alexandria. Present systems of geometry are largely based on his methods and his *Elements of Geometry* was, until quite recently, a standard textbook.

Euripides (480–406 B.C.) was a Greek poet and tragedian. His plays were far less religious and far more humanistic than those of his fellows. Among the many fine plays that survive are *Alcestis, Medea,* and the *Bacchae*.

Faraday, Michael (1791–1867), one of Britain's most distinguished scientists, discovered the principles of electro-magnetism. His work on electrochemistry was also outstanding.

Fawkes, Guy (1570–1606), was one of a group of Roman Catholics who conspired to blow up King James I and the House of Lords on November 5, 1605. Fawkes was discovered on the scene of the crime, captured and later hanged.

Fleming, Sir Alexander (1881–1955), was the distinguished British bacteriologist whose accidental discovery of penicillin proved a milestone in the history of medicine. Howard Florey and Ernst Chain were fellow pioneers in the development of the drug.

Sir Alexander Fleming

Ford, Henry (1863–1947), an American automobile manufacturer, developed assembly-line methods of production and mass-produced the Model T Ford, affectionately known as the 'Tin Lizzie'.

Freud, Sigmund (1856–1939), holds an important place in the history of psychology. He founded the technique of psycho-analysis and developed the theory of the unconscious mind. He suggested three basic divisions of the mind—the *id,* the *ego* and the *super-ego.*

Freud was born in Freiburg, and lived most of his life in Vienna.

Fry, Elizabeth (1780–1845). This celebrated English reformer did much to alleviate the dreadful conditions in prisons, especially for women. She was a member of the Society of Friends.

Gagarin, Major Yuri Alexeyevich (1934–1968), became world famous when he made the first manned space flight in Vostok I on April 12, 1961. The Russian cosmonaut made one orbit of the Earth in a 108-minute flight.

Gainsborough, Thomas (1727–1788), is one of the greatest names in British painting. His landscapes, such as *The Watering Place*, and portraits, such as *The Blue Boy*, are almost without equal. He was a founder member of the Royal Academy.

Detail from a painting by Gainsborough. The delicacy and sensitivity of Gainsborough's portraits vividly recall the elegance of the age in which he lived.

Galileo (1564–1642) This great Italian scientist made many important discoveries in the fields of astronomy, mathematics and physics. He discovered the law of the pendulum and the law of falling bodies. He supported the Copernican theory—that the Earth revolves around the Sun—and the improvements he made to the telescope gave him further evidence. With his telescope he also discovered the moons of Jupiter.

Gama, Vasco da (1469–1524), a Portuguese navigator, was the first person to sail around the Cape of Good Hope to India and back (1497–1499).

Gandhi, Mohandas Karamchand (1869–1948), was the great Indian spiritual leader and reformer who waged a campaign of passive resistance against British rule in India. He did much to improve the lot of the 'untouchables' and he strove for harmony between Hindus and Muslims. He was assassinated in New Delhi on his way to a prayer meeting.

Garibaldi, Giuseppe (1807–1882). This celebrated Italian patriot fought to free Italy from Austria and make it one country. After fleeing to South America he returned in time for the outbreak of war in 1859. Whilst his comrade, Cavour, fought for the northern states, Garibaldi, aided by only 1,000 volunteers, set off to capture the south. This valiant deed did much to inspire his countrymen to fight even harder for liberty.

Genghis Khan (1162–1227), was one of the world's greatest conquerors. He established a vast Mongol empire extending across the whole of Northern Asia. He turned the hordes of savage barbarians into a well-organized, effective army. He was a brilliant, but extremely cruel general.

Gladstone, William Ewart (1809–1898), was the great Liberal statesman who became prime minister of Britain four times. He was a supporter of Free Trade and Home Rule for Ireland, and a violent opponent of Disraeli.

Goethe, Johann Wolfgang von (1749–1832), is regarded as one of the most imaginitive and versatile writers in western literature. Dramatist, writer and poet, his great masterpiece is the dramatic poem *Faust*. Goethe was also an earnest student of the natural sciences.

Handel, George Frederick (1685–1759), was a German-born English composer who was renowned for his operas, concertos and oratorios. Although he wrote many operas he is most famed for his oratorio *The Messiah*, which has a unique place in English music.

Hannibal (247–183 B.C.), was the great Carthaginian soldier who fought the Romans with inventive genius. He is remembered especially for his unique exploit of taking elephants with him across the Alps into Italy.

Hardie, James Keir (1856–1915), was founder of the Independent Labour Party and the first leader of the Party in Parliament.

Harvey, Sir William (1578–1657), an English physician, discovered how the blood circulates in the body.

Herodotus (485?–424? B.C.), was the world's first major historian. He travelled extensively in Greece, Asia and North Africa gathering material for the history he wrote in old age. Cicero, the Roman orator, called him the 'father of history'.

Hillary, Sir Edmund (b. 1919), a New Zealand mountain-climber and explorer, and Sherpa Tensing Norgay were the first men to climb Mount Everest (1953).

Hippocrates (460–377 B.C.), was the celebrated Greek physician, known as the 'father of medicine'. He established medicine as a science, divorced from philosophy and superstition. Amongst his many writings is the Hippocratic Oath, the code of ethics of the medical profession, which is still widely adhered to.

Hitler, Adolf (1889–1945), became dictator of Germany in 1934. A brilliant and persuasive orator, he became known as the Fuehrer (leader). His Nazi Party eliminated any opposition and ruthlessly persecuted the Jews. He led Germany into World War II by attacking Poland in 1939. His political ideas can be read in his book *Mein Kampf* which he wrote while in prison as a young man.

Homer (800's? B.C.) was the famous author of the magnificent poems *The Iliad*, which tells of the seige of Troy, and *The Odyssey*, which tells of the travels of Ulysses.

Ivan the Terrible (1530–1584), crowned first Tsar of Russia, was a tyranical ruler, who, in his later years, pursued a policy of terror against his subjects which earned him his name.

Ivan the Terrible

Jefferson, Thomas (1743–1826), was author of America's Declaration of Independence. He played a leading part in America's struggle for independence and became the third President of the United States.

Jenner, Edward (1749–1823), was the English physician who pioneered vaccination against smallpox. He made his first vaccination in 1796.

Jesus (4 B.C.?–A.D. 30 or 33), was the founder of Christianity. He is believed by Christians to have been the son of God. He was born in Bethlehem and brought up at Nazareth. At the age of 30, He became a rabbi (teacher) and went from place to place preaching and performing miracles. His following grew but this only alarmed the Jewish rulers. Betrayed by Judas, one of his apostles, he was crucified. Three days later, he is said to have risen from his grave. He spent 40 days on Earth and then ascended into Heaven.

Statue of Christ at Rio de Janeiro.

Joan of Arc (1412–1431), known as the Maid of Orleans, led the French to victory over the English at Orleans in 1429. During a later battle, Joan was captured and sold to the English, who burnt her as a witch in the market place at Rouen. After her death she became the heroine of France and the Pope reversed the verdict of her trial. In 1920 the Church declared her a saint.

Johnson, Samuel (1709–1784), was the famous English writer, critic and lexicographer, who was immortalized by his friend Boswell's biography of him.

His *Ode to a Nightingale, Ode to Autumn,* and *Ode on a Grecian Urn* are renowned for their beauty and sensitivity.

Kennedy, John Fitzgerald (1917–1963), was the youngest American ever to be elected President and also the first Roman Catholic president. His assassination at Dallas, Texas, less than three years after his election, shocked the world.

Khrushchev, Nikita Sergeyevich (1904–1971), was master of Russia from the mid-1950's until 1964. He became First Secretary of the

His genius seems universal. He was an imaginitive designer, inventor, engineer and architect. Amongst the finest examples of his work are *The Mona Lisa, The Virgin of the Rocks* and the magnificent mural *The Last Supper.*

Lincoln, Abraham (1809–1865), was one of the greatest figures of American history. In 1861 he became President of the United States. His opposition to slavery and his refusal to allow the Southern states, who wanted to keep their slaves, to secede led to the Civil War (1861–1865). His famous Gettysburg Address, spoken on one of the bloodiest battlefields of the war, has inspired his countrymen ever since. Lincoln was assassinated in a theatre box by John Wilkes Booth, a leading actor.

Lister, Joseph (1827–1912), the great Scottish surgeon was the first to pioneer antiseptic methods in surgery. The use of these methods dramatically reduced the number of deaths during operations.

Livingstone, David (1813–1873), was a Scottish medical missionary and explorer. He was the first man to travel the length of Lake Tanganyika. He discovered the Victoria Falls and set out to discover the source of the Nile. Henry Morton Stanley was sent to look for him on this expedition and uttered the now famous greeting 'Dr Livingstone, I presume' Unfortunately, Livingstone's health failed him and he died before he achieved his aim.

Louis XIV (1638–1715) ruled France absolutely for 72 years. He is credited with the famous remark, 'L'état, c'est moi' (I am the state). His reign was magnificent and literature and art flourished under him.

Luther, Martin (1483–1546), led the Protestant Reformation in Germany. He attacked the corruptions of the Church of his day in the revolutionary '95 theses' which he pinned to the church door in Wittenberg. As a result terrible religious wars were fought, but Protestantism survived together with many of Luther's doctrines.

Machiavelli, Niccolo (1469–1527), an Italian statesman and political philosopher, asserted in his book *The Prince* that a ruler should use any means within his power to advance his political ends. This unscrupulous disregard for justice and humanity has given the word *Machiavellian* its derogatory sense.

Magellan, Ferdinand (1480?–1521), was the Portuguese navigator who led the first expedition to sail round the world. He discovered the Magellan Strait and named the Pacific Ocean. He was killed in the Philippines, but one of his ships did manage to complete the voyage.

Mao Tse-tung (b. 1893) is chairman of the Chinese Communist Party and leader of the government. He has recently persecuted his political opponents in China and challenged Moscow's supremacy in world communist affairs.

Marconi, Guglielmo (1874–1937), was the Italian electrical engineer who developed the so-called wireless telegraphy—radio. He carried out his first successful experiments in 1895.

Marco Polo (1254–1324) was the famous Venetian traveller and explorer, whose accounts of his journeys in the East and his

Dr Samuel Johnson (far right) dominated conversation with his sagacity and wit.

Julius Caesar (102?–44 B.C.) was a Roman statesman and general. He was extremely popular with the people and made himself dictator. The senate feared his popularity would make him a tyrant and a small group of his friends, including Brutus, decided to assassinate him. On the Ides of March they stabbed him to death at the foot of Pompey's statue.

Julius Caesar

Keats, John (1795–1821), was one of the finest English poets. He died tragically young.

Communist Party on the death of Stalin in 1953 and Russian Premier in 1958. He relaxed Stalin's reign of terror and pursued peaceful co-existence with the Western world.

Knox, John (1505-1572), was the religious reformer who established Protestantism in Scotland. He was bitterly opposed by the Catholic Mary Queen of Scots.

Kublai Khan (1216–1294) This famous Mongol emperor was the grandson of Genghis Khan. Under his rule the empire reached its peak of civilization and power.

Lawrence, Thomas Edward (1888–1935), better known as 'Lawrence of Arabia', led the Arab revolt against Turkey in World War I. His exploits made him a legendary figure and won him much influence amongst the Arabs. After his triumph he retired to write his fascinating account of his adventures, the *Seven Pillars of Wisdom.*

Lenin, Vladimir (1870–1924), was founder and leader of the Communist Party. He spent most of his life working towards revolution, organizing the Bolshevik Party. In 1917 the Russian revolution took place and Lenin headed the government until his death, when Stalin succeeded him.

Leonardo da Vinci (1452–1519) is considered one of the greatest painters of all time.

service with Kublai Khan astounded his European contemporaries. His writings constitute a unique chronicle of the period.

Marx, Karl (1818–1883), was the German philosopher who propounded the theories on which Communism is based. He was supported and influenced in his work by his friend Friedrich Engels (1820–1895). Together they wrote the celebrated *Communist Manifesto* (1848). He enlarged on his theories in *Das Kapital.* Marx spent most of the latter part of his life in London, but his works have been admired by people in all parts of the world and have a profound influence in politics and economics.

Mata Hari (1876–1917) was a Dutch dancer who became a famous (if not terribly successful) German spy. She was executed by the French towards the end of World War I.

Melville, Herman (1819–1891), was an American author who wrote the famous novel *Moby Dick.*

Mendel, Gregor (1822–1884), an Austrian monk and botanist, first propounded the laws of heredity. The importance of his work was not recognized until much later.

Metternich, Clement (1773–1859), was an Austrian statesman who played a critical role in European politics during the first half of the 19th century. He strove to unite the aims of European countries and to halt as far as he could the movement towards democracy. His influence lasted until 1848 when revolution finally overthrew him.

Michelangelo (1475–1564) the Italian painter, sculptor and architect was a member of the Buonarroti family but he is always known by his Christian name. He built the great dome of St Peter's and spent over four years painting the ceiling of the Sistine chapel in the Vatican. His fresco *The Last Judgement* and his superb statue of David are masterpieces.

Milton, John (1608–1674), the English poet, is remembered mainly for his great epic poem *Paradise Lost.* As well as this he wrote many great poems and was very active in politics. He wrote several pamphlets advocating divorce and one, the *Areopagitica,* on the freedom of the press. His last and greatest works were written while he was blind.

Mohammed (A.D. 570–632) was a great religious leader and founder of the faith called Islam. He was born in Mecca. At first his preaching met with great opposition but eventually he was hailed as a great prophet.

Molière (1622–1673) was the stage name of Jean Baptiste Poquelin, the French playwright, actor and theatre manager. His comedies are among the world's greatest, especially *Tartuffe* and *Le Misanthrope.*

Montfort, Simon de (1208–1265), has claim to be the founder of the British Parliament. He led the English barons against King Henry III in an attempt to bring about political reforms. In 1264 he summoned representatives from the towns and shires of England to an assembly. A short time afterwards he was defeated and killed in battle.

More, Sir Thomas (1478–1535), was an English statesman and writer, whose refusal to acknowledge Henry VIII as head of the Church led to his execution. The title of his

book about an imaginary ideal world, *Utopia,* has passed into the English language.

Mozart, Wolfgang Amadeus (1756–1791), was a famous Austrian composer. There are few branches of music in which he did not excel. His operas, including *The Magic Flute* and *Don Giovanni,* abound in exquisite music. He also wrote many wonderful symphonies.

Mussolini, Benito (1883–1945), became Fascist dictator of Italy in 1922. In 1940 he entered World War II on Hitler's side, but, after defeats all round, was overthrown in 1943.

Napoleon I (Bonaparte) (1769–1821), a Corsican by birth, became emperor of France in 1804. His military genius won him brilliant victories throughout Europe until his invasion of Russia in 1812 ended in disaster. Exiled to Elba he returned to France and was finally defeated at Waterloo by Wellington and Blücher. Napoleon died in exile on the lonely island of St Helena.

Napoleon Bonaparte

Nelson, Horatio (1758–1805), Britain's foremost naval hero, led the British fleet and defeated the combined fleets of France and Spain at Trafalgar. Blind in one eye and with his right arm missing, Nelson directed the battle from the flagship *Victory* until he was mortally wounded.

Lord Nelson

Newton, Sir Isaac (1642–1727), was perhaps the greatest English scientist. His work encompassed physics, astronomy and mathematics. His book *The Principia,* published in 1687, documents his outstanding discoveries of the laws of motion and the theories of gravitation. His other towering achievements include the development of calculus, the investigation of the spectrum, and the invention of the reflecting telescope.

Nightingale, Florence (1820–1910), was a dedicated nurse and hospital reformer. As a nurse she made a study of hospital management, and in spite of fierce opposition she

organized a staff of nurses to alleviate the terrible conditions in the military hospitals during the Crimean War where she became known as 'the lady with the lamp.'

Omar Khayyám (1050?–1123?) was the celebrated Persian poet who wrote the famous *Rubáiyat.* The poem, translated by Edward Fitzgerald, was published in English in 1859.

Pankhurst, Emmeline (1858–1928), led the fight for 'Votes for Women' in Britain. She and her fellow suffragettes were often imprisoned for their militant behaviour.

Pasteur, Louis (1822–1895), a French chemist, established the science of bacteriology with his brilliant researches. His study of disease and theory of germ life made it possible to prevent many disease formerly thought to be incurable. The process of heating milk to kill bacteria is called pasteurization, after his name.

Paul, St (A.D. 16?–67?) Named Saul, this great saint was at first a merciless persecutor of the first Christians. He was converted on the road to Damascus when he is said to have been blinded by a dazzling light and to have heard the voice of Christ. After this he became the most important preacher and organizer of the early Church.

Peary, Robert Edwin (1856–1920), an American Arctic explorer, was the first man to reach the North Pole, in 1909.

Pepys, Samuel (1633–1703), was the author of the famous *Diary* which contains humorous and fascinating accounts of his personal life, court intrigues, the theatre and music. His diary is of great interest also for the eye-witness accounts of the Plague and the Great Fire of London. He was Secretary of the Navy during the reigns of Charles II and James II.

Pericles (495?–429 B.C.) was an Athenian statesman under whose rule Athens achieved her greatest glory. Art, architecture, industry and commerce flourished.

Pétain, Henry Philippe (1856–1951), a French national hero of World War I, was imprisoned for treason after World War II for collaborating with the Germans.

Peter, St (?–A.D. 64?) was the most important of the apostles of Jesus of Nazareth. After the Crucifixion he set out to preach Christianity but was himself put to death in Rome. Roman Catholics regard him as the first Pope.

Peter the Great (1672–1725) became Tsar of Russia at the age of 22. He built the country up into a great power. He founded the great city of St Petersburg (now Leningrad) in 1703 and made it Russia's capital.

Plato (427–347 B.C.) was one of the greatest Greek philosophers. He was the pupil of Socrates and the teacher of Aristotle. He wrote a great many 'dialogues', amongst them his famous *Republic.*

Pythagoras (580?–500? B.C.) was the Greek mathematician and philosopher who is best remembered today as the author of Pythagoras's Theorem—that the square on the hypotenuse of a right-angled triangle is equal to the sum of the squares on the other two sides.

Raleigh, Sir Walter (1552–1618), was the English soldier and scholar who became a favourite of Queen Elizabeth I. He sent expeditions to North America and established a colony at what he called Virginia, after the 'virgin queen'. He fell out of favour when he married one of the queen's maids and was imprisoned in the Tower of London.

Raphael (1483–1520) was one of the greatest painters of the Italian Renaissance. He was a contemporary of Da Vinci and Michelangelo. He painted frescoes in the Vatican. Amongst them is the much admired *Sistine Madonna*.

Rasputin, Grigori Yefimovich (1871–1916), was a Russian monk who gained great influence at the Russian court and was believed by some to have miraculous powers. But he had many enemies and was assassinated.

Rembrandt (1606–1669) was an exceptional Dutch painter. He was a superb portrait painter and some of his greatest and most sensitive works are self-portraits. One of his best-known pictures is *The Night Watch*.

Rhodes, Cecil John (1853–1902), was an Englishman who became a South African statesman. He made a vast fortune from the diamond fields of South Africa and established the colony of Rhodesia. He endowed part of his fortune to provide scholarships to Oxford University.

Richelieu, Cardinal (1585–1642), one of France's most gifted statesmen, was chief adviser to Louis XIII and the 'power behind the throne'. He did much to strengthen the monarchy at home and France's power abroad. He also founded the French Academy.

Robespierre, Maximilien (1758–1794), was one of the leaders of the French Revolution. Originally an advocate and judge, he became prominent in the Jacobin Party and was elected a member of the Assembly. During the so-called Reign of Terror he condemned many people to death but was himself guillotined not long afterwards.

Roosevelt, Franklin Delano (1882–1945), was a great American statesman. He became President in 1933 and led his country through the Second World War. He, Churchill and Stalin became known as 'The Big Three'. His achievements were especially remarkable because he was disabled.

Rousseau, Jean Jaques (1712–1778), was a French writer and philosopher whose works greatly influenced the writers and thinkers of his time. He discusses his political philosophy in *Du Contrat Social*. Perhaps his most interesting work is his autobiography *Confessions*.

Rutherford, Lord (1871–1937), was the distinguished British physicist who developed the nuclear theory of the atom and in 1919 produced the first artificial transmutation of nitrogen (i.e. changed the nitrogen atom to a different atom).

Saladin (1137–1193) was Sultan of Egypt. He led the Moslems against the Christians in the Third Crusade. He was a magnificent soldier and a wise and able ruler.

Schweitzer, Albert (1875–1965), was an almost legendary figure during his own life-time. Born in Germany, he was a writer, philosopher and doctor. He devoted most of his life to medical missionary work in equatorial Africa.

Scott, Robert Falcon (1868–1912), was a British naval officer and Antarctic explorer. He led two important polar expeditions. His party reached the South Pole a month after Amundsen but they died on the return journey.

Shakespeare, William (1564–1616), the English poet and playwright, was one of the world's greatest and most renowned writers. His creative genius was unique. He was a master of both tragedy and comedy, and has had a profound influence on world literature.

William Shakespeare

Shaw, George Bernard (1856–1950), was a brilliant Irish playwright and critic. In his many outstanding plays he attacked the society of his day with penetrating wit. Amongst his finest works are *Man and Superman, Pygmalian, Major Barbara* and *Saint Joan*.

Socrates (469–399 B.C.) was one of the greatest Greek philosophers. He wrote nothing himself but his teachings were set down in the writings of his pupils, especially Plato. He was unjustly accused of opposing religion and was condemned to either death or banishment. He calmly chose death rather than leave his beloved Athens.

Sophocles (496–406 B.C.) was one of the three most distinguished Athenian tragedians. His plays surpassed even those of Aeschylus and Euripides. Of the 123 plays he is believed to have written only seven survive—amongst them *Oedipus Tyrannus* and *Electra*.

Stalin, Joseph (1879–1953), became master of Russia on the death of Lenin in 1924, and ruthlessly eliminated his opponents. He established Communist control over eastern Europe after World War II and instigated the 'Cold War' with the West. After his death he was denounced by Khrushchev as a tyrant.

Stephenson, George (1781–1848), was the British railway pioneer who developed the locomotive into a reliable machine. His most famous engine was the *Rocket*.

Sun Yat-Sen (1866–1925) was a Chinese revolutionary leader who founded the Chinese Republic and became its first president.

Tchaikovsky, Peter Ilich (1840–1893), was a Russian composer. His immensely varied works have achieved great popularity. His ballets *Swan Lake, The Sleeping Beauty* and *The Nutcracker* are universally acclaimed.

Tennyson, Alfred Lord (1809–1892), succeeded Wordsworth as poet laureate of England. He was immensely popular and widely read in his own day, for his works closely reflected the feelings and aspirations of Victorian society. Among his best poems are *The Lotus Eaters, Mariana, Ulysses* and *Morte d'Arthur*.

Thucydides (460–400 B.C.) was an Athenian historian. His history of the Peloponnesian War between Athens and Sparta is one of the first examples of accurate, impartial historical writing.

Tolstoy, Leo Nikolayevich (1828–1910), was one of Russia's greatest writers. His most famous works are the epic *War and Peace*, which is set against a background of the 1812 Napoleonic invasion, and *Anna Karenina*, a poignant love story.

Tutankhamen (1358?–1340? B.C.) was an Egyptian pharaoh. Howard Carter, a British archaeologist, uncovered his untouched tomb in 1922. It was the only Egyptian tomb ever discovered that had not been looted.

Twain, Mark (1835–1910), was the pen-name of Samuel Langhorne Clemens, the author of two great American classics. *The Adventures of Tom Sawyer* and *The Adventures of Huckleberry Finn* are based on his own boyhood experiences.

Tyndale, William (1494–1536), a leader of the Protestant Reformation in England, translated the Bible from Greek into English. His translation was denounced by the English clergy, and he fled to Antwerp. There he was seized for heresy, and met a martyr's death by strangling and burning.

Van Gogh, Vincent (1853–1890), was a Dutch painter, whose canvases were as brilliant as his life was tragic. He suffered from severe depression and insanity and once cut off one of his ears. He committed suicide. *The Chair and the Pipe, Sunflowers* and *Wheatfields and Cypress Trees* are among his most popular works.

Virgil (70–19 B.C.) was Rome's greatest poet. His masterpiece is *The Aeneid*. This magnificent epic tells of the wanderings of Aeneas after the fall of Troy and his settlement in Italy.

The poet Virgil sits between his muses, Clio and Melpomene.

Voltaire (1694–1778) was the pen-name of François Marie Arouet, one of France's most renowned writers and philosophers. He was sharply critical of the politics, society, and religion of his day. His writings helped to feed the discontent that led to the French Revolution.

Washington, George (1732–1799), was the first President of the United States. He commanded the victorious American army during the American War of Independence. After his death he was venerated as the 'father of his country'.

Watson-Watt, Robert Alexander (b. 1892), a British engineer, played a leading role in the development of radar in the 1930's

Watt, James (1736–1819), was a Scottish engineer who developed the steam engine into a really practical source of power. He also invented the governor, one of the first control devices.

Webb, Sidney James (1859–1947), was an eminent British Socialist and economist who was a founder member of the Fabian Society. His wife Beatrice (1858–1943) was also a dedicated Socialist and helped him in his work.

Wellington, Duke of (1769–1852), born Arthur Wellesley, was the British soldier who defeated Napoleon at the Battle of Waterloo. The 'Iron Duke', as he was called later became prime minister.

Wesley, John (1703–1791), was a British evangelical leader who founded the Methodist Church in Britain and America. He was a man of great energy and a powerful preacher.

Wilberforce, William (1759–1833), was a British reformer who led the movement to abolish slave trading in the Empire.

Arthur Wellesly, the Duke of Wellington rides to his great triumph at Waterloo.

Wilde, Oscar (1854-1900), was a brilliant and eccentric Irish poet and dramatist. He is well known for his comedies, such as *The Importance of Being Earnest*, which abound in wit. His poem *Ballad of Reading Gaol*, written while he was in prison, is widely admired.

Wolsey, Cardinal Thomas (1475?–1530), was the brilliant English statesman who, as Chancellor to Henry VIII, controlled the fortunes of England for many years. His inability to obtain for Henry a divorce from Catherine of Aragon led to his sudden fall from power.

Cardinal Wolsey

Wordsworth, William (1770–1850), was one of the greatest British Romantic poets. His nature poetry has seldom, if ever, been equalled. In 1798, together with his friend Coleridge, he published the *Lyrical Ballads*, an important landmark in English poetry.

Wren, Sir Christopher (1632–1723), was the eminent English architect who designed St Paul's Cathedral and many other London churches after the Great Fire of London. He was originally an astronomer and it was his design for the Sheldonian Theatre in Oxford that first brought him fame.

Wright, Wilbur (1867–1912), with his brother Orville (1871–1948), built the first successful powered, heavier-than-air flying machines, or aeroplanes. Orville made the first ever aeroplane flight at Kitty Hawk, North Carolina on December 17, 1903.

Wycliffe, John (1320–1384), was a leading religious reformer, who vigorously criticised the abuses of the Church. He was one of the first to translate the Bible into English.

Xenophon (430?–355? B.C.) was a notable Greek general and historian who studied under Socrates.

Xerxes (519?–465? B.C.) was a great Persian king who, with a vast army, defeated the Spartans at Thermopylae, but at Salamis his fleet was defeated. Xerxes was not a popular ruler and was assassinated.

Zeppelin, Count Ferdinand von (1838–1917), pioneered the development of airships in Germany. His massive craft flew successfully for a number of years and were used for bombing in World War I.

Zoroaster (700's B.C.) was the Persian prophet who founded the religion called Zoroastrianism, now practised by the Parsees of India.

Government

Early man had no proper government, nor any written laws. The earliest and simplest form of government arose from the customs of tribal groups – rule by the head of the family. Such a system, where the over-ruling power is in the hands of one person, is called a *monarchy*. Usually a monarchy is hereditary. A monarch whose power is unlimited is called an *absolute* monarch, or *autocrat*. The rule of a *constitutional* monarch, such as the British sovereign, is limited by parliament.

The beginnings of modern ideas about government came from the early Greek and Roman systems. The Greeks soon realised that an absolute monarch might rule justly and wisely, but, with no limits to his power, he might also become a tyrant. They devised a new form of government, with a larger number of citizens involved. When this government was by a few citizens, who were the oldest and best citizens, whether chosen by birth or by education, it was called an *aristocracy*. Often, however, power fell into the hands of a few men who sought power for its own sake and became tyrants. This sort of government was called *oligarchy*.

Eventually the Greeks realised that the fairest method of government was one in which all the citizens took part. This kind of government is called *democracy* (in Greek 'demos' means 'the people'). Although, in Athens in the year 5 B.C., all citizens had the right to vote, only a small minority of the population qualified as citizens. Women, foreigners and slaves were not classed as citizens. However, in most modern democracies every sane, law-abiding adult has the right to vote.

There are still, however, many countries which do not have democratic governments. Often power is in the hands of a *dictator*, who has usually usurped power and holds on to it with the backing of the army. In *totalitarian* states, such as Russia, although elections may be held regularly, there is only one party and it permits no opposition. Some people believe that there should be no government at all, that each individual should govern himself by reason. This absence of government is called *anarchy*. Some countries, such as the U.S.A. and France, are *republics* with an elected president, who may hold a great deal of power.

Elections

Because it is physically impossible for everybody in a country to vote over every

Above: Cicero, the great Republican orator and philosopher, addresses the Roman senate.

Below: Rome achieved her greatest glory under the dictatorships of the first Caesars. But their wise rule was turned to the worst kind of tyranny on the succession of Caligula.

Below: General De Gaulle who was President of the French Republic until 1969.

issue, various methods have been devised for people to elect representatives. In Britain, the U.S.A. and many British Commonwealth countries, the country is divided into areas where two, three or more candidates stand for election. The one with the largest number of votes is elected. One of the disadvantages of this system is that the member returned to parliament may represent only a minority of the electorate – the other candidates having polled more votes between them than the winning candidate. Also it means that over the whole country candidates from small parties may never be elected. However, in most of western Europe and Scandinavia a voting system is used which does allow for adequate representation of small parties. They are given seats in proportion to the number of votes they poll over the whole country. This is called *proportional representation*.

Political Parties

A political party consists of people with more or less the same views. In Britain there have always been only a few large parties – usually only two. One party forms the government and the others, the opposition. In western Europe, the system of proportional representation in elections makes for many more parties. Often in these countries no party wins a big enough majority to form the government and a coalition government is formed.

Administration

Government in Britain, as in most countries, can be divided into three areas – the *legislative*, the *executive* and the *judicial*. In Britain, all the members of parliament make the laws. They are the legislature. The cabinet and the ministers appointed by the prime minister administer the laws and decide on policies. They are the executive and they are responsible to the legislature –

the whole of parliament. The judiciary, which consists of all the courts of law in the country, is also responsible to parliament.

In the United States of America, the executive, legislative and judicial branches of government are separate. The head of state is an elected President, and neither he nor his cabinet are members of Congress, the legislative branch of Federal government. Congress is composed of two houses – the Senate and the House of Representatives. The judiciary is headed by the Supreme Court whose members are appointed by the President with the advice and consent of the Senate.

The task of running a country is very complex. The government is divided into various departments, with a minister responsible for each. The government has to pay for the upkeep of the army, for universities, for hospitals, for the police force and for many other essential services. To do this it needs money. In Britain, one department, the Treasury, handles all the finance. The minister, the Chancellor of the Exchequer, decides how much money all the departments need and also how to raise the money – whether by borrowing or by taxation. He also decides what method of taxation to use – *direct* (e.g. income tax) or *indirect* (e.g. purchase tax).

Civil Service

Apart from needing money, the government needs people to handle all the work involved in the various departments. In Britain, this is done by an independent body of trained civil servants, who do not change with the government. In some countries, when the government changes civil service posts are given to supporters of the new government.

Local Government

Because the task of the central government is so great, most countries have local governments as well. Local governments are usually elected, although in some countries they are appointed by the central government. Local governments also collect their own taxes to pay for the upkeep of local amenities, such as roads, housing, fire services and, in Britain, education.

Trade Unions

Apart from representation in parliament, there are other ways in which people can defend their rights. Trade unions are formed to protect the working conditions and to increase the wages of workers. The right to strike is a necessary democratic right. The workers band together to bargain with employers to reach agreement on fair rates of pay.

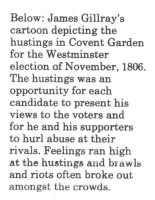

Below: James Gillray's cartoon depicting the hustings in Covent Garden for the Westminster election of November, 1806. The hustings was an opportunity for each candidate to present his views to the voters and for he and his supporters to hurl abuse at their rivals. Feelings ran high at the hustings and brawls and riots often broke out amongst the crowds.

Great Religions

There have been many religions in the history of the world. From the earliest times people have believed in and worshipped a god, or more than one god. Primitive man worshipped simple things, such as stones, the Sun, or a river. But since that time men have evolved many different faiths which encompass a wide variety of beliefs. These are some of the most widespread and influential religions today.

Christianity

Christianity is the religion of those who follow the teaching and example of Jesus Christ. Jesus preached a doctrine of universal love and brotherhood. His teachings and the story of his life are related in the New Testament. Despite the simplicity of Christ's doctrines, the religion has been complicated by the many interpretations put upon them. In 1504, after a long dispute with Rome, the centre of Christianity, Eastern Christians broke away to form the Eastern Orthodox Church. In the 1500's the Reformation brought about the division of Western Christians into Roman Catholics and Protestants. Today there are almost 1,000 million Christians, divided into more than 300 denominations.

Islam

In all there are over 460 million Muslims. Muslims are followers of Mohammed (A.D. 570–632), whom they regard as the last great prophet and messenger of Allah (God). The sacred book of Islam is the Koran. All good Muslims must observe the 'five pillars' of their faith – the first is confession of faith in one God and Mohammed. The second is prayer, five times a day. The third is almsgiving. The fourth is fasting. And the fifth is pilgrimage to Mecca, the birthplace of Mohammed.

Hinduism

More than four-fifths (about 417 million) of the people of India are Hindus. Hinduism is both religion and a way of life. Union with Brahma, the supreme, all-embracing spirit, is the goal of the Hindu. He can achieve this by practising *yoga* and self-discipline. If a man fails to achieve this union he is reborn, either to a higher or lower form of life, depending upon the way he has led his former life. Hindu society is divided into ranks, or castes. Those without caste are pariahs (untouchables). Caste can only be changed through rebirth.

Above: Icons, depicting sacred subjects such as the madonna and child, were often themselves regarded as sacred in the Eastern Orthodox Church, and were the subject of great religious devotion.

Right: The Archbishop of Canterbury is the spiritual leader of the Church of England and the Anglican community throughout the world.

Above: Hindus regard the River Ganges as sacred. Hindu pilgrims bathe and drink the water off the ghats (steps) which line the waterfront.

Right: In Japan, Shinto families often worship at their private 'temples' where, they believe, the spirits of their ancestors are enshrined.

Below: A young Muslim kneels and prays to Allah. Muslims must always face in the direction of Mecca when they pray.

Confucianism

Confucianism is not really a religion but a philosophy. Confucius was an ancient Chinese scholar. The basis of his teaching was the Golden Rule: 'Do not do unto others as you would not have others do unto you'. Although Confucius had few followers during his lifetime, after his death his philosophy spread. Today there are over 300 million Confucianists.

Buddhism

Buddhism is the religion of over 160 million people. Buddhists do not worship a god, but seek to attain the state of *nirvana* (enlightenment) in which there is no desire, no suffering, and no existence as we know it. According to Siddhartha Gautama, (the Buddha who founded the religion) the way to this state is by the 'noble eightfold path' whose steps comprise a code of conduct covering all aspects of a man's life. Like Hindus, Buddhists believe that all creatures are born many times and that the evils of a man's past life explain the sufferings of his present life.

Judaism

Judaism is based on the teachings of the Old Testament and the Talmud. Many of its beliefs concerning God and morals are shared by the Christians. Jews believe that they are God's chosen people and that one day a Messiah will come to establish God's kingdom on Earth. Judaism has its centre in Palestine but the 13 million Jews are scattered throughout the world.

Other Important Faiths

Jainism and **Sikhism** are two widespread Indian sects which practise much modified forms of Hinduism. Neither sect adheres to the Hindu caste system.

Shintoism is a Japanese religion based on nature and ancestor worship.

Taoism is a mystical Eastern religion which preaches a creed of compassion, humility and non-violence.

Zoroastrianism is an ancient Persian religion whose creed is based on the fight between good and evil in man.

Types of Belief

Animism Belief that objects and natural phenomena possess souls of their own.

Pantheism Belief that God exists everywhere and all things are divine.

Monotheism Belief in one supreme God as in Christianity, Judaism and Islam.

Polytheism Belief in several gods as found in Hinduism.

Dualism Belief in equal forces of good and evil as found in Zoroastrianism.

Atheism Disbelief in the existence of a god and rejection of religion.

Agnosticism Neither belief nor disbelief in a god.

Right: The sound of the Ram's Horn ushers in the Jewish New Year (Rosh Hashanah) and the start of ten days of penitence, ending with the Day of Atonement (Yom Kippur) – a day spent in fasting and prayer in the synagogue.

Below: Although there is no concept of a god in the Buddhist religion, statues of the Buddha or Enlightened One, who founded the religion, play a great part in the devotions of Buddhists.

Money

At one time, when people wanted to buy anything they had to give something else in exchange for it. For example, if a farmer wanted to buy bread from a baker, he offered him eggs in exchange. The baker would accept them because he needed eggs. At this period, a person's 'money' consisted of the goods that he possessed or could produce. As communities became larger and trade developed, this method of buying, called *barter,* appeared to be a clumsy way of carrying on buying and selling. Some people then had the idea of using token goods for trade, things that all people considered precious and would accept. In many parts of the world, cattle were used as token goods or money. Today, in parts of Africa, they are still considered to be the only real wealth. The English word 'pecuniary' (consisting of money) comes from the Latin word *pecus*. meaning 'cattle'.

The first people who are known to have used coins as money were the Lydians, who lived in Asia Minor. They began using stamped pieces of metal as a medium of exchange (that is, for buying and selling) as early as the 7th century B.C. But it is believed that the Chinese may have made coins at an even earlier date than that. The early coins were of irregular shapes and were stamped with rough designs. At one period of history, the Chinese shaped each coin into the form of the article it would

buy. For example, the coins used for buying clothes were shaped like the human body.

Token Money
Until recent times, the money value of coins (the amount coins were worth when used as money) depended on the value of the metal that the coins were made of. But today most governments issue *token coins*. This means that the value stamped on a coin is not the same as the value of the metal in the coin. People accept a coin in payment not because they value the coin itself but

Tetradrachm of Tyre (1st century B.C.), the 'thirty pieces of silver' of Biblical fame.

Bronze coin of Herod the Great (37-4 B.C.).

Demetrius Poliorcetes of Macedon (4th century B.C.).

Stater of Bahrain (3rd or 4th century A.D.).

Left: Cowrie shells are used as money in some primitive parts of the world.

Modern U.S. 50-cent coin. The Dollar is the basis of the world's most powerful monetary system.

because they have confidence in the authority that issued the coin. Because coins are heavy and bulky, they are chiefly used for making only small payments. Larger payments are made in paper money which is issued by banks authorized to do so by the government.

Banking
Banks are institutions which take care of people's money, and use it to earn more money. They do this by lending it to people who want to borrow money and by charging interest on the loan. By receiving money from those who can spare it and lending it to those who can make use of it, banks play a very important part in the economic affairs of a country.

Commercial banks are the banks that we can see in the High Street of any small town or in many places in large cities. People deposit their savings and their earnings in such banks, and the banks help them by taking care of their money, by making it easy for them to pay bills, and by giving them advice. A person who has an *account* with a bank (that is, who has placed money in the bank) does not have to carry his money around with him and can withdraw money from his account whenever he needs it. Most banks offer two kinds of accounts: current accounts and deposit accounts. A customer who has a current account can withdraw money from his account at any time during the business hours of the bank. A person who has a deposit account must give the bank notice before withdrawing it.

Savings banks, such as the Post Office Savings Bank, accept deposits of money from the public and pay interest on it. They do not lend money, and they do not make any profit. Their purpose is to encourage people to save.

Central banks, such as the Bank of England, carry out banking business for the government and also do business for other banks. They help the government to control the country's financial affairs.

Banks are not the only institutions which borrow and lend money today. There are many finance corporations which do so. Examples of these institutions are the building societies which specialize in lending money to people who wish to build or buy their own house, and the hire-purchase companies which advance money to people who wish to buy furniture or a car and spread their payments over a period of time. Naturally, buying things in this way means paying more in the long run Interest has to be paid on all the money that remains to be repaid.

Insurance Companies

Insurance companies are a rather different type of finance institution. They offer to pay a money sum to compensate an individual for loss or damage to himself or his property. They calculate the risk involved and are then able to tell the would-be insurer how much must be paid at regular intervals to entitle him to compensation in the event of an accident. The money which the insurance companies receive they use to invest and finance a wide variety of undertakings.

Trade

Alongside the great growth in banking and finance in the modern world, there has been a great growth in trade. In early times most exchanges were between neighbouring communities—objects which came a long way were few and very costly. It is difficult to realize today how many of the most commonplace purchases have travelled thousands of miles before coming into our pos-

Above: A selection of modern bank-notes. A country's government decides what paper money shall be made and circulated.

Right: Early eighteenth century fire-mark of the Sun Fire Office. This was fixed to a property to show the firemen that it was insured with them. Fire brigades were set up by insurance companies after the Great Fire of London.

Left: A two million mark German banknote of 1923. During periods of inflation, the real value of money falls because it will purchase fewer goods. In 1923, inflation in Germany became so great that it cost millions of marks merely to post a letter. The previous year it had cost less than one mark.

session. Practically every country finds it necessary to import certain goods from abroad. To pay for these imports a country must export its own goods to other countries.

Many governments charge a fee, or *duty*, on goods which come into the country from abroad. Besides providing the nation with a considerable income, these duties usually mean that a foreign product will cost more than a similar home-made one. This is a form of protection for home producers who do not have import duty to pay. Import duties also enable a government to regulate the amount of money spent on goods from abroad. This may be very necessary at times to ensure that the value of imports does not soar above the value of exports.

Chemistry

All substances are chemicals. The study of chemistry is the study of every substance, its structure, its composition and, perhaps more important, the reactions in which it takes part.

The overwhelming variety of materials occurring in Nature are made up from ninety-two basic ingredients called *elements*. There are in fact over a hundred elements known at present but the artificial ones made in the laboratory exist in such small quantities that their chemistry is not yet of practical importance.

Each element contains atoms of one size only. An *atom* is defined as the smallest part of an element which shows the chemical properties of that element. Atoms join together to form what we call *molecules*. The number of groups which can be arranged out of 92 distinct atoms is almost incalculable. That is why there is such a vast range of known substances and many still to be discovered. A substance built up chemically from more than one element is called a *compound* (not a mixture).

Branches of Chemistry

Because nearly half a million compounds are known to contain the element carbon they are given a branch of chemistry to themselves called *organic chemistry*. The name comes from the carbon compounds produced by living organisms. The study of elements other than carbon is called *inorganic chemistry*. A third great division is that concerned with the structure of matter and the laws governing chemical reactions. It is called *physical chemistry,* a name which rightly suggests the application of both physics and chemistry. Analytical chemistry is concerned with the identification of the various ingredients of a compound *(qualitative analysis)* and finding out the quantity of each present *(quantitative analysis).*

A chemical reaction involves energy as well as a rearrangement of atoms. The heat of a fire, for example, is energy released when coal combines with oxygen. Sometimes this chemical energy is turned into electrical energy, and just as heat splits up some substances so we can decompose certain compounds by passing a current of electricity through them. Those substances which can be split by a current are called *electrolytes* and the process is called *electrolysis*. Electrical chemistry is of great industrial importance in the extraction of such reactive metals as sodium and aluminium.

Above: Different elements are made of different atoms, the difference being in the numbers of protons and neutrons in the nucleus (the mass number) and the number of orbiting electrons (the atomic number).

Below: Servicing a chemical reaction vessel. The technician wears special clothing and breathing apparatus to protect himself from fumes.

The manufacture of chemicals has increased enormously in the last hundred years or so, and is now one of the largest industries in the world. Chemists are also employed in the making, packaging and storing of textiles, foodstuffs, medicines etc.

Chemical Compounds

If a crystal of common salt could be ground into particles smaller than those of the finest talcum powder, it would still behave as salt. We believe that the smallest particle which can show the behaviour of common salt is the sodium chloride *molecule*. This can only be broken down further into an *atom* of sodium and an *atom* of chlorine. Sodium chloride is a *compound;* sodium and chlorine are its *elements*. The properties of compounds are quite different from those of the elements they contain. For example, sodium is an inflammable metal and chlorine is a pungent greenish gas.

In describing a chemical change or 'reaction' it is convenient to employ symbols and formulae instead of writing the names in full. Each of the elements is represented by one or two letters: for example, H = hydrogen, O = oxygen, Na = sodium, Cl = chlorine. A molecule of common salt consists of an atom of sodium joined to an atom of chlorine, so its symbol is NaCl. Similarly a hydrogen chloride (hydrochloric acid) molecule is HCl, but a molecule of water is H_2O because there are *two* hydrogen atoms joined to each atom of oxygen. Sodium hydroxide (caustic soda) contains three elements (sodium, hydrogen and oxygen), so its formula is NaOH. When hydrochloric acid is added to caustic soda a chemical reaction takes place. Although no change may be apparent, salt and water are produced. This can be put into words as: hydrogen chloride and sodium hydroxide produce sodium chloride and water. But it is both quicker and more informative to make use of the symbols:

$$HCl + NaOH \rightarrow NaCl + H_2O.$$

To explain how elements such as sodium and chlorine join up to form a compound we must bear in mind that atoms contain charged electrons. One of the electrons in a sodium atom is easily removed; in fact, the remainder of the atom (called the sodium ion) is more stable without it. But an atom which has lost a negative electron is no longer electrically neutral; it has acquired a positive charge. On the other hand the chlorine atom is more stable after it has gained an electron. This 'ion' of chlorine is negatively charged. When a sodium atom comes into contact with a chlorine atom, the sodium transfers its unwanted electron to the chlorine and the two charged ions are held together by the attraction which exists between unlike charges. Most metals form compounds in this way. It is called *ionic bonding.* Calcium has two unwanted electrons and therefore forms two bonds.

In some cases, however, there is no actual transfer of electrons. Instead the atoms *share* a pair (or pairs) of electrons, each atom donating one electron to the bond. This is called *covalent bonding,* and examples of it are shown in water, oxygen, carbon dioxide, and hydrogen chloride.

Where both the electrons are provided by the same atom the bond is known as a *co-ordinate* covalence. This type of bond is found in ammonium salts.

The *valency* of an element is its combining power, indicating the numbers of atoms of different elements which will combine together. To help in understanding valency, it can be thought of as the number of combining 'hooks' that an element has available for making chemical bonds.

For example, sodium (Na) and chlorine (Cl) have a valency of one; oxygen (O) and zinc (Zn) have a valency of two; and aluminium (Al) has a valency of three. It follows that the compound formed between sodium and chlorine – sodium chloride (or common salt) – consists of one atom of sodium linked to one atom of chlorine, and its formula is NaCl. However, zinc chloride is $ZnCl_2$ (one atom of zinc + two atoms of chlorine) since zinc has two combining arms, each of which can link to a chlorine atom. In the same way, aluminium chloride is $AlCl_3$, zinc oxide ZnO and aluminium oxide Al_2O_3.

Types of Chemical Reaction

There are a number of different types of chemical reaction. The *combination* reaction is the simplest. The reacting substances combine, adding together to form a new chemical compound, e.g. sulphur combines with oxygen to form sulphur dioxide:

$$S + O_2 \rightarrow SO_2$$

A *decomposition* reaction means the splitting of a compound by the action of heat, e.g. mercuric oxide decomposes to mercury and oxygen on heating:

$$2HgO \rightarrow 2Hg + O$$

In a *double decomposition* reaction, two metallic radicals exchange their radical partners, e.g. silver nitrate reacts with potassium chloride to form silver chloride and potassium nitrate:

$$KCl + AgNO_3 \rightarrow AgCl + KNO_3$$

A *replacement* reaction is one in which an atom (or group of atoms) takes the place of another atom (or group of atoms) in a compound. For instance, when the iron blade of a penknife is dipped into a solution of copper sulphate, the iron takes the place of the copper in the copper sulphate and the displaced copper is deposited on the blade of the knife as a red-brown layer:

$$Fe + CuSO_4 \rightarrow FeSO_4 + Cu$$

Oxidation is a reaction in which a substance gains oxygen. In burning, the oxygen is gained from the air, but in other oxidation reactions it is gained at the expense of another chemical compound known as an *oxidising agent.* The oxidising agent is itself *reduced,* i.e. it loses oxygen. For instance, red hot carbon reduces carbon dioxide to carbon monoxide. In doing so, the carbon gains oxygen and is oxidised to carbon dioxide:

$$CO_2 + C \rightarrow 2CO$$

Below: Molecules of elements.

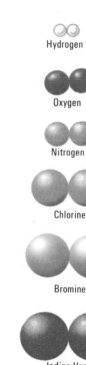

Hydrogen

Oxygen

Nitrogen

Chlorine

Bromine

Iodine Vapour

White Phosphorus
(just above boiling point)

Sulphur

Household Chemicals

Salt cellars and bottles of vinegar were common to most households long before anyone knew that their contents were chemical compounds. They were both used simply because they helped to preserve food and gave it a pleasant flavour. Neither was difficult to obtain.

Common salt occurs naturally and has only to be removed from the ground and purified. Although it is commonly known as salt, chemically speaking, there are many salts (compounds which are part metallic and part acid radical). This particular one is sodium chloride.

Vinegar is dilute acetic acid. It is not a corrosive one like sulphuric acid, but a dilute organic acid. There are no 'vinegar wells', but nevertheless it is not difficult to make. Just leave the cork out of a bottle of wine and some bacteria will do the job for you, oxidizing the ethyl alcohol in the wine to acetic acid. Vinegar is easily made from ethyl alcohol. There are many substances like this around the household – chemical substances which quite by accident have been found useful for certain purposes. If they worked, that was enough. One of these chemicals was Epsom salt. A spring at Epsom, Surrey, had so much of this salt dissolved it in that even the cows refused to drink there. No one knew what was wrong with the water, but its effect on humans was as a purgative. In 1695, Nehemiah Grew became the first person to extract crystals of the salt from water. The crystals were very much later found to be hydrated magnesium sulphate:

$$(MgSO_4.7H_2O)$$

Several sodium compounds are to be found around the house. Soap is one example.

Salt

Vinegar

Soap

Washing Soda

BAKING POWDER

Baking Soda

It usually is sodium stearate, made by boiling fat with sodium hydroxide. The glyceryl stearate (fat) is split up in the manufacture to form glycerine and soap (sodium stearate).

Another is washing soda, sodium carbonate crystals ($Na_2CO_3.10H_2O$). A handful of these glassy crystals in the washing water softens it, preventing a nasty scum from forming and sticking to the washing. The sodium ions from the soda change places with the metallic ions in the water responsible for its hardness. Bath salts have a similar water-softening action but they are less harsh. They consist chiefly of sodium sesquicarbonate ($Na_2CO_3.NaHCO_3.2H_2O$). This is a double salt, part carbonate, part bicarbonate.

Baking soda is entirely sodium bicarbonate ($NaHCO_3$). When this compound is heated, it decomposes, giving off the gas, carbon dioxide. Bubbles of carbon dioxide trapped in the cake, as it cooks, give it extra lightness. Because a small amount of powder gives off a large volume of gas, only a little bicarbonate of soda need be used to make the cake rise sufficiently.

As well as salts, both acids and alkalis find their places on household shelves. Sticks of sodium hydroxide and bottles of ammonia solution are useful in the kitchen. The alkali ammonia is used as a sink and pipe cleaner because it attacks particles of fat and converts them into a soap which itself helps to clean the dirty parts. A stick of sodium hydroxide is more drastic in its action of attacking grease to form soap. For this reason it is used for cleaning dirty ovens. After the grease has been converted to soap it is easier to wipe off. (The sodium hydroxide in the stick is usually mixed with soap.)

Again, with weed-killers, at one time, the salt sodium chlorate was in great favour. Now compounds such as salts of chlorophenoxyacetic acid are on the market.

Below: Common salt deposits in western Uganda

Above: Plastics can be moulded into intricate shapes, such as toy building bricks.

Plastics

Plastics, broadly speaking, are substances that can be moulded into shape when they are heated. Though the term 'plastics' is normally used in relation to man-made substances, there are a number of naturally-occurring plastic substances, such as amber, resin and rubber. Man-made plastics are of two kinds. Some are made from substances obtained from natural sources. Celluloid, for instance, is made from cellulose which occurs in plants. Others, such as polythene, are made entirely from chemicals.

Many plastics, after they have been moulded, can be softened again by heating. These are called *thermoplastics*. Some, however, remain rigid on reheating. These are called *thermosetting* plastics. A third type, used mainly in bonding materials, set chemically when two constituents are brought together, and form a new material.

The most useful raw materials for making synthetic plastics are petroleum (crude oil) and coal. They both yield a wide range of useful chemicals, although coal is a much less important source than it used to be. Manufacturers turn these relatively simple chemicals into the complicated ones known as plastics by means of a process called *polymerization*.

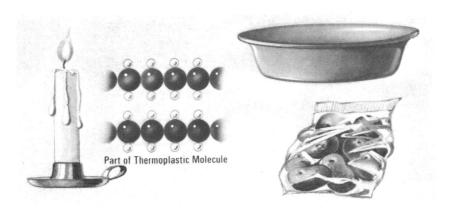

Above: Thermoplastics soften and melt when they are heated, rather like candle wax. They can easily be shaped when hot, and set rigid as they cool. Polyethylene is a thermoplastic. The molecules of thermoplastics consist of long separate chains of atoms, that bend easily. As a result, most thermoplastics are flexible materials, useful for making such products as bowls and bags.

Right: Producing a plastic cistern by injection moulding.

Below: Thermosetting plastics are soft or liquid when they are manufactured, and set hard when they are heated, rather like an egg does when it is hard boiled. They are shaped by heating, usually in hot moulds. The chains of molecules are linked together, and so do not bend. As a result, thermosetting plastics are hard and inflexible materials that withstand heat, useful for making cups and telephones.

Part of Thermoplastic Molecule

Shaping Plastics

There are a great many ways of shaping plastics. Solid objects can be turned out in huge numbers by *injection moulding*, where the softened plastic is forced under pressure into a mould, cooled rapidly, then ejected already finished. Rods, beading, and the fine filaments for yarns and fabrics are produced by *extrusion*, where molten plastic is forced through a hole. Sheets of material for rainwear or vehicle covers are *calendered* through rollers to the required thickness.

Very tough plastic 'board' can be made by sandwiching, or *laminating*, several layers of plastic material together. Awkwardly-shaped plastic objects can be joined by welding in much the same way as metal can.

Plastics have an enormous range of uses. They are used in clothing, furnishing fabrics and carpets. In engineering they are used for bearings that require little or no lubrication. Plastics are the basis of many modern paints and varnishes, and substitutes for glass where unbreakability is an important factor. Because plastic materials do not rust, rot, or react to most acids and alkalies, they are excellent for the packaging of foodstuffs.

Part of Thermosetting Plastic Molecule

Europe

The Continent

Europe is the smallest of the continents with the exception of Australia, but it is second only to Asia in population. One person in five lives in Europe. It is known as the birthplace of western civilization. Its art, political ideas, and scientific discoveries have spread all over the world. Among the 34 countries that make up Europe are the world's largest (Russia), and the smallest (Vatican City).

The continent of Europe forms the western peninsula of the great Europe/Asia land mass. Its eastern limits are the Ural Mountains, and its south-eastern boundary is the frontier between Russia and Turkey and Iran. A small part of Turkey, north-west of the Sea of Marmara, is in Europe. Everywhere else Europe is surrounded by sea. The continent has an area of 4,063,000 square

Above: An unruly cluster of houses surrounding a church or a castle is typical of many villages in western Europe.

Right: The Parthenon, a relic of the glory of Ancient Greece. Europe has a rich and varied cultural history.

Left: Tending sheep in southern Greece, a way of life that has remained unchanged for centuries.

Above: Much about Europe is picturesque. At the same time, the continent contains some of the greatest industrial concentrations in the world.

Right: Offering excellent opportunities to climbers and skiers, the Alps have become a major playground of Europe.

Left: The Eiffel Tower, Paris, one of Europe's most famous landmarks.

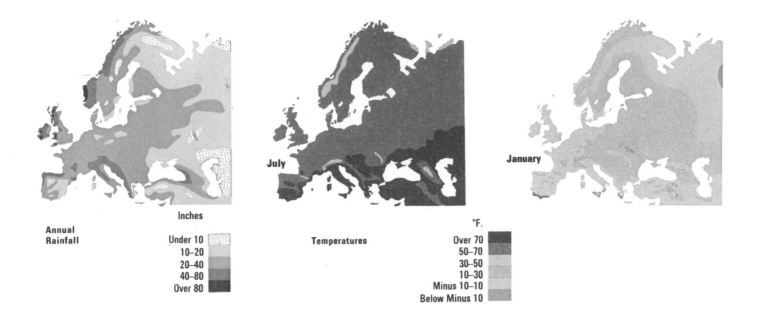

Annual Rainfall

Inches

Under 10
10–20
20–40
40–80
Over 80

July

January

Temperatures

°F.

Over 70
50–70
30–50
10–30
Minus 10–10
Below Minus 10

Above: Most of Europe has a moderate rainfall. North West Europe has rain at all seasons. The Mediterranean region has its chief rain in winter. The continental interior has more rain in summer than in winter.

Below: The Ponte Vecchio, with its tiny shops, crosses the River Arno in Florence. The city is rich in art and architectural treasures, the Uffizi Galleries and the Pitti Palace containing some of the world's most famous paintings and sculptures

Above: Though Europe displays a normal range of temperatures, the warm waters of the North Atlantic Drift give North West Europe very mild winters. Norway has an ice-free port (Narvik) north of the Arctic Circle.

miles. Its greatest length is 4,000 miles, and its greatest width 3,000 miles. It has a population of 621,000,000.

The Land

There are four main land regions. *The Alpine Mountain System* runs across southern Europe and includes the Caucasus, the Balkans, the Carpathians, the Apennines, the Alps, the Pyrenees and the Sierra Nevada. The highest peak is Mt Elbrus (18,481 ft) in southern Russia. *The Central Uplands* are densely forested, but they also contain some of Europe's most productive coalfields. The uplands run from Czechoslovakia, through southern Germany, central France, central Spain and Portugal. *The Central Plains* rarely rise more than 500 feet above sea level. They extend from the foothills of the Ural Mountains in Russia, through Poland, northern Germany, The Netherlands, Belgium, northern France and south-eastern England. Farming is the chief occupation of this broad, fertile area. *The North-West Highlands* are craggy and steep. The soil is too poor for large-scale farming. The highlands extend from northern Finland, through Sweden, Norway, northern and western Britain, Ireland and western France.

Europe is well served with rivers. Most of the main ones are used as major transport routes. The longest river in Europe is the

Above: Austrian traditional costume. The people of Europe are made up of a large number of different nationalities, each with its own way of life and traditions.

Below: Part of the Ruhr, the industrial heartland of Europe and one of the greatest concentrations of heavy industry in the world. During World War II, the Ruhr was devastated by Allied bombing, but it was rapidly reconstructed in the post-war years. The steel industry is based on extremely rich coal deposits.

Volga which flows through Russia for 2,290 miles before emptying into the Caspian Sea. Other important rivers are the Rhine, which flows through West Germany and The Netherlands into the North Sea; the Danube, which flows eastwards from West Germany through Austria, Hungary, Yugoslavia and Rumania to the Black Sea; the Seine, on which Paris stands; and the Thames.

Lakes are plentiful in Europe. Finland alone has some 60,000. The largest lake in the world, the salt-water Caspian Sea, lies between Asia and Europe.

Most of Europe has a mild climate. In winter, large areas of the continent are warmed by westerly winds blowing off the Atlantic Ocean. Warm ocean currents keep most of Norway's coasts ice-free all the year round, although a third of the country lies within the Arctic Circle. In the summer, the same westerly winds keep the continent cool.

Farther south, the Mediterranean countries have mild, wet winters and hot, dry summers. Eastern Europe has colder winters and short, hot summers. The average rainfall for Europe is between 20 and 40 inches a year.

Flora and Fauna

A large proportion of Europe's wild animals have been wiped out by the increasing human population and the spread of built-up areas.

Above: Europe does not produce enough food to feed its dense population and much has to be imported. The export of manufactured goods pays for these imports. As a result, the harbours of Europe are amongst the busiest in the world.

use advanced methods and are able to produce a very high yield of crops per acre. Important crops are barley, oats, beet sugar, beans, peas, and tobacco. Wheat is the chief grain crop. Dates, figs, grapes, and olives flourish in the Mediterranean countries.

Dairy farming is an important part of European agriculture. Denmark, Britain and The Netherlands specialize in the production of butter, cheese, and milk. Half the exports of Denmark, Greece, Spain and Ireland consist of foodstuffs.

Europe possesses enormous centres of mining and manufacturing. The greatest of these is the Ruhr Valley, in West Germany, where vast amounts of coke, chemicals, heavy machinery and iron and steel are produced. Switzerland specializes in the production of watches, and Belgium turns out quantities of fine lace. France's wines and perfumes are renowned throughout the world. The automobile industry accounts for a large proportion of the exports of West Germany, Britain, France, Italy and Sweden.

Three-fifths of the world's coal is mined in Europe. The richest coalfields lie in Britain, Russia, West Germany and Poland. The leading iron ore producers are Britain, France, Russia, West Germany and Sweden. Half of the world's iron ore is produced in Europe. *Bauxite* (aluminium ore) is mined in France, Greece, Hungary and Russia.

Survivors include wolves, bears, wild boars, beavers, elk, foxes, hares and rabbits. The *chamois* (a species of antelope) makes its home in the Alps. Reindeer live in large herds in the northern forests. In the colder regions a number of valuable fur-bearing animals such as lynx, marten and ermine still survive. Birds are numerous, and include eagles, falcons, storks and owls.

Although vast forests have been cut down to make way for cities and other man-made developments, there are still thickly forested areas in parts of Europe. Notable among these are Germany's Black Forest, and the plantations of olive and cork trees in the Mediterranean regions. Huge grassy plains are found in Russia (*steppes*), and in parts of Hungary, Rumania and Spain.

Farming and Industry
Most European farms are small but well run. Farm workers make up about a third of Europe's people. Western European farmers

Right: Population distribution map of Europe. Though Europe is the smallest continent with the exception of Australia, it is second only to Asia in population. One person in every five lives in Europe. The greatest concentrations of people are in the industrial areas of western Europe.

The People
The people of Europe are made up of a large number of different nationalities. They each have their own ways of life, languages, literatures, customs and traditions. Today, Europe is divided into two main political camps: Western Europe and Eastern or Communist Europe.

An *iron curtain* (rigid frontier barriers) divides the rival sections. There are 9 communist countries and 25 countries of Western Europe, and trade, communications, and travel between them is greatly hindered by this division.

During the present century, Europe has had to recover from two world wars, mainly fought on its soil, and a number of smaller battles. As part of the postwar recovery, 17 Western European nations founded the Organization for European Economic Co-operation (OEEC) in 1948. The European Economic Community was formed in the 1950's by France, West Germany, Belgium, Italy, Luxembourg and The Netherlands. The member countries, which now include Denmark, Britain and Ireland, share a parliament and a court of justice.

165

Reykjavik

ICELAND

Bergen

NORWAY

SWEDEN

FINLA

Oslo

Turku

Helsinki

Stockholm

Tallinn

Glasgow

Edinburgh

Göteborg

Riga

Belfast

Eire

Newcastle

Aarhus

DENMARK

Copenhagen

Kaunas

Dublin

U. K.

Kiel

Kaliningrad

Cork

Liverpool

Manchester

Hamburg

POLAND

Minsk

Birmingham

Amsterdam

Bremen

Berlin

Szczecin

Gdánsk

Cardiff

NETHERLANDS

Elbe

Poznan

Bristol

London

The Hague

GERMANY

Warsaw

Southampton

Rotterdam

Rhine

Essen

Leipzig

Dresden

Wroclaw

Lodz

Le Havre

Antwerp

BELG.

Cologne

Oder

Vistula

Brussels

Bonn

Rhiems

LUX.

Frankfurt

Prague

Katowice

Cracow

Lvov

Seine

Paris

CZECHOSLOVAKIA

Rennes

Nancy

Strasbourg

Nantes

Loire

Dijon

Basle

Zurich

Munich

Vienna

FRANCE

Garonne

Limoges

Geneva

Bern

Salzburg

Bratislava

Debrecen

Corunna

Bordeaux

Lyons

SWITZERLAND

AUSTRIA

Budapest

Gijón

Santander

Rhône

Milan

Graz

HUNGARY

Cluj

Vigo

San Sebastian

Turin

Po

Venice

Zagreb

Oporto

Bilbao

Padua

Trieste

RUMANIA

Valladolid

Ebro

Saragossa

Marseilles

Nice

Genoa

Belgrade

Madrid

Douro

Toulon

Leghorn

Florence

Bucharest

PORTUGAL

SPAIN

Barcelona

Sarajevo

YUGOSLAVIA

Danub

Guadiana

Valencia

ITALY

Córdoba

Rome

Sofia

BULGAR

Seville

Guadalquivir

Majorca

Belgrade

Skopje

Plovdi

Cadiz

Granada

Alicante

Naples

Bari

Tirana

Gibraltar

Malaga

Cartagena

Taranto

ALBANIA

Salonika

TU

Cagliara

GREECE

Palermo

Messina

Reggio di Calabria

Athens

100   200   300   400   500   600   700   800   900   1,000

Scale in Miles

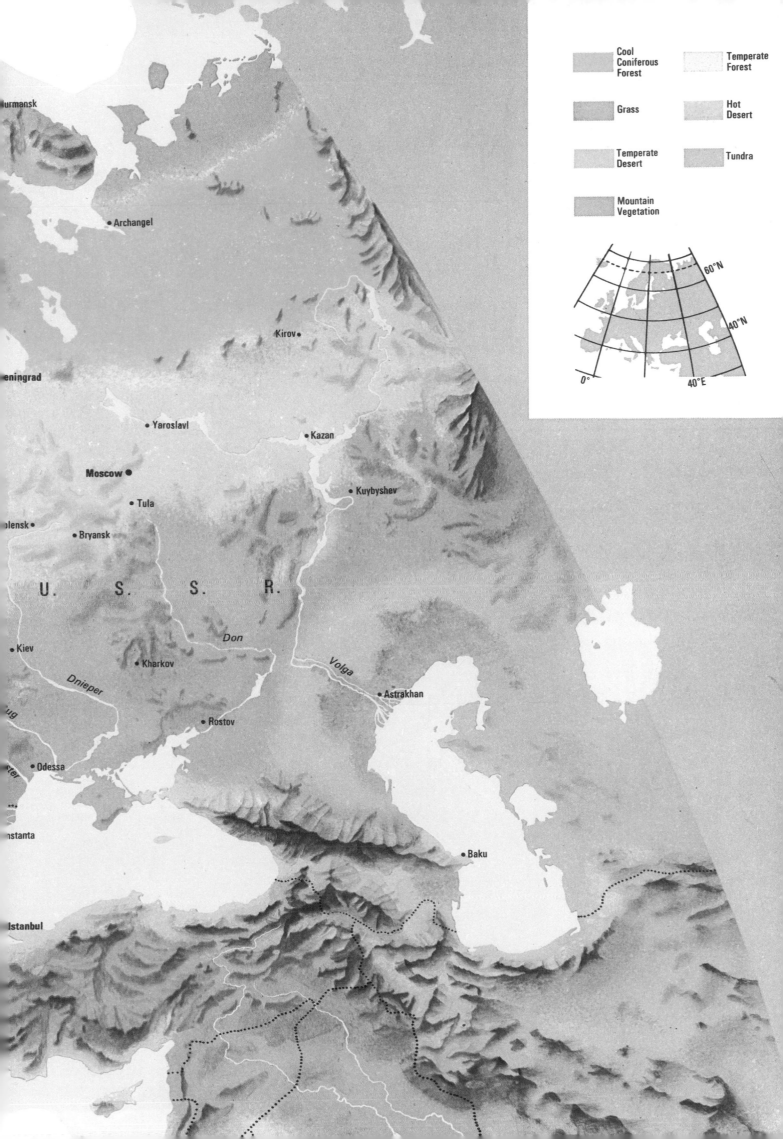

Cool
Coniferous
Forest

Temperate
Forest

Grass

Hot
Desert

Temperate
Desert

Tundra

Mountain
Vegetation

60°N

40°N

0°

40°E

Murmansk

Archangel

Kirov

Leningrad

Yaroslavl

Kazan

Moscow

Tula

Kuybyshev

Smolensk

Bryansk

U.   S.   S.   R.

Don

Kiev

Kharkov

Volga

Dnieper

Astrakhan

Bug

Rostov

Dniester

Odessa

Constanta

Baku

Istanbul

Inventions

Throughout the ages men's inventive minds have produced all kinds of things that have made life easier or improved it in some way. Often a need prompts an invention. On the other hand, an invention often creates a need. Kay's invention of the flying shuttle greatly increased the speed of weaving, which created a need for more yarn. As a result of this need, Hargreaves, Arkwright and Crompton all invented machines to spin yarn more quickly.

Sometimes it is difficult to credit one particular person with an invention. Two people may produce virtually the same invention at the same time. Or the invention may combine the work of many people. Early cars, for instance, were developed by putting together a great number of inventions. The following table lists some of the notable inventions of modern times.

Above: The famous *Rocket*. The invention of the steam locomotive was destined to revolutionize transport throughout the world during the last century.

Above: An early sewing machine.

Left: Spinning Jenny.

Above: A model of Bell's first telephone.

Date	Invention	Inventor
1450	Movable Type	Johannes Gutenberg (Ger.)
1550	Spinning Wheel	China?
1590	Compound Microscope	Zacharias Janssen (Dutch)
1593	Thermometer	Galileo Galilei (Ital.)
1608/9	Refracting Telescope	Hans Lippershey (Dutch) Galileo Galilei (Ital.)
1643	Barometer	Evangelista Torricelli (Ital.)
1670	Reflecting Telescope	Isaac Newton (Brit.)
1681	Pressure Cooker	Denis Papin (Fr.)
1698	Steam Pump	Thomas Savery (Brit.)
1712	Beam Engine	Thomas Newcomen (Brit.)
1733	Flying Shuttle	John Kay (Brit.)
1760	Lightning Conductor	Benjamin Franklin (U.S.)
1767	Spinning Jenny	James Hargreaves (Brit.)
1768	Spinning Frame	Richard Arkwright (Brit.)
1779	Spinning Mule	Samuel Crompton (Brit.)
1780s	Double-acting Steam-Engine/ Governor	James Watt (Brit.)
1783	Hot-air Balloon	Montgolfier Brothers (Fr.) Joseph Michel Jacques Etienne
1787?	Power Loom	Edmund Cartwright (Brit.)
1790s	Cotton Gin	Eli Whitney (U.S.)
1800?	Electric Battery	Alessandro Volta (Ital.)
1800	Lathe	Henry Maudsley (Brit.)

Date	Invention	Inventor
1804	Glider	George Cayley (Brit.)
1804	Canning	Francois Appert (Fr.)
1804	Steam Locomotive	Richard Trevithick (Brit.)
1807	Steamboat	Robert Fulton (U.S.)
1812	Mechanical Printing	Friedrich König (Ger.)
1815	Safety Lamp	Humphry Davy (Brit.)
1816	Stethoscope	René T. H. Laënec (Fr.)
1818	Tunnelling Shield	Marc Isambard Brunel (Brit.)
1827	Friction Match	John Walker (Brit.)
1830s	Photography	Joseph Nicephore Niépce (Fr.) Louis J. M. Daguerre (Fr.) William Fox Talbot (Brit.)
1836	Revolver	Samuel Colt (U.S.)
1836	Screw Propeller	John Ericsson (Swed.)
1837	Telegraph	William Cooke (Brit.)
1839	Steam Hammer	James Nasmyth (Brit.)
1839	Vulcanized Rubber	Charles Goodyear (U.S.)
1845	Sewing Machine	Elias Howe (U.S.)
1849	Safety Pin	Walter Hunt (U.S.)
1852	Safety Lift	Elisha Graves Otis (U.S.)
1865	Yale Lock	Linus Yale (U.S.)
1867	Dynamite	Alfred Nobel (Swed.)
1867	Typewriter	Christopher L. Sholes (U.S.) Carlos Glidden (U.S.) Samuel W. Soule (U.S.)
1868	Air Brake	George Westinghouse (U.S.)
1876	Four-Stroke Internal Combustion Engine	Nikolaus August Otto (Ger.)
1876	Telephone	Alexander Graham Bell (U.S.)
1877	Phonograph	Thomas Alva Edison (U.S.)
1878	Cathode Ray Tube	William Crookes (Brit.)
1878/9	Electric Lamp	Joseph Swan (Brit.) Thomas Alva Edison (U.S.)
1880s	Machine Gun	Hiram Stevens Maxim (U.S.)
1884	Steam Turbine	Charles Algernon Parsons (Brit.)
1885	Petrol Engine	Karl Benz (Ger.) Gottlieb Daimler (Ger.)
1888	Pneumatic Tyre	John Boyd Dunlop (Brit.)
1891	Roll Film	George Eastman (U.S.)
1893	Diesel Engine	Rudolf Diesel (Ger.)
1895	Radio	Guglielmo Marconi (Ital.)
1903	Powered Aircraft	Wilbur Wright (U.S.) Orville Wright (U.S.)
1904	Diode Radio Valve (Tube)	John Ambrose Fleming (Brit.)
1907	Triode Radio Valve (Tube)	Lee De Forest (U.S.)
1925	Quick Freezing of Food	Clarence Birdseye (U.S.)
1926	Liquid-Propelled Rocket	Robert Hutchings Goddard (U.S.)
1926-28	Television	John Logie Baird (Brit.) Vladimir Zworykin (U.S.)
1930	Cyclotron	Ernest Orlando Lawrence (U.S.)
1930	Nylon	W. H. Carothers (U.S.)
1935	Radar	Robert Watson-Watt (Brit.)
1936/9	Helicopter	Heinrich Focke (Ger.) Igor Sikorsky (U.S.)
1937	Jet Engine	Frank Whittle (Brit.)
1944	Digital Computer	Howard Aiken (U.S.)
1947	Polaroid Camera	Edwin H. Land (U.S.)
1948	Transistor	John Bardeen (U.S.) William Shockley (U.S.) Walter Brattain (U.S.)
1950s	Rotary Petrol Engine	Felix Wankel (Ger.)
1955	Hovercraft	Christopher Cockerell (Brit.)

Computers

In July 1969, an Apollo spacecraft carrying three American astronauts was hurtling past the Moon at a speed of 6,000 miles an hour. At precisely the right moment, the craft's retro-rocket fired to slow the spaceship down and drop it into orbit round the Moon. If the rocket engine had not fired at precisely the right time, the astronauts might have crashed on to the Moon, or they might have gone right past to be lost in outer space.

How did they know the exact moment to fire the rocket engine? A computer told them. Only a computer could do the necessary complex calculations quickly enough. In fact, practically every move on a space mission from launch to splash-down is controlled by computers.

A computer is really a very speedy, accurate calculating machine. In a way, the cash register which automatically adds up a shopper's bill in a supermarket is a simple sort of computer. But the name is now reserved for the complicated electronic 'brains' that are being used more and more in industry and commerce. Computers work out people's wages, electricity bills and airline bookings. They control machines in factories to produce articles automatically and efficiently. Computers can even set type for books and magazines, help doctors examine patients and diagnose disease, control traffic flow and produce weather forecasts.

In order to get information in and out of a computer, engineers use a special 'language'. Numbers are expressed in *binary code,* which uses only the figures 1 and 0. These figures can be represented by on-and-off pulses of electric current—an 'on' pulse corresponding to 1 and an 'off' pulse to 0. Because they use electric currents, computers work extremely fast. A calculation that would take a mathematician hours to do using pencil and paper can be completed in a fraction of a second by a computer. And the computer cannot make a mistake.

Digital and Analogue Computers

There are two main types of computers: *digital* computers and *analogue* computers. Digital computers deal in separate numbers, like the cash register or the abacus (bead frame) used in China and Japan. They are therefore used in accounting, banking and to do all sorts of high-speed mathematical calculations. The separate numbers are represented by streams of separate on-and-off electrical pulses.

Analogue computers, on the other hand, deal in continuously varying information which is represented by physical quantities the computers can handle. A simple example is the slide rule, in which a number is represented by a marked-off length of wood or plastic. In electronic analogue computers, quantities are represented by electric voltages which may vary continuously. They are used, for example, in *simulators* used for training pilots of aircraft or spacecraft. When the pilot moves the controls in the cockpit of the simulator, varying electric signals pass to the analogue computer which works out what would happen to a real craft.

Above: Replica of an adding machine designed by Pascal in 1652.

Below: A modern computer.

Below: The information fed into a modern computer may be stored in memory cores. It is translated into a series of electrical pulses which magnetize the cores. The cores are connected in memory units.

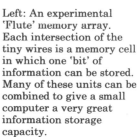

Left: An experimental 'Flute' memory array. Each intersection of the tiny wires is a memory cell in which one 'bit' of information can be stored. Many of these units can be combined to give a small computer a very great information storage capacity.

169

Amphibians

Amphibians are the class of animals that includes frogs, toads, newts, and salamanders. Amphibians first appeared on the Earth about 400 million years ago. They evolved from fishes that came out of the water and developed air-breathing lungs. Many amphibians are equally at home in fresh water and on land, but almost all amphibians breed in water. And if they live on land, it is usually near water.

Most amphibians lay eggs that float in water or are attached to stones or water plants. The way in which the *larvae* (the young amphibians) grow into adults is like the evolution process by which amphibians came into being. A frog larva or *tadpole* has gills with which it obtains oxygen from the water to breathe. It swims by using its tail, like a fish. But as the tadpole grows, it loses its fish-like character. Lungs and limbs

Right: The axolotl is an unusual amphibian which rarely grows into an adult salamander. It spends the whole of its life as a tadpole.

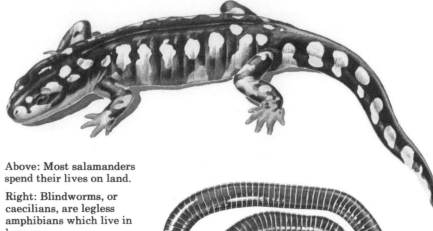

Above: Most salamanders spend their lives on land.

Right: Blindworms, or caecilians, are legless amphibians which live in burrows.

Most frogs and toads lay their jelly-covered eggs in fresh water. The eggs hatch into tadpoles with external gills. The tadpoles grow and lose their external gills. They grow first hind legs and then front legs. Finally they lose their tails and become adult frogs.

develop until it is able to leave the water and climb onto the land and breathe air.

Some amphibians, such as newts, spend most of their time in the water. Others, such as frogs and toads, are at home on land and in the water, and some, like the salamanders, live mainly on land.

Amphibians are cold-blooded animals and usually small in size, although the largest, the giant salamander of Japan, is six feet long. There are three main kinds of amphibians: tailed amphibians, tail-less amphibians, and caecilians.

Tailed amphibians include the newts and salamanders. Newts live mostly in water, whereas salamanders are found mainly on land. They have long tails and four short limbs, and are found all over the world except in polar regions.

Tail-less amphibians include frogs and toads. They have large and powerful hind limbs with which they propel themselves through water and jump about on land. They, too, are found in most regions of the world.

Caecilians are legless amphibians. They live in burrows in moist soil. Some lay eggs, but others produce live young. Caecilians are found in tropical regions around the world.

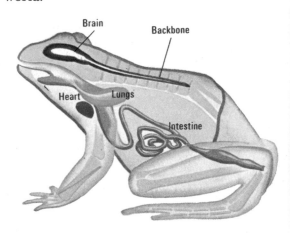

Above: The body plan of an amphibian. The skin of an amphibian is moist and not waterproof. Amphibians breathe through their skins as well as through their lungs.

Below: Fowler's toad, a North American amphibian. It uses its vocal sac to make a bleating croak.

Reptiles

Reptiles are the class of animals that includes lizards and snakes, crocodiles and alligators, and turtles. Reptiles evolved from amphibians about 250 million years ago. They differ from amphibians in that their skin is scaly and the young are born resembling their parents.

From the time of their appearance on the Earth to about 70 million years ago, reptiles dominated the land. Some, the *dinosaurs,* grew to a great size. Others, the *pterosaurs,* flew in the air. But these creatures died out suddenly. Today, reptiles live on land and in water, and some, such as the giant crocodiles and snakes, grow as large as 30 feet. The smallest reptiles are lizards about two inches long.

Reptiles are cold-blooded animals – their body temperature is the same as the temperature of their surroundings. For this

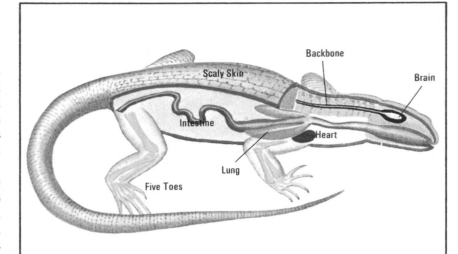

The body plan of a typical reptile. Reptiles are vertebrate animals. They have a backbone protecting the nerve cord and a skull protecting the brain. The skin of reptiles is scaly and waterproof. They breathe through their lungs. Most reptiles have four legs, but some lizards and all the snakes are legless forms.

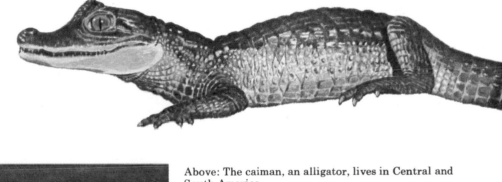

Below: The tuatara which lives on small islands off the coast of New Zealand is a 'living fossil'. It is the only living member of a group of reptiles related to the dinosaurs. The other members of this group died out millions of years ago.

Above: The caiman, an alligator, lives in Central and South America.

reason, reptiles are not found in polar regions, where they would become too cold to survive. In tropical regions, they can often be seen sunning themselves and then moving into the shade when they become too hot. In regions with a cold winter, reptiles hibernate. Most reptiles lay eggs, but a few bear living young.

Orders of Reptiles
There are four main groups or *orders* of living reptiles: the crocodiles and alligators; the turtles, tortoises, and terrapins; the lizards and snakes; and the tuatara.

Crocodiles and alligators make up the order *Crocodilia.* This order also includes the caimans and gavials. They are all large animals with cigar-shaped bodies and long, powerful tails. Their jaws are lined with rows of sharp teeth. They live in fresh water or salt water in tropical regions around the world, feeding on animals such as fish, birds, and small mammals.

Turtles, tortoises, and terrapins make up

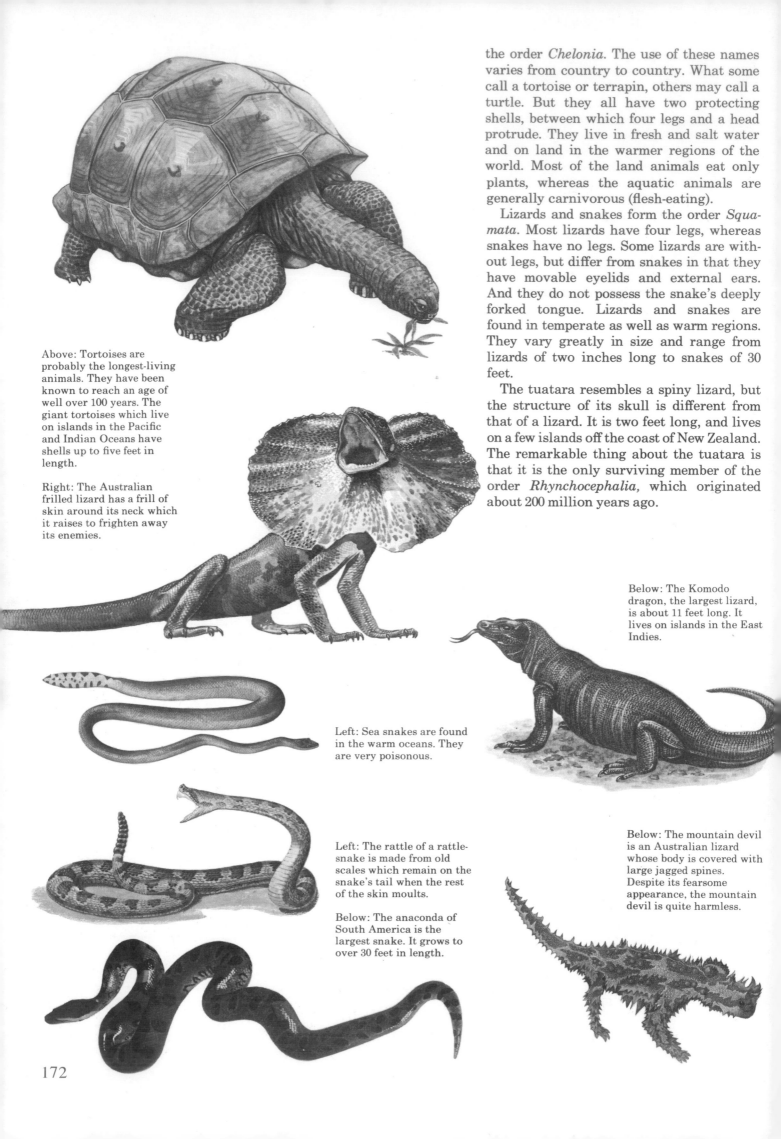

the order *Chelonia*. The use of these names varies from country to country. What some call a tortoise or terrapin, others may call a turtle. But they all have two protecting shells, between which four legs and a head protrude. They live in fresh and salt water and on land in the warmer regions of the world. Most of the land animals eat only plants, whereas the aquatic animals are generally carnivorous (flesh-eating).

Lizards and snakes form the order *Squamata*. Most lizards have four legs, whereas snakes have no legs. Some lizards are without legs, but differ from snakes in that they have movable eyelids and external ears. And they do not possess the snake's deeply forked tongue. Lizards and snakes are found in temperate as well as warm regions. They vary greatly in size and range from lizards of two inches long to snakes of 30 feet.

The tuatara resembles a spiny lizard, but the structure of its skull is different from that of a lizard. It is two feet long, and lives on a few islands off the coast of New Zealand. The remarkable thing about the tuatara is that it is the only surviving member of the order *Rhynchocephalia,* which originated about 200 million years ago.

Above: Tortoises are probably the longest-living animals. They have been known to reach an age of well over 100 years. The giant tortoises which live on islands in the Pacific and Indian Oceans have shells up to five feet in length.

Right: The Australian frilled lizard has a frill of skin around its neck which it raises to frighten away its enemies.

Below: The Komodo dragon, the largest lizard, is about 11 feet long. It lives on islands in the East Indies.

Left: Sea snakes are found in the warm oceans. They are very poisonous.

Left: The rattle of a rattlesnake is made from old scales which remain on the snake's tail when the rest of the skin moults.

Below: The anaconda of South America is the largest snake. It grows to over 30 feet in length.

Below: The mountain devil is an Australian lizard whose body is covered with large jagged spines. Despite its fearsome appearance, the mountain devil is quite harmless.

Radio and Television

Radio

Many people contributed to the development of radio – there is no one single inventor. The existence of radio waves was predicted by the British mathematician Clerk Maxwell in the middle of the 19th century. Hertz, a German scientist was the first man to generate radio waves – that was in 1888. The first 'wireless' message is claimed to have been sent across a laboratory by the Russian scientist Popov in 1896. Later that year the first experiments aimed at turning radio into a practical communication medium were carried out by Marconi in the garden of his father's villa in Italy. Several years later, Marconi astounded the scientific world by transmitting a message across the Atlantic from Cornwall to Newfoundland – a feat thought to be impossible.

Radio waves are generated by oscillatory electric currents. An important characteristic of them is their frequency which is the number of oscillations a second. Each station has its own particular frequency. A tuned circuit in the receiver selects the particular station we want. This circuit consists of a coil of wire and a component known as a *capacitor* which resonates at, and therefore gives preference to, one particular frequency. Varying the value of the capacitor alters the resonant frequency and therefore the station to which the receiver is tuned. The radio signal selected by the tuned circuit is very weak and must be amplified up to many times its original strength before it can operate a loudspeaker. Amplification is provided by transistors or radio valves (tubes). A receiver also has a valve (tube) or transistor that extracts the voice or music from the radio wave.

The heart of a radio transmitter is a valve (tube) or transistor that generates an oscillatory current of precisely controlled frequency. The vibrations of a piece of quartz are normally used to control the frequency. After being amplified several times, the current is fed to the antenna which converts it into a radio wave.

Before reaching the antenna, however, the speech, music or telegraph signals to be carried by the radio wave are impressed on it by a process known as *modulation*. In one technique, the amplitude of the radio wave is made to vary in step with the variations in the amplitude of the speech or music. This is known as *amplitude modulation* (AM). In an alternative technique, which gives better quality, the frequency of the radio wave

varies in step with the variations of the speech or music. This is called *frequency modulation* (FM). Telegraph signals can either switch the radio wave on and off or switch its frequency back and forth between two valves.

Transmission

Strange though it may seem, radio waves travel only in straight lines. Transatlantic transmissions are possible because the radio waves are bounced round the curvature of the Earth by the ionosphere. This is a layer of electrically charged (ionized) gases in the upper atmosphere. They are ionized by radiation from the Sun. Only radio waves which cannot carry TV are reflected in this way. Today, telecommunications satellites in orbit round the Earth are used to relay microwave signals carrying TV programmes around the world.

Microwaves are also used on the ground

Above: Marconi with equipment similar to that with which he first transmitted a message across the Atlantic in 1901.

Below: A microcircuit compared with the tip of a ball-point pen (highly magnified). Microcircuits have allowed the development of very small radio and television equipment.

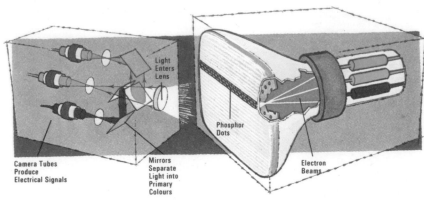

Above: In a colour television camera (left), electrical signals are produced by each of the three primary colours of light (red, green and blue). In the receiver these signals actuate electron beams that cause dots of phosphor in the screen to glow red, green or blue accordingly.

A three-valve radio receiver of 1922 compared with a modern nine-transistor model. Despite the complicated array of wires and components, the circuit of the early radio is much simpler than that of a modern model.

to carry the many thousands of telephone conversations and TV programmes between large cities. Dish-shaped antennas on towers beam the signals from hilltop to hilltop.

Television

Before moving pictures can be transmitted by a TV broadcasting station they must be converted into electrical signals. The early experimenters very quickly realized that there was no economic way of transmitting the whole of each picture in one go. To overcome this they hit on the idea of dividing each picture up into a number of small areas and transmitting the light value, or degree of brightness, of each of these areas one at a time. In the TV receiver, a beam of electrons strikes a coating of *phosphors* on the screen and the coating glows. The beam travels rapidly over the screen, so that each of the areas is reconstructed in its correct place and at the appropriate brightness, and the viewer sees the complete picture.

To convert the light value of each area into an electrical signal we make use of the *photo-electric effect*. Certain metals, including selenium, produce an electric potential when light falls on them. The picture is scanned electronically by a system that looks at a small area of the picture at a time. Scanning begins in the top left hand corner of the picture. In a simple system the light from the top left hand corner of the picture falls onto a cell containing selenium, which sends a current to the transmitter that is proportional to the brightness of that part of the picture. The scanning system then moves along the top of the picture until it reaches the right hand corner. It is then switched off and moves rapidly back to the

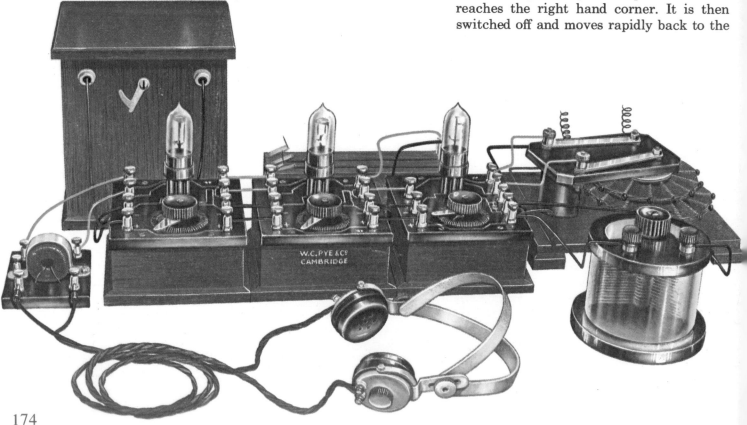

Above: A television production in progress at a modern studio. The camera and sound recording equipment can be seen in the foreground.

left hand side of the picture to a point just below its original starting point. It is then switched on again and moves along to the right hand side of the picture following a line just below the first one. The process is repeated until the bottom of the picture is reached.

In modern TV cameras the scene to be televised is focused by a lens onto an array of photo-electric elements. Scanning is carried out by a beam of electrons. In the United States the picture is divided up into 525 horizontal lines and 30 complete pictures are transmitted each second. In Europe the number of lines is 625 and there are 25 complete pictures a second. The United Kingdom is gradually changing over to the European standard from the earlier standard of 405 lines and 25 pictures.

There are three separate camera tubes in a colour TV camera. Special mirrors split up the light from the scene into its red, green and blue components, and direct each component into its tube. In the TV receiver the

signals that have come from each tube control three beams of electrons. One beam is adjusted to strike dots of phosphor on the face of the *cathode-ray tube* in the receiver that glows red. The second beam strikes dots that glow green; the third one strikes dots that glow blue.

Scanning is carried out in the same way as in black and white TV. There are over one million phosphor dots, and the viewer sees a full colour picture which if examined in detail under a microscope is seen to be made up of many small glowing red, blue and green dots.

There are not enough TV channels to allow each colour signal to be transmitted in its own channel. Instead, all three signals are transmitted in one channel using in the United States a highly sophisticated system known as N.T.S.C. Slightly different systems known as PAL and SECAM are used in Europe. All the systems produce a black and white picture on a black and white TV receiver.

Asia

The Continent
Asia is the largest of the continents and has more people than any other continent. It covers about 17,153,000 square miles – almost one-third of the land area of the world. Its greatest distance, east to west, is 6,000 miles, and north to south about 5,400 miles. Its population is about 1,887,500,000. This means that 57 out of every 100 people live in Asia.

Asia is a continent of extremes. It has the highest mountains and the lowest depths. Parts of the continent are colder than the North Pole but other areas are among the hottest places on Earth. More rain falls in parts of southern Asia than anywhere else in the world, but some Asian deserts are among the driest places on Earth.

Asia extends from the Ural Mountains in the west to the Pacific Ocean in the east:

The rivers of northern Asia empty into the Arctic Ocean. In spring, when their mouths are still blocked by ice, the rivers flood the land.

and from the Arctic Ocean in the north to the Indian Ocean in the south. Its south-western frontier with Europe runs along the shores of the Caspian Sea, Black Sea and Mediterranean. Asia is joined to Africa by the isthmus of Suez, which is cut in two by the Suez Canal. It is separated from North America by the Bering Strait in the north-east, only 45 miles wide at its narrowest part.

The Land
Asia can be conveniently divided into six major regions. Central or Inner Asia is a triangular mass of mountains and high, remote plateaus. It includes Tibet, Mongolia and parts of western China. Many ranges of mountains meet in the *Pamir Knot,* sometimes called the *Roof of the World.* The Himalaya range includes Mt Everest (29,028 ft), the world's highest peak.

Northern Asia includes the vast Russian lowlands of Siberia. The region stretches from the Ural Mountains in the west to the Pacific Ocean in the east. It is drained by a number of huge rivers. *Eastern Asia,* or the *Far East,* is a mountainous area that includes most of China, Japan, Korea and Formosa. This is where nearly half the Asian people live.

Southern Asia is the region that lies to the south of the Himalaya mountains. It includes the ancient plateaus of Afghanistan, Bhutan, India and Pakistan. *South-western Asia* is a dry region that includes Turkey, Iran and the Arabian Peninsula. *South-eastern Asia* includes the land south of China and east of India, and the Indonesian, Malaysian and Philippine islands.

There are some large bodies of inland water in Asia. The Caspian Sea, the world's largest inland sea, lies between Asia and Europe. The shore of the Dead Sea, partly in Israel and partly in Jordan, lies about 1,300 feet below sea level.

Among many huge rivers in Asia the Lena, Yenisei, and Ob are frozen for part of their courses during six months of each year. In the spring, when the rivers are full, and their mouths are still ice-bound, great floods occur. Other important rivers are the Jordan, that flows southwards from Lebanon to the Dead Sea; the Tigris and Euphrates, which drain Iraq; the Brahmaputra and the Ganges that empty into the Bay of Bengal through a common delta; and the Indus, which rises in western Tibet and flows into the Arabian Sea.

In China the chief rivers are the Hwang, the Si-Kiang, and the Yangtze. The plain of Manchuria is drained by the Amur and its tributary, the Sungari. The mountains in or near Tibet give rise to several major rivers,

Stretching from the Arctic to the Equator, Asia has many contrasting climates. The rainfall varies from over 450 inches per year in Assam to less than one inch in parts of the Gobi and Arabian deserts. Most of the rain in southern Asia falls during the summer months when 'monsoon' winds blow onto the land.

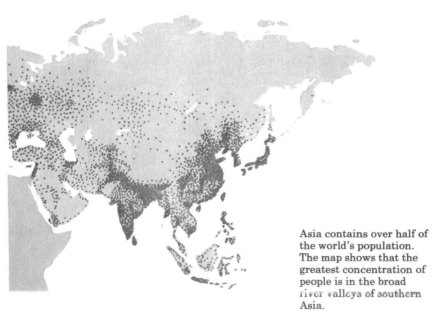

Below 10
10-20
20-40
40-80
Over 80

Inches

Asia contains over half of the world's population. The map shows that the greatest concentration of people is in the broad river valleys of southern Asia.

Above: Threshing the harvest by hand. In many parts of Asia, farming has remained unchanged for centuries.

Below: The scarcity of good farmland makes fish a vital part of the diet in many areas.

among them the Brahmaputra, Hwang, Indus, Mekong, Salween and Yangtze.

Deserts are plentiful throughout Asia. Most of the Arabian Peninsula is desert, and the Gobi desert occupies an enormous plateau in central Asia.

The far north of Asia has an arctic climate, and the southern regions are equatorial. The interior of the continent suffers great extremes of climate. Winters are bitterly cold but summers produce a fierce heat. These extremes cause great differences in pressure and wind systems and are the cause of the violent *monsoons* (seasonal winds) that bring heavy rain to all of south-east Asia from May to October.

Flora and Fauna
Asian wild animals include tigers, monkeys, rhinoceroses, bears, deer, mongooses, and many kinds of poisonous and non-poisonous snakes. Some wild animals, such as the

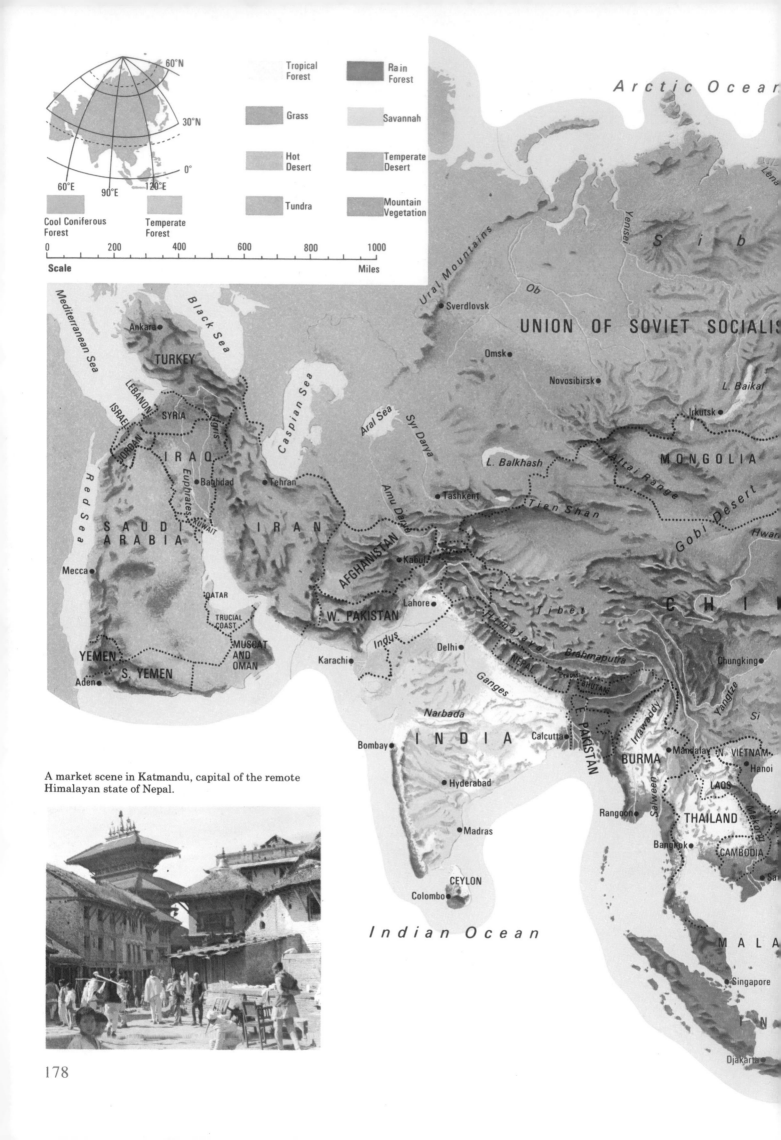

A market scene in Katmandu, capital of the remote Himalayan state of Nepal.

Above: Rice is the great cereal crop of Asia. It yields more food per acre than other cereals. The rice-fields, called paddies, must be flooded because rice grows in standing water.

Left: Independence Day celebrations in India. Since World War II many Asian nations have achieved independence.

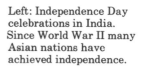

Left: Street scene in downtown Tokyo, the city claimed to have the largest population of any in the world. Below: In the hot, wet lands of southern Asia, people still build houses on stilts over rivers.

179

elephant and the water buffalo, have been tamed and trained to work in the forests and fields.

Vegetation varies with the climate. Northern Asia contains the world's largest fir and pine forest. Temperate grasslands and desert scrub cover some other parts of the continent.

Resources and Industry

Most people in Asia eat rice as their main food. Rice grows in the wet, tropical regions. In drier areas other cereals such as maize, wheat, millet and soya beans are grown. Timber is a valuable product. The tropical regions yield quantities of teak, pine wood comes from Siberia, and hardwoods from the forests of China. Other important agricultural products are tea, tobacco, rubber, dates, jute, cotton and olives.

Much Asian industry consists of handicrafts produced in small factories and workshops. The great exception is Japan. Japan leads the world in shipbuilding and is also a leading steel producer. Northern China, parts of India, and central Siberia also have modern, well-equipped factories that produce a wide range of goods. But most Asian nations export few manufactured goods because they are unable to meet the needs of their own people. Many exports are minerals. A quarter of the world's petroleum comes

Religion plays an important part in the daily lives of people over much of Asia. Top left: Every Burmese boy spends at least seven days in a Buddhist monastery during his early life. Bottom left: Hindus bathe in the Ganges, a river sacred to their faith.

Above: Cows are sacred to Hindus. They can often be seen wandering freely through the cities of India.

from south-eastern and south-western Asia. Turkey and the Philippines export chromite, and nearly two-thirds of the world's tin comes from south-eastern Asia.

The People

Most of the world's earliest civilizations and all the world's great religions began in Asia. More than 2,000 years ago powerful empires flourished in the continent. Their peoples reached a high development in the arts and sciences. They began to influence Europe, especially through contact with the ancient Greeks, from about 300 B.C. But because the various Asian peoples were separated from each other by vast deserts and lofty mountain ranges, they never became as closely knit as some of their western neighbours. They gradually developed different languages, customs and ways of life.

After World War II the political map of Asia was profoundly altered. Many nations once subject to colonial rule achieved their independence.

Right: The main range of the mighty Himalaya mountains towers above the terraced foothills in Nepal. The Himalaya sweep in a great arc 1,500 miles from the Pamir Knot in the west to the borders of China and Assam in the east.

Below: Asia was the birthplace of all of the world's great religions and consequently contains the shrines of many faiths. The grotto at Bethlehem, the birthplace of Christ, is a hallowed shrine of Christendom.

INDEPENDENT COUNTRIES OF ASIA

Country	Area (sq. mi.)	Capital
Afghanistan	253,861	Kabul
Bangladesh	55,000	Dacca
Burma	261,789	Rangoon
Cambodia	69,898	Phnom Penh
Ceylon	25,332	Colombo
China	3,691,502	Peking
Cyprus	3,572	Nicosia
Formosa (Taiwan) [Nationalist China]	13,885	Taipei
India	1,262,274	New Delhi
Indonesia	735,269	Djakarta
Iran (Persia)	636,294	Tehran
Iraq	173,260	Baghdad
Israel	7,992	Jerusalem
Japan	142,726	Tokyo
Jordan	34,750	Amman
Korea, North	46,540	Pyongyang
Korea, South	38,004	Seoul
Kuwait	6,000	Kuwait
Laos	91,429	Vientiane
Lebanon	4,015	Beirut
Malaysia	128,430	Kuala Lumpur
Maldive Islands	115	Male
Mongolia	592,665	Ulan Bator
Nepal	54,362	Katmandu
Pakistan	312,000	Islamabad
Philippines	115,707	Quezon City
Russia (Asiatic)	6,498,500	Moscow
Saudi Arabia	870,000	Riyadh
Singapore	224	Singapore
South Yemen	112,000	Aden
Syria	71,000	Damascus
Thailand (Siam)	198,456	Bangkok
Turkey (Asiatic)	292,260	Ankara
Vietnam, North	61,294	Hanoi
Vietnam, South	65,948	Saigon
Yemen	75,290	Sana

Right: In most parts of Asia articles are still handmade by individual craftsmen. Every village in India, for instance, has its own potter, carpenter, and so on. Japan is one of the main exceptions. It is the industrial giant of Asia and one of the world's leading manufacturing nations with factories as fully automated as any in the Western hemisphere.

181

Peoples of the World

Human beings living on our planet all belong to the same species. But varying geographical conditions and climates have resulted in the *evolution* (development by change) of different groups called races.

It is believed that all people originally came from one common ancestral type, but the various groups now have distinct and characteristic differences. However, we should not think of racial differences as being hard and fast, because the races often overlap, and there is no such thing as a pure race.

Nevertheless, some humans are tall, faired-skinned, and blue-eyed, often with light-coloured wavy hair; and others are very dark-skinned, or black, and have short woolly hair, and deep brown eyes. Some, again, are small and slimly built, with long straight black hair, and slanting almond-shaped eyes. Such variations are not in fact any more extreme and remarkable than those found between the draught-horse, the slim speedy race-horse, or even the small Shetland pony, which are all descended from the prehistoric horse.

These broad physical types of the human family hand down their characteristics to their children. But, because men move, either singly or in groups, from one part of the globe to another, and intermarry, most countries have a mixture of types.

In addition to differences in colours of the skin, eyes, and hair, there can be characteristic differences in the shape of the head and nose, and in the bulk and average height of people.

Caucasoid People: An Arab of Egypt (left), a woman of Bulgaria (centre), and a woman of India (right).

Races of Man

In Europe, most nations are a mixture of several races. The Nordic types are found mainly in the north and west, and as a rule these people have long narrow heads, fair colouring, and blue eyes, and are quite tall. The Alpine type is darker than the Nordic, having a rounder head, and is shorter on the whole, and often has brown eyes. This type is found chiefly in central Europe and in a broad belt of land stretching from western

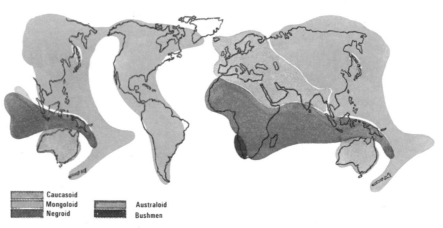

Caucasoid
Mongoloid
Negroid
Australoid
Bushmen

Peoples of the World

Above: A map of the world showing the distribution of various races before recent migration.

Mongoloid People: Two women of Japan (left), a man of Hong Kong (centre), and an Indian farmer of Peru (right).

France as far as Persia in the east. Around the Mediterranean, people are dark-haired, but inclined to be short, and slightly built.

Mongoloid races are found all across the continent of Asia, and have spread east, through migrations, to become the Eskimos and American Indians; south-east into the Pacific Islands; and west to become the Lapps of Europe. Their heads are round, covered in long straight hair, and their skins are yellow or brown. As a rule, they have short flat noses and slanting eyes.

In Africa south of the Sahara the people are of the Negroid type (short woolly hair, black skin and eyes). Farther south still, the Congo pygmies, Bushmen and Hottentots of southern Africa differ greatly and are thought to be of different races.

Both North and South America are believed to have been peopled originally by very early migrations from eastern Asia, where the Mongoloid race is dominant. The many tribes of American Indians are descended from these early migrants. The majority of white Americans are descendants of the European types who settled there.

The Australian aborigine is of the Australoid type, with dark skin, wavy hair, and overhanging eyebrows. Similar types are found in some Indian jungle tribes. New Zealand Maoris are Polynesians, mainly Mongoloid, but taller than average. This type is found all over the Pacific. Papuans and Melanesians, who live from New Guinea to Fiji, are Negroid types, though their noses are long and they have long mop-like hair.

Negroid People: A warrior and his wife of New Guinea (right), and an African Negro (below).

Population

The world population is at present reckoned to be over 2,600 millions. It is still rising rapidly, especially in Asia, and may well reach over 6,300 millions by the end of the present century. Advances in medical knowledge, improved sanitation, and superior technical developments all contributed to a rapid increase in the population in Europe in the 17th century. Between 1650 and 1900 it increased fourfold. But since the turn of the century the birthrate in Europe has steadily fallen, and the great increase, sometimes called the 'population explosion', has come about in the under-developed countries of Asia, Africa and Latin America.

Most of the world's population is concentrated on a fraction of the Earth's surface, in those parts where soil and climate make it comparatively easy to live. If people were spread evenly over the globe there would be about 50 people to every square mile. The world population is most densely massed in western Europe, the United States, the Nile Valley, India, Java, China and Japan.

Other People: Two aborigines of Australia (left), a group of Maoris of New Zealand (right), and a group of pygmies of Congo (below).

Textiles

As far back as 5000 B.C., the Egyptians and other ancient peoples were weaving fine linen and woollen cloth. In about 3000 B.C., the Chinese discovered how to weave beautiful cloth from the delicate threads spun by the silkworm. The Indians began making cotton cloth very soon afterwards.

Spinning and weaving were done by hand at home until the 1700's. Then, the invention of machines such as the spinning jenny, the spinning mule, and the power loom led to the development of textile-making as a large-scale industry. People left their homes to spin and weave in factories.

The discovery of synthetic dyes and artificial silk in the 1800's and synthetic fibres in the 1900's gave textile manufacturers a much wider range of materials to work with. Today, we can buy brightly coloured fabrics which do not crease or shrink, which dry quickly, and which do not need ironing. They may contain fibres made from glass, coal, oil, or even rock.

Natural Fibres

A wide variety of different fibres are used in making textiles. Most of them are natural fibres, which come from certain plants, animals, and even minerals, but some do not occur in nature at all. They are called *artificial,* or *man-made* fibres.

Cotton and flax are the most common plant fibres. Like all plant fibres, they are made up

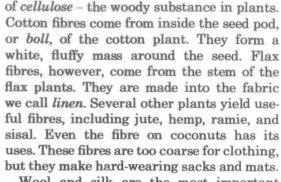

Below: Prior to spinning, loose *slivers* of combed fibres are fed to drawing frames where they are drawn out thinner and twisted. They emerge from the frames as *rovings* ready for spinning.

of *cellulose* – the woody substance in plants. Cotton fibres come from inside the seed pod, or *boll,* of the cotton plant. They form a white, fluffy mass around the seed. Flax fibres, however, come from the stem of the flax plants. They are made into the fabric we call *linen.* Several other plants yield useful fibres, including jute, hemp, ramie, and sisal. Even the fibre on coconuts has its uses. These fibres are too coarse for clothing, but they make hard-wearing sacks and mats.

Wool and silk are the most important animal fibres. All animal fibres are made up of complicated substances called proteins. Wool, as we all know, comes from sheep. It is a special kind of curly hair. The hair of goats, too, can be made into textiles. The finest, wool-like fibres come from Cashmere and Angora goats. They are softer and more lustrous than wool. Hair from the Angora goat is better known as mohair. The hairy coats of camels and the camel-like llamas and alpacas are also used to make cloth.

Fine threads of silk are spun by the silkworm when it makes a cocoon around itself. The threads from several cocoons go into the silk threads used for weaving. Silk is the only natural fibre that is produced in a long, continuous thread. The other natural fibres consist of short, or *staple* fibres.

The only minerals which occur naturally in fibre form are those known as asbestos.

Man-made Fibres

There are two main kinds of man-made fibres. Some, such as rayon, are made by processing a natural substance and then re-forming it. Others are made entirely from chemicals produced by man. They are called *synthetic* fibres. Nylon was the first and is still the most important one. Fibre-glass is a syn-

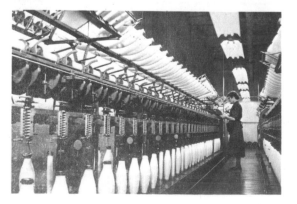

Left: On a weaving loom, alternate warp threads are raised or lowered and a *shuttle,* carrying the weft thread, shoots through the gap between them. A comb-like *reed* packs the weft threads tightly together. Then the process is repeated.

Left: In spinning, the roving is drawn into finer and finer yarn and wound on revolving bobbins.

Left: A mechanical harvester moves through the cotton fields. It sucks the bolls from the plants like a giant vacuum cleaner.

Left: Sorting silk cocoons.

Below: Filaments of viscose rayon are extruded through tiny holes in 'jets' submersed in an acid bath. The filaments are seen leaving the acid bath and being gathered into a *tow*.

thetic fibre made from glass.

Each kind of fibre has its own particular properties and advantages. For example, cotton is strong and hard-wearing. Wool is warm and resists creasing because it has natural elasticity. Silk is soft and lustrous. Linen is crisp and shiny. Synthetic fibres are very strong and absorb little water.

To make textiles from the fibres, we spin yarn and then interlace it in various ways.

Spinning

All the natural textile materials, except silk, are made up of fairly short, fine fibres. Cotton, for example, has fibres up to 2 inches long. Wool fibres are a little longer. Individual fibres are too short, too fine, and too weak to be woven into cloth. They must first be gathered together, drawn out into a long 'rope', and then twisted tightly together to make yarn. Making yarn from the raw fibres is called *spinning*.

Weaving

The method of weaving every kind of yarn, both natural and man-made, is basically the same. One set of threads is passed crosswise under and over a set of lengthwise threads. The crosswise threads are called the *weft*, and the lengthwise threads, the *warp*.

Weaving in this up-and-down way would be very slow. It is far easier to raise and lower different warp threads and pass the weft thread between them. This is what happens on the weaving machine, or *loom*. At the end of a weft line, the up-and-down warp threads are changed and the weft thread is again passed through to make another line. This process is continued until the cloth is finished.

Knitting and Twisting

Clothing such as vests, sweaters, and socks, which needs to be loose and comfortable, is made by *knitting*. In weaving, the fabric is made from two sets of yarns. One is threaded under and over the other to make the fabric. In knitting, however, only one yarn is used. The fabric is formed by making loops and 'hanging' one row of loops upon another.

Weaving and knitting are the two most important methods of making textiles, but there are several others. Lace and all kinds of netting, from net curtains to fishermen's nets, are made by twisting one set of yarns around another. Felt is made by pounding hot, wet fibres together.

Fabrics go through a variety of finishing processes to make them more attractive. They are bleached white, dyed, and treated so that they dry quickly and do not crease or shrink.

Ships and the Sea

Inscriptions show that by 3000 B.C., the Egyptians were travelling over the sea to Crete in slender, many oared ships with a single square sail to help if the wind was in the right direction. These ships were called galleys. The oarsmen were usually slaves.

Later, the Phoenicians, the Greeks and the Romans developed the galley into a powerful fighting ship. Their galleys had two, three, and sometimes more rows, or *banks*, of oars. The two-banked vessel was called a *bireme*, and the three-banked a *trireme*. The combination of oars and sail continued up until about A.D. 1000. One of the last fast fighting vessels of this kind was the Viking longship, with a single bank of oars. These remarkable ships voyaged to Iceland and the New World.

The Age of Sail
In about A.D. 1000, a new kind of sail appeared, called the *lateen* sail. It was triangular and enabled boats to sail close to the wind as well as with the wind. This led to the development of the classic full-rigged ships, around A.D. 1400. They had a mainmast and foremast with square sails and a mizzenmast at the rear with a lateen sail. The square sails were split into two – a mainsail and a topsail – for greater flexibility.

This arrangement was used in Christo-

Ancient Egyptian trading vessel.

Viking longship.

Medieval ship with lateen sails.

Early steamship.

pher Columbus's tiny ships, *Santa Maria, Pinta,* and *Nina,* in which he sailed to America in 1492, and in the larger, heavier, and armed galleons, such as Francis Drake's *Golden Hind.*

The famous ships of the seventeenth and eighteenth centuries, which became the standard warships of the period, had basically the same arrangement of masts. But the sails were usually split into three on each mast. The clipper ships of the 1800's, which were the last great sailing ships, had their sails split up into four, five, and even more sections. These long, graceful vessels were built with a very large sail area, purely for speed. They were used, for example, to carry tea from China and wool from Australia to Europe.

The Age of Steam
By the mid-1800's, steam-engined ships burning wood and coal were rapidly replacing sailing vessels. The days of sail were nearly over. At first, steamships were driven by paddle-wheels at the sides. Then the screw propeller was invented, and proved to be far superior. At the same time, iron was replacing wood as the main material for ship construction. The most spectacular iron ship built was I. K. Brunel's *Great Eastern,* which was 700 feet long, with room for 4,000 passengers. By 1890, iron was itself being replaced by steel, which is the main material used for shipbuilding today.

A wonderful new kind of engine propulsion came in 1894, when Charles Algernon Parsons installed one of his steam turbines

Top left: Robert Fulton's first steamboat, the *Clermont,* makes its historic voyage down the Hudson River from New York to Albany.

Bottom left: *The Savannah* was the first ship to use steam during an Atlantic crossing. Her voyage took 29 days.

Below: The last of the great sailing ships were the graceful clippers of the 1800's. One of the most famous was the *Cutty Sark.*

186

1   2   3   4   5

Above: Stages in ship-building: 1. First stage with plating complete; 2. Main watertight bulkheads erected; 3. Completing plating and bulkheads for F deck; 4. Deckhouse bulkheads in position on E deck; 5. B and C decks and the stern take shape.

in a launch, *Turbinia*. Within a few years, every fast ship was built with efficient steam turbines, including the famous liners, *Mauretania* and *Lusitania* (1907). The steam turbine remains unsurpassed for marine propulsion.

Since the First World War, oil has replaced coal as fuel for the furnaces of ships. Some of the latest ships have a nuclear reactor to raise steam for the turbines. The United States submarine *Nautilus* (1955) was the first nuclear-powered vessel. The first nuclear surface ship was the Russian icebreaker *Lenin* (1959).

Shipbuilding

Building a modern ship is a very complicated and expensive process, but it need not take a long time. Using modern materials and the latest methods of construction, ship-builders can complete a ship in a remarkably short time. Some shipyards, operating as-

sembly-line methods of construction, can build an 800-foot tanker in under four months.

The shipyard, which is often in a river estuary, covers a large area. It has drawing offices, assembly and workshops, and sloping concrete ramps reaching down to the water's edge. These are the *building berths* where the ships are actually constructed.

In the *drawing office,* the designer, or *naval architect,* works out a suitable design for a new ship. He prepares detailed drawings of the whole and of each part of the ship, and shows how all the parts fit together.

The prepared drawings go to the *mould loft,* where skilled men prepare patterns called *templates* for the steel plates which make up the ship. In the plate shop, powerful gas cutting torches follow the line of the patterns and cut the steel to shape.

Plates for the curved parts of the ship's

187

hull, especially the bow (front) and the stern (rear), have to be bent. This operation is carried out by massive hydraulic presses which bend the thick steel plates as though they were sheet tin. The properly shaped and curved plates are then welded into sections in the *assembly shop.*

In the past, the hull of a ship was made by riveting hundreds of steel plates together one by one. This method is still sometimes used. To make the joint, the plates have to overlap. The rivets are hot when they are hammered through holes in the overlapping plates. They shrink as they cool and squeeze the plates tightly together. Teams of riveters, using power hammers, can work at an incredibly fast rate.

Most ships today, however, are built by welding the plates together. The edges of the plates to be joined are fiercely heated by a gas or electric welding torch. As the edges soften, molten metal is added to the joint. A strong, continuous joint forms when the metal cools. A great deal of metal, and therefore weight, is saved by this method because no overlap is needed.

The hull is usually constructed by *prefabrication.* Whole sections of it are welded together, under cover, in an assembly shop, and the hull is built up section by section instead of plate by plate.

During construction, the ship is supported by heavy wooden blocks under the keel. Travelling cranes along each side of the berth swing the prefabricated sections into position. An army of goggled welders joins the sections together. Gradually the ship takes shape. The keel, the sides, the side-to-side bulkheads, and the deck plates are put together. The ship is enveloped in a network of scaffolding from which welders and painters work.

When the basic construction is finished, and the hull painted, the ship is ready for launching. A greased, wooden slipway is built beneath it to guide it into the water. It is usually launched stern first, but sometimes sideways if space is limited.

After launching, the vessel is towed to the *fitting-out yard* to be finished. There the engines, the boilers, and all the other machinery are installed, the superstructure is completed, and the cabins furnished and decorated. Within a few months, the ship is ready for its sea trials, and if these are successful it is ready for its first, or *maiden,* voyage.

The Compass
Sailors use several means of *navigating,* or finding their way across the featureless oceans. The most essential instrument for

navigation is the *compass,* which always points in the same direction. In the past, ships used a special kind of magnetic compass, called a *mariner's compass.* It was designed so that the ship's motion would affect it as little as possible.

Most modern ships, however, have a very accurate *gyrocompass,* which contains a rapidly spinning gyroscope wheel. It is completely unaffected by the movement of the ship. In some ships, this compass can be coupled with the steering gear to make steering automatic.

Navigation
There are basically four different methods navigators use to find their position at sea. They are generally used in combination so that each one serves as a check on the others.

Dead reckoning is really the basis of all navigation. The navigator finds the ship's position at any time by plotting on a chart the distance and direction the ship has travelled. He knows the direction from the ship's compass. He calculates the distance by means of the ship's *log,* which is a device for measuring the speed and the distance travelled.

Navigators frequently check their position by observing the position of the heavenly bodies in the sky – the sun during the day and the stars and planets during the night. This is called *celestial navigation.* The navigator observes the direction of, say, several stars and the angle they make with the horizon. The instrument he uses is called a *sextant.* By consulting a book of tables called the *Nautical Almanac* and a very accurate clock, or *chronometer,* he can find how far he is from the so-called earthly position of each star at any time. He draws *lines of position* based on each star 'fix', and the point where they intersect gives the ship's exact position.

Electronic methods of navigation are becoming increasingly important. Ships have *radio direction finders,* which 'fix' onto the signals from radio beacons on lighthouses, for example. By obtaining 'fixes' from two such beacons, the navigator can find his exact position.

Radar is another valuable navigational aid. This electronic device sends out radio waves. When they hit an object, they are reflected back as an echo. The echo shows up on a radar screen as a visible dash, or 'blip'. The distance and direction of the object can be calculated from the position of the blip on the screen. By showing the ship's position in relation to other ships in the area, radar reduces the danger of collisions in darkness or fog.

Nocturnal or Star Dial

Astrolabe

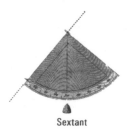

Sextant

Davis' Quadrant

Cross Staff

Some early navigation instruments.

Lighthouses and Lightships

Navigating a ship close to shore is difficult enough in the daylight. In the dark and in fog it can be very dangerous. Lighthouses are built at ports and harbours, on headlands, or on rocks some way from shore, to warn sailors that they are approaching land or dangerous water.

Lighthouses are tall, usually round towers with a steady or flashing light at the top. The light, of course, is not much use in the fog. For this reason, most lighthouses also have a foghorn and a radio beacon, which sends out radio signals.

Lighthouses are recognized by the kind of beams, or *signals*, they give out. The flashing lighthouse, which is the most common type, gives out a series of flashes, alternating with periods of darkness. Each lighthouse has its own characteristic 'pattern' of flashes, which makes it instantly recognizable to the ship's navigator.

The light in the lighthouse is provided by a lamp and a lens system, or *optic*, which concentrates the light into a strong beam. It is housed in a glass-and-steel lantern room. In most lighthouses, the light is made to flash by rotating the optic around the lamp. The lamp may be lit either by electricity or by acetylene gas.

It is not always practical to have a lighthouse where there are dangers to navigation so *lightships* are used instead. Lightships are anchored near sandbanks, wrecks and other obstructions. They are simply floating lighthouses, with flashing lights, foghorns, and radio beacons. They are very strongly built to survive the worst storms.

Above: The mariner's compass.

Left: Lightships are floating lighthouses anchored near sandbanks, wrecks and other obstructions.

Below: A traditional method of sending messages from ship to ship using signal flags is called semaphore.

The *echo-sounder,* or *fathomer,* which indicates what depth of water lies beneath the vessel, is essential for coastal navigation. This is a device in the keel of the vessel which transmits sound waves down into the water and receives back the echo as the waves are reflected from the sea bed. The time the echo takes to return is an indication of the depth of the water at that point.

When navigating close to shore, the navigator watches for landmarks, lighthouses and buoys. This method is often called *piloting.*

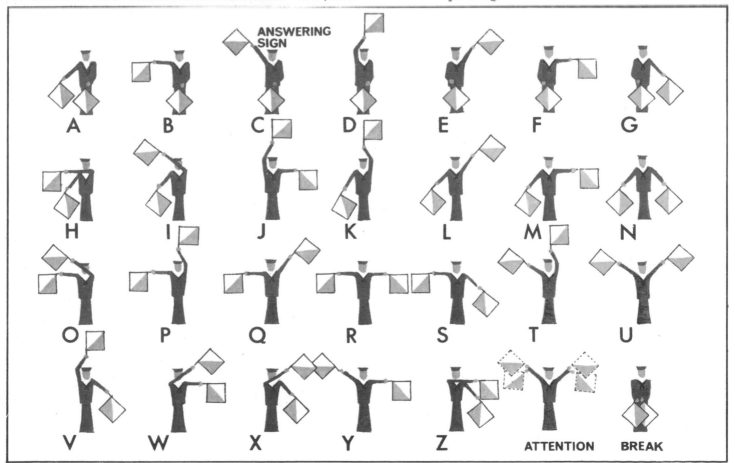

189

Above: Tankers which carry crude oil are the largest vessels afloat.

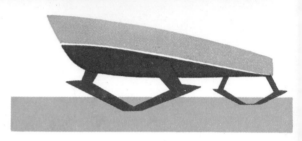

Above and right: Hydrofoils lift a boat clear of the water as it gathers speed, thus reducing the drag of the water.

Salvage

Despite the latest improvements in ship construction and navigation, disasters still happen at sea. A gale, a shifting cargo, a collision or a fire may bring a ship into a dangerous condition. When this happens, an SOS is sent out on the radio-telegraph and signal rockets are fired into the air. Ships in the vicinity of the distressed vessel rush to its aid, and if the accident occurs not far from the coast, the local lifeboats are called out.

Saving or recovering ships or their cargo is called *salvage*. If the crippled ship sinks in deep water, there is little that can be done. Recovery is only possible down to about 400 feet by deep-sea divers in cumbersome suits, or lighter clad skin divers if the water is shallower.

If the ship is not badly damaged, the salvage crew may try to refloat it. Divers first repair the damaged hull. Then they may try to pump air into it from the surface until it rises, or they may try to lift it with wires slung between two floating pontoons.

The most exciting salvage work, however, is concerned with the past rather than the present. Through the ages, many ships have sunk to the bottom of the sea, taking with them fabulous treasure. The Caribbean Sea, for example, is littered with the wrecks of Spanish galleons. A number have been found and precious jewellery and coins have been salvaged from some of them.

The Fastest Ships

Conventional ships expend a lot of power overcoming the drag, or resistance, of the water. The *hydrofoil* boat is designed to reduce this drag greatly, and it can travel much faster as a result.

The hydrofoil itself is a device like an aircraft wing which tends to 'lift' when it travels through the water, just as an aircraft wing tends to lift when it travels through the air. As the boat gathers speed, the hydrofoils near the bows and stern gradually lift it out of the water until the hull is clear.

Even faster than the hydrofoil boat is the hovercraft, a machine designed to skim smoothly over the surface of the water (or the ground) supported by a cushion of air. The air cushion is maintained by blowing air from inward-pointing jets beneath the body. The latest commercial hovercraft have maximum speeds approaching 100 m.p.h.

Below: The air-cushion on which a hovercraft rides is maintained by blowing air from inward-pointing jets beneath the body.

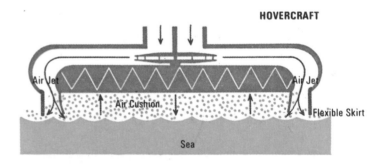

HOVERCRAFT

Air Jet — Air Cushion — Air Jet — Flexible Skirt — Sea

Above: Tugs are small, sturdy and highly manoeuvrable vessels.

Left: Fast motor boats are used as patrol vessels. One of their uses is to prevent smuggling.

Below: The world's largest liner, the *France*, leaving the world's busiest port, New York.

Ocean Liners

The most magnificent ships of all are the sleek ocean liners such as the *France, United States* and *Queen Elizabeth 2* which rival the most exclusive hotels in luxury. A passenger liner can be distinguished from other vessels by the extent of the superstructure rising above its hull. This may house five or more decks containing public rooms, cabins, sun decks and so on. In modern ships, the superstructure is made of aluminium to reduce top-weight and therefore make the vessel more stable. To increase the comfort of the passengers, most passenger liners are fitted with *stabilizers* to reduce the rolling motion of the ship in rough weather.

Huge ocean liners are seldom manoeuvrable enough to enter harbour by themselves. A number of small, sturdy tugs are used to pull and nudge the liners into position. In addition to these harbour tugs, there are the ocean-going and salvage tugs specially designed and equipped for towing crippled ships back to port.

The Oceans

Water covers nearly three-quarters of the Earth's surface. Large areas of water are called *oceans,* and they usually separate the continents. Smaller areas separating islands or enclosed by land on several sides are called *seas, gulfs* or *bays, channels,* or *straits.* The waters separating Britain from the mainland of Europe are called the English Channel and the North Sea. The Gulf of Mexico and the Caribbean Sea separate North and South America from the West Indies.

There are five oceans. The Pacific Ocean, between America and Asia, is the largest and deepest, covering a third of the world's surface. It extends one-third of the way around the world at the Equator. The Atlantic Ocean separates America from Europe and Africa. The Indian Ocean is bordered by Africa, Asia and Australia. The Arctic Ocean lies between the land masses around the North Pole, and is covered mostly by ice. The waters around the Antarctic continent are called the Antarctic Ocean, but they do not have bordering land masses like the other oceans.

Around most coasts there is a shelf of land extending out from the coast under the sea. This shelf, called a *continental shelf,* has a depth of up to 600 feet. It may extend for several hundred miles, and then the sea-floor falls steeply away to the ocean bottom or the *abyss.* The abyss is about 12,000 to 16,000 feet deep. It consists of great plains, called *abyssal plains,* crossed by ridges and mountains and by deep trenches. Islands occur where the undersea mountains, often volcanic, break the surface. The deepest known spot on earth is the bottom of the Mindanao Trench off the Philippine Islands in the Pacific Ocean. It is 37,782 feet deep, over seven miles.

Ocean currents are general movements of warm and cold water throughout the world's oceans. There are several great systems of ocean currents, affecting life in the sea and the climates of bordering lands.

Tides

Tides are the regular rise and fall that occur in sea-level twice a day. Tides are caused by the forces of gravity exerted on the Earth by the Sun and Moon. These bodies tend to pull the water in the oceans up towards themselves. As the Earth rotates, the rise in level moves around the world, following the Moon. Another rise in level, opposite to that beneath the Moon. This rise balances the first rise. When these rises in level meet the shore, a *high* tide occurs. Midway between the two, the level falls to *low* tide.

The Sun also has an effect on the tides, but this effect is much smaller than the Moon's, because the Sun is so far away.

Spring Tide (High)

Neap Tide (Low)

Above: Tides are caused by the pull of the Moon and, to a lesser extent, by the pull of the Sun. The highest tides occur when the Sun and Moon are both pulling in the same direction. The smallest tides occur when they are pulling at right angles.

Below: Map of ocean currents.

Birds

It is impossible to mistake a bird for any other kind of animal because birds are the only animals that have feathers. Scientists believe that birds have descended from reptiles and that the feathers have developed from scales. There is strong evidence for this belief in the scales that still remain on birds' legs. In spite of their reptile ancestors, birds are warm-blooded, like human beings. They keep their bodies at a fixed high temperature whether the air is hot or cold. The feathers help to keep them warm in cold weather.

A bird's wings are specially constructed front legs, and they bear the long, sturdy feathers which are necessary for flight. Not all birds fly, however, and their wings may be poorly developed or, as in penguins, used for a completely different job: penguins use their stumpy wings for swimming.

Unlike most back-boned animals, modern birds have no teeth. They rely on their beaks for catching and cutting their food, and their beaks vary according to the type of food they eat. Birds' feet also vary according to the sorts of places in which they live – ducks' feet are webbed, for example. One can tell a great deal about the life of a bird by just looking at its beak and feet.

Because of their great mobility, birds can live almost anywhere on earth. Nevertheless, birds as a whole are mainly tree-dwelling animals because this is where they first came into being and where, in the absence of competitors, they established themselves. Many groups have taken to living wholly or partly on the ground, and others live on and around the water. The majority of birds, however, live in trees.

Adaptations for Flight

The skeleton of a bird is well built for flight. The bones are small and thin, and therefore light, although they are strong. The long bones are hollow and are often given extra strength by criss-crossed 'struts' inside. More than half of a bird's weight is muscle, and the largest muscles are those that move the wings. These are very powerful muscles and must have good anchorage. This an-

The wing of a bird is a modified forelimb. Here it is compared with a human arm.

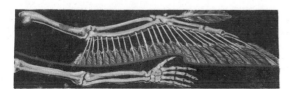

Right: Breathing in birds. The position of the ribs and breastbone of a bird during inspiration (left) and expiration (right) are shown by the dotted line. The respiratory movements are produced by the rib and abdominal muscles which alternately enlarge and reduce the body cavity.

Below: The sequence of wing movement of a bird in flight.

chorage is provided by the breast-bone which has a large, thin *keel* projecting from the underside, just like the keel of a yacht. The muscles are attached to this keel. Flightless birds have only a small keel, and some of them have no keel at all.

Food and Digestion

Most birds are very active animals, and they use up a lot of energy. In order to get this energy they have to spend a great deal of time eating. Many birds, especially the seed-eaters, have a stretchable bag near the beginning of their food canal. This bag is called the *crop,* and quite a lot of food can be swallowed and stored there. This is particularly useful for birds like pheasants and pigeons that have many enemies and have to get as much food as they can when their enemies are not around. The food collected in the crop can be digested later. Seed-eating birds and some others also have a very muscular region in the food canal which is called the *gizzard.* Seeds are ground up here, often with the aid of grit swallowed by the bird, before passing further down the canal for digestion.

As well as plenty of food, birds need a good oxygen supply to meet their energy needs. Their lungs are specially built. When men breathe in and out, a lot of stale air remains in their lungs. Birds, however, have air sacs beyond their lungs. When they breathe in, the air rushes *through* the lungs and into the air sacs. When the birds breathe out again, the air rushes back through the lungs. There is always fresh air in the lungs and they have a large supply of oxygen. The sacs also help to buoy the bird up.

Birds also have a good blood system, with a four-chambered heart giving an efficient circulation very similar to man's.

The Life of a Bird

All birds reproduce by laying eggs, and they usually lay their eggs in spring or early summer. Egg-laying time is called the breeding season. The birds start by choosing their mates. Male birds often have bright colours and frequently use attractive call songs which attract mates and may also frighten other males from the chosen territory. There is a good deal of courtship and display by one or both birds, and this eventually leads to nest-building and mating. Nests are mainly places to lay eggs and rear young: they are not permanent homes. Some birds do not even bother to make a proper nest. They use a hollow in the ground or a rocky ledge.

Some birds lay as many as 20 eggs, but half a dozen is more usual. Many birds of prey lay only one or two eggs. After laying, the eggs have to be kept warm or *incubated,* and the birds do this by sitting on their eggs. Sometimes only one parent will sit on the eggs, sometimes both parents take it in turns. The sitting bird is fed by its partner. The eggs generally hatch in two to three weeks, although some kinds of birds need longer.

Many ground-nesting and water-nesting birds already have feathers when they hatch and they can leave the nest right away, although they still have to be looked after by their mother. Ducks and chickens are examples. Tree-living birds, however, are generally very poorly developed when they hatch, completely naked and blind and quite unable to move about. Young chicks are always very hungry, and their parents bring them a constant supply of food. Nestling birds grow and develop very rapidly as a result of the endless feeding and are ready for their first flying lesson after a few weeks. The mother encourages her offspring to fly by flying a short distance herself and then calling to the young ones. When once the young have mastered the art, the family breaks up and leaves the nest.

Some birds pair for life and may return year after year to the same nest. More often, a new nest is made each year. The length of a bird's life varies. Ravens have been kept for 70 years and parrots for more than 60, but they probably have much shorter lives in the wild.

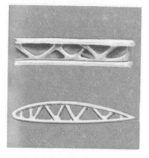

Above: The skeleton of a bird is well built for flight. The long bones are hollow and often have criss-crossed 'struts' inside. This structure, like that of a girder, saves weight without losing strength.

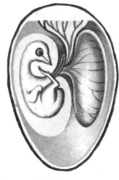

Above: A bird's egg has a rich supply of yolk for the developing embryo. The developing egg must be kept warm and this is performed by one or both parents who incubate them while sitting on the nest. Special bare patches of skin – the brood patches – are well supplied with blood and are applied closely to the eggs.

Left: A young stork in a typical resting posture.

Brown Pelican
Length : 50 Inches

Wandering Albatross
Length- 48 Inches

Willow Warbler
Length : 4½ Inches

Great Tit

Varied Tit

Blue Tit

Lengths : All about 5 Inches

Golden Eagle
Length : 32 Inches

Black Cap
Length : 5½ Inches

Black-Naped Oriole
Length : 9 Inches

Peregrine Falcon
Length : 15 Inches

Tailorbird
Length : 5 Inches

Osprey, or Fish Hawk
Length : 23 Inches

Chough
Length 15 Inches

Scarlet Macaw

Fantail Pigeon

African Grey Parrot
Length : 13 Inches

Scarlet Ibis
Length : 24 Inches

The Dodo, an Extinct
Member of the
Pigeon Family
Length :40 Inches

Crowned Crane
Length : 38 Inches

Sarus Crane
Length :60 Inches

Canada Goose
Length : 36–40 Inches

Roseate Spoonbill
Length : 30 Inches

Adelie Penguins

Common Dipper
Length : 7 Inches

Heron
Length :36 Inches

Moorhen
Length : 13 Inches

195

South America

South America is the fourth largest continent, covering 14 per cent of the Earth's land area. It is almost twice the size of the United States, but is sparsely populated.

South America is joined to Central and North America by the Isthmus of Panama, and lies almost entirely to the east of them. It has an area of 6,870,000 square miles, and a population of 168,200,000.

The Land
The land can be divided into three main regions running north and south: in the west, the Andes, running parallel to the Pacific coastline; in the centre, the great central plains, stretching from the Orinoco Basin to Patagonia; and in the east, the eastern highlands.

The Andes rise to more than 20,000 feet in places, and stretch from Panama to Tierra del Fuego in the south. Many important rivers, including the Amazon, start in the foothills of the Andes. The plains in the centre of the continent go by various names, according to their latitude. In the north, on the borders of the Guianas and Brazil, they form the Llanos. The Brazilian jungles are called *selvas*. Farther south, the *Gran Chaco*, comprising hundreds of thousands of square miles of grasslands, swamps and lakes, stretches across parts of Bolivia, Paraguay, and Argentina. From the Gran Chaco to Patagonia in the far south are the *pampas*, the farming and grazing lands from which Argentina gets most of its wealth.

The eastern highlands are much lower than the Andes. They consist of the Guiana

Above: Simon Bolivar liberated north-western South America from the Spaniards.

Above: Spreading coffee beans to dry in the sun. South America produces two-thirds of the world's coffee.

Below: Brasilia, the futuristic capital of Brazil, was built in a wilderness.

Highlands, the Brazilian Highlands and the Patagonian Plateau.

South America's river system is dominated in the north by the immense Amazon basin. In the north-west, the rivers Magdalena and Cauca join in the north of Colombia and empty into the Caribbean Sea. The Orinoco, fed by more than 400 tributaries, flows through the middle of Venezuela into the Atlantic Ocean. The eastern Brazilian Highlands are drained by the 1,800-mile-long São Francisco that also flows into the Atlantic. The most important waterway system in South America is the Río de la Plata. This is a broad estuary formed by the rivers Paraná, Paraguay, and Uruguay. It serves Argentina, Brazil, Bolivia, Paraguay and Uruguay.

Climate
Most of South America lies within the tropics, and its climate is generally warm and sunny throughout the year. Seasonal extremes of temperature are not as great as they are in parts of Asia and North America. In the Brazilian jungles, on the Equator, it is always hot and humid. High in the Andes the snow never melts. In the south, summers (December to March) are cool, and winters (June to September) are mild. The heaviest rainfall (more than 60 inches a year) occurs in the Amazon valley, the coasts of the Guianas, Colombia and Ecuador, and in south-western Chile. But strips of northern Chile and Peru, and Patagonia get practically no rainfall, and are virtually deserts. The icy Peru Current of the Pacific Ocean swirls along the coasts of Chile and Peru and keeps them cool.

Flora and Fauna
Although about a quarter of all the world's known animals live in South America, there are no large herds of game such as are found in North America and Africa. Most of the animals are found in the rain forests of the Amazon Basin. There are no very large animals to rival the elephant and giraffe. The largest animal in South America is the tapir, which is about the size of a small pony. The anaconda is one of the world's largest snakes, and the piranha probably the most ferocious fish. Sloths, armadillos and giant anteaters are all unique to the continent. Birds are particularly abundant and colourful, ranging in size from gem-like hummingbirds the size of a bumble-bee, to the giant condor, with its 10-foot wing span.

Some 2,500 kinds of trees flourish in South America's rain forests, and the list of orchids is almost endless. Some of the most valuable woods are *quebracho* the hardest timber in the world; *cinchona,* whose bark yields the

Pre-Columbian statue from Colombia of a masked divinity.

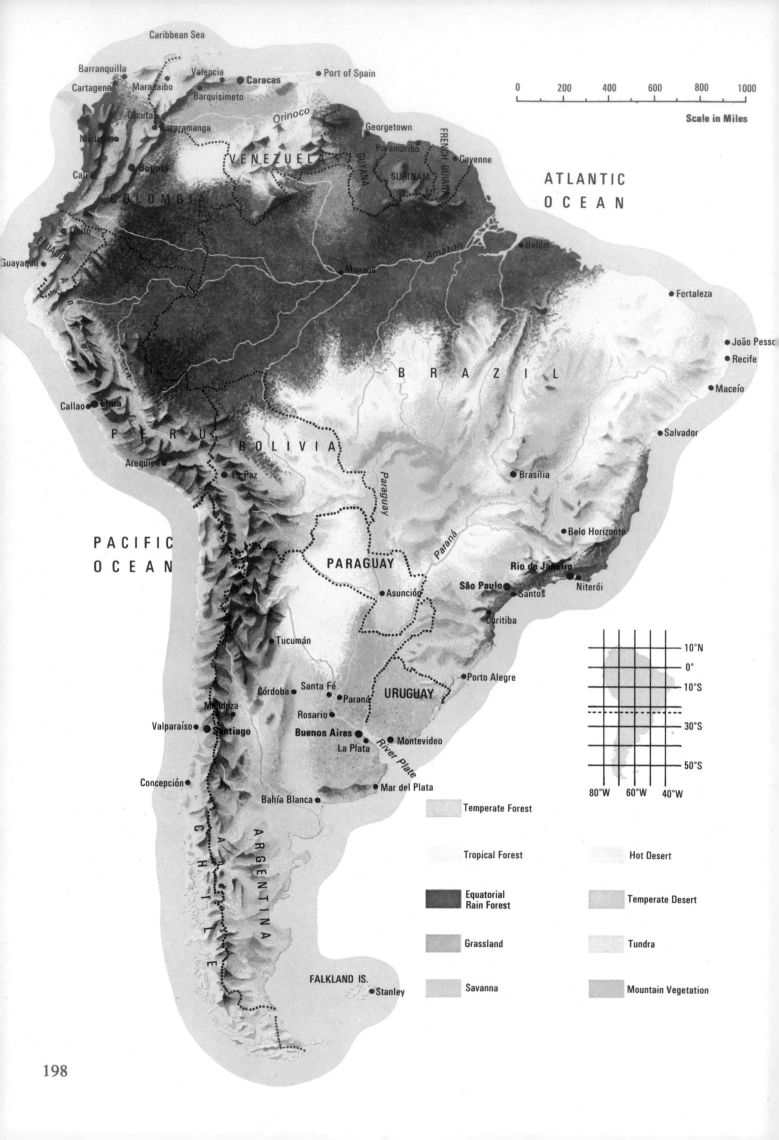

Caribbean Sea

Barranquilla
Cartagena
Maracaibo
Valencia
Cúcuta
Bucaramanga
Medellín
Cali
Bogotá

Barquisimeto
Caracas
Port of Spain

Georgetown
Paramaribo
Cayenne

VENEZUELA
Orinoco

COLOMBIA

GUIANA
SURINAM
FRENCH GUIANA

ATLANTIC
OCEAN

EQUADOR
Quito
Guayaquil

Manaus
Amazon
Belém

Fortaleza

João Pesso
Recife

BRAZIL

Maceío

Callao Lima

PERU

Salvador

Arequipa
BOLIVIA
La Paz

Brasília

Paraguay

Belo Horizonte

PACIFIC
OCEAN

Paraná

PARAGUAY

Rio de Janeiro
São Paulo Santos
Niterói

Asunción
Coritiba

Tucumán

10°N
0°
10°S

Córdoba
Santa Fé
Paraná

URUGUAY

Porto Alegre

30°S

Mendoza
Rosario

Valparaíso Santiago

Buenos Aires
La Plata

Montevideo
River Plate

50°S

Concepción

Bahía Blanca
Mar del Plata

80°W 60°W 40°W

CHILE
ANDES
ARGENTINA

Temperate Forest

Tropical Forest

Hot Desert

Equatorial
Rain Forest

Temperate Desert

Grassland

Tundra

FALKLAND IS.
Stanley

Savanna

Mountain Vegetation

0 200 400 600 800 1000
Scale in Miles

quinine used in fighting malaria; and *balsa,* one of the lightest woods in the world.

People and Products

There are 11 independent countries in South America. The largest is Brazil, the smallest is Guyana. In addition, Surinam (an overseas territory of the Netherlands) and French Guiana (an overseas department of France) occupy the north-east coast of the continent. The people of all these countries speak Spanish except for those of Brazil (Portuguese), Guyana (English), French Guiana (French), and Surinam (Dutch).

More than half the people of South America are farmers, but there is still an enormous amount of land that is unused or used wastefully. In some countries there are millions of people living in poverty, while a comparatively small number of wealthy families live in luxury. But many South American governments are beginning to break up the large estates and trying to share their countries' wealth more fairly.

Above: Population distribution map of South America. The heart of the continent is the sparsely populated Amazonian Basin.

Although manufacturing is growing rapidly, many manufactured articles have still to be imported. Exports are mainly agricultural: coffee, beef, cotton, sugar, cereals, bananas and wool.

History

South America is part of a larger cultural region called *Latin America.* This includes nearly all of Central America, Mexico, some Caribbean islands, and the whole of South America, with the exception of Surinam and French Guiana.

Latin America was originally discovered and explored by Spanish and Portuguese explorers in the 1500's. In the early 1800's most countries, inspired by the Venezuelan general, Simón Bolívar, fought for and achieved their freedom from colonial rule. The following 100 years were years of revolution and bloodshed. Today, the continent is outwardly peaceful, but a number of countries lie uneasily under military dictatorships.

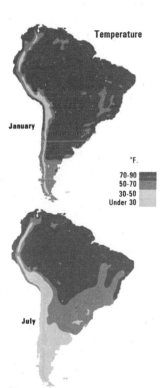

Temperature

January

°F.
70-90
50-70
30-50
Under 30

July

Annual Rainfall

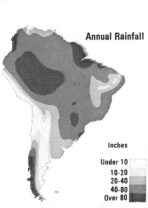

Inches
Under 10
10-20
20-40
40-80
Over 80

Right: The ruins of Machu Picchu, a fortress city of the ancient Incas.

Left: The face of a Bolivian boy reflects his Mongoloid ancestry. The original inhabitants of South America migrated from Asia.

Below: The sturdy but irritable llama is used as a pack animal in the Andes.

Weather and Climate

An Ocean of Air

The atmosphere is a transparent envelope of gas, hundreds of miles thick, surrounding the Earth and held to it by the force of gravity (the Earth's attraction). It is really a collection of gases, with nitrogen making up about 78% and oxygen about 21%. Minute quantities of a number of other gases, particularly argon, carbon dioxide, hydrogen, neon and helium, account for the remaining 1%.

It is impossible to exaggerate the importance of the atmosphere in our lives. Without it, life just would not exist. Not only would there be a complete absence of oxygen, the gas vital to life, but the direct rays of the sun would sear the Earth during the day, while at night temperatures would fall far below freezing point. The atmosphere acts as a shield during the day to protect the Earth from most of the sun's rays and as a blanket at night to hold the heat in.

Below: The world wind belts caused by heated air rising at the equator and cooler air moving in to take its place. The hot air moves towards the poles but sinks to the ground at about latitude 30°, only to rise again over colder air spreading out from the polar regions at about latitude 60°.

The Weight of Air

Because the air does not appear to press down on us, it seems impossible that it could weigh anything. But it certainly does. The total weight of the atmosphere reaches the staggering figure of 6,000,000,000,000,000 tons. With all this weight pressing down (because everything is drawn towards the Earth by the force of gravity) it is clear that the air nearest the Earth's surface must be tightly packed under great pressure (dense) and that at higher levels pressure will be less and the air only loosely packed (rarefied). Pressure does indeed fall off with height, and, moreover, very rapidly. The air pressure at sea-level is almost 15 pounds per square inch, but at 18,000 feet (a height exceeded by many mountain peaks) it is only half that figure, and at a height of 30 miles only one-thousandth the pressure at sea-level.

Atmospheric Layers

The atmosphere can be divided into three main 'layers': the troposphere, the stratosphere and the ionosphere. The troposphere, the lowest layer, is the region of weather.

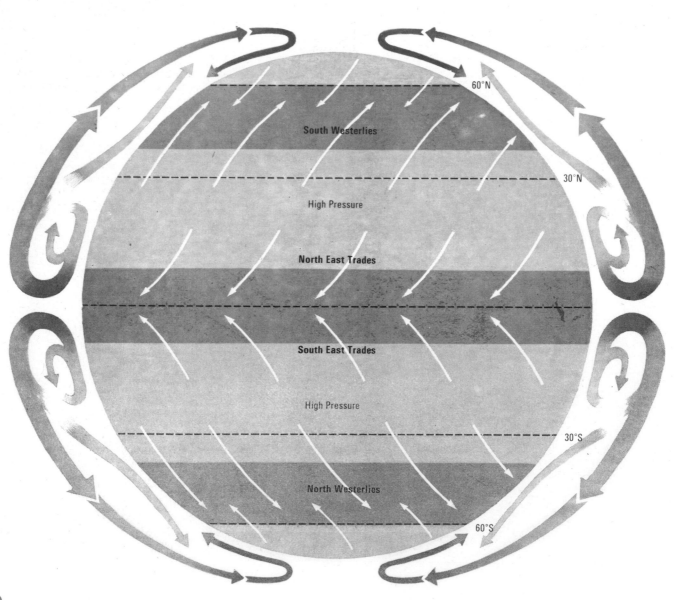

60°N

South Westerlies

30°N

High Pressure

North East Trades

South East Trades

High Pressure

30°S

North Westerlies

60°S

This is where the air is packed tightest, in fact 90% of the atmosphere's total mass is contained within its narrow boundaries. On the average, temperatures decrease everywhere in the troposphere with height at the rate of 3·5°F. for every thousand feet (6°C. per thousand metres).

Above the troposphere lies the second layer of the atmosphere – the stratosphere. Icy winds sweep its lowest levels but the air above is perfectly calm and 'weather' ceases to exist.

Above the stratosphere lies the ionosphere, the rarefied outer layer of the Earth's atmosphere. The ionosphere is important in radio communications. It reflects long and medium radio waves back to the ground. In this way, radio messages can be transmitted round the curve of the Earth.

Weather in the Making

Different parts of the world receive different amounts of heat from the sun. Generally speaking, the amount of heat received from the sun depends upon latitude, and temperatures decrease away from the equator. In high latitudes, a similar amount of the sun's rays is spread over a greater surface area than in low latitudes (owing to the curve of the Earth), and the rays have to travel through a greater thickness of atmosphere before reaching the ground.

This unequal heating of the Earth's surface causes movements of air – the winds. Warm air at the equator moves towards the poles, and cold air at the poles moves towards the equator. In addition, the Earth's rotation deflects the winds (to the right in the northern hemisphere, to the left in the southern hemisphere). But this regular wind pattern is complicated because the Earth's surface is made up of both land and water. Land heats up more quickly than water, but also loses its heat more quickly. This sets up pressure differences in the air over various parts of the world. The Earth's motion round the Sun, causing the seasons, further complicates matters.

As a result of all these influences, masses of air 'wander' about the Earth's surface. It is these wandering air masses that are responsible for changes in weather: they meet up with each other, they rise and fall, they are warmed and cooled, and, most important of all, they carry rain.

Clouds and Rain

By a process called *evaporation,* water on the Earth's surface turns into a gas – water vapour – and is held in the air. The amount of water vapour a body of air can hold depends upon its temperature. The warmer

Right: Rain is caused by the rising and cooling of moist air. Convectional rain results when heated air, rising of its own accord, expands and cools.

Right: Orographic or relief rain is caused by air being forced to rise to colder levels by high land lying in its path.

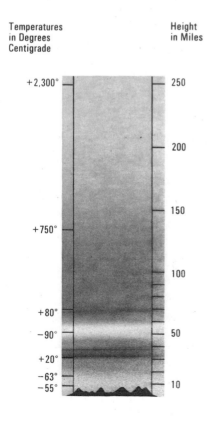

Right: Cyclonic rain is caused by a mass of warm air riding up over a 'mountain' of cold air or being lifted by a 'wedge' of cold air.

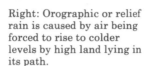

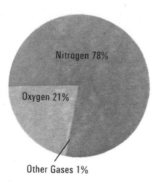

Above: The composition of air.

Right: Temperatures in the atmosphere. The rise in temperature at a height of about 16-35 miles is caused by a layer of ozone which absorbs ultra-violet radiation emitted by the sun.

Nitrogen 78%

Oxygen 21%

Other Gases 1%

Temperatures in Degrees Centigrade

Height in Miles

+2,300°   250

200

+750°   150

100

+80°
−90°   50

+20°
−63°
−55°   10

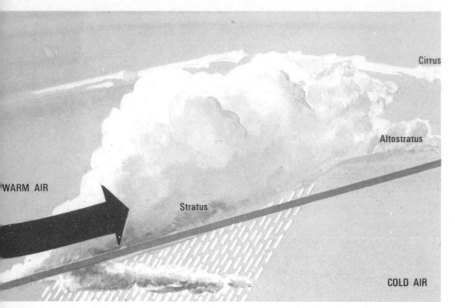

Cross-section of warm front. Warm air, overtaking cooler air, rises gradually over it. The front is the surface of separation between the two.

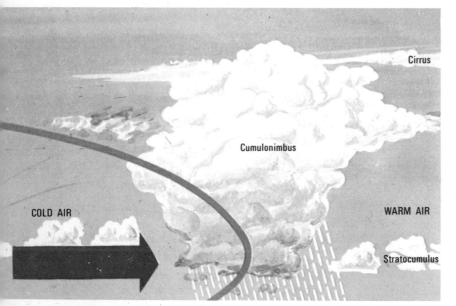

Cross-section of a cold front. Cold air, overtaking warmer air, burrows underneath to form a wedge.

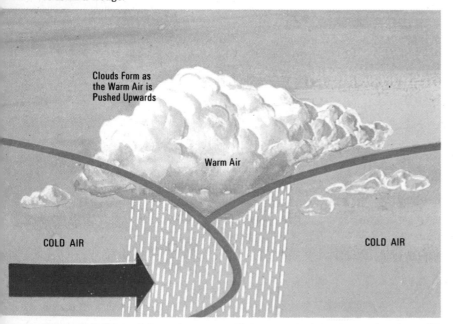

An occluded front is formed when a cold front catches up with a warm front. The warm air in between is pushed up away from the ground.

the air the more moisture it can hold in the form of vapour.

When a body of air is cooled, there comes a point, known as the *dew point,* below which it is unable to hold all of its moisture in the form of vapour. The excess water vapour then *condenses* on the small particles of dust and pollen that are always to be found floating in the air to form water droplets, or, if the dew point temperature is low enough, ice crystals. Condensation in the atmosphere produces cloud, or, at low levels, fog.

Rain results from the rising and cooling of moist air. When air rises it expands (because pressure is lower at higher levels of the atmosphere) and cools. Moisture in the air condenses into water droplets or ice crystals to form clouds.

But the cloud particles are a long way from being raindrops, which are about a million times larger. The cloud particles get bigger as they collide with each other or as more moisture condenses on them. Then, when they reach a certain size, they tend to fall towards the ground under their own weight. But they will reach the ground only if they are heavy enough to overcome the resistance of the upward air currents from the surface of the Earth.

Thunderstorms

All thunderstorms form in similar conditions – where large pockets of moist air rise through cooler air. They usually develop in summer, when a mass of warm humid air lies above the heated ground. The heated air rises, at the same time expanding and cooling. For the formation of a thundercloud, the surrounding air must be cooler than the rising column.

As the rising air cools, its vapour condenses into millions of tiny droplets to form at first a white, fluffy cloud and eventually a black, menacing thundercloud. The water droplets turn to ice crystals, which grow until they are big enough to fall. As they fall, they melt into raindrops. Only the largest raindrops are heavy enough to force their way through the violent upflow of air travelling at speeds of 20 to 60 m.p.h.

The thunder and lightning produced in a thunderstorm are caused by electrical discharges between clouds or between a cloud and the ground. You can estimate how far away a thunderstorm is by counting the seconds between the flash and the thunder – every 5 seconds represents a mile.

Thunderstorms are most common in the tropics and over land with a mild summer climate. A typical thunderstorm is from 3 to 5 miles across, but clusters of thunderstorms called *squall lines* may stretch for several hundred miles.

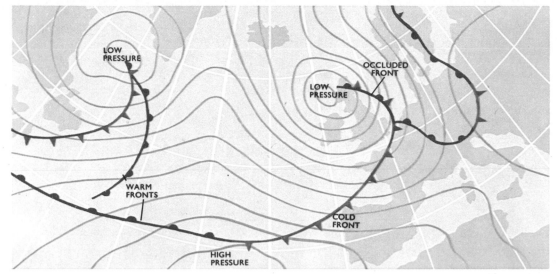

Left: Cold, warm and occluded fronts are invariably present on weather maps in temperate latitudes.

Hurricanes

A hurricane is a violent, whirling storm in which winds blow spirally inwards towards a centre of low pressure. Hurricanes form over the sea within 20 degrees of the equator. The heat of the tropical sun evaporates large amounts of water from the sea to form a deep layer of warm, moist air. Some meteorologists believe that a depression forms in the upper air (above 10,000 feet), breaking the barrier separating the moist air below from the dry air above. This allows the surface air to rise rapidly to great heights like a pillar from the sea. As the air rises, it cools, and the water vapour it contains condenses to form thousands of tons of rain. In this way the hurricane is 'fed' because during this process the moisture gives up the heat that caused it to evaporate from the sea. Enormous quantities of heat are fed back to the air, making the upflow even greater.

In the northern hemisphere, because of the spin of the Earth, the winds blow in an anti-clockwise direction around the centre of the hurricane. Wind speeds range from 75 miles an hour to almost 200 miles an hour. Hurricanes may be 300 miles across and may travel at about 20 miles an hour. They cause tremendous damage, and leave a wide trail of destruction behind them.

At the heart of the storm lies a region of calm air, about 15 to 30 miles across. This is called the *eye* of the hurricane. It is ringed by howling winds and towering clouds.

Right: A depression is born when a wave develops in the polar front (1). Cold air wraps around the back and two clearly defined fronts develop (2). The cold air begins to overtake and burrow under the warm air (3). The warm sector is gradually lifted off the ground until the depression is occluded (4).

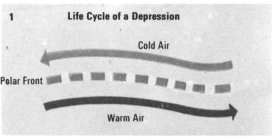

1 Life Cycle of a Depression

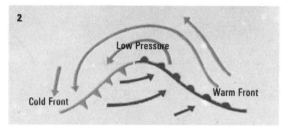

2

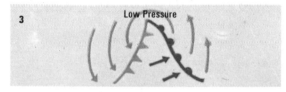

3

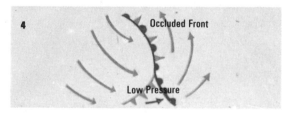

4

Depressions

Depressions occur when cold air masses from the polar regions meet warm air masses from the tropics. In the northern hemisphere, the cold masses from the polar regions tend to move in a westerly direction, and warm masses from the equator in an easterly direction. When two such opposing air masses meet, there is a great deal of turbulence. Warm air and cold air have different densities and do not mix easily. Cold air may curl round the back of the warm mass, and a depression is created — perhaps several hundred miles from end to end. The cold air is moving faster than the warm air, and eventually forces it upwards. The two wedges of cold air come together, and all that is left is a slowly revolving mass of cold air. The depression, at this stage, is said to be *occluded*.

One of the most important functions of weather forecasting is the prediction of the formation of depressions and of their movements. Conditions alter greatly week by week and very many factors have to be taken into account.

Left: Electrical charges in a thundercloud are caused by friction between colliding water droplets, ice crystals and gas molecules. The top of a cloud usually becomes positively charged and the bottom negatively charged. The electricity is discharged as a flash of lightning.

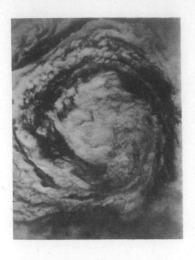

Right: Looking down on the central eye of a hurricane. It is ringed by boiling clouds and lashing rain.

Above: For its size, a tornado is the most destructive of storms. Winds rush at 300 miles per hour in a tight spiral around a partial vacuum. The twisted black funnel is rarely more than 200 yards across.

The few hurricanes which actually cross the coast have a devastating effect but usually die down fairly rapidly over the land, partly through friction with the ground and partly through a lack of 'fuel' i.e. enormous quantities of moisture-laden air. In the Pacific these violent storms are called typhoons.

Changeable weather

Men have studied the weather for thousands of years, looking for indications of good weather or of rain in the cloud formations, the colour of the sky, and the direction of the wind, and so on. And they have made up sayings about the weather, such as: 'Red sky at night, shepherd's delight; red sky in the morning, shepherd's warning.' In many parts of the world, the weather is predictable up to a point – the icy polar wastes, the deserts, the tropical rain forests. But in the so-called *temperate zones*, between the polar regions and the tropics, weather conditions may change greatly from day to day. Hot and cold air masses meet, forming regions of low-pressure spiralling winds called *depressions*, stretching for hundreds of miles. These bring long periods of unsettled weather, which is difficult to predict with any degree of certainty.

Weather Forecasts

Men who study weather and produce forecasts are called *meteorologists*. They make measurements of temperature, pressure, precipitation, cloud formation, wind force and direction, and *humidity* (the amount of water vapour in the air). They attach complex instruments called *radio-sondes* to balloons to obtain information about the upper air. And they draw up weather charts from all the information received from weather stations on land, at sea, and in the air, and make their predictions with the help of computers.

Climate

The climate of a region is its general pattern of weather over a long period of time. It is the average of many small variations. No matter what part of the world we live in, our way of life is affected by the climate. It influences how we dress, what we eat, and the type of houses we live in.

Some parts of the world have hotter climates than others. Temperatures usually decrease away from the equator. But temperatures are affected by altitude (temperatures decrease with height), by ocean currents (which may increase or lower the temperature of coastal lands), and by distance from the sea (areas far inland tend to have warmer summers and colder winters than coastal lands).

Rainfall is a major feature of climate. The wettest regions are generally those reached by winds which have blown for long distances across the sea. Hilly regions tend to receive more rain than lowlands, particularly on the windward slopes.

CLOUD TYPES

There are two distinct forms of cloud – *cumuliform* (heap) clouds and *stratiform* (layer) clouds. Their formation depends on how quickly the air rises.

Cumuliform clouds are associated with strong convection currents and quickly rising air. They usually have a fairly level base, but a fluffy and often dome-shaped upper part. This is where the convection currents are 'boiling over'.

Stratiform clouds form when the upward currents of air are very weak, their tops usually being marked by a temperature inversion. They have a notable lack of distinctive features. The usual form is a uniform blanket which may stretch unbroken across the sky.

Cirrus: Delicate, white detached clouds with fibre-like appearance. Its many forms include 'mares'-tails'.

Cirrocumulus: Thin sheet or patch of cloud in the form of ripples or rounded small masses often merged together. Can produce a 'mackerel sky'.

Cirrostratus: Transparent film of fibre-like, whitish cloud. Frequently seen before a depression. Generally the cause of halo round Sun or Moon (effect of ice crystals on light).

Altocumulus: Greyish-white sheet or patch of cloud, with shading, made up of rounded heaps often merged together.

Altostratus: Greyish sheet of cloud, either fibre-like or uniform. Often produces 'watery sky' seen before depressions.

Stratocumulus: Greyish-white sheet of cloud, with shading, made up of rounded masses often merged together.

Stratus: Uniform, grey cloud layer, similar to fog. May envelop high ground.

Nimbostratus: Grey, often dark, layer of cloud, sometimes blurred by falling rain or snow.

Cumulus: Detached cloud heaps, developing upwards; brilliant white when lit by Sun.

Cumulonimbus: The thunder-cloud. Dense, with upper portion usually flattened out in shape of anvil; base may be very dark.

Mammals

Mammals are the most successful of all animals. They are the dominant animals on Earth today. There are more insects, but the insects do not affect their surroundings to the same extent.

One of the reasons for the success of the mammals is their adaptability as a group. They are found in the icy polar seas and in the tropical rain forests. They can live in deserts and in the seas. There are flying mammals – the bats – and swimming mammals – the whales. There are also flesh-eating, fruit-eating, and grass-eating mammals.

A second reason for the success of the mammals is their ability to control their body temperature. Mammals can keep warm in cold places and can keep cool in warm places. Mammals and birds are the only animals that can do this. Other animals go cold when their surroundings go cold.

The largest animal ever to have lived is a mammal – the blue whale. The giant dinosaurs were not as large as the Blue Whale. The most intelligent animal ever to have lived on Earth is a mammal – Man.

Above: A rabbit is a typical mammal. Its body is covered with hair, it gives birth to live young and suckles them with milk.

The Body of a Mammal

The mammals are easy to recognise, because most of them are covered by hair, fur or wool. The fur grows from the skin, and under the skin there is a layer of muscle, and of fat. The muscles are attached to the skeleton. The mammal's skeleton is much the same as the reptile and amphibian skeletons, but it is more suitable for the land. Mammals have a skull which protects the brain, a backbone which both supports the body and protects the nerve cord, ribs which protect the heart and the lungs and help the animal to breathe, and four limbs. Most mammals' bodies are really carried on a girder – the backbone – resting on four supports – the limbs. A few, like Man and the apes, balance on their back legs, but the upright position does not support the body as well as the four-legged, or quadrupedal, position does.

The mammal's body is controlled by its brain and its nervous system. The nerves run from the brain to all the parts of the body. There is a second nervous system which comes from the spinal nerve cord, and controls the movements like the beating of the heart. This system continues to work when the animal is unconscious, or asleep.

Food is taken in through the mouth and digested in the stomach. It moves into the animal's intestines, where the digestion

continues, and the food passes through the intestine wall into the blood stream. The blood carries the food to storage organs, like the liver, and to the rest of the body.

Air is taken into the animal's body through the nostrils. It passes into the lungs, where the oxygen in the air is dissolved in the moisture in the lungs, and passes into the blood stream. The carbon dioxide, which is left over when the food has been used, passes out of the blood into the lungs, and it is forced out of the body. Sea animals, like the whale and the seals, are able to 'clean' the carbon dioxide out of their bodies before they dive. They collect a great deal more carbon dioxide in their lungs while they are underwater and blow it out when they surface. When the whale 'spouts' it has just come up from a dive, and is shooting the warm, wet, carbon dioxide-laden air from its lungs.

The food and the oxygen are carried round the body in the blood. The blood is pumped through the arteries – the blood vessels coming from the heart – by the heart. It is pushed along in the veins – the blood vessels going to the heart – by the blood behind it. The blood in the veins can only run towards the heart. There are valves in the tubes which stop it running backwards.

Right: The body plan of a rabbit.

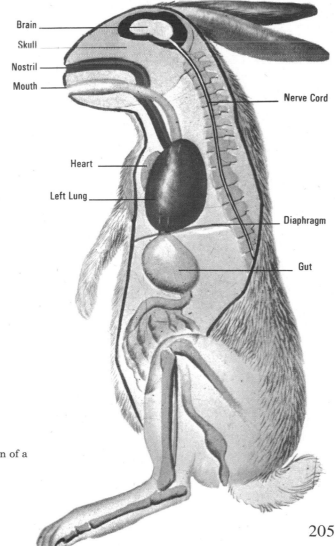

Brain
Skull
Nostril
Mouth
Nerve Cord
Heart
Left Lung
Diaphragm
Gut

Groups of Mammals

The mammals evolved from the reptiles many millions of years ago. The reptiles reproduce by laying eggs protected by shells.

One group of mammals lays eggs as its reptilian ancestors did. This is the monotreme group, which lives in Australia. There are only a few monotremes living today. They are the duck-billed platypus and the spiny ant-eater. These animals both have fur and feed their young on milk, like other mammals.

Australia is the home of another unusual group of mammals, the marsupials. Marsupials also live in America. They are the animals which keep their young in pouches. Kangaroos, opossums and the koala bear are marsupials. Many marsupial animals look like the true mammals. There is a marsupial wolf, a marsupial mole and a marsupial cat.

The true mammals give birth to fully formed live young. There are fifteen groups or orders of true mammals.

Insectivora – This is a group of small animals which includes the shrews, the hedgehogs and the moles. They are insect-eating animals, but many of them eat eggs, roots and shoots as well as insects. They have a very high body temperature and they have to eat very frequently in order to maintain it.

Hedgehog

Chiroptera – This is the bat group. The bats are the only mammals that actually fly. Their arms and hands are adapted to form wings, with leathery skin stretched over the bones. Bats are interesting because they have their own particular form of radar. As they fly they squeak. The echoes of the squeaks bounce back from any object in front of the bats so that they are warned of its presence.

Bats

Edentata – This group includes the ant-eaters, the armadilloes and the sloths. The ant-eaters have a long snout and a long, sticky tongue. This helps them to catch the ants on which they feed. The sloths live in trees hanging upside-down on the branches.

Sloth

They hang by all four feet. Sloths eat leaves. The armadillo is protected by bony plates in the skin. When it is frightened it rolls itself into a ball, so that it is completely covered by its armour.

Pholidota – This is a small group containing the pangolins, or scaly ant-eaters. The pangolin's body is covered by horny scales.

Pangolin

Rodentia – The rodents include the rats, mice, gophers and squirrels. They all have four very unusual teeth in the front of their jaws. The chisel-like teeth are open-ended. They continue to grow throughout the rodent's

Rat

European Lemmings

American Woodchuck

Porcupine

life. They are constantly worn away by gnawing. Some rodents are pests. Rats cause a great deal of damage. Rodents such as beavers, however, are attractive and usually harmless.

Rabbit

Lagomorpha – This group includes the rabbits and hares. They have open-ended teeth; they have six, however, two more than the rodents. Rabbits are very successful mammals.

206

Tubulidentata – This is a small order containing only the aardvark. The aardvark is an African ant-eater.

Sirenia – This group is the sea-cows. These are marine animals which live near the coasts, feeding on the seaweeds.

Hyracoidea – This small group contains the rock conies of Africa. They look rather like rabbits.

Proboscidea – This is the elephant group. The elephants are herbivores which live in Africa and India. They are large mammals. Their lower front teeth grow to form tusks.

Cetacea – This group is the whales. Whales are completely marine animals, except for a freshwater dolphin. They spend all their lives in the water. They do not even come ashore for the birth of their young.

Whales' bodies are completely adapted for life at sea. They are streamlined, like a fish. Their limbs are reduced to one pair of flippers. Whales are intelligent animals. Recent experiments show that they can be trained as easily as dogs.

Artiodactyla – This group includes the pigs, hippopotamuses, camels, deer, giraffes, yaks, sheep, cattle, goats and antelopes. It is an important group to man, as many of his domestic animals belong to it.

Yak

Hippopotamus

Cow

Whale

Carnivora – This large group includes cats, dogs, bears, otters, weasels, seals and walruses. Most of the group are flesh-eating animals. They are the hunters. The carnivores either have sharp claws or strong teeth with which to hunt their food.

Stoat

Leopard

Zebras at a Waterhole

Perissodactyla – This group includes the horses, zebras, rhinoceros, and tapirs. They are all herbivores. The horses and zebras are swift runners.

Primates – This group includes monkeys, apes, and Man himself. It is the most intelligent mammalian group. The members have eyes which face forward and mobile hands.

Tapir

Gibbons

207

Photography

The History of Photography

No one man can be credited with the invention of photography. It was a slow process of discovery, which began in earnest in the early 19th century. Long before that, however, the Greeks and Chinese had discovered the principle of what was called the 'camera obscura'. The word comes from the Latin meaning 'dark room', and the device consisted of a light-sealed room or box with a small hole at one side. The light passed through this hole to cast an upside-down impression on the opposite side. Although very limited, it was the forerunner of the modern camera.

The chief problem, however, was how to fix the image in the camera so that it was permanent. It was not until the early 19th century that an attempt was made at recording the image permanently on material which was sensitive to light.

In 1839, a Frenchman, called Daguerre, developed a silver copper plate coated with chemicals which, when exposed in a camera and treated in the dark with more chemicals, could produce a permanent image. The limitation of this was that each plate could produce only one positive. In the same year, and Englishman called Fox Talbot announced a method which used specially treated paper, instead of plates, and by which any number of prints could be made. His system was not adopted, however, until many years after his death.

Right: Early photography was a cumbersome business, requiring much on-the-spot equipment.

Below: The diaphragm, which is made of over-lapping leaves, can be adjusted to alter the size of the aperture.

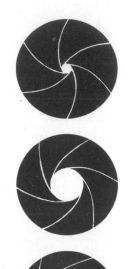

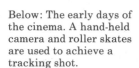

Below: The early days of the cinema. A hand-held camera and roller skates are used to achieve a tracking shot.

The next stage was the invention of a glass plate which was more highly sensitive to light and which therefore could record better images. Then, in 1891, a flexible roll film was developed by an American, George Eastman, which took the place of the cumbersome and fragile glass plates. This was the discovery which made possible Edison's early experiments in cine photography in 1894. In 1888, Eastman started the Kodak firm which was to lead to the development of the modern photographic industry. It was the same firm that developed the first commercially successful colour film in 1935.

How a Camera Works

The modern camera is a light-sealed box whose most important features are: a lens, an aperture, a shutter, and a light-sensitive material which records what the camera 'sees'.

The *lens* focuses the image on the film at the back of the camera. As light rays from an object enter the camera, they are bent by the lens so that they come together at a particular point. At this point, the image of the object will be in focus.

The *aperture* is the device on the camera which controls the amount of light which reaches the film. It is in the shape of a circular hole which can be opened or closed. It is used together with the *shutter,* which is a mechanism for letting the light into the camera for the length of time chosen by the photographer. Since the amount of light reaching the film affects the quality of the photograph, the selection of shutter speed and size of aperture is very important.

The *film* is the light-sensitive material which makes a permanent record of the image focused by the lens. It usually consists of a transparent base coated with chemicals which change when light is let in through the aperture by the shutter. When developed, fixed and printed on paper, the image recorded on the film is permanent and can be viewed in daylight.

Developing and Printing

Because film is sensitive to light, the first stages of processing it must be done in

darkness. The film is taken from its protective container or covering and placed in a light-sealed tank into which a *developing* chemical is poured. This is stirred and kept at a certain temperature, then rinsed away. The process is repeated with the *fixing* fluid. The strip of film is then removed and hung to dry in a dust-free place.

This strip of film consists of 'negatives' – transparent pictures which are the reverse of the image seen by the photographer, bright objects being produced as dark areas. This is because the silver bromide particles, of which the film is made, darken on contact with the light let in by the camera. Developer converts the crystals which have been exposed to a dark, metallic silver; fixer dissolves away the other, unexposed crystals; and water rinses out any remaining, unwanted chemicals.

Printing is the process which converts the negative into a photograph. A special paper which darkens on contact with light is placed behind the negative in a frame. Light is then let in. The length of exposure and strength of the light are carefully controlled as these affect the quality of the print. Too much light makes the print too dark; too little leaves it too pale. The light does not penetrate the dark areas of the negative so these appear as white on the print. It only penetrates the paler parts of the negative which therefore print as black or grey depending on their shade. In this way, the negative is reversed to give the original image. The paper is then developed, fixed, washed and dried in the same way as the negative.

What is left is a permanent record of the image which the photographer saw. It can be enlarged and any number of prints can be made.

Cinematography

Cine photography is an important modern development which has created the cinema and greatly affected television. In the late 19th century, exposures took too long for any sort of actions to be recorded. When films became more sensitive to light, however, shutter speeds increased and it became possible to record actions which occurred too fast for the human eye to see properly. For example, a series of photographs solved an artists' controversy in 1872 by showing that a horse moves all four legs separately when it gallops. It was discovered that if a number of pictures of a moving object were taken in quick succession, then viewed rapidly one after the other, an impression of movement could be produced. When roll film was made in 1889, Edison invented a

Left: Rays of light are shown passing through the lens and forming an inverted image on the film at the back of the camera.

Below: An Agfa miniature camera showing the various adjustments. The aperture is set at stop f8 and the lens is focused on an object 10 feet away. The marks opposite the f8 positions on the depth-of-field scale show that the depth of field is from 8 to 15 feet.

projector which could create this effect. Cinematography developed rapidly from then. Special cameras were made which could expose several hundred pictures in quick succession on a long roll of film. Edison's projector was improved, so that it could show the pictures on a white screen, stopping for a fraction of a second between each, and giving a very realistic effect. This was improved further in the late 1920's by the addition of sound recorded on the film, and a little later by colour photography.

Today, 35 or 70 millimetre width film is used for professional pictures. The number of pictures (or 'frames') taken is 24 per second. 16 millimetre width film is used by advanced amateurs and some professionals. Small sizes such as 8 mm and 'Super Eight' (a new, slightly larger version of the 8 mm type) are used by amateur cinematographers who make their own films.

High speed cinematography of more than a million frames per second is possible with modern equipment. When a film of an explosion or any other rapid event is filmed at this rate, and then projected at the normal speed of 24 or 16 frames per second, things which occur in a fraction of a second, last for minutes on the screen.

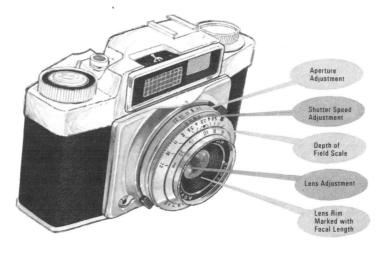

Aperture Adjustment

Shutter Speed Adjustment

Depth of Field Scale

Lens Adjustment

Lens Rim Marked with Focal Length

o

Exploration

The first explorers to leave any record of their travels were the people living in Mediterranean lands who ventured out into the Atlantic. In 500 B.C., Hanno of Carthage sailed down the north-west coast of Africa and formed a small colony. Two hundred years later, Pytheas, a Greek, sailed north to trade with the Tin Isles, as Britain was then called. He may even have reached Iceland.

New technical discoveries aided the progress of exploration. Maps and navigating instruments and new designs for ships enabled men to travel further afield.

Route to the East

The desire to reach India and Cathay had inspired European traders and travellers for centuries. Ever since men like Marco Polo returned from China with tales of the precious jewels, silks and spices to be found there, they had been risking their lives and fortunes.

When the fierce Mohammedans came to power in the lands east of the Mediterranean, the overland caravan routes to the East were closed to Christian traders. The two great seafaring nations, Spain and Portugal, competed fiercely in seeking a sea

Above: Captain James Cook, the English explorer and navigator.

Below: Sir Henry Morton Stanley, the British explorer and journalist, who found Livingstone.

route to India. Spain ignored the belief that the Earth was flat and sent Christopher Columbus in search of a westward route. He found land and named it the West Indies, believing he had reached India. But he had discovered America. Shortly afterwards, the Portuguese found the eastward route to India round the coast of Africa.

The Spanish and Portuguese defended their territory fiercely so other nations turned to other places in search of new lands. The French explored Canada and many brave sailors went in search of the North West Passage. They hoped to find a way to China round the north of the American continent, similar to the North East Passage to Russia. The Russians explored the Arctic and set up trading posts in North America and China.

Dutch traders sighted Australia before Captain Cook landed there and claimed it for England. Whalers and sealers sighted the Antarctic. Many nations have surveyed and explored stretches of this land of snow and ice.

During the nineteenth century, the heart of Africa was penetrated and thoroughly explored by Europeans. Traders, missionaries, surveyors and archaeologists all contributed to the list of new discoveries. In America and Australia, mineral wealth attracted many prospectors during the gold rush.

Opposite: Map depicting Marco Polo's journey to the Orient.

Left: Map showing the voyages of discovery and the extent of the known world at various dates.

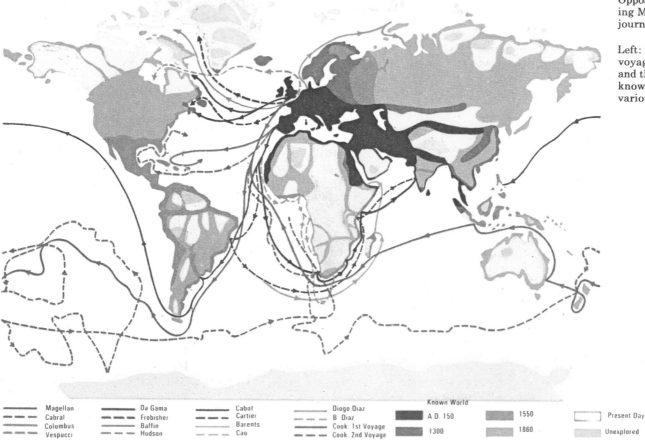

					Known World			
Magellan	Da Gama	Cabot	Diogo Diaz		A.D. 150	1550		Present Day
Cabral	Frobisher	Cartier	B. Diaz					
Columbus	Baffin	Barents	Cook, 1st Voyage		1300	1860		Unexplored
Vespucci	Hudson	Cao	Cook, 2nd Voyage					

A New Age of Exploration

Every part of the world has now been photographed and mapped from the air, and although there are areas of unexplored territory, these places no longer offer the same challenge to explorers as they did in an earlier age. Now, we think we know what is there, even if nobody has actually been to look. In olden days men did not know, they had to go and find out for themselves.

Today man is probing in other directions. There are projects being prepared for investigating the Earth's core. Great advances are being made in undersea exploration by Captain Jacques Cousteau and others.

The greatest challenge remaining to man today is the conquest of outer space. Men are again facing unknown dangers and obstacles in their attempts at exploration this time, the world beyond the Earth.

Scott's party at the South Pole. All tragically perished on the return journey.

Africa — The Dark Continent

It was not until the fifteenth century that the outline of Africa was slowly mapped by European navigators. This was when Spain and Portugal backed attempts to discover a sea route to India, since the overland trade route across Asia Minor put the valuable camel caravans at the mercy of the Turkish rulers and fierce wandering tribes. On several occasions, Portuguese captains sailed down the western coast, but it was only in 1497 that Vasco da Gama finally rounded the Cape of Good Hope and sailed on to India. Soon, a few trading posts and coastal settlements were established but for a long time little was known about the interior of the 'dark continent'.

It was a very difficult task to explore Africa. Everywhere the coastal plain was backed by high ground, either arid, or so thickly forested as to be impassable. Even the rivers were of little use, as rapids and waterfalls made voyages upstream impossible. It is hardly surprising that parts of the mysterious interior remained unmapped until late in the nineteenth century.

In 1795, Mungo Park set out to trace the course of the Niger river. He was drowned after being attacked by hostile natives in 1805 while on a second expedition attempting to find the mouth of the same river. Many years later, between 1857 and 1863, Burke, Speke and Grant in several journeys from the east coast discovered the Lakes Tanganyika and Victoria (the source of the Nile).

The most famous explorer of all was Livingstone, a medical missionary, whose main aim was to help and teach the primitive natives rather than discover new lands. In a series of remarkable expeditions from 1849 to 1873, he crossed the Kalahari Desert from south to north, followed the course of the Zambesi to its mouth, crossed South Africa from the east coast to Portuguese Angola and explored the land around Lake Tanganyika. Finally he died of a fever in 1873 while trying to find the source of the Congo. Stanley, the last of the great explorers, followed the Congo from its source in Lake Tanganyika to its mouth on the west coast of Africa.

The last great areas to be surveyed were the Sahara and Libyan deserts. The first man to visit Timbuktu was René Caillé. By 1930 the whole of Africa had been explored, but there are still frequent expeditions to find out more about tropical diseases, the wild life and the anthropology in certain areas, as well as map-making.

South America

The first man to explore the coast of South America is reputed to be Amerigo Vespucci. He certainly made several voyages to South America but there are not many good records of them. He is remembered because the continent was named after him.

Many parts of America became part of the Spanish Empire. The fierce conquistador, Cortés, conquered the Aztecs in Mexico. In the high Andes, another Spaniard, Pizarro, found the rich Inca Empire. He too overcame the people and destroyed their king and city. Pizarro's brother crossed the Andes with a great army in search of more riches in the Cinnamon Lands. One of his lieutenants, de Orellana, sailed down the Amazon to the Atlantic. The rivers of South America have continued to attract explorers right up to the present day.

Australia

During the sixteenth century, the big shipping companies encouraged exploration. They hoped to find new areas for trade and new sources of gold and other valuables. Employees of the Dutch East India Company charted the coasts of Australia and in 1642 Tasman sailed round Australia and sighted Tasmania.

The first man to land was William Dampier who visited Western Australia during the first scientific expedition to be commissioned by Britain. Captain Cook landed on the east coast of Australia and claimed it as British territory. The first settlers were convicts who had been deported from Britain and landed in Botany Bay.

For nearly 150 years nothing was known of the interior of Australia. The coastline and the fertile lands of Victoria Land and Queensland had been surveyed but no one had passed west of the Blue Mountains.

The route inland was found by way of the great rivers, the Darling, the Murray and the Murrumbidgee. They were navigated by Charles Sturt. The interior proved to be a vast desert. It was first crossed from south to north in 1862 by John Stuart, a bushman looking for good cattle raising country.

North America

The first Europeans to cross the Atlantic were the Norsemen in their open longboats. From the Norse Sagas we know how Eric the Red set up a colony in Greenland and his son Lief Ericson sailed further west to the coast of Newfoundland and Nova Scotia.

About four hundred years later Christopher Columbus made his epic voyage to the New World. But the first sailor to chart the coast of North America was John Cabot.

Soon after the Spaniards claimed Central America, French explorers established settlements in Canada. Jacques Cartier sailed down the St. Lawrence and a few years later de Champlain discovered Lake Ontario and they began to explore the Great Lakes. René de Salle discovered the Niagara Falls.

The first European to cross the continent north of Mexico was Alexander Mackenzie. He was one of the many employees of the Hudson's Bay Company who helped to chart these parts while carrying out their work as hunters and fur traders.

South of the Great Lakes, the West was slowly opened up. Lewis and Clark went up the Missouri and across the Rockies to the Pacific. Pioneers journeyed to the Pacific coast to found new settlements. The North American continent was not completely explored until the end of the nineteenth century.

Antarctica

Antarctica was the last continent to be discovered and explored. The British seaman, Captain James Cook, sailed around the continent between 1772 and 1775. He did not reach the mainland, but saw much of the rich life in the seas. Hearing his reports, many sailors began to hunt seals and whales in the region.

In 1820 the coast of Antarctica was sighted. The first landing was probably made by an American sailor, John Davis, in 1821. The British explorer Robert Falcon Scott made the first major inland journey in 1901-4. But the first man to reach the South Pole was the Norwegian Roald Amundsen, who planted his country's flag there on December 14, 1911. A British team led by Scott arrived about a month later. But Scott and his companions died in the cold on their return.

The development of aircraft speeded the exploration of Antarctica. In 1929 the American Richard E. Byrd became the first man to fly over the South Pole. In 1959 an agreement was signed by 12 nations ensuring the use of Antarctica for peaceful purposes only.

The Human Body

The human body is made up entirely of tiny cells. There are millions of these cells, arranged in numerous groups. Groups of similar cells which work together are called *tissues,* and different tissues are united to form *organs.*

There are five main types of tissue: *skeletal,* as in bone; *epithelium,* which provides lining and covering; *connective,* which binds organs together and packs the spaces between them; *muscle;* and *nerve.*

The study of the cells, tissues and organs is called *histology.* Histology was not possible until the microscope had been invented, although there was some knowledge of *anatomy* before the microscope. Anatomy is the study of the organs of the body in relation to one another.

The eye is an important sense organ. It is well protected by the skull and is lubricated by the eyelid. The eyes are more important to Man than smell or hearing. Many animals can smell and hear better than they can see, but, when Man was a hunting animal, he hunted by sight. The eye itself is covered by a tough, light-proof coat, called the sclera, with a transparent 'window' – the cornea.

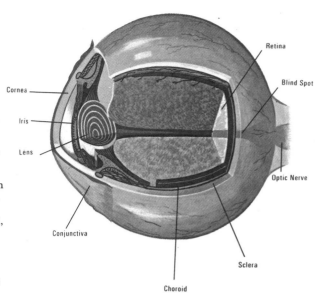

Retina

Blind Spot

Cornea

Iris

Lens

Optic Nerve

Conjunctiva

Sclera

Choroid

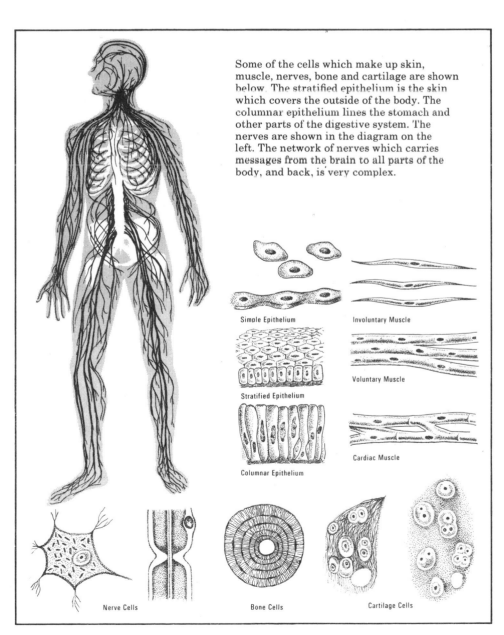

Some of the cells which make up skin, muscle, nerves, bone and cartilage are shown below. The stratified epithelium is the skin which covers the outside of the body. The columnar epithelium lines the stomach and other parts of the digestive system. The nerves are shown in the diagram on the left. The network of nerves which carries messages from the brain to all parts of the body, and back, is very complex.

Simple Epithelium

Involuntary Muscle

Stratified Epithelium

Voluntary Muscle

Columnar Epithelium

Cardiac Muscle

Nerve Cells

Bone Cells

Cartilage Cells

Nerves

The brain and its various parts, together with the spinal cord, consist of millions of nerve cells. They may be compared to a central switch-board which receives and transmits signals. Jointly they are termed the *central nervous system.*

The brain is made up of separate grey matter (thinking) cells and white matter (pathway) cells, and the surface is elaborately folded. Together with the spinal cord, the brain controls all the conscious and unconscious thinking and movement of the body.

The central nervous system is linked to the rest of the body by the *peripheral nervous system,* a complicated network which carries signals to and fro between the brain and the other organs.

The body maintains a number of special sense organs which enable the central nervous system to make an exact response to a given stimulus.

The skin, which is in direct contact with the surroundings, possesses free nerve endings which respond to touch, pain and temperature.

The eye, protected with a bony cavity in the front of the skull, is of particular importance in providing the brain with precise information about surrounding conditions. It possesses light-sensitive cells which transmit signals to the brain by way of the *optic* nerve. In the brain, the signals are interpreted as light.

The ear is the body's organ of hearing. It receives sound waves which are transmitted as signals along the auditory nerve to the brain. The ear also possesses a mechanism which controls the body's sense of balance. This is maintained by means of a complicated signalling system, much of which is automatic.

The *olfactory* cells provide the body with its sense of smell. These *chemoreceptors* (sense organs dealing with chemicals) are embedded in the epithelial lining of the nose and are directly connected to the central nervous system.

The tongue also possesses chemoreceptors in the form of *taste-buds* embedded in its tissue. The taste-buds detect chemicals and then transmit signals which are interpreted in the brain as salty, sweet, sour, or bitter.

Vertebrae

Spinal Cord

Bone and Cartilage

The human body is supported by a skeleton of hard bones. These not only carry the full weight of the body, but also help to protect the body's delicate and sensitive organs. The brain, for example, is enclosed in the bony skull, and the heart and lungs are protected by a cage of ribs. The skeleton also provides a solid base to which muscles are attached.

A bone consists of layer upon layer of hard calcium phosphate and other materials. It has a rich blood supply, and the hollow cavity running through the centre of long bones and spaces in other bones are filled with a fatty marrow in which red blood corpuscles are produced.

Cartilage is also a skeletal tissue. It acts as a shock absorber for the body. It is tough and very strong, resists compression and extension, and yet is slightly elastic. Cartilage surrounds the ends of bones; it cushions the bony joints and absorbs the shock of a jolt.

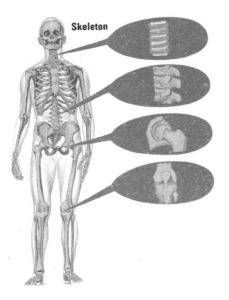

Skeleton

Skin

The outer covering of the body is known as skin. It consists of a sheet of epithelial cells cemented together. Skin acts as a protective coat for underlying muscles, and a body may have up to twenty square feet of skin. Skin also helps to regulate the body temperature. Evaporation of water (perspiration) from the sweat glands that open onto the skin's surface cools the body when it gets hot.

Section of Skin

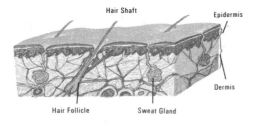

Hair Shaft
Epidermis
Dermis
Hair Follicle
Sweat Gland

Muscle

Every movement of the body is due to the pulling action of muscles working in small groups or complicated combinations. Muscles also hold parts of the body in position to provide its posture.

Three kinds of muscles provide all the body movements. *Involuntary*, or *unstriped*, muscles include those over which we generally have no conscious control. These are found, for example, in the walls of the intestine and blood vessels, and the pupil of the eye. *Voluntary*, or *striped*, muscles include those which we can consciously control. Muscles of the limbs, neck and abdomen are of this type which accounts for the largest number of muscles in the body. *Heart*, or *cardiac*, muscle is striped and of a special branched kind that joins to form an elaborate network.

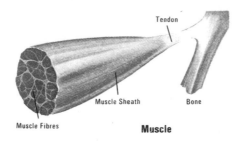

Tendon
Muscle Sheath
Bone
Muscle Fibres

Muscle

Digestion and Absorption

The human body needs food to live. The foods we eat are made up of sugary and starchy carbohydrates, fats, proteins, minerals, vitamins and water. The body digests (breaks down) these foods to provide energy and body building materials.

The purpose of digestion is to break down sugars and starch to glucose, proteins to amino acids, and fats to fatty acids and glycerol. The end products of digestion are molecules small enough to be absorbed into the body and used by its cells.

Food enters the body through the mouth, where the chewing action of the teeth grinds it into smaller particles. This allows the first digestive juice in saliva to act. Saliva, a watery fluid secreted by glands in the mouth, contains a substance called *ptyalin* which converts starch to sugary maltose.

After the food has been mixed, partly digested and thoroughly wetted by saliva, it is swallowed and passes down a thick tube *(oesophagus)* to the stomach. In the muscular bag of the stomach, the food is sterilized by hydrochloric acid, and attacked by more digestive juices which start the break-down of proteins. Small quantities of digested food (mainly glucose) are absorbed through the stomach lining into the blood, and the remainder travels into a long, narrow tube, the *small intestine*.

In the small intestine, various glands pour their secretions onto the food to continue the digestive process. The liver produces bile which enters the intestine, via the gall bladder, through the bile duct. The bile salts split up large fat droplets into smaller ones by emulsification, rather similar to the way in which detergents break up grease in washing-up water. The pancreas releases its alkaline juice which contains substances *(enzymes)* able to break down proteins to smaller units, starch to maltose, and fats to fatty acids and glycerol. The first loop of the small intestine *(duodenum)* contains glands in its walls that also produce an alkaline digestive juice.

Between them, the various juices complete the break-down of the fats, carbohydrates and

proteins, and in the process the digested food becomes more and more liquid. When the food has been broken down completely, it is absorbed through the thin walls of the small intestine. Amino-acids (from proteins) and glucose pass into a network of tiny blood vessels which then join up and carry the food to the liver. The fatty acids and glycerol, obtained from fatty foods, reach the liver by an indirect route through the lymph vessels and the heart. The liver acts rather like a warehouse, holding back much of the digested food and releasing it gradually as the body needs it.

When all the food materials have been absorbed, the small intestine is left with a watery residue containing a large amount of cellulose and other indigestible plant material. This residue passes to the *large intestine* which is concerned mainly with the absorption of water. When most of the water has been taken back into the body, the residue is passed out of the body as *faeces*.

The *liver* is the largest gland in the body. It lies under the diaphragm close to the intestines. Its main role is of a chemical laboratory, storing and converting foods absorbed into the body. By this and other activities, the liver controls the blood composition. A further important function is that of *detoxication*, or conversion of harmful substances in the blood to harmless ones.

Digestive Tract

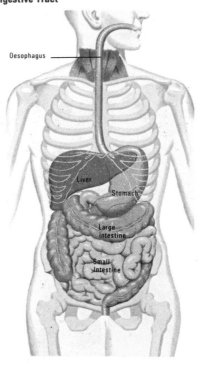

Oesophagus
Liver
Stomach
Large Intestine
Small Intestine

Excretion

The removal of waste products from the body (excretion) is the main function of the kidneys. This pair of bean-shaped organs lie one on each side of the spine. The kidneys also play a role in controlling the loss of body water, and regulating the acid and alkaline level of the whole body fluid.

Kidney

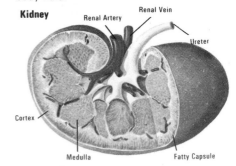

Renal Artery
Renal Vein
Ureter
Cortex
Medulla
Fatty Capsule

Blood passes through the kidneys, which filter out excess water and waste materials such as ammonia and urea. This filtered material is known as urine and it is carried from the kidneys in two tubes *(ureters)* which take it to the bladder. From there it passes to the outside through a tube called the *urethra*.

Glands

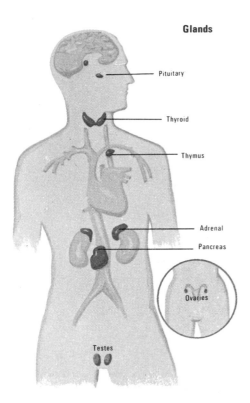

Glands

Glands

The body contains a number of important glands which produce chemical substances and release them into the body. There are two main types: *exocrine* glands which release their secretions for local action into a duct that connects the organ to a site in or outside the body (e.g. the sweat glands, salivary glands, liver and pancreas); and *endocrine*, or *ductless*, glands which release their fluids directly into the blood stream to affect a distant part or the body as a whole (e.g. the pituitary, adrenals, thyroid and parathyroid). The pancreas has both endocrine and exocrine regions.

The endocrine organs produce secretions called *hormones*. These act as chemical messengers and are carried around the body in the blood to stimulate some distant part to action.

The *pituitary*, suspended from the underside of the brain, is called the master gland. It weighs only one-sixth of an ounce, yet it has a great effect upon the whole body. The hormones it secretes affect: growth and the building up and breaking down processes of the body *(metabolism)*; water and salt loss through the kidneys; the sex glands; the thyroid and adrenal glands; and the smooth muscle in the walls of blood vessels.

The *thyroid* gland, an 'H'-shaped structure situated in the neck in front of the wind-pipe, secretes *thyroxin*. This hormone causes an increase in the rate of chemical reactions within cells by promoting the activities of chemical catalysts *(enzymes)*.

The *parathyroid* glands, attached to each lobe of the thyroid gland, are concerned with the body's use of calcium and with the proper working of nerves and muscle.

The *pancreas*, situated underneath the stomach, produces, besides digestive juices, the hormone *insulin* which regulates the blood sugar level and controls the rate at which glucose is released from the liver.

Adrenal glands, which are loosely attached to the upper side of each kidney, secrete adrenalin which increases the heartbeat and prepares a frightened person for action. It tenses the muscles and, by diverting blood from the digestive system, it gives you 'butterflies' in your stomach.

Male and female bodies possess glands for reproduction. The female reproductive organs consist of almond-shaped ovaries which produce unfertilized eggs *(ova)* at regular intervals. The ovaries lie in a cavity inside the lower part of the body, protected by the hips *(pelvis)*. Male glands of reproduction are the testes which produce millions of spermatozoa (sperm). As well as producing eggs and sperms, the reproductive organs also produce hormones which control the growing-up' process.

The Blood System

The blood acts as the body's transport system, connecting up the various parts of the body and carrying oxygen and food cells. Waste products of metabolism are also carried by the blood to the kidneys for elimination from the body. The blood also helps to keep the body at an even temperature, and it helps to fight invading germs.

The body contains about nine pints of blood which is driven at a high pressure to the tissues. The fluid part *(plasma)* contains the food supply needed by the body cells. In the plasma float millions of red and white blood corpuscles.

The red corpuscles, manufactured in bone marrow, contain a pigment *(haemoglobin)* which carries oxygen from the lungs to the tissues where it is released. Carbon dioxide, formed when food is used up in the body, dissolves in the blood plasma and is carried back to the lungs where it escapes into the air.

The white corpuscles in blood help to combat disease by destroying bacteria. Substances produced by bacteria may also kill white blood cells, which sometimes appear as pus.

The blood is pumped around the body by the heart. The human heart is a muscular, four-chambered 'bag' situated in the chest cavity between the lungs. The two upper chambers are called *auricles* and the two lower ones, which have the thickest walls, are called *ventricles*.

The blood vessels carrying blood away from the heart are called *arteries*. They branch to all parts of the body and, as they get further from the heart, they get smaller and smaller until they become minute *capillaries*. These capillaries spread through all the tissues, giving up food and oxygen, and then they join up again to form *veins* which carry the blood back to the heart.

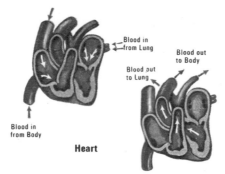

Heart

Blood which has been round the body and which has given up its oxygen returns to the heart in large veins which open into the right auricle. The pumping action of the heart, controlled by numerous valves, forces this blood into the right ventricle and then along the pulmonary arteries to the lungs. Here the blood receives a fresh supply of oxygen and it then returns to the heart, this time entering the left auricle. The blood then passes into the left ventricle, which contracts strongly and sends the blood on its journey around the body again.

During its passage through the tissues, the blood loses a lot of its water by seepage out of the capillaries. This fluid bathes the tissues and carries food to them. It then drains into another set of tubes, called lymph vessels, which carry it back to the main veins entering the heart. Bacteria and worn out cells often find their way into the lymph vessels but they are filtered out and destroyed in the lymph nodes, or lymph glands, which are situated at various points along the lymph vessels. If you have an infected hand, you might be able to feel a swelling in your armpit. This swelling is the lymph node destroying the germs before they can get into the main blood stream.

Respiration

All human activities require energy. In the body, the energy required for growth and movement is obtained by the 'burning' *(oxidation)* of food materials within the body tissues. The oxygen essential for this process is found in air. It is absorbed into the blood stream in the lungs. At the same time, the blood gives up the waste carbon dioxide it has brought from the tissues.

The lungs are situated in a cavity which is surrounded below by a muscular upward-domed sheet *(diaphragm)* and on all other sides by the ribs. They open to the air by way of the windpipe and the nose and mouth.

Lungs

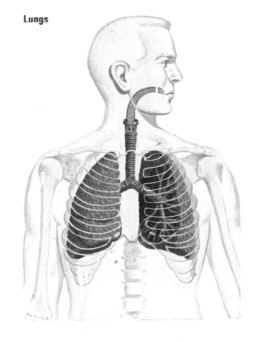

During the inhaling of air *(inspiration)*, the diaphragm muscles contract, so flattening the sheet, and the ribs are pulled out by muscles to enlarge the lung cavity. When exhaling *(expiration)*, the muscles relax, the lung cavity becomes smaller, and air is forced out of the lungs. This is the process of breathing, which is normally controlled automatically by the brain but can be consciously controlled.

The voice is produced in the *larynx* which is a special part of the wind-pipe in the throat. Inside the larynx are two sheets of tissue (vocal cords) which are responsible for the actual production of sound. The act of speaking is controlled by the brain.

Men of Medicine

Medicine is concerned with the science of healing involving the prevention and cure of disease. Its practice has been known in various forms for thousands of years. The following is a list of some of the people who have played a notable role in this field.

Imhotep, a physician, lived in ancient Egypt about 2980 B.C. He became worshipped as a god of medicine. It is said he used drugs and instruments to treat disease. Many ancient cures were attributed to him.

Moses, the Jewish philosopher, did much to prevent illness by his laws, many of which form the basis of present-day hygiene.

Hippocrates, born in 460 B.C. separated the study of disease from its philosophy. Known as the 'father of medicine' he defined the aims of medicine in his Hippocratic Oath. His code of medical conduct is accepted still today.

Aristotle (384–322 B.C.), the Greek philosopher, brought new direction to medical thinking by introducing the study of anatomy by observation and comparison. His teachings influenced the world for 2,000 years.

Herophilus (320 B.C.), an Egyptian known as 'father of anatomy', taught at the Alexandria Medical School. He was one of the first to dissect the human body in public and identified the brain as the centre of the nervous system and the 'seat of intelligence'.

Erasistratus (300–250 B.C.), the Roman 'father of physiology', distinguished the main parts of the brain and noted their separate nerve channels.

Aulus Cornelius Celsus (about 37 A.D.) wrote 'De re medica' as an assembly of medical knowledge which, when printed in 1478, became one of the first medical text books.

Galen (130–200 A.D.), a Greek physician, distinguished between muscle, nerve and tendon. His writings on anatomy and science became a text book which was used in Europe for 1,300 years.

Avicenna (979–1037), a Persian doctor, wrote 'The Canon of Medicine' which became a standard medical text book in the West until about 1650.

Leonardo Da Vinci (1452–1518), the famous painter, studied and dissected the human body. His anatomical drawings became classics.

Andreas Vesalius (1514–64) transformed surgical practice. He published 'De humani corporis fabrica', an illustrated book on human anatomy.

Ambroise Pare (1517–90), a French army surgeon, first tied bleeding blood vessels instead of applying hot irons to them, which had been the practice until then.

Jerome Fabricius (1537–1619), considered the founder of modern embryology (study of the unborn animal), wrote the first illustrated book on the subject.

Sanctorius (1561–1636), an Italian professor, invented and described the thermometer in 1610, and developed apparatus for measuring pulse.

William Harvey (1578–1657), an Englishman, discovered the circulation of blood and demonstrated the function of the heart. His notes were published in 1628 as 'De mortu cordis'.

Rene Descartes (1596–1650), a French philosopher, wrote 'De Homine', the first modern book of physiology.

Giovanni Alphonso Borelli (1608–79) described the mechanical principles of muscular movement.

Franciscus Sylvius (1614–72) added to the knowledge of physiological activity by the examination of digestive juices.

Thomas Sydenham (1624–89), an English physician, first used Laudanum (tincture of opium) to treat smallpox. His book 'Methodus curandi febres' was not based on theory but the study and observation of epidemic diseases.

Marcello Malpighi (1628–94), an Italian, first used a microscope to demonstrate the blood movement from arteries to veins through capillaries. He developed theories of respiration, gland secretion, and grey (thinking) matter of the brain.

Robert Boyle (1629–91) changed attitudes towards chemistry. He conceived the principle of chemical elements and recommended their detection by experiment.

Anton van Leeuwenhoek (1632–1723), an uneducated Dutch linen draper, developed the single lens microscope in 1680 with which he discovered, described and first drew bacteria, and detailed red blood corpuscles.

John Mayow (1640–79) first recognised the existence of a substance (oxygen) concerned with combustion, respiration, and the conversion into arterial blood.

GALIEN PRYNCE OF PHISYCKE

Above: The writings of Galen became a textbook used in Europe for 1,300 years.

Right: Harvey demonstrates the circulation of the blood to King Charles I.

Sir John Floyer (1649–1734) introduced the first one-minute watch for regular observation of pulse rate.

Reverend Stephen Hales (1677–1761) invented the first pressure gauge. He computed the circulation rate and velocity of blood in veins and arteries.

Giovanni Battista Morgagni (1682–1771) demonstrated in 1761 the necessity of basing diagnosis and treatment on knowledge of anatomical conditions.

Lady Mary Wortley Montague (1689–1762) first introduced into England from Turkey inoculation against smallpox in 1718.

Albrecht von Haller (1708–77) worked on physiological functions of the human body including the mechanism of respiration and automation of the heart. His understandings remain the basis of much modern-day physiological thinking.

James Lind (1716–94) discovered that scurvy (a vitamin deficiency disease) could be prevented by eating fresh fruit or lemon juice.

Lazaro Spallanzani (1729–99) discovered that microscopic organisms did not develop in vegetable matter that had been boiled and sealed.

Edward Jenner (1749–1823) discovered in 1796 cowpox serum for smallpox vaccination.

Edward Jenner

Rene H. Laënnec (1781–1826) invented the stethoscope in 1816.

William Beaumont (1785–1853), an American, demonstrated the workings of the digestive system and the significance of gastric (stomach) juices.

James Blundell (1790–1877) carried out the first successful blood transfusion in the curing of disease.

Charles Pravaz (1791–1853) and **Alexander Wood** (1817–84) first used a hypodermic syringe in 1853.

Sir James Simpson (1811–70) was first to use chloroform as an anaesthetic in England in 1847.

Sir James Simpson

Ignaz Semmelweiss (1818–65), an Austrian, first introduced the principle of asepsis (the complete exclusion of germs) by insisting that doctors wash in disinfectant before touching patients.

Louis Pasteur (1822–95) established in 1864 his theory that bacteria cause disease by multiplying, and founded bacteriology. He discovered the vaccine for rabies.

Gregor Mendel (1822–84), an Austrian Abbe, discovered the principles of heredity and formed the basis of genetics.

Thomas Morton (1819–68), an American, first introduced sulphuric ether into surgical practice in 1842. In the same year **Crawford Williamson Long** (1815–78) first used ether as an anaesthetic during an operation.

Joseph Lister (1827–1912) introduced the antiseptic technique to surgery in 1865, using carbolic acid to free the air of microbes. He first used catgut in surgery for stitching wounds.

Robert Koch (1843–1910) found the tuberculosis bacillus in 1882. He also discovered the cholera bacterium and anthrax bacillus, and developed the blood serum jelly in which to grow them.

Elie Metchnikoff (1845–1926) found the white cells in blood.

William Röntgen (1845–1923) discovered the X-rays in 1895.

Walter Reed (1851–1902), an American army doctor, discovered the mosquito parasite that carries yellow fever.

Emil von Behring (1854–1917) discovered the antitoxins for inoculation against diphtheria and tetanus.

Shibasaburo Kitasato, a Japanese scientist, isolated the bacilli for bubonic plague in 1894 and dysentry in 1898.

Sigmund Freud (1856–1939) introduced the approach of psycho-analysis to mental illness.

Sir Ronald Ross (1857–1932) discovered the anopheles parasite in the malaria carrying mosquito.

Sir Frederick Gowland Hopkins (1861–1947) discovered vitamins.

Sir Alexander Fleming,
the discoverer of Penicillin

Sir William Maddock Bayliss (1866–1924) and **Ernest Henry Starling** (1866–1927) jointly isolated hormones.

Marie (1867–1934) and **Pierre** (1859–1906) **Curie** isolated polonium and radium from pitchblend. They discovered radioactive elements in radium that could be used to treat disease.

Frederick Banting and **Charles Best**, two Canadians, in 1921 discovered and isolated insulin, the sugar regulating hormone.

Sir Alexander Fleming (1881–1955) discovered Penicillin in 1928 and **Sir Howard Florey** and **Ernest Chain** introduced it in 1941 for the treatment of disease.

Gerhard Domagk produced 'Prontosil' in 1935, the first of the sulphonamide drugs.

Selman Waksman discovered 'Streptomycin' in 1944, used in the treatment of tuberculosis.

Jonas E. Salk produced the poliomyelitis (infantile paralysis) vaccine injection in 1955, and **A. B. Sabin** produced the oral vaccine for it.

Jonas Salk

217

Metals

Man first began using metals at least 5,000 years ago. He found that they could be hammered into tools and weapons that remained sharp. From small beginnings the use of metals has grown to such an extent that civilization as we know it today could not exist without them.

Over 400 million tons of steel alone are used throughout the world in a year. It is used for its strength in large buildings and bridges, and for motor cars, railways, and ships. Most of the machinery that makes practically everything we use is made of iron or steel. The 'tin' cans for food are made from steel coated with tin. The knives and forks we eat with are made of stainless steel.

Many other metals are important to us. We cook in aluminium saucepans. Copper cables carry electricity to light our homes.

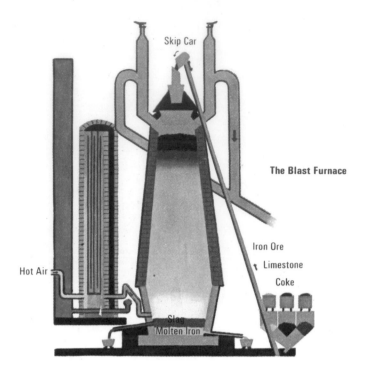

The Blast Furnace

The Blast Furnace

Smelting iron ore is one of the most important metal-making processes in the world. It takes place in a *blast furnace*, so called because a blast of hot air passes through it.

Iron ore — a compound of iron and oxygen — is heated in the furnace with coke. The oxygen combines with the carbon in the coke to form a gas, which escapes. The iron remains behind. The hot-air blast through the furnace makes the coke burn fiercely. The temperature is high enough to melt the iron. Limestone is added to the furnace to help remove impurities. It combines with them to form a molten *slag*.

The blast furnace is a brick-lined cylinder as much as 100 feet high. Coke, iron ore, and limestone are fed into the top of the furnace. They are called the *charge*. The air blast is heated in huge brick stoves before it enters the bottom of the furnace. The stoves are themselves heated by burning gases that have come from the top of the furnace. The heat from the burning coke melts the iron, which runs down to the bottom of the furnace. The molten slag containing some impurities forms a layer on top of the iron.

Every few hours the molten iron is drawn off, or *tapped*. It is either poured into moulds or taken while still molten for further refining. The iron produced in the furnace is called *pig iron*. It contains carbon and other impurities.

Blast furnaces operate continuously day and night until the furnace lining wears out. Many of the larger furnaces produce well over a quarter of a million tons of pig iron a year. In Britain alone, over 30 million tons of iron ore are processed in blast furnaces every year.

Left: Miners operate a powerful drilling tool to remove metal ores from deposits deep underground.

We wear jewellery made of the precious metals gold, silver, and platinum. The coins we carry in our pockets contain copper, nickel, and zinc. Our newspapers are printed from type containing mainly lead. The list of the uses of metals is endless.

Metals from the Earth

Metals make up a large part of the Earth's outer layer, or *crust*. But only a few of them appear in the metal form we are familiar with. The precious metals gold and platinum, for instance, are always found in this metallic form.

However, most metals, such as iron and tin, are found combined with other chemical 'units', or *elements*. Most of these compounds do not look anthing like metals. They are often lumps of rock. But many of them can be treated to produce the metal. These are called *ores*.

Metals and compounds of metals are not generally found in all parts of the world.

They occur in certain regions in limited deposits. Taking these ore deposits from the ground is called *mining*. Sometimes the deposits occur on or near the surface. In this case, mining involves simply scooping up the deposit with giant shovels. Iron ore is often mined in this way. But sometimes the deposits lie hundreds or even thousands of feet below the ground, and deep shafts must be sunk to reach them. In South Africa, for example, gold is mined almost two miles below the surface.

Right: A sheet of hot metal passes over rollers and under a water spray to cool it.

Left: A large steel ingot is forged into shape under an 8,000-ton press.

Right: Cutting torches burning oxygen and propane automatically cut out girders from a thick sheet of steel.

Below: Men pour molten metal into moulds to cast a large object. The metal solidifies into shape inside the moulds.

Extracting and Purifying

The metal ores coming from the ground must pass through many stages before pure metal is obtained. Unwanted material with the ore must first be removed. Sometimes this is done simply by washing. Often more complicated treatments are needed. These include crushing, heating, and floating in a frothing liquid.

Ways of getting the metal from this *concentrated* ore depend on what the metal is combined with in the ore. But many of the common ores, such as iron ore, are heated with coke in a huge *smelting* furnace. Some are first roasted in air. Smelting produces an impure metal that must be purified by *refining*.

Methods of refining, too, vary with the metal. Some involve heating the impure metal in a furnace with substances which remove the impurities. Steel is refined in this way. Some metals, such as copper, are refined by passing electricity through them in a solution.

A uranium prospector uses an instrument to detect radiation coming from rock. If he finds any radiation, the rock may contain uranium ore.

Sometimes chemical elements other than metals are included in alloys. The most important is carbon. Steel, our most useful metal, is an alloy of iron and carbon.

The reason behind alloying is to give the pure metal more useful properties. For example, pure iron is weak and not very hard. But when a small amount of carbon is added, it becomes *steel,* which is both strong and hard.

The way in which the properties improve depends largely on the metal or metals being added. A metal that is, say, stainless will tend to make the alloy stainless too. *Stainless steel* is made by adding chromium to steel. The properties of alloys can be further improved by heat treatment, such as heating and then dipping in water.

By far the most important alloys are the *alloy steels.* Adding nickel to steel makes it hard and strong. Chromium makes it hard and resistant to corrosion. Manganese makes it hard-wearing and less brittle.

Shaping and Finishing

The purified metal from the refining operations can be shaped in various ways. Sometimes it is used hot, sometimes cold.

Molten metal is shaped by *casting.* It is poured into a mould of the required form and allowed to cool. Hot but solid metal can be shaped in several ways. It can be pressed into shape by *forging.* It can be formed into sheets by *rolling.* Rods and tubes can be made by forcing the metal through holes. This is called *extrusion.* Wires are made by *drawing* the cold metal through holes. Cold metal also can be rolled.

Sometimes objects are made by joining several pieces of metal together. This can be done by *soldering* and *welding.* Molten metal formed at the joints binds the pieces together. Another method of making objects is to mould them in metal powder and then press and heat the moulded powder.

Most metal parts are given their final shape by *machining.* This includes drilling holes, cutting and grinding. Many metals, especially steel, are coated with other metals for protection and for decoration. Some are merely painted.

Alloys

Not many metals are used widely in their pure state. Other metals are usually added to them to form mixtures called *alloys.* The copper alloys are well known – *brass* (with zinc), *bronze* (with tin), and *cupronickel* (with nickel). Bronze and cupronickel are familiar to us as 'copper' and 'silver' coins.

SOME IMPORTANT METALS

Aluminium (Al) is a light metal which is resistant to corrosion and forms strong alloys. It conducts heat and electricity well. Aluminium alloys have many uses, ranging from utensils to vehicle bodies.

Antimony (Sb) is a hard, brittle metal which is alloyed with lead in printers' type metal.

Boron (B) is added to steel to make it extremely hard.

Cadmium (Cd) is used to electroplate iron to prevent rusting. This metal is used in the control rods of nuclear reactors.

Chromium (Cr) is added to provide a shiny, non-tarnishing coating on other metals. It is also used in the manufacture of stainless steels.

Cobalt (Co) is used in the production of powerful magnets and cutting tools.

Copper (Cu) conducts heat and electricity better than any other metal except silver. It is used a great deal for wires and cables carrying an electric current.

Germanium (Ge). Crystals of germanium form the tiny transistors in transistor radio sets.

Gold (Au) is a precious metal which can be drawn or beaten into extremely thin wire and sheets. It is usually alloyed with other metals such as copper and silver.

Iron (Fe) is the most useful of all metals. Steel is basically an alloy of iron and carbon. Special alloy steels are formed by the addition of other metals, such as tungsten and vanadium.

Lead (Pb) is a soft, heavy metal with a low melting point and a good resistance to corrosion. It is used for the plates of storage batteries, cable sheathing and roofing.

Lithium (Li) is the lightest of all metals. Lithium-lead alloys are used in radiation shielding.

Magnesium (Mg) is a light metal which burns in air with a brilliant white flame. The chief use of magnesium is in the production of light, strong alloys.

Manganese (Mn) is a hard, brittle metal which is used to produce tough, steel alloys.

Mercury (Hg) is the only metal which is liquid at normal temperatures. One of the uses of mercury is in thermometers.

Molybdenum (Mo) is a strong, hard metal with a high melting point. It is used in the manufacture of tool steels.

Nickel (Ni) is widely used in the production of special alloy steels, particularly stainless steels.

Platinum (Pt) is a precious metal with remarkable resistance to corrosion.

Silver (Ag) is a precious, white metal which is resistant to corrosion, though sulphur fumes tarnish it. It conducts heat and electricity extremely well.

Sodium (Na) is a very soft metal which reacts with water and corrodes quickly in air. It is used in liquid form to extract heat from some forms of atomic reactor.

Tin (Sn) is so soft that it can be cut with a knife. Most tin is used to plate other metals, such as steel, to prevent rusting.

Titanium (Ti) is a strong metal which is very resistant to corrosion. It is used in turbine compressor blades, engine cowlings and on the leading edges of aircraft wings.

Tungsten (W) has the highest melting point of all metals (3,380°C). A familiar use of tungsten is as the filament of an electric light bulb.

Uranium (U) is a heavy, radioactive metal which is a source of nuclear power.

Vanadium (V) is used in special alloy steels for such things as axles and springs.

Zinc (Zn) is used mainly to form a rust-free coating on iron.

Archaeology

The archaeologist reconstructs the lives and activities of past peoples – how they made a living, what tools they used, what skills they had acquired, even what diseases afflicted them. The clues for building up these pictures are the traces such peoples have left behind – bones, tools, ornaments, pottery and buildings.

The archaeologist works mainly by excavating a deserted site, from which he collects all the evidence of human occupation. Excavation today is a highly professional and scientific business, though the voluntary help of amateurs is often welcome. Often it is not possible to dig up the whole site, so the excavator plans trenches across it, perhaps at the corners, or straight through the middle. Each trench is marked out and its position on the map recorded. The trench is then sunk until virgin soil, earth untouched by man, is reached. First, the top layer of soil is carefully removed. Then each level or layer of earth underneath is carefully scraped away with builders' trowels. Different layers are revealed by changes in the colour of soil. The position of everything found is carefully recorded, and important finds are photographed in position.

From these records the archaeologist draws plans of what was found in each level. Objects from the lower levels will be older than objects from the higher ones. The archaeologist knows that one kind of broken pottery is older than another kind. But how much older? Occasionally a coin with a date is found with a particular type of pottery in one place. This gives a date for that kind of pottery wherever it is found. But much archaeology depends on arranging artefacts (pottery, flints, brooches, jewellery) into types, and trying to decide which type developed out of which other type, and when.

Scientific Dating Techniques
Recently a whole series of scientific techniques have aided the archaeologist to date his finds. One of the most accurate is the carbon-14 method. Carbon-14 is a radioactive form of carbon found in plants and animals. When living things die the radioactive carbon that has been taken in *decays*, breaking down to form nitrogen. The rate of this breakdown is constant. After 5,568 years half of the radioactive carbon has decayed. After another 5,568 years half as much again has disappeared. By measuring the quantity of radioactive carbon left in

Right: A fragment of one of the Dead Sea Scrolls, which were discovered in 1947. The scrolls date from between the first century B.C. and the first century A.D. Some of them throw new light on the development of Jewish and Christian beliefs.

Below: A bundle of papyri is discovered in Israel. Much painstaking work will be needed to separate and unroll them.

old wood, bones, peat, antlers and grain, their age can be estimated.

A method of telling the relative age of human and animal remains involves testing the amount of fluorine they contain. Bones and teeth buried in the ground gradually absorb traces of fluorine. If bones found together contain the same amount of fluorine they are of the same age. This method proved the Piltdown skull to be a fake.

The Ancient World

Ancient Egypt

One of the earliest civilizations known to man began in the valley of the Nile, when wandering tribes settled along the banks of this great river. The Nile was the source of their livelihood. Each year, in June, heavy rain falling on the mountains to the south caused the river to rise and burst its banks, flooding the surrounding countryside. As the water subsided in October, the land was coated in a black layer of mud. In this fertile soil they began to plant their crops of emmer wheat and barley. From these early settlements grew one of the greatest and most brilliant civilizations the world has ever seen. Though Egypt was conquered a number of times, the ancient culture survived until after the fall of the Roman Empire, when Arabs overran the land.

The scattered villages of the Nile valley

Above: Osiris, the Ancient Egyptian god of the underworld, was linked with the doctrine of immortality.

Below: The valley of the Nile contains many impressive remains of one of the earliest civilizations.

were united around 3000 B.C. by Menes (or Narmer) who became the first pharaoh of Egypt. The early pharaohs held absolute rule, and in them were united the political, civil and spiritual powers of the nation. With subsequent dynasties (families of rulers) the power of the pharaoh waned, though he was retained as a figurehead.

The Egyptians were preoccupied with death. They mummified their dead and placed them in rich, ornately carved coffins. In the tombs they placed the earthly belongings of the dead person, believing that they would be needed in an afterlife. Owing to Egypt's dry climate, many of the contents of these tombs have been preserved, to be discovered many centuries later. They reveal to modern eyes the beauty of Egyptian artistry, and much can be learned from them about the way of life in Ancient Egypt.

The Egyptians also developed a style of picture writing called *hieroglyphics*. This was used mainly for sacred purposes, but adapted from it for everyday use was a form

of writing called *hieratic* which contained between 700 and 800 signs. The discovery of the Rosetta Stone in 1799 made it possible to decipher Egyptian writing.

The Golden Age of Crete
Midway between the continents of Africa and Europe lies the island of Crete which saw the flowering of a highly developed civilization between 2800 and 1400 B.C. The Cretans, who lived in squat, square houses grouped around magnificent stone palaces, were a race of adventurous seagoers and brilliant craftsmen. The ships of Crete carried their culture over the Aegean Sea, notably to Mycenae and Tiryns.

Archaeologists found at Cnossus evidence of a high standard of living which included indoor sanitation, exquisite frescoes, beautiful pottery and golden jewellery. About 1400 B.C., invaders, probably Greeks from the mainland, destroyed the palaces at Cnossus and Phaestus and the Cretan civilization rapidly declined.

The Homeric City of Troy
Troy was a city state situated on a hillside at the mouth of the Hellespont. The original city was probably founded by traders in touch with Crete. By 2500 B.C., it had developed into a prosperous independent outpost. Troy probably derived much of its wealth from a tax levied on all tin trade passing from the Black Sea into the Mediterranean. The city was attacked and destroyed many times. When a German called Schliemann excavated the site in 1872-4, he found traces in all of nine cities. The sacking of Troy by the Greeks in 1184 B.C., traditionally after a ten-year war, has been made famous by Homer's *Iliad*.

Civilizations of the Two Rivers
In the Tigris and Euphrates basin, another great civilization developed contemporary with that in Egypt. In the delta of these two rivers, nomadic sheep and cattle herders, the Sumerians, built thriving city-states. Ur, Lagash and Uruk were flourishing by 3500 B.C. They irrigated the marshy ground and developed prosperous agricultural communities. Surrounding the Sumerians were many other peoples, including the Assyrians, Hittites, Elamites, Amorites and Hebrews.

At first, Ur became the chief town. Then Lagash replaced it about 2400 B.C. In the next century, Sargon founded Akkad and conquered the Sumerians and their neighbours. Sargon created a great empire and spread the civilization of Sumer throughout the plain. This period of prosperity and development ended about 2000 B.C. The

Above: The huge temple, built by Rameses II at Abu Simbel, was recently moved piece by piece to save it from the rising waters behind the Aswan dam.

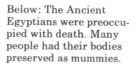

Right: The Kephren pyramid. The pyramids were built to preserve the mummified bodies of the dead god-kings for eternity.

Below: The Ancient Egyptians were preoccupied with death. Many people had their bodies preserved as mummies.

Amorites, who next held sway, built the fine city of Babylon, and under an able administrator, Hammurabi, instituted a legal and judicial system.

About 1097 B.C., the Assyrians, the strongest military force the world had yet seen, asserted themselves in the north. One of their kings, Sennacherib, constructed the earliest known aqueduct which carried water to the city of Nineveh. The Assyrian empire reached its height of splendour and learning during the reign of Assurbanipal (668–626). But soon after his death Nineveh fell to the Chaldeans (612 B.C.). Under Nebuchadnezzar, the Chaldeans built another magnificent city at Babylon, where the Israelites were held in captivity. About 539 B.C., Babylon fell to the Persians.

The Hittites
About 1800 B.C., the Hittites, a race of shepherds and farmers, established a powerful kingdom on the high plateaux of Anatolia. Records show that they were wise and

the tribes were led away to Babylon. When this city fell to the Persians, in 538 B.C., they were allowed to return, but were subjected to a succession of foreign masters – the Persians, Greeks, Ptolemies of Egypt, Seleucids and Romans.

The Phoenicians

As the maritime power of Egypt waned, the Phoenicians, a race of skilled craftsmen and merchant adventurers living in coastal cities along the eastern Mediterranean, took advantage of the situation. From the eighth century B.C., they traded throughout the Mediterranean and even reached Britain. Along the northern coast of Africa they founded several colonies, notably at Carthage, which in later centuries was itself to become a powerful commercial and political rival to Rome. The maritime power of the Phoenicians was destroyed by the Persians and Greeks.

The Persian Empire

The early Persians were nomadic tribes living on the Iranian plateau. In the mid-sixth century B.C., Cyrus the Great made himself ruler of Media and in a series of rapid conquests founded the great Persian empire, reaching from the banks of the Danube to North-West India. The Persians borrowed from the conquered nations and fused their many cultures into a unified whole. The empire was ruled wisely and well. Fine roads were built, with stations for royal messengers, and each province was ruled by a satrap, the 'eyes and ears of the king'.

Under Darius, the Persians entered a long, unsuccessful conflict with the Greek city states (499–449 B.C.). The first Persian expedition ended when a storm crippled the fleet. The second was defeated at Marathon by a smaller Athenian force. The third, under Xerxes, was checked by an heroic band of Spartans at Thermopylae, and the Persian Empire was finally destroyed by Alexander the Great in three great victories – Granicus (334 B.C.), Issus (333 B.C.) and Gaugamela (331 B.C.).

Ancient Greece

Greece was invaded and settled by a number of peoples, including Minoans, Achaeans and Dorians, who intermingled and developed the Greek language. By 1500 B.C., there were flourishing cities inhabited by Greek-speaking people on the mainland of Asia Minor as well as in Greece.

Owing to the difficulty of communications in this mountainous land, separate city-states gradually grew up. The Greek word for city-state is *polis* and the word 'politics' comes from this. The practice of politics was

humane law-givers, while their sculpture, influenced by Egypt, was copied by the Assyrians. In 1271, the Hittites concluded a treaty of peace and alliance with Rameses II of Egypt by which the Hittite conquests in Syria were recognized. The Hittite kingdom was destroyed in the late twelfth century by Thracians, Phrygians and Assyrians.

The Hebrews

The Hebrews, groups of wandering herdsmen, traced their ancestry back to Abraham, a citizen of Ur. Some of them became slaves in Egypt. Under Moses, their leader, they were led away and eventually reached the 'Promised Land' – Palestine. There they found the Canaanites, but under a poet king, David, the nations were united. Less than a century later, the kingdom was again split into two – Israel and Judah. Israel, the northern kingdom, was destroyed by the Assyrians and many of its people taken into captivity. In 586 B.C., Judah, the southern kingdom, was crushed by the Chaldeans and

Above: The snake-goddess, a small statuette found at Cnossus.

Below: Statuette of Ashur-nasir-pal II, king of Assyria (883–859 B.C.).

224

the outstanding Greek gift to the world. The city-states tried every form of government, including monarchy, aristocracy and tyranny, and they first experimented with democracy. In Athens, for example, every male citizen had a voice and a vote in running the city.

In the fifteenth century B.C., the Greek city-states engaged in a long conflict with the mighty Persian Empire from which they emerged victorious. After the defeat of Persia, there was a marvellous flowering of Greek culture, above all in Athens. The Parthenon, a perfectly proportioned temple, was built on the Acropolis between 447 and 432 B.C.

Athens built up an Empire, the Confederacy of Delos, whose members had to pay for a common fleet, but in doing so she made enemies. In 431 B.C. Sparta joined the Athenians' enemies and the long Peloponnesian War began. Under the outstanding statesman Pericles, Athens was at first successful, but she was ultimately defeated in 405 B.C. and had to admit a Spartan garrison.

The Greek city-states never learned to live together in peace. Wars continued until Philip, King of Macedon, defeated Thebes and Athens and united Greece in 338 B.C.

Philip's son, Alexander the Great, embarked upon a series of conquests which in the short space of thirteen years created an empire reaching eastwards to India. Alexander died at the age of 33 in 323 B.C., and his empire crumbled even more rapidly than it had been created. But the Hellenistic culture he helped to spread survived and was absorbed by the Roman civilization.

The Roman Empire

Rome began as a village on the banks of the River Tiber. Traditionally, it was founded by Romulus in the year 753 B.C. Rome gradually became the leader of nearby towns which were formed into the *Latin League*. In the sixth century, the Etruscans conquered Rome, but in 509 B.C. they were driven out and Rome became a republic.

Republican Rome was ruled by two elected consuls who were chosen from the patricians or richer citizens. They were helped to govern by various assemblies of which the most important was the senate. The head of every leading family was a member of this assembly. The poor citizens, the plebeians, struggled for centuries to gain equal rights. By 287 B.C. they had won the struggle and tribunes protected their rights.

After 450 B.C., Rome began to expand. By 270 B.C., she had established her power throughout much of Italy. By 120 B.C., much of Spain, southern France, Greece, Sicily,

Above: Examples of Greek pottery.

Below: The rise of the Roman Empire.

Corsica, Sardinia and present-day Tunisia lay under her rule.

As Rome's colonies increased, her citizens grew richer, and the old Roman way of life changed for the worse. The citizens began to rely heavily on slave labour, and farming became neglected because cheaper corn could be imported from North Africa. A century of civil war ensued as a struggle for power took place.

The victor in this struggle was Julius Caesar. By 45 B.C., he had become dictator of the Roman state for life. He was too cautious to call himself king, but his enemies feared his power and assassinated him. Caesar's nephew Octavian seized power after his uncle's death. He became the first Emperor of Rome under the name of Augustus. Under his wise rule, the *Pax Romana* (Roman Peace) was maintained and the rivers Rhine and Danube fixed as the northern limits of the Empire.

Towards the end of Augustus' reign, Christianity grew up as a religion. Later Emperors persecuted Christians until, in A.D. 313, the Emperor Constantine announced that they were to be allowed freedom of worship. He also established the city of Byzantium (later Constantinople, today Istanbul) as the capital of the eastern half of the Empire. After A.D. 395, rule over the Empire was divided between two emperors, one in Rome, the other in Byzantium.

From the fifth century A.D., the Empire began to decline. Barbarian tribes had long been attacking her northern and eastern frontiers. Within the Empire there were many problems: people were discontented because of high taxes; the government

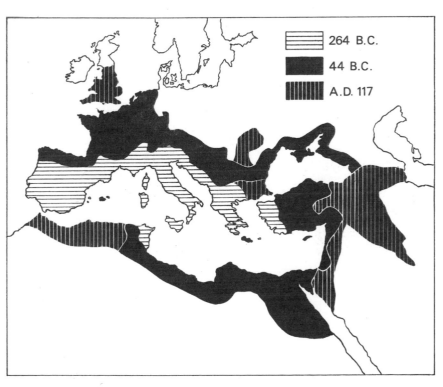

☰	264 B.C.
■	44 B.C.
▥	A.D. 117

Above: Roman ruins in northern Africa, the granary of the empire.

Above: Early Chinese craftsmen produced delicately fashioned china vessels.

officials were no longer efficient and honest; and a huge slave population meant constant fear of rebellion.

Waves of invaders now began to break through the defences. The Visigoths, under Alaric, sacked Rome in A.D. 410. Other invaders, Franks, Vandals and Huns, swept into the Empire and ravaged it. Only the eastern half of the Empire remained free until the Turkish conquest of 1453. The western half split into many small kingdoms which developed over the centuries into modern nations such as France and Spain.

The Valley of the Indus

The earliest known cities in India were in the valley of the Indus. The two largest, Mohenjo-daro and Harappa, were inhabited from 2500 to 1700 B.C. or later. Archaeologists have discovered a great deal about the daily life of these people. They could spin and weave and used a potter's wheel. They also used bronze and made jewellery of silver, ivory and gold. Seals with picture writing have been found, but nobody has yet been able to decipher this writing. Invaders from the Persian plateau probably made the inhabitants desert the cities.

China

China has the oldest *continuous* civilization in the world, dating back to about 2200 B.C. The earliest recorded dynasty, the Shang, lasted from *c.* 1750–*c.* 1122 B.C. The Chou dynasty which followed united most of China but the empire split up into a number of warring states in 479 B.C. It was reunited in 221 B.C. by the Chins who built the Great Wall of China to keep out invaders. Under the Han dynasty (206 B.C.–A.D. 220), Chinese society reached its height. Roads were built across an empire larger than present-day China, with inns and post offices at regular intervals, a civil service chosen not by birth but by examination was established; and trade was developed with India and even Rome. The Chinese still call themselves 'sons of Han'.

Chinese civilization continued and developed through successive dynasties – the Tang, Sung, Yuan and Ming. In 1644, a branch of the nomad Mongols set up the last dynasty, the Manchu, which ruled until 1911–12 when China became a republic. In 1948, the Communists came to power and radically changed the ancient culture of China.

World Gazetteer

In order to make the gazetteer as comprehensive as possible, the information has been presented in note form. The following symbols should be noted: *c*, capital city; *a*, area; *p*, population.

Current estimates have been used for the population figures of countries. All other population statistics have been taken from the latest census figures available.

A

Abidjan, *c* and port of Ivory Coast. *p* 400,000. Major export city for crops.

Accra, *c* of Ghana, W Africa. *p* 522,000.

Aconcagua, mt. in Argentina, 22,834 ft. Highest in S. America.

Addis Ababa, *c* of Ethiopia, E Africa. *p* 560,000. Commercial city. Handicrafts.

Adelaide, *c* of S. Australia. *p* 771,000. Car, flour and knitting industries.

Aden, port in South Yemen. *p* about 60,000.

Aegean Sea, part of Mediterranean Sea between Greece and Turkey. Has many islands.

Afars and Issas, French terr. in NE Africa *c* Djibouti; *a* 8,900 sq. mi.; *p* 86,000. Once called French Somaliland.

Afghanistan, landlocked monarchy in S Asia. *c* Kabul; *a* 253,861 sq. mi.; *p* 17,141,000. Bordered by USSR, China, India, Pakistan, and Iran. Products include cotton, wool, karakul pelts. Afghanistan became fully independent by 1923.

Africa, see under separate countries.

Ahmedabad, city in NW India. *p* 1,317,000.

Alabama, S state, US. *c* Montgomery. *a* 51,609 sq. mi.; *p* 3,558,000. Chemicals, coal, crops, fertilizers, iron.

Alaska, northernmost and largest state of US. *c* Juneau. *a* 586,400 sq. mi.; *p* 274,000. Fishing, forest products, furs, mining, oil.

Reaping a harvest of barley in Alaska.

Albania, mountainous republic in SE Europe. *c* Tirana; *a* 11,000 sq. mi.; *p* 2,154,000. Bordered by Yugoslavia, Bulgaria, Greece, and Adriatic Sea. Products include tobacco and petroleum. Won independence from Turkey in 1912.

Albany, *c* of New York State, US. *p* 130,000. Shipping, printing and publishing.

Alberta, province, SW Canada. *c* Edmonton. *a* 255,285 sq. mi.; *p* 1,561,000. Cattle, cereals, coal, natural gas, petroleum.

Alderney, see Channel Islands.

Aleutian Islands, US terr. near Alaska. *a* 6,821 sq. mi.; *p* 6,000. Fishing, sheep.

Alexandria, chief port of UAR. *p* 1,801,000. Once area of Greek-Egyptian culture.

Algeria, second largest republic in Africa. *c* Algiers; *a* 917,537 sq. mi.; *p* 13,152,000. Most Algerians are Arabs or Berbers who are Moslem in religion. Most people live in the small hilly strip between the coast and the Atlas Mts. Languages: Arabic and Berber. Bordered by Mediterranean Sea and seven countries. Products are fruit, cattle and oil. Won independence from France in 1962.

Algiers, *c* and major port of Algeria. *p* 943,000. Commercial, cultural city.

Alice Springs, town in Northern Territory, Australia. *p* 5,000. Transport centre.

Alps, largest European mtn range. Covers parts of Austria, France, Germany, Italy, Rumania, Switzerland, Yugoslavia.

Altai, Asian mtn range running across part of Mongolia-USSR border.

Amazon, longest river in western hemisphere, flows 3,900 mi. across South America.

Amman, *c* of Jordan. *p* 330,000. Crops, leather and textile industries.

Amsterdam, *c* and port of The Netherlands. *p* 1,715,000. Cultural city. Diamond polishing, petroleum refining, shipbuilding.

Amsterdam has many canals and fine buildings.

Amur, Asian river, 2,700 miles, flows partly along China-USSR border to the Pacific.

Anatolian Plateau, mountainous area covering most of Asiatic Turkey.

Andes, longest mtn range in world, in S. America. Runs N to S through Venezuela, Colombia, Ecuador, Peru, Bolivia, Chile, Argentina. Many peaks over 20,000 ft.

Mount Osorno a volcanic peak in Chile.

Andorra, state in Pyrenees under control of France and Spain. *c* Andorra. *a* 175 sq. mi. *p* 14,000. Livestock, tobacco, wines.

Angola, Portuguese territory in W Africa. *c* Luanda; *a* 481,352 sq. mi.; *p* 5,734,000. Located S of Congo on Atlantic Ocean. Products include fish, minerals, petroleum.

Anguilla, W. Indian I., part of St Kitts-Nevis-Anguilla group. *a* 35 sq. mi.; *p* 5,000.

Ankara, *c* of Turkey. *p* 1,067,000. Grain and fruit market. Mohair cloth.

Annapolis, *c* of Maryland, US. *p* 23,000. Naval academy. Sea foods.

Antarctic Circle, corresponds to the 66½°S line of latitude.

Antarctic Ocean, surrounding Antarctica, is often regarded as part of the Atlantic, Indian and Pacific oceans.

Antarctica, ice-bound continent surrounding S. Pole. *a* between 5,000,000 and 6,000,000 sq. mi. No permanent inhabitants. Several countries claim parts.

Antigua, W. Indian island state in association with Britain. *c* St John's; *a* 170 sq. mi.; *p* 64,000. Agriculture, cotton, rum.

Antwerp, Belgian port. *p* 253,000. Gothic cathedral and Renaissance town hall.

Apennines, mtn range, runs from N to S of Italy.

Appalachian Mtns run along E coast of N. America through Canada and US.

Arabia, vast desert peninsula in SW Asia, S of Iraq and Jordan. Mainly in Saudi Arabia. *a* about 1,185,000 sq. mi.

Arabian Sea, part of Indian Ocean between Africa and India.

Aral Sea, salt lake in SW Russia. *a* 26,166 sq. mi.

Arctic Circle corresponds to the 66½°N line of latitude.

Arctic Ocean surrounds the North Pole. *a* 5,440,000 sq. mi. Large frozen areas.

Argentina, second largest republic in S. America. *c* Buenos Aires; *a* 1,072,000 sq. mi.; *p* 24,178,000. People are mostly of Spanish and Italian descent, or are *mestizos* (mixed Amerind and European). Language: Spanish. With Chile forms S part of continent. On the central plains, called the pampas, farmers produce cattle, sheep and grain, to provide three-quarters of Argentina's wealth. Won independence from Spain in 1816.

Arizona, SW state, US. *c* Phoenix; *a* 113,909 sq. mi.; *p* 1,663,000. Agriculture, copper, gold, lead, silver, uranium. Famed for magnificent Grand Canyon.

Arkansas, S state, US. *c* Little Rock; *a* 53,104 sq. mi.; *p* 1,986,000. Cotton, rice, bauxite, coal, natural gas, petroleum.

Arkansas, river in S US, 1,450 mi. long.

Ascension, British island in Atlantic Ocean. *a* 34 sq. mi.; *p* 1,200.

Asia, see under separate countries.

Asunción, *c* and main port of Paraguay. *p* 305,000. Food, paper, textile industries.

Athens, *c* of Greece. *p* 1,853,000. Cultural, business and tourist city. Site of Parthenon and similar buildings.

Atlanta, *c* of Georgia, US. *p* 1,258,000. Cultural and trade city. Communications point.

Atlantic Ocean touches Africa, Americas, and Europe. *a* 31,530,000 sq. mi.

Atlas, mtn range in NW Africa running through Morocco, Algeria and Tunisia.

Auckland, city of New Zealand. *p* 588,000.

Augusta, *c* of Maine, US. *p* 22,000.

Austin, *c* of Texas, US. *p* 247,000. Educational city. Bricks, furniture.

Australia, Commonwealth monarchy, is the world's largest island. *c* Canberra; *a* (including Tasmania) 2,967,741 sq. mi.; *p* 12,588,000. Almost all Australians are of European origin — mainly British. Language: English. Religions: Protestantism and Roman Catholicism. Half of Australia's people live in 6 cities. Inhabited only by aborigines until the 1600's, Australia developed into an independent British nation by 1900. Temperate SE Australia is the most, and tropical N Australia the least developed. Because Australia was cut off from other land masses in early times, it has some animals, such as kangaroos, which are found in no other country.

Although most of Australia is desert, or semi desert, the fertile area is bigger than many European countries. Sheep and wheat are important. Minerals include coal, gold, lead, petroleum, silver, uranium, zinc. Manufacturing industries are developing fast to supply Australia's needs. S Australia has many lakes, including Eyre, Frome, Gairdner, Torrens. Australia has 6 states, 2 mainland territories, and several overseas territories.

Above: A view over Canberra, the capital of Australia.

Below: Kangaroos are marsupials found only in Australia. There are over 20 different species, the smaller ones being known as wallabies.

Austria, European republic in Alps. *c* Vienna; *a* 32,374 sq. mi.; *p* 7,437,000. Austrians are a German speaking people, and mainly Roman Catholic. One third of the country is forest. Chief river: Danube. Most farms are small. Main products are crude oil and machinery. Austria lost its great empire in defeat in 1918.

Azores, Portuguese islands in mid Atlantic. *a* 922 sq. mi.; *p* 337,000. Fruit, wine.

B

Baffin Bay, Canada, lies W of Greenland.

Baghdad, *c* of Iraq. *p* 1,745,000. Site of city of Arabian Nights. On Tigris river.

Bahamas, W. Indian Is. British territory. *c* Nassau; *a* 4,404 sq mi; *p* 164,000. Fish, fruit, handicrafts, salt, sponges.

Bahrain, island sheikdom in Persian Gulf. *c* Manama; *a* about 213 sq. mi.; *p* 227,000. Rich in petroleum. Pearl fisheries.

Baku, city in SW USSR. *p* 1,218,000. Main port for surrounding petroleum producing area.

Bali, Indonesian island. *a* about 2,200 sq. mi.; *p* 1,783,000. Famous native dancers. 30,000 temples. Indian in culture.

Balkans, term used to describe peninsula containing Albania, Bulgaria, Greece, Rumania, Turkey (in Europe), Yugoslavia.

Balkhash, lake in S USSR. *a* 6,680 sq. mi.

Baltic Sea, N Europe. *a* 160,000 sq. mi.

Baltimore, port in Maryland, US. *p* 1,980,000. Shipbuilding, shipping, manufacturing.

Bamako, *c* of Mali, W Africa; *p* 165,000.

Banff National Park, SW Alberta, Canada. Located in Rockies. *a* 2,564 sq. mi.

Bangkok, *c* and leading port of Thailand. *p* 1,608,000. Cultural, economic city. Many tourist attractions, including temples.

Bangladesh, republic in S. Asia, *c* Dacca; *a* 55,000 sq. mi.; *p* 59,000,000. Formerly East Pakistan, Bangladesh achieved independence in 1971. The land is fertile and densely populated. It is watered by the Ganges and Brahmaputra rivers. Products include rice, jute and tea.

Bangui, *c* of Central African Republic, *p* 111,000. Trading town linked to Congo River.

Barbados, W. Indian island. Independent state, *c* Bridgetown; *a* 166 sq. mi.; *p* 254,000. Cotton, fruit, rum, sugar.

Barcelona, largest port in NE Spain. *p* 1,697,000. Food processing, textiles.

Basra, major port of Iraq. *p* 404,000.

Bathurst, *c* of Gambia, W Africa. *p* 28,000.

Baton Rouge, *c* of Louisiana, US, *p* 152,000. Cotton, petroleum refining.

Baykal, large deep freshwater lake in SE Siberia, USSR. *a* 12,150 sq. mi. Depth reaches 5,712 ft. in places.

Beirut, *c* and chief seaport of Lebanon; *p* 700,000. Site of Phoenician city.

Belfast, *c* of N. Ireland; *p* 380,000.

Belgium, monarchy in NW Europe. *c* Brussels; *a* 11,779 sq. mi.; *p* 9,759,000. Belgians in the north are Flemish speaking. In the south, the Walloon people speak French. Bordered by Netherlands, Germany, Luxembourg and France. Two thirds of Belgium is fertile farmland, but manufacturing provides the main income. Chief port: Antwerp. Products include cereals, flax, handicrafts, machinery and minerals. Won independence in 1830.

Belgrade, *c* and port on Danube river, Yugoslavia; *p* 585,000. Food processing.

Bengal, Bay of, part of N Indian Ocean between India and Burma. *a* 339,280 sq. mi.

Ben Nevis, mt. in Invernesshire, Scotland, 4,406 ft. Highest peak in Britain.

Bering Sea, N Pacific, between Alaska and USSR. *a* about 878,000 sq. mi.

Berlin, former capital of all Germany. Since 1945, divided into W. (now part of W. Germany) and E. (now capital of E. Germany). *p* 3,270,000 (E. 1,079,000; W. 2,191,000).

Bermuda, British territory. 360 islands in W Atlantic. *a* 21 sq. mi.; *p* 54,000.

Berne, *c* of Switzerland; *p* 167,000. Chocolate, dairy products, watches.

Bhutan, independent state in E Himalaya. *c* Thimbu; *a* 18,147 sq. mi.; *p* 805,000. Cloth, forestry, grains. People mainly nomadic.

Bikini, island in central Pacific. *a* 2 sq. mi. People moved to Kili and Rongerik because of US atomic bomb test on island, 1946.

Birmingham, city in central England. *p* 1,075,000. Great industrial area.

Below: The small deepwater harbour at Bridgetown handles most of Barbados's exports.

Biscay, Bay of, stormy part of Atlantic W of France, N of Spain.

Bismarck, c of North Dakota, US. p 33,000.

Black Sea, inland sea between USSR, Turkey, Bulgaria, Rumania. a 170,000 sq. mi.

Bloemfontein, c of Orange Free State, S. Africa. p 146,000. Court of Appeals located in city. Cattle and marketing point.

Bogotá, c and largest city of Colombia; p 2,206,000. Cultural and social city.

Boise, c of Idaho, US; p 99,000. Food processing. Hot springs nearby.

Bolivia, landlocked republic in S. America. c La Paz (actual), Sucre (official). a 424,163 sq. mi.; p 3,965,000. People are of Amerind or European descent or are *mestizos* (mixed). Language: Spanish. Bordered by Peru, Brazil, Paraguay, Argentina, Chile. The Andes cover W Bolivia, which contains Lake Titicaca (12,500 ft.). Mainly agricultural. Several minerals extracted. Won independence from Spain by 1825.

Bombay, port in W India. p 4,784,000. Cultural city and trade point. Chemicals, grain, metals, shipbuilding.

Bonn, c of W. Germany; p 144,000. Birthplace of Beethoven. Cultural city.

Borneo, island divided between Brunei, Indonesia and Malaysia. a 285,000 sq. mi. Diamonds, petroleum, rice, rubber, teak.

Bosporus, strait linking Asian and European Turkey. Between Black Sea and Sea of Marmara.

Boston, c and port of Massachusetts, US; p 697,000. Many historical places.

Botany Bay, shallow inlet 5 mi· S of Sydney, Australia. Site of first British landing by Captain Cook in 1770.

Botswana, Commonwealth republic in southern Africa. c Gaberones; a 275,000 sq. mi.; p 655,000. Borders S. Africa. Includes Kalahari desert. Cattle and tourism. Called Bechuanaland until independence in 1966.

Brasilia, c of Brazil; p 200,000. Outstanding modern architecture. Interior capital since 1960, replacing Rio de Janeiro.

Brazil, largest republic in S. America. c Brasilia; a 3,286,478 sq. mi.; p 95,000,000. Most people are of Portuguese, the rest of Amerind, Negro or mixed descent. Language: Portuguese. Bordered by Atlantic Ocean and all S. American countries except Chile and Ecuador. The Amazon's tropical forests cover N Brazil. Most Brazilians live in the central and S plateaus. Brazil grows half the world's coffee, and has lumber, iron ore and manganese. Many resources unexploited. Brazil won independence from Portugal in 1822.

Brazzaville, c of Congo (Brazzaville); p 136,000. Commercial city.

Brisbane, c and port of SE Queensland, Australia; p 778,000. Trading city.

Bristol, England. p 428,000. Port and cultural city.

British Columbia, province, SW Canada. c Victoria; a 355,855 sq. mi.; p 2,067,000. Agriculture, canning, fishing, minerals.

British Honduras, Brit. territory in Central America. c Belize; a 8,666 sq. mi.; p 123,000. Agriculture, fishing, forestry.

British Indian Ocean Territory, formed in 1965 from Chagos Archipelago, Aldabra, Farqhar and Des Roches. p 1,500.

Brunei, British protected state in Borneo. c Brunei; a 2,226 sq. mi.; p 122,000. Pepper, petroleum, rubber, timber.

Brussels, c of Belgium; p 1,074,000. Carpets, lace, textiles.

Bucharest, c of Rumania; p 1,247,000. Cultural and industrial city.

Budapest, c of Hungary; p 1,970,000. Communications city on Danube. Grain, metals, textiles, wine.

Buenos Aires, c of Argentina; p 2,967,000. Main port, business and social city.

Buffalo, port in New York State, US. p 1,323,000. Aircraft, petroleum refining, textiles.

Bujumbura, c of Burundi, E Africa; p 71,000.

Bulgaria, republic in SE Europe (Balkans). c Sofia; a 42,729 sq. mi.; p 8,525,000. People are mainly of Bulgar-Slav origins. Most people are farmers who live in small villages. Products include grain, livestock, minerals, rose oil, salt, textiles and tobacco. Bulgaria united and achieved independence in 1885.

Traditional Bulgarian folk dancing at a village festival.

Burma, republic in SE Asia. c Rangoon; a 261,789 sq. mi.; p 27,327,000. Most Burmese are farmers. Buddhism is the main religion. Chief products include grain, petroleum, rubber, teak, textiles, minerals (including precious stones).

Burundi, republic in E central Africa. c Bujumbura; a 10,747 sq. mi.; p 3,544,000. Bordered by Rwanda, Tanzania and Congo. Main product, coffee. Independent from Belgium since 1962.

C

Cairo, c of UAR. Main port on Nile; p 4,197,000. Handicrafts, paper, textiles. Pyramids nearby, at Giza.

Calcutta, chief port of NE India, in Ganges delta. p 4,703,000. Food processing, jute, mineral and textile industries.

California, W state, US. c Sacramento; a 158,693 sq. mi.; p 19,300,000. Fruit, fishing, lumber, minerals. Famous places include Death Valley and Hollywood.

The campus of Berkeley University, California.

California, Gulf of, lies between California and Mexico.

Cambodia, monarchy in SE Asia. c Phnom Penh; a 69,898 sq. mi.; p 7,003,000. Most people are Buddhists. Cambodia is a tropical country. Rice, rubber and textiles are the main products. Fishing and forestry are also important industries. Buddhist temples provide tourist attraction.

Cambridge, Cambridgeshire, Britain. p 100,000. Famous university town.

Cameroon, federal republic in W Africa. c Yaounde. a 183,569 sq. mi.; p 5,837,000. Bordered by Nigeria, Chad, Central African Republic, Congo (Brazzaville), Gabon, Eq. Guinea. Products include cocoa, coffee and lumber. Independent from France since 1960.

Canada, monarchy in N. America. c Ottawa; a 3,851,809 sq. mi.; p 21,477,000. Languages: English, French. Main religions: Protestantism, Roman Catholicism. Canada's 10 provinces and 2 territories lie north of its 4,000 mile southern border with the US. Alaska and the Pacific lie to the W, Greenland and the Atlantic to the E. Only Russia is bigger. Due largely to its cold climate, Canada developed slowly. British and French trappers and farmers settled southern Canada from E to W during the 1800's. In the 1900's, the population trebled. Canada developed prosperous farming, fishing, forestry, mining and manufacturing industries.

The Rocky Mts rise in the W. Several huge lakes lie between the Great Lakes (shared with the US) and the Arctic Ocean NE of Alaska. To the E, Hudson Bay is partly iced up between September and May. Canada's great rivers include Mackenzie, St Lawrence, Yukon. Each province has its own prime minister with limited powers under the federal system.

Canary Islands, N Atlantic, form two Spanish provinces. a 2,807 sq. mi.; p 987,000. Agriculture. Largest island: Tenerife.

Canberra, c of Australia in Australian Capital Territory; p 107,000. Cultural, educational, and science city.

Cancer, Tropic of, latitude 23½°N marks the northern limit of the tropics.

Canterbury, city and county borough, England. p 33,000. Famous Gothic cathedral dates from 11th-15th centuries.

Canton, port in S China. p 1,840,000. Chemicals, chinaware, machines, textiles.

Cape Cod, peninsula in W Massachusetts, US. Codfish and cranberries.

Cape Horn, southernmost tip of S. America. Stormy, feared by early navigators.

Cape Kennedy, missile base in Florida, US.

Cape of Good Hope, S. Africa. Southernmost tip of Africa.

Cape Province, S. Africa. c Cape Town; a 278,465 sq. mi.; p 5,363,000. Copper, diamonds, fruit, sheep, tobacco, wheat.

Cape Town, port and c of Cape Province, S Africa; p 625,000. Legislative c of S. Africa. Food processing, fishing, wine.

Cape Verde Islands, Portuguese terr. in Atlantic. c Praia; a 1,557 sq. mi.; p 220,000. Copper, diamonds, sugar, wine.

Capricorn, Tropic of, latitude 23½°S marks the southern limit of the tropics.

Caracas, c of Venezuela; p 1,695,000; Cultural and trading city.

Cardiff, c and largest city of Wales; p 287,000. Important communications and industrial city.

Caribbean, sea between W. Indies and mainland Americas. a 750,000 sq. mi.

Carlsbad Caverns, SE New Mexico, US. a 71 sq. mi. Limestone decorations.

Caroline Island, US Pacific Trust Terr. in Pacific. a 462 sq. mi. Copra, phosphate.

Carpathian Mtns, range in central and eastern Europe, mainly forested.

Carson City, c of Nevada, US; p 5,000.

Carstensz, mt., New Guinea. Highest island peak in world, 16,500 ft.

Casablanca, largest city and port of Morocco. *p* 1,085,000. Mineral industries.

Caspian Sea, world's largest inland body of water. Iran-USSR. *a* 170,000 sq. mi.

Caucasus, mtn range bordering Europe and Asia, in USSR. Highest peak: Elbrus.

Cayman Islands, three British islands S of Cuba. *a* 100 sq. mi. *p* 46,000.

Celebes, island of Indonesia. One of the Greater Sunda islands.

Central African Republic, *c* Bangui; *a* 227,118 sq. mi.; *p* 1,511,000. Landlocked between Chad, Sudan, both Congos, Cameroon. Products include diamonds, cotton. Independent from France since 1960.

Ceylon (Sri Lanka), island commonwealth monarchy in Indian Ocean. *c* Colombo; *a* 25,332 sq. mi.; *p* 12,743,000. Main religion: Buddhism. Main language: Sinhala. Products include coconuts, graphite, precious stones and rubber. Tea is the main export. Became independent from Britain in 1948.

Chad, landlocked desert republic in N central Africa. *c* Fort-Lamy; *a* 495,793 sq. mi.; *p* 3,568,000. Lake Chad in W. Products include cotton, cattle. Independent from France since 1960.

Channel Islands, British islands with limited self-government off NW France. *a* 75 sq. mi.; *p* 119,000. Cattle, tomatoes, tourism. Islands include Alderney, Guernsey, Jersey, Sark.

Charleston, *c* of West Virginia, US; *p* 245,000. Coal, lumber, petroleum.

Charlottetown, *c* and port of Prince Edward Island, Canada; *p* 18,000. Fish, shipyards.

Chatham Island, E of, and belonging to, New Zealand. *a* 372 sq. mi.; *p* 490.

Chengtu, port in S China. *p* 1,107,000.

Cheyenne, *c* of Wyoming, US; *p* 44,000. Transport point for livestock.

Chicago, city in Illinois, US, on Lake Michigan *p* 6,632,000. Grain, livestock, steel mills. Airport is among world's largest. Many colleges, universities.

Chile, coastal republic in S. America. *c* Santiago; *a* 286,397 sq. mi.; *p* 9,583,000. Chileans are mainly *mestizos* (of mixed Spanish and Amerind descent). Bordered by Peru, Bolivia, Argentina, Pacific. Andes run along border. Three-quarters of exports are minerals, including copper, iron ore, and nitrates. Won independence from Spain in 1818.

China, communist republic in E Asia. *c* Peking; *a* 3,691,502 sq. mi.; *p* about 753,568,000. Main language: Chinese. Most people are Chinese. Traditional religions, Confucianism, Taoism, Buddhism, are in decline.

China borders 11 other countries and the Pacific Ocean. China's 21 provinces are the home of its 3,500 year-old culture based upon careful farming, which developed around the Yangtze and Hwang rivers. China absorbed outlying deserts and plateaus to form its 5 outer regions of Kwangsi Chuang, Tibet, Sinkiang Uighur, Inner Mongolia and Ningsia Hui. *Loess* (wind-swept yellow fertile dust) covers much of NE China and gives the Yellow Sea its name. Since 1949, China has attempted a 'great leap forward' to catch up with the West industrially.

Christchurch, *c* of Canterbury, New Zealand; *p* 258,000. Cultural and industrial city.

Christmas Island, in E Indian Ocean, belongs to Australia. *a* 62 sq. mi.; *p* 3,000.

Christmas Island, central Pacific, claimed by both Britain and US. *a* 220 sq. mi.; *p* 52.

Chungking, city in SW China. *p* 2,121,000. Wartime capital. Chemicals, metals, textiles.

Cincinnati, city in Ohio, US; *p* 1,353,000. Meat packing, machines, plastics.

Cleveland, port in Ohio, US. *p* 2,004,000. Factories and steel mills.

Colombia, republic in S. America. *c* Bogotá;

a 455,335 sq. mi.; *p* 21,154,000. People are mainly of Spanish descent, or are *mestizos* (mixed European and Amerind). Language: Spanish. Bordered by Venezuela, Brazil, Peru, Ecuador, Pacific Ocean, Panama, Caribbean Sea. Products include coffee, petroleum and other minerals. Won independence from Spain in 1819.

Workers tend young rubber tree seedlings on a plantation in Colombia.

Colombo, *c* and main port of Ceylon. *p* 511,000. Coconuts, rubber and tea.

Colorado, US state in Rocky Mts. *c* Denver; *a* 104,247 sq. mi.; *p* 2,043,000 Cattle, cereals, precious metals, petroleum.

Columbia, *c* of South Carolina, US; *p* 289,000. Cotton mills, ironworks.

Columbus, *c* of Ohio, US; *p* 851,000. Chemicals, machinery and paper goods.

Comoro Islands, French territory in SE Africa. *c* Dzaoudzi; *a* 830 sq. mi.; *p* 250,000.

Conakry, *c* of Guinea, W Africa; *p* 175,000. Exports include bauxite and coffee.

Concord, *c* of New Hampshire, US; *p* 29,000. Granite, textiles. Skiing nearby.

Congo (Brazzaville), republic in equatorial Africa. *c* Brazzaville; *a* 132,046 sq. mi.; *p* 906,000. Bordered by Atlantic Ocean, Congo (Kinshasa), and four other countries. Timber. Independent from France since 1960.

Congo (Kinshasa), republic in equatorial Africa. *c* Kinshasa; *a* 905,563 sq. mi.; *p* 17,440,000. Congo has a tiny Atlantic coastline, and is bordered by Lake Tanganyika, Congo (Brazzaville) and nine other countries. River Congo and rain forests dominate much of the country. Katanga highlands are rich in cobalt, diamonds, and copper – the main source of income. Independent from Belgium since 1960. Became involved in bitter civil wars. Renamed Zaire Republic in 1971.

Congo, W African river. 2,718 mi. long.

Connecticut, NE state, US. *c* Hartford; *a* 5,009 sq. mi.; *p* 2,963,000. Aircraft engines, fishing, machines, watches. Yale University founded at Branford in 1706.

Cook Island, New Zealand dependency in S Pacific. *c* Avarua; *a* 90 sq. mi.; *p* 20,000.

Copenhagen, *c* and largest port of Denmark; *p* 1,378,000. Dairy products, furniture.

Cork, city in Republic of Ireland. *p* 122,000 Many Roman Catholic churches.

Corsica, French island in Mediterranean. *c* Ajaccio; *a* 3,368 sq. mi.; *p* 275,000. Sheep, wine. Birthplace of Napoleon.

Costa Rica, small republic in central America. *c* San José; *a* 19,600 sq. mi.; *p* 1,746,000. Bordered by Nicaragua, Caribbean Sea, Panama, Pacific Ocean. Products include bananas and coffee. Independent since 1844.

Coventry, England. City with outstanding modern cathedral. *p* 336,000.

Crete, Greek island in Mediterranean. *a* 3,235 sq. mi.; *p* 483,000. Centre of an ancient civilization.

Cuba, island republic in West Indies. *c* Havana; *a* 44,218 sq. mi.; *p* 8,579,000. Cubans are of Spanish, Amerind, Negro or mixed descent. Language: Spanish. Location, about 150 mi. S of Florida. Half the land is flat. The rest is hilly with mountains in SE. Main products include minerals, sugar, tobacco. Cuba gained independence in 1898 after Spanish-American War.

Curacao, Dutch Island N of Venezuela. *a* 210 sq. mi.; *p* 145,000. Petroleum refineries.

Cyprus, island republic in Mediterranean. *c* Nicosia; *a* 3,572 sq. mi.; *p* 627,000. Most Cypriots follow Greek Orthodox religion and speak Greek. Some are Turkish Moslems. Products include cereals, copper, fruit, iron ore and vegetables. Won independence from Britain in 1960.

A market stall in Cyprus. Great poverty still exists in many parts of the island.

Czechoslovakia, mainly industrial republic in central Europe. *c* Prague; *a* 49,370 sq. mi.; *p* 14,643,000. People are mainly Czech and Slovak. Danube flows through the south. Soil is fertile and rich in minerals. Products include coal, glassware, grain, iron ore, machinery and uranium. Won independence, mainly from Austria, in 1918.

D

Dahomey, republic in W Africa. *c* Porto Novo; *a* 43,483 sq. mi.; *p* 2,681,000. Bordered by Togo, Upper Volta, Nigeria, Gulf of Guinea. Nuts and palm oil. Independent from France since 1960.

Dakar, *c* of Senegal, W Africa; *p* 375,000.

Dallas, city in N Texas, US. *p* 1,352,000. Aircraft, cotton, machinery industries.

Damascus, *c* of Syria. *p* 600,000. Among oldest cities in world. Famous for metalwork, mosaics and silk brocades.

Danube, second longest river in Europe, flows 1,750 mi. through 8 countries.

Dardanelles, strait linking Sea of Marmara to Aegean. Commands entrance to Black Sea/Mediterranean. 40 mi. long.

Dar-es-Salaam, *c* of Tanzania, E Africa. *p*. 273,000. Petroleum refining, textiles.

Dartmoor, plateau in SW Devon, England. *a* 220 sq. mi. Ponies, deer, wild life.

Darwin, *c* and port of Northern Territory, Australia. Communications point. *p* 20,000.

Dead Sea, lake between Israel and Jordan. *a* 340 sq. mi. (25% salt).

Death Valley, E California, US. Lowest point in western hemisphere. 282 ft. below sea level. Extreme temperatures.

Delaware, NE state, US. *c* Dover; *a* 2,057 sq. mi.; *p* 534,000. Chemicals, dairy foods, fishing, furs, lumber, minerals.

Delhi, c of India. p 2,441,000. City is in two parts, old and new. Jewellery, metal and textile industries.

Denmark, monarchy in NW Europe. c Copenhagen; a 16,619 sq. mi.; p 4,913,000. Language: Danish. Denmark consists of a peninsula and many islands. Bordered by Germany and the Baltic and North seas. Dairy farming, fishing, furniture and ship-building are the main industries. Danish Vikings explored and settled in many parts of the western world by 1000 A.D.

Denver, c of Colorado, US; p 1,081,000. Skiing resort.

Des Moines, c of Iowa, midwest US. p 271,000. Manufacturing city.

Detroit, port in Michigan, US. p 4,060,000. World-famed for automobiles.

Doha, c of Qatar, Persian Gulf. p 28,000.

Dom, Swiss mt., 14,913 ft.

Dominica, W. Indian island state in association with Britain. c Roseau; a 298 sq. mi.; p 74,000. Fruit, spices, sugar.

Dominican Republic, state in W. Indies. c Santo Domingo; a 18,704 sq. mi.; p 4,320,000. Covers two-thirds of island of Hispaniola. Cocoa, coffee and sugar are grown. Under Spanish, French, Haitian and US rule until final independence achieved in 1924.

Dover, c of Delaware, US. p 15,000.

Dover, port in England. p 36,000.

Drakensberg, S African mtn range running between Natal and Orange Free State.

Dublin, c of Republic of Ireland. p 569,000. Administrative, communications and cultural city. Clothing, electrical goods, glass, stout.

Durban, city in South Africa. p 663,000. Agriculture, textiles.

E

Easter Island, E Pacific. Governed by Chile. a 45 sq. mi.; p about 250. Many mysterious stone statues.

Ecuador, equatorial republic in S. America. c Quito; a 104,506 sq. mi.; p 6,064,000. Bordered by Colombia, Peru and Pacific Ocean. Half the people are Amerind, the rest are of Spanish or *mestizos* (mixed) descent. Exports include bananas and balsa. Independent since 1830.

Edinburgh, c of Scotland. p 466,000. Annual festival attracts many visitors.

Edmonton, c and port of Alberta, Canada. p 377,000. Farming, petroleum.

Egypt (UAR), republic in N Africa. c Cairo; a 386,100 sq. mi.; p 33,277,000. People are Moslems of Arab, Negro, or mixed descent. Bordered by Mediterranean Sea, Israel, Red Sea, Sudan and Libya. 95% of Egyptians live on the 3% of fertile land in the Nile Valley, where

Barren deserts cover 97 per cent of Egypt. The donkey and the camel are still the only available transport for many people.

many grow cotton or grain, the staple produce. Egypt attracts many tourists. Independent since 1922.

Elbrus, mt. in Caucasus, NW Georgia, USSR. Highest point in Europe, 18,481 ft.

Elburtz, mtn range in N Iran.

El Salvador, smallest republic in Central America. c San Salvador; a 8,260 sq. mi.; p 3,472,000. Bordered by Guatemala, Honduras, Pacific Ocean. Products include coffee and rubber. Gained final independence in 1841.

English Channel, narrow sea between England and France, about 300 miles long.

Equatorial Guinea, republic in W Africa. c Santa Isabel; a 10,832 sq. mi.; p 293,000. Bordered by Cameroon and Gabon. Coffee grown. Called Rio Muni and Fernando Po until independence from Spain in 1968.

Erie, one of Gt Lakes, N. America. a 9,940 sq. mi. Ports include Buffalo, Cleveland, Port Colbourne, Toledo.

Ethiopia, monarchy in NE Africa. c Addis Ababa; a 398,350 sq. mi.; p 24,604,000 (including Eritrea). Most Ethiopians are Coptic Christians, some are Moslems. Language: Amharic. Bordered by Red Sea, Afars and Issas, Somalia, Kenya, Sudan. Products are coffee, livestock and minerals. Ancient empire.

Ethiopian Highlands, mtn range covering whole of north and west Ethiopia.

Euphrates, W Asian river flowing 1,700 mi. through Armenia, Turkey, Syria, Iraq.

Europe, see under separate countries.
Everest, mt. in China – Nepal. Highest in the world, 29,028 feet.
Everglades National Park, S Florida, US. *a* 1,719 sq. mi. Lakes and swamps. Famed for wildlife.

F

Falkland Is, British territory in S. Atlantic. *c* Port Stanley. *a* 4,618 sq. mi.; *p* 2,000.
Faroe Islands, in N Atlantic. Danish territory with limited self government. *a* 540 sq. mi.; *p* 39,000.
Fiji, group of islands in S Pacific, British territory. *c* Suva; *a* 7,056 sq. mi.; *p* 544,000 Bananas, cotton, sugar.

Above: Fijian natives prepare for the ritual fire-walking ceremony.

Finland, republic in N Europe. *c* Helsinki; *a* 130,120 sq. mi.; *p* 4,789,000. Official languages: Finnish and Swedish. Finland is bordered by Sweden, Norway, USSR, Baltic Sea, Gulf of Bothnia. Finland has many lakes and forests. Timber is the chief source of income, cereals and potatoes the main crops. Won independence from Russia in 1917.
Flinders Chase National Park, Kangaroo Island, Australia. *a* 212 sq. mi.
Florida, SE state, US. *c* Tallahassee; *a* 58,560 sq. mi.; *p* 6,151,000. Fish, fruit, lumber, minerals, sponges, sugar. Contains Cape Kennedy and Miami Beach.
Folkstone, port in SE England. *p* 44,000.
Formosa, see Taiwan.
Fort Lamy, *c* of Chad, Africa. *p* 35,000.
France, republic in W Europe. *c* Paris; *a* 211,207 sq. mi. (including Corsica); *p* 51,814,000. Language: French. Main religion: Roman Catholicism. Bordered by Belgium, Luxembourg, Germany, Switzerland, Italy, Mediterranean Sea, Spain, Bay of Biscay, English Channel. N and W France is mainly flat. S and E lie the Massif Central and the Vosges, Jura Alps and Pyrenees mountains. Rivers include the Garonne, Loire, Rhône and Seine.

Mild climate, fertile soil and natural resources make France a leading farming and industrial country. Products include automobiles, coal, iron, wheat, wine. An ancient country, France held a world empire until the 1960's. Since 1957, increasingly integrated in EEC and other European organizations.

Below: Notre Dame Cathedral is built on a small island in the River Seine in France's capital.

Frankfort, *c* of Kentucky, US. *p* 18,000.
Fredericton, *c* of New Brunswick, Canada. *p* 22,000. Leather goods, lumbering.
Freetown, *c* and main port, Sierra Leone. *p* 148,000. Commercial city.
French Guiana, territory in NE S. America. *c* Cayenne; *a* 34,740 sq. mi.; *p* 36,000.
French Oceania, group of islands in Pacific. Includes Gambier, Marquesas, Society, Tuamotu and Tubai Is. *c* Papeete, on Tahiti; *a* 1,554 sq. mi.; *p* about 90,000.
Friendly Islands, see Tonga.

G

Gabon, equatorial republic in W Africa. *c* Libreville; *a* 103,089 sq. mi.; *p* 497,000. Bordered by Cameroon, Equatorial Guinea, Congo (Braz.), Atlantic. Timber and manganese. Independent from France since 1960.
Galapagos Islands, in E Pacific belong to Ecuador. *a* 2,868 sq. mi.; *p* 2,500. Named after Spanish word for turtles.
Galway, port in Republic of Ireland. *p* 25,000. Fishing, textiles.
Gambia, small republic in W Africa. *c* Bathurst; *a* 4,005 sq. mi.; *p* 362,000. Bordered by Senegal, Atlantic. Products include groundnuts, rice. Independent from Britain since 1966.
Georgia, SE state, US. *c* Atlanta; *a* 58,876 sq. mi.; *p* 4,568,000. Corn, cotton, fruit, lumber, peanuts, steel, tobacco.
Germany, East, republic in central Europe. *c* Berlin; *a* 41,659 sq. mi.; *p* 15,860,000 (excluding Berlin). Language: German. Bordered by Poland, Czechoslovakia, W Germany, Baltic Sea. The Elbe river divides E. Germany from W. The Oder and Neisse rivers form the border with Poland. Since its separation from W. Germany in 1945, E. Germany has become an important industrial country.
Germany, West, republic in central Europe. *c* Bonn; *a* 95,928 sq. mi.; *p* 60,294,000 (excluding Berlin). Language: German. Religions: Protestantism and Roman Catholicism. W. Germany borders E. Germany and eight other nations, and has short coastlines on the Baltic and North seas. Flat in the N, Germany becomes increasingly mountainous to the S. Mts include Alps, Harz, Schwarzwald (Black Forest). Rivers include Danube, Elbe, Ems, Rhine, Weser. All are important commercially. Defeated and occupied after 1945, W. Germany is now one of the greatest industrial nations and a member of EEC.
Ghana, republic in W Africa. *c* Accra; *a* 92,100 sq. mi.; *p* 8,838,000. People are mainly of the Adansi, Akwamu and Ga tribes. Main language: English. Bordered by Ivory Coast, Upper Volta, Togo, Gulf of Guinea. Lake Volta lies to E. Products include cocoa, diamonds, gold and lumber. Called Gold Coast until independence from Britain in 1957.
Gibraltar, British territory bordering S Spain. *a* 2·25 sq. mi.; *p* 26,000.
Gilbert and Ellice Islands, British territory in SW Pacific. *c* Tarawa; *a* 375 sq. mi.; *p* 60,000.
Glacier National Park, NW Montana, US. *a* 1,560 sq. mi. Over 200 glacier-fed lakes.
Glasgow, Scotland's greatest industrial city. *p* 937,000. Engineering, printing and shipbuilding.
Gobi, Chinese–Mongolian desert, bleak, cold and stony. *a* 500,000 sq. mi.
Gorki, city in SW USSR. *p* 1,140,000.
Grand Canyon, Arizona, US. 217 mi. long; 1 mi. deep. Many layers of rock are exposed where worn away by Colorado river.
Gt Australian Bight, bay south of Australia. *a* about 570,000 sq. mi.
Great Basin, plateau and desert on western US. *a* about 210,000 sq. mi.
Greater Antilles, island group in W. Indies.

Includes Cuba, Jamaica, Hispaniola, Puerto Rico and smaller islands.

Gt Lakes, in N America, are: Erie, Huron, Michigan, Ontario, Superior. *a* 94,000 sq. mi. Largest group of freshwater lakes in world.

Greece, monarchy in SE Europe. *c* Athens; *a* 50,944 sq. mi.; *p* 8,856,000. Greeks call themselves *Hellenes* after the goddess Helen. Greece is composed of a peninsula and 437 islands. More than half the people are farmers. Main products include fruit, livestock, olive oil wine, lignite, marble. Ancient Greek civilization flourished 2500 years ago. Many modern technical terms are based on old Greek words.

Greenland, largest island in N. America. Danish territory. *c.* Godthaab; *a* 840,000 sq. mi.; *p* 48,000. Density, 5 people to 100 sq. mi. Cryolite mined.

A young mother from Thule in Greenland carries her baby in its strange, but practical 'pram'.

Grenada, W. Indian island state in association with Britain. *o* St Georgo'o; *a* 138 sq. mi.; *p* 105,000. Spices and other foods.

Guadalajara, city in W Mexico; *p* 1,138,000. Agriculture, pottery. Rail and road hub.

Gaudeloupe, French island in W. Indies. *c* Basse-Terre; *a* 687 sq. mi.; *p* 355,000. Products include bananas, cocoa, coffee, rum, sugar cane.

Guam, US territory in Mariana Islands, N Pacific. *a* 209 sq. mi.; *p* 86,000.

Guatemala, mountainous republic in Central America. *c* Guatemala; *a* 42,042 sq. mi.; *p* 5,170,000. Half the people are descended from Maya Indians. Chief products include coffee, bananas, cotton. Final independence gained in 1839.

Guatemala City, *c* of Guatemala, Central America. *p* 577,000. Coffee, minerals.

Guernsey, see Channel Islands.

Guinea, republic in W Africa. *c* Conakry; *a* 94,925 sq. mi.; *p* 4,029,000. Bordered by Portuguese Guinea, Senegal, Mali, Ivory Coast, Liberia, Sierra Leone, Atlantic. Products include bananas, bauxite and other minerals. Independence gained from France in 1958.

Guyana, Commonwealth republic in S. America. *c* Georgetown; *a* 83,000 sq. mi.; *p* 739,000. Bordered by Venezuela, Surinam, Brazil. Products include bauxite, rice, sugar. Called British Guiana until independence in 1966.

H

Hainan, island off S China. *a* 13,000 sq. mi.

Haiti, mountainous republic in W. Indies. *c* Port-au-Prince. *a* 10,714 sq. mi.; *p* 4,949,000. Shares island of Hispaniola with Dominican Republic. Language: French. Main product: sugar. Won independence from France in 1804.

Halifax, *c* of Nova Scotia, Canada. *p* 87,000. Foundries, petroleum refining. Atlantic port.

Hanoi, *c* of North Vietnam, SE Asia. *p* 644,000. Metals, rice and textiles. Once capital of French Indo-China.

Harrisburg, *c* of Pennsylvania, US. *p* 392,000. Cigarettes, metals, textiles.

Hartford, *c* of Connecticut, US. *p* 777,000. Seat of Trinity College.

Havana, *c* and major port of Cuba. *p* 1,517,000. Business and cultural city.

Hawaii, westernmost state of US, made up of islands in Pacific. *c* Honolulu; *a* 6,421 sq. mi.; *p* 780,000. Agriculture, fishing. Famous for pineapples, surfing.

Hebrides, group of British islands off W coast of Scotland. Sheep and weaving.

Helena, *c* of Montana, US. *p* 20,000.

Helsinki, *c* and port of Finland. *p* 528,000. Machinery, textile and wood industries.

Himalaya, highest mtn range in world, bordering Pakistan, Kashmir, India, Tibet, Nepal, Sikkim, Bhutan. Highest peak: Everest.

Hindu Kush, mtn range in central Asia, bordering Afghanistan and Pakistan. W of Himalaya range.

Hispaniola, W. Indian island divided into Haiti and Dominican Republic. *a* 29,536 sq. mi.

Hobart, *c* and port of Tasmania, Australia. *p* 141,000. Fruit, minerals.

Hokkaido, most northerly island of Japan.

Honduras, mountainous republic in Central America. *c* Tegucigalpa; *a* 43,277 sq. mi.; *p* 2,691,000. Coastline on both Caribbean Sea and Pacific. Products include bananas and coffee. Gained independence in 1838.

Hong Kong, British territory bordering China. *c* Victoria; *a* 391 sq. mi.; *p* 4,248,000. Market for Chinese goods. Many industries. Includes mainland territory. Hong Kong and 235 other islands.

Honolulu, *c* of Hawaii, US. *p* 585,000. Fruit and sugar industries. Resort.

Honshu, largest island of Japan. *a* 88,000 sq. mi.

Houston, port in S Texas, US. *p* 1,740,000. Chemicals, machinery, petroleum refining.

Hsian, city in central China. *p* 1,310,000

Huascarán, Peruvian mt. 22,542 ft.

Hudson Bay, inland sea in E Canada. Empties into Atlantic. *a* about 470,000 sq. mi.

Hudson, river flowing 350 mi. through NE US. Early trade route for settlers.

Hungary, republic in central Europe. *c* Budapest. *a* 35,919 sq. mi.; *p* 10,343,000. Hungarians are descended mainly from Magyar and German peoples. Language: Magyar. Danube passes through Budapest. Carpathian mts lie in the north. Manufacturing provides the chief income. Products include cereals, lignite, peppers, sugar beet. Magyars, nomads from Asia, settled in Hungary from the 800's A.D.

Huron, one of Gt Lakes, N. America. *a* 23,010 sq. mi. Ports include Bay City, Cheboygan, Collingwood, Midland.

Hwang Ho, Chinese river 2,700 miles long. In English, called Yellow river.

Hyderabad, city in W India. *p* 1,261,000.

I

Iceland, island republic in N Atlantic. *c* Reykjavik; *a* 39,768 sq. mi.; *p* 209,000. Most Icelanders live in Reykjavik. Iceland has over 200 volcanoes. Fishing and fish canning are the chief industries.

Idaho, NW state, US. *c* Boise; *a* 83,557 sq. mi.; *p* 703,000. Dairy products, livestock, lumber, minerals.

Ifni, since 1969, part of Morocco.

Illinois, midwest state, US. *c* Springfield; *a* 56,400 sq. mi.; *p* 10,991,000. Dairy products, livestock. Chicago, in north, is main market and transport hub.

India, republic in S Asia. *c* Delhi; *a* 1,262,274 sq. mi.; *p* 556,321,000. Main languages include Hindi, English and 13 important local languages. Religions include Hinduism, Islam, Christianity, Sikhism, Buddhism, Jainism. Most people live in India's half-million villages. The ancient caste system became illegal in 1950. From the Himalayan mts in N India, the Brahmaputra and Ganges rivers flow S.

Among the world's poorest countries, India possesses much fertile land and many minerals. Often short on food, India is slowly developing great industries. Each of its 17 states has limited self government. India ended nearly 200 years of British rule in 1947.

Visitors are shown around the interior of the Taj Mahal at Agra.

Indian Oooan touches Africa, Asia and Australia. *a* 28,350,000 sq. mi.

Indiana, midwest state, US. *c* Indianapolis; *a* 36,291 sq. mi.; *p* 5,061,000. Farming and manufactured goods.

Indianapolis, *c* of Indiana, US. *p* 1,027,000. Famous for automobile races.

Indonesia, island republic in SE Asia, N of Australia. *c* Djakarta; *a* 735,269 sq. mi.; *p* 118,045,000. Main islands: Bali, Borneo, Celebes, Java, Sumatra. Also includes W. Irian, in New Guinea. Most people are Moslems. Language: Indonesian. Products include coffee, minerals, rubber, soya beans, spices and tea.

Indus, Asian river flowing 1,700 mi. from Tibet through Pakistan into Arabian Sea.

Inner Mongolia, autonomous region of N China. *c* Huhehot; *a* 230,000 sq. mi.; *p* 9,200,000.

Iowa, midwest state, US. *c* Des Moines; *a* 56,290 sq. mi.; *p* 2,774,000. Automobiles, cereals, machinery, meat packing.

Iran, monarchy in SW Asia. *c* Tehran; *a* 636,294 sq. mi.; *p* 28,478,000 Iranians speak Persian and most are Moslems. Iran lies between Caspian and Arabian seas. Iran is a plateau surrounded by Centrai, Elburz and Zagros mts. Products include carpets, dates, petroleum, tobacco. Iran was once called Persia. Ruins of ancient Persepolis lie in SW Iran.

Iraq, republic in SW Asia. *c* Baghdad; *a* 173,260 sq. mi.; *p* 9,421,000. Most Iraqis speak Arabic. Most are Moslems. Main rivers: Tigris, Euphrates. Chief products include cotton, dates, petroleum. Once called Mesopotamia, it was site of several ancient civilizations.

Ireland, Republic of, covers most of the island in NE Atlantic. *c* Dublin; *a* 27,135 sq. mi.; *p* 2,884,000. Most Irish are Roman Catholic. Languages: English and Gaelic. Ireland has many lakes and rivers. Farms cover two-thirds of the fertile soil. Exports include butter, livestock and stout. Won independence in 1921.

Irish Sea, lies between Britain and Ireland.

Irtysh, river in Siberia, 1,840 mi. long.

Islamabad, c of Pakistan (replaced Karachi). Began to be built near Rawalpindi in 1961.

Israel, republic in W Asia. c Jerusalem; a 7,992 sq. mi.; p 2,017,000. Most Israelis are Jews, who speak Hebrew but migrated from other countries. Bordered by four Arab states and the Mediterranean. Products include chemicals, citrus fruit, grains, olives, salt. State came into being in 1948.

Istanbul, chief port of Turkey, on Bosporus. p 1,751,000. Commercial city and transport hub. Old Byzantine city, also old capital of Turkey.

Italy, mountainous republic in S Europe. c Rome; a 116,303 sq. mi. (including Sardinia, Sicily); p 53,327,000. Language: Italian. Religion: Roman Catholicism. The Alps form most of Italy's borders with France, Switzerland, Austria, Yugoslavia. The Apennines form a 'backbone' N to S, where Italy lies between the Tyrrhenian and Adriatic seas. The Po river flows through Italy's fertile N plain, where Milan, Turin and other industrial cities lie. Florence, on the Arno river, is a great cultural city. Rome, on the Tiber river, was the centre of the Roman empire. Italy won unity and independence mainly from Austria between 1860–71.

Brunelleschi's magnificent dome towers over his native Florence. It is only one of Italy's splendid Renaissance treasures.

Ivory Coast, republic in W Africa. c Abidjan; a 127,520 sq. mi.; p 4,422,000. On Gulf of Guinea, bordered by five countries and Atlantic. Products include coffee, cocoa, timber. Independent from France since 1960.

J

Jackson, c of Mississippi, US. p 250,000. Named after Andrew Jackson.

Jakarta, c of Indonesia in NW Java. p 2,907,000. Textiles, mixed industries.

Jamaica, island, Commonwealth monarchy in W. Indies. c Kingston; a 4,411 sq. mi.; p 1,991,000. People are mostly of Negro descent. Located 90 mi. S of Cuba. Products include bananas, bauxite, sugar. Became independent from Britain in 1962.

Japan, island monarchy in E Asia. c Tokyo; a 142,726 sq. mi.; p 102,879,000. People are almost entirely Japanese, except for 15,000 Ainu on Hokkaido. Language: Japanese. Main religions: Shinto and Buddhism. Japan lies in N Pacific Ocean, separated from mainland Asia by Sea of Japan. Its four islands, (N to S) Hokkaido, Honshu, Shikoku and Kyushu, form a mountain chain broken only by sea. Volcanic eruptions and earthquakes are common. Japan has no long rivers but many swift streams fed by heavy falls of rain and snow.

Isolated and feudal until 1868, Japan then developed fast. It built a great empire but lost it in World War II. By 1970, Japan's gross national product ranked third after US and Russia.

Japan, Sea of, part of Pacific Ocean between Korea, USSR and Japan.

Jasper National Park, in Rockies, W Alberta, Canada. a 4,200 sq. mi.

Java, Indonesian island. a 50,390 sq. mi.; p 63,060,000. Volcanoes have made island fertile.

Jefferson City, c of Missouri, US.; p 28,000.

Jersey, see Channel Islands.

Jerusalem, holy city for Christians, Jews and Moslems, was divided between Israel and Jordan until 1967, when p was 234,000. c of Israel. Jordanian sector taken by Israel in 1967 war.

Jidda, port in Saudi Arabia. p 150,000.

Johannesburg, largest city in S. Africa. p 1,295,000. Rail, commercial and industrial city for gold fields. Machinery.

Jordan, Arab monarchy in SW Asia. c Amman; a 34,750 sq. mi. (before 1967); p 2,314,000. Most people are Moslems who speak Arabic. Chief river, Jordan. Products include chemicals, grains, grapes, livestock and wool. Became independent in 1948, after union of Trans-Jordan with part of Palestine.

Juneau, c of Alaska. p 7,000. Fish, furs.

K

K2 (Mt Godwin-Austen), Kashmir, 28,250 ft.

Kabul, c of Afghanistan. p 292,000. Cultural, economic and political city.

Kalahari Desert, southwestern Africa. a about 20,000 sq. mi.

Kampala, c of Uganda, E Africa. p 47,000.

Kanchenjunga, Himalayan mt on Nepal-Sikkim border, 28,208 ft.

Kanpur, city in N India. *p* 1,012,000.

Kansas, midwest state, US. *c* Topeka; *a* 82,276 sq. mi.; *p* 2,293,000. Aircraft, cattle, metals, processed foods, wheat.

Karachi, chief port and former capital of Pakistan. *p* 1,913,000. Crop processing, handicrafts, engineering and metal works.

Kashmir, border region of India and Pakistan divided between both countries.

Katmandu, *c* of Nepal, S Asia. *p* 123,000.

Kentucky, E central state, US. *c* Frankfort; *a* 40,395 sq. mi.; *p* 3,220,000. Cattle, coal, maize, tobacco, whiskey. Famous for thoroughbred horses and Derby.

Kenya, Commonwealth republic in E Africa. *c* Nairobi; *a* 224,960 sq. mi.; *p* 10,811,000. Bordered by Ethiopia, Somalia, Indian Ocean, Tanzania, Uganda, Sudan. Products include coffee, hides and tea. Won independence from Britain in 1963.

Kenya, Mt, extinct volcano, central Kenya, 17,058 ft.

Kharkov, city in SW USSR. *p* 1,148,000.

Khartoum, *c* of Sudan, NE Africa. *p* 135,000. Ivory, gum, ostrich feathers.

Khyber Pass, in Himalaya, connects W Pakistand and Afghanistan. 33 mi. long.

Kibo, peak of Kilimanjaro mt. in Tanzania, 19,340 ft.

Kiev, city in SW USSR. *c* of Ukraine. *p* 1,457,000. Important industrially.

Kigali, *c* of Rwanda, E Africa. *p* 4,000.

Kilimanjaro, highest mt. in Africa, 19,565 ft. See also Kibo, Mawenzi.

Killarney, 3 lakes in Republic of Ireland near town of Killarney.

Kingston, *c* and port of Jamaica. *p* 494,000. Food processing. Resort.

Kinshasa, *c* and largest city of Congo Kinshasa. *p* 508,000.

Kita Kyushu, Japanese city formed in 1963 by combining Wakamatsu, Yauata, Tobata, Kokura and Moji. *p* 1,042,000.

Kobe, port in S Honshu, Japan. *p* 1,217,000. Shipbuilding, sugar refining, textiles.

Korea (North), communist republic in E Asia. *c* Pyongyang; *a* 46,540 sq. mi.; *p* 13,902,000. Language: Korean. The land is mountainous and rich in minerals. Products include barley, cotton, iron ore, tungsten and wheat. An ancient country, Korea regained independence as two countries (N and S) by 1949.

Korea (South), republic in E Asia. *c* Seoul; *a* 38,004 sq. mi.; *p* 32,483,000. Language: Korean. Main religions: Buddhism, Christianity. South Korea has many bays and islands. Products include cotton, graphite, rice, silk, tungsten and wheat. Korea regained independence (lost to Japan in 1910) as two countries (N. and S.) by 1949.

Kosciusko, Australia's highest mt, New South Wales, 7,310 ft.

Kra, Isthmus of, in Thailand, connects Malaya with Asian mainland.

Krakatoa, volcanic island in SE Asia Eruption in 1883 was perhaps world's biggest explosion.

Kruger National Park, S. Africa. *a* 8,000 sq. mi. Crocodiles, elephants, giraffes, hippopotami, lions, monkeys, zebras.

Kuala Lumpur, *c* of Malaysia, SE Asia. *p* 316,000. Communications point.

Malaysia's capital, Kuala Lumpur, is the site of many new buildings, like this one built in the classical style.

Kuibyshev, wartime capital of USSR. *p* 1,080,000. Industrial city.

Kunlun, Asian mtn range, mainly in Tibet.

Kuril Is, USSR group in N Pacific. *a* 6,000 sq. mi.; *p* 15,000. Fish, furs, wood.

Kuwait, *c* of Kuwait. *p* 100,000. Port.

Kuwait, independent state in N Arabia. *c* Kuwait City; *a* 6,000 sq. mi.; *p* 732,000. Most people Arabs and Moslems. World's richest state per head of population, because Kuwait is second largest exporter of petroleum in world. Gained independence in 1961.

Huge pipelines and oil tankers at Ahmadi Port reflect the mineral wealth which has brought riches to Kuwait.

Kyoto, city and former capital of Japan. *p* 1,365,000. Ancient cultural city.

Kyushu, southernmost island of Japan.

L

Lake District, NW England, has 15 lakes. Mountainous beauty spot.

Lagos, *c* of Nigeria, W Africa. *p* 665,000. Exports crops and leather. Port.

Lahore, city in W. Pakistan. *p* 1,296,000. Food processing, handicrafts, machinery. Cultural and religious city.

Lansing, *c* of Michigan, US. *p* 336,000. Vehicle manufacturing.

Laos, monarchy in SE Asia. *c* Vientiane; *a* 91,429 sq. mi.; *p* 2,980,000. Language: Lao. Bordered by China, Vietnam, Cambodia, Thailand and Burma. Products include cattle, cotton, rice, sugar and tin. Independent from France since 1954.

Las Vegas, city in Nevada, US. *p* 65,000. Famed for gambling and nightclubs.

Lebanon, Mediterranean republic in SW Asia. *c* Beirut; *a* 4,015 sq. mi.; *p* 2,726,000. Most Lebanese are Christians or Moslems who speak Arabic. Products include fruit, metal goods, nuts, textiles. Lebanon gained independence from France in 1946. In ancient times it was the site of Phoenicia.

Leeds, city in Yorkshire, England. *p* 506,000. Clothing and furniture industries.

Leeward Is, in W. Indies, include Anguilla, Antigua, Guadeloupe, Montserrat, Nevis, St Kitts, Virgin Is. *a* 1,324 sq. mi.; *p* 505,000. Foods, textiles, tobacco.

Leicester, England. *p* 280,000. Chemicals, knitware and shoe industries.

Lena, Asian river flowing 2,645 miles through Siberia, USSR, into Arctic Ocean.

Leningrad, port on Baltic Sea, USSR. *p* 3,341,000. Chemicals, engineering, machines, textiles. Old capital of Russia. Once called St Petersburg, also Petrograd.

Lesotho, Commonwealth monarchy in southern Africa. *c* Maseru; *a* 11,716 sq. mi.; *p* 974,000. Entirely surrounded by Republic of S. Africa, where 40% of its men work. Independent since 1966. Formerly called Basutoland.

Lesser Antilles, island group in W. Indies. Includes Barbados, Leeward and Windward Is, Trinidad and Tobago, and other islands.

Liberia, Negro republic in W Africa. *c* Monrovia; *a* 43,000 sq. mi.; *p* 1,161,000. Founded by Negroes freed from slavery in US in 1820's. Bordered by Sierra Leone, Guinea, Ivory Coast, Atlantic. Large proportion of world's shipping flies Liberian flag. Iron ore, rubber. Became fully independent state in 1847.

Libreville, *c* of Gabon, W Africa. *p* 46,000.

Libya, republic in N Africa. *c* Tripoli and Benghazi; *a* 679,378 sq. mi.; *p* 1,939,000. Bordered by Mediterranean Sea, Egypt, Sudan, Chad, Niger, Algeria, Tunisia. Products include fruit and petroleum. Gained independence in 1952.

Liechtenstein, small European principality between Austria and Switzerland. *c* Vaduz; *a* 62 sq. mi.; *p* 22,000.

Lima, *c* and largest city of Peru. *p* 1,436,000. Business and cultural city.

Limerick, port in Republic of Ireland. *p* 56,000. Settled by Danes in 800's A.D.

Lincoln, *c* of Nebraska, central US. *p* 161,000. Food processing.

Line Is, group in central Pacific, divided between Britain and US. Includes Caroline, Christmas, Fanning, Flint, Jarvis, Malden, Palmyra, Vostok, Washington is. Also called Equatorial Is.

Lisbon, *c* of Portugal. *p* 822,000. Commercial port, cultural and industrial city.

Little Rock, *c* of Arkansas, US. *p* 279,000. Cotton, livestock and petroleum.

Liverpool, city in Lancashire, England. *p*

688,000. England's second greatest port.

Loch Ness, 24 mi. long, in Invernesshire, Scotland. Claimed by some to be home of Loch Ness 'monster'.

Logan, highest mt. in Canada, 19,850 ft.

Lomé, c of Togo, W Africa. p 86,000.

London, port and c of Britain. a 620 sq. mi., p 7,764,000. Administrative, cultural, fashion, industrial, social metropolis. One of world's chief financial cities. Rich in history.

Los Angeles, port in S California, US. p 6,789,000 (includes Long Beach). Cultural and social area. Aircraft, chemicals, filming, manufacturing.

Louisiana, S state, US. c Baton Rouge; a 48,523 sq. mi.; p 3,726,000. Cotton, lumber, minerals, petroleum, rice, sugar, tobacco. Named after Louis XIV of France.

Lourdes, S France. p 16,000. Place of religious pilgrimages for Roman Catholics.

Lusaka, c of Zambia, Africa. p 138,000.

Luxembourg, independent duchy in NE Europe. c Luxembourg; a 988 sq. mi; p 349,000. People are of mixed descent. Bordered by Belgium, Germany and France. Iron and steel industries are the chief sources of income. Luxembourg became completely independent by 1890.

Luxembourg, c of Luxembourg. p 78,000. Engineering, metal and paper industries.

M

Macao, Portuguese colony on southern coast of China. a 6 sq. mi.; p 174,000. Fishing.

Mackenzie, Canada's longest river, flowing 2,635 miles through North West territories.

McKinley, mt. in S Alaska, 20,320 ft. Highest peak in North America.

Madagascar, island republic off SE Africa coast. c Tananarive; a 228,000 sq. mi.; p 7,845,000. Agriculture main occupation. Also called Malagasy Republic.

Madeira, group of Portuguese islands in Atlantic. c Funchal; a 308 sq. mi.; p 269,000.

Madeira, river flowing 2,000 miles through South America, mainly in Brazil.

Madison, c of Wisconsin, US. p 260,000. Food processing, tool making.

Madras, port in SE India. p 1,896,000. Leather, mineral and textile industries.

Madrid, c of Spain. p 2,599,000. Communications point. Museums include Prado, Royal Armoury.

Maine, NE state, US. c Augusta; a 33,215 sq. mi.; p 976,000. Paper and lumber. Leather, processed foods, woollens.

Malagasy Republic, see Madagascar.

Malawi, landlocked republic in E Africa, alongside Lake Nyasa. c Zomba (prospective c Lilongwe); a 46,066 sq. mi.; p 4,437,000. Fishing, maize and tea. Gained independence from Britain in 1966.

Malaya, W part of Malaysia. a 50,840 sq. mi.; p 10,957,664. Most people are Malay Chinese. Main city Kuala Lumpur.

Malaysia, tropical Commonwealth monarchy in SE Asia composed of Malaya, Sarawak and Sabah. c Kuala Lumpur; a 128,430 sq. mi.; p 10,957,664. Most people are Malay Chinese, or Indian. Products include rubber, tin, palm oil, pineapples. United as an independent state in 1963.

Maldive Is, independent country in Indian Ocean. c Malé; a 115 sq. mi; p 108,000.

Malé, c of Maldive Is, S Asia. p 12,000.

Mali, landlocked republic in W Africa. c Bamako; a 464,874 sq. mi; p 5,077,000. Lies between Senegal and Niger. Millet, livestock and rubber. Called French Sudan until independence from France in 1960.

Malta, island Commonwealth country in Mediterranean. c Valetta; a 122 sq. mi.; p 314,000. People speak Maltese and English.

Cereals and fruit grown. Good weather makes Malta a popular tourist resort. Completely independent from UK by 1964.

Man, Isle of, British island in Irish Sea with limited self government. c Douglas. a 227 sq. mi.; p 50,000. Farming, tourism.

Managua, c of Nicaragua, Central America. p 262,000. Crops, precious metals.

Manchester, city in Lancashire, England. p 603,000. Metal products, textiles.

Manchuria, old name for NE part of China now divided into Heilungkiang, Kirin, Liaoning provinces. p 52,000,000.

Manila, port in SW Luzon, Philippines. p 3,100,000. Former capital, commercial and cultural city. Food processing, textiles.

Manitoba, province, central Canada. c Winnipeg; a 246,512 sq. mi.; p 979,000. Furs, lumber, minerals, petroleum, wheat.

Margherita, mt. on border of Uganda and Congo (Kinshasa), 16,763 ft.

Mariana Is, US Pacific Trust Terr. in N Pacific. a about 370 sq. mi., p 76,000.

Marquesas, group of French islands in S Pacific. a about 480 sq. mi.; p 5,000.

Marshall Is, US Pacific Trust Terr. in N Pacific. a about 150 sq. mi.; p 14,000.

Martinique, French Is. in W. Indies. c Fort-de-France; a 385 sq. mi.; p 362,000. Rum is chief product.

Maryland, E state, US. c Annapolis; a 10,577 sq. mi.; p 3,754,000. Coal, crops, metals, salt. Largest city: Baltimore.

Maseru, c of Lesotho, p 3,500. E terminal of railway from S. Africa. Trade point.

Massachusetts, NE state, US. c Boston; a 8,257 sq. mi.; p 5,469,000. Small farms, fishing, leather, machinery, paper. Harvard University at Cambridge.

Mato Grosso, plateau in W Brazil. Rich in diamonds and gold.

Matterhorn, mt. in Swiss-Italian Alps, 14,690 ft. Famous in mountaineering history.

Mauritania, republic in NW Africa. c Nouakchott; a 419,230 sq. mi.; p 1,140,000. Borders Senegal. Agriculture, copper and iron. Gained independence from France in 1960.

Mauritius, island republic in Indian Ocean 550 mi. E of Malagasy. c Port Louis; a 720 sq. mi.; p 848,000. Exports include rum and sugar. Gained independence from Britain in 1968.

Mawenzi, peak of Kilimanjaro mt. in Tanzania, 16,896 ft.

Mecca, holy city in W Saudi Arabia. p 200,000. Forbidden to non-Moslems.

Medina, holy city in Saudi Arabia. p 50,000.

Mediterranean, sea dividing Africa and Europe. a 965,000 sq. mi.

Mekong, river flowing 2,600 mi. through Tibet, China, Burma-Thailand border, Laos, Cambodia, S. Vietnam into South China Sea.

Melanesia, one of 3 main divisions of Pacific is. Includes Fiji, New Caledonia, New Hebrides, Solomons. a about 60,000 sq. mi.

Melbourne, c and chief port of Victoria, Australia. p 2,232,000. Aircraft, engineering, flour and textile industries.

A board rider is carried ashore on the crest of a wave at Torquay, a popular surfing beach near Melbourne. Surfing is one of Australia's most popular sports.

Memphis, city in Tennessee, US. p 752,000. Cotton, lumber, country and western music.

Mexico, mountainous republic in N America. c Mexico City. a 761,602 sq. mi.; p 50,462,000. Mexicans are mostly *mestizos* (of mixed European and Amerind descent). Language: Spanish. Bordered by US, Gulf of Mexico, British Honduras, Guatemala, and Pacific Ocean. Sierra Madre mts cover two thirds of Mexico. Several active volcanoes. Coffee, maize, silver and tourism provide most of the income. Independence won from Spain in 1821.

Mexico City, c of Mexico. p 6,815,000. Once Aztec c of Tenochtitlan. Largest cultural, industrial city. Spanish colonial architecture.

Mexico, Gulf of, W part of Atlantic between Mexico and US. a 700,000 sq. mi.

Michigan, midwest state, US. c Lansing; a 58,216 sq. mi.; p 8,739,000. Automobiles, chemicals, furniture, metals, processed foods.

Michigan, one of Gt. Lakes, N. America. a 22,400 sq. mi. Ports include Chicago, Gary, Michigan City, Milwaukee.

Micronesia, one of 3 main divisions of Pacific is. Includes Carolines, Marianas, Marshall Is. a about 1,300 sq. mi.

Middlesbrough, city in England. p 393,000.

Milwaukee, city and port in Wisconsin, US. p 1,331,000. Brewing, meat-packing.

Minneapolis and St Paul (twin cities), Minnesota, US, near Great Lakes, p 1,629,000. Manufacturing industries.

Minnesota, midwest state, US. c St Paul; a 84,068 sq. mi.; p 3,647,000. Agriculture, iron ore, livestock, metals and paper. Lakes and forests attract many tourists.

Mississippi, S state, US. c Jackson; a 47,716 sq. mi.; p 2,344,000. Cotton, livestock, lumber, petroleum, pecan nuts.

Mississippi, second longest river in US, 2,350 miles. Links with Missouri river.

Missouri, longest river in North America, flowing 2,714 miles through the US.

Missouri, S state, US. c Jefferson City; a 69,674 sq. mi.; p 4,625,000. Cattle, cereals, coal, iron, tobacco, zinc.

Mogadishu, c and port of Somalia, NE Africa. p 170,000. Fish canning, hides.

Molucca (or Spice) Islands, Indonesia.

Monaco, principality on Mediterranean coast of France. c Monaco; a less than 1 sq. mi.; p 23,000. Resort.

Mongolia, republic in E central Asia. c Ulan Bator; a about 600,000 sq. mi.; p 1,283,000.

Monrovia, c of Liberia, Africa. p 81,000.

Mont Blanc, highest mt. in Alps, 15,771 ft.

Montana, NW state, US. c Helena; a 147,138 sq. mi.; p 675,000. Cattle, coal, copper, gold, petroleum, wheat.

Monte Carlo, Monaco. p 8,000. Popular gambling casino. Notable aquarium.

Monte Rosa, Alpine peak between Italy and Switzerland, 15,203 ft.

Montevideo, c of Uruguay. p 1,159,000. Business and cultural city. Major port.

Montgomery, c of Alabama, US. p 207,000. Cotton, food packing, lumber.

Montpelier, c of Vermont, US. p 9,000.

Montreal, city in Quebec, Canada. p 1,222,000. Cultural and business city. Port. Mainly French-speaking.

Montserrat, British W. Indian island. c Plymouth; a about 36 sq. mi.; p 15,000. Cotton, farming.

Morocco, monarchy in N Africa. c Rabat; a about 172,000 sq. mi.; p 14,905,000. People are Arabs and Berbers. Most people are Moslems. Bordered by Mediterranean Sea, Algeria, Spanish Sahara and Atlantic Ocean. Atlas Mts cover most of Morocco. Varied crops, many minerals. Gained independence from France in 1956.

A horse-drawn sleigh train in a Moscow park.

Moscow, c of USSR. p 6,507,000. Commercial, cultural and technology city. Famous for Bolshoi Ballet, Gorki Park, the Kremlin, Red Square, St Basil's Church.

Mosul, city in Iraq on Tigris. p 341,000.

Mourne Mountains, range in Northern Ireland. Highest peak, 2,796 ft.

Mozambique, Portuguese territory in E Africa. c Lourenco Marques, a 302,329 sq. mi.; p 7,413,000. Agriculture and trade are main occupations.

Munich, city in S Germany. p 1,232,000. Cultural city. Beer, handicrafts.

Murray, Australia's longest river, 2,310 mi. Hydroelectric plants and reservoirs.

Muscat and Oman, Arabian sultanate. c Muscat; a 82,000 sq. mi.; p 572,000. Camels, dates, fish, pearls, petroleum.

Traditional robes and rifles contrast with the modern vehicles of an oil exploration party in Muscat and Oman.

Muscat, c of Muscat and Oman, E Arabian Peninsula. p 5,000. Pearl fisheries.

N

Nagoya, port on Honshu, Japan. p 1,935,000. Chemical, porcelain, textiles.

Nairobi, c of Kenya, E. Africa. p 315,000. Meat packing, food processing, paper.

Nanking, former c of China. p 1,419,000. Cultural city on Yangtze. Textiles.

Naples, port in S Italy. p 1,245,000.

Nashville, c of Tennessee, US. p 523,000. Industrial and cultural city.

Natal, S. African province. c Pietermaritzburg; a 33,578 sq. mi.; p 2,980,000. Cereals, minerals, petroleum, sugar, tea.

Nauru, small independent island state in W Pacific. c Nauru; a 8 sq. mi.; p 6,000.

Nebraska, midwest state, US. c Lincoln; a 77,227 sq. mi.; p 1,439,000. Cattle, dairy products, food processing.

Nelson, river in central Canada, 1,600 mi.

Nepal, monarchy in Himalayas, SE Asia. c Katmandu; a 54,362 sq. mi.; p 11,055,000. Most Nepalese are Gurkhas who speak Nepali. Religion: Buddhism-Hinduism. Nepal has many forests. Most of its trade is with India. Main products are cattle and skins, drugs, quartz, rice, timber.

Netherlands, monarchy in NW Europe. c Amsterdam; a 12,978 sq. mi.; p 13,167,000. People and language called Dutch. Netherlands also called Holland. Bordered by Germany, Belgium, North Sea. Land protected from sea by dikes. Main rivers: Rhine, Maas, Scheldt. Main exports: dairy products, flowers. Manufacturing and shipbuilding are important industries. Won full independence from Spain by 1648.

Nevada, W state, US. c Carson City; a 110,540 sq. mi.; p 449,000; Mining, cattle, sheep. Gambling at Las Vegas and Reno.

New Brunswick, province, SE Canada. c Fredericton; a 27,985 sq. mi.; p 625,000; Farming, fishing, forestry, mining.

New Caledonia, French island in S Pacific. c Nouméa; a 7,336 sq. mi.; p 103,000.

New Guinea, Pacific island NE of Australia. a 342,915 sq. mi.; p 2,927,000. There are 3 political divisions: Papua; Trust Territory of New Guinea; and West Irian (Indonesia). See separate entries.

New Guinea, Trust Territory of, Australian part of island. c Port Moresby; a 93,000 sq. mi.; p 1,719,000. Agriculture, rubber.

New Hampshire, NE state, US. c Concord; a 9,304 sq. mi.; p 702,000. Agriculture, machinery, paper, shoes, textiles.

New Hebrides, Pacific is. British and French condominium. a 5,700 sq. mi.; p 78,000

New Jersey, NE state, US. c Trenton; a 7,836 sq. mi.; p 7,093,000. Chemicals, minerals, textiles. Largest city: Newark.

New Mexico, SW state, US. c Santa Fe; a 121,666 sq. mi.; p 1,006,000. Copper, cotton, uranium. Largest city: Albuquerque.

New Orleans, port in Louisiana, US. p 1,044,000. Cotton. Famous for jazz.

New South Wales, state in SE Australia. c Sydney; a 309,433 sq. mi.; p 2,541,000. Coal, crops, sheep, steel, timber.

New York, NE state, US. c Albany; a 49,596 sq. mi.; p 18,078,000. Niagara Falls in W. Many educational institutes. Chief cities include Buffalo, New York City, Rochester, Schenectady, Syracuse. Agriculture, mainly fruits. N.Y. has been the leading manufacturing state since 1840.

New York, largest city and port of US. p 11,410,000. Major financial, business and cultural area of US. Manhattan Island, heart of the city, contains UN building.

New Zealand, monarchy, more than 1,000 miles SE of Australia. c Wellington; a 103,736 sq. mi.; p 2,777,000. Most New Zealanders are of British origins, some are Maoris (Polynesians who settled NZ before the British). Main language: English. Religions: Protestantism and Roman Catholicism.

NZ is made up of North Island, South Island, and many smaller islands. Most people live in N. Island. The S. Alps cover much of S. Island. NZ has 2 active volcanoes, hot springs, lakes and waterfalls. NZ's mild climate, fertile soil and small population have enabled it to become a leading sheep and dairying country. One fifth of NZ is forest. NZ became independent of Britain in 1907. Ties with Britain are very strong, but less so than in the past. NZ is taking an increasingly important part in world affairs.

Newcastle, city in Australia. p 328,000.

Newcastle-on-Tyne, city in England. p 245,000.

Newfoundland, province, E Canada (includes Labrador). c St John's; a 156,185 sq. mi.; p 514,000. Fishing, forestry, minerals. Discovered by Cabot for England in 1497.

Niagara Falls, between Canada and US. Height ranges from 186 to 193 ft.

Niamey, c of Niger, W Africa. p 262,000. Terminus for trans-Sahara routes.

Nicaragua, largest republic of Central America. c Managua; a 57,143 sq. mi.; p 1,945,000. People are of Spanish, Negro, or Amerind (mixed) descent. Language: Spanish. Lake Nicaragua is 3,060 sq. mi. Main products are cotton, gold and timber. Won independence from Spain in 1821.

Nicosia, c of Cyprus. p 106,000.

Niger, landlocked republic in W Africa, lying N of Nigeria. c Niamey; a about 480,000 sq. mi.; p 3,894,000. Livestock, peanuts and uranium. Gained independence from France in 1960.

Niger, W African river, 2,600 miles long.

Nigeria, Commonwealth republic in W Africa. c Lagos; a 356,669 sq. mi.; p 63,431,000. The main tribes are Hausa, Yoruba, Ibo and Fulani. Main language: English. Bordered by Dahomey, Niger, Chad, Cameroon and Gulf of Guinea. Nigeria occupies the lower basin of the Niger with forests in S and plains in N. Products include cocoa, tin and oil. Gained independence from Britain in 1960.

Nile, world's longest river, flowing 4,160 mi. through NE Africa, fertilizes much of Sudan and Egypt.

Niue Island, in Pacific, belongs to New Zealand. a 100 sq. mi.; p 5,000. Bananas.

North America, see under separate countries.

North Carolina, E state, US. c Raleigh; a 52,712 sq. mi.; p 5,122,000. Cotton, lumber, maize, peanuts, tobacco.

North Dakota, N state, US. *c* Bismarck; *a* 70,665 sq. mi.; *p* 627,000. Cattle, cereals, coal, grain, processed foods.

North Island, New Zealand. *a* 44,281 sq. mi.; *p* 1,963,000. Hot springs, volcanoes.

North Sea, NE Atlantic between Britain and mainland N Europe. *a* 222,000 sq mi.

Northern Ireland, part of UK. *c* Belfast; *a* 5,462 sq. mi.; *p* 1,502,000. Six NE counties of Ireland. Flax, aircraft industry.

Northern Territory, Australian state. *c* Darwin; *a* 520,280 sq. mi.; *p* 44,000 (including about 17,000 aborigines). Cattle, copper, gold, silver, tin, uranium. Pearl fishing.

Northwest Territories, Canada, are composed of Franklin, Keewatin, Mackenzie. Governed directly from Ottawa. *a* 1,304,913 sq. mi.; *p* 32,000. Fishing, furs, gold and silver, petroleum. About half of the territory lies within Arctic Circle.

Norway, monarchy in N Europe. *c* Oslo; *a* 125,181 sq. mi; *p* 3,875,000. Norwegians are descendants of Norsemen. Languages are Nynorsk and Bokmål. Norway has many islands. With Denmark and Sweden it forms the Scandinavian peninsula. Fishing, forestry, manufacturing, minerals. Skiing draws many tourists.

Nottingham, city in England. *p* 305,000.

Nouakchott, *c* of Mauritania, NW Africa. *p* 35,000. Livestock and millet.

Nova Scotia, province, SE Canada. *c* Halifax; *a* 21,068 sq. mi.; *p* 763,000. Consists of many islands. Agriculture, coal, fishing, forestry, minerals.

Novosibirsk, city in USSR. *p* 1,080,000.

O

Ob, Asian river flowing 2,500 miles through western Siberia, USSR.

Oceania, general name for Australia, New Zealand and surrounding territories.

Ohio, midwest state, US. *c* Columbus. *a* 41,222 sq. mi.; *p* 10,588,000. Cereals, cattle, iron and steel works, machinery, salt. Main cities: Cincinnati, Cleveland.

Oklahoma, S state, US. *c* Oklahoma City; *a* 69,919 sq. mi. *p* 2,520,000. Cattle, cereals, cotton, lead, petroleum, zinc.

Oklahoma City, *c* of Oklahoma, US. *p* 588,000. Metal, petroleum industries.

Old Faithful, geyser in Wyoming part of Yellowstone National Park, US.

Olympia, port and *c* of Washington, US. *p* 18,000. Agriculture, seafood.

Oman, see Muscat and Oman.

Ontario, smallest of Gt Lakes, N. America. *a* 7,450 sq. mi. Ports include Hamilton, Kingstown, Ottawa, Toronto.

Ontario, south central province, Canada. *c* Toronto; *a* 412,582 sq. mi; *p* 7,452,000. Leading agricultural and industrial province. Contains one of world's largest uranium sources.

Orange Free State, S. African province. *c* Bloemfontein; *a* 49,866 sq. mi.; *p* 1,387,000. Drakensberg mts in NE.

Oregon, NW state, US. *c* Salem; *a* 96,981 sq. mi.; *p* 2,008,000. Crops, fruit, fishing, meatpacking, metals, lumber, uranium.

Orinoco, S. American river flowing 1,700 miles through Brazil, Colombia, Venezuela to Atlantic.

Orizaba, Pico de, mt. in Mexico, 18,700 ft.

Orkney, Scottish county consisting of 68 islands in North Sea. *a* 360 sq. mi.; *p* 19,000.

Osaka, chief port of Honshu, Japan. *p* 3,156,000. Machinery, shipbuilding, textiles. Has a rich cultural tradition.

Opposite: The Empire State Building dominates part of New York's skyline.

Oslo, *c* and port of Norway. *p* 483,000. Fish, paper and textile industries.

Ottawa, *c* of Canada in SE Ontario. *p* 291,000. Cultural city. Bookbinding, food processing, printing.

Oxford, Oxfordshire, Britain. *p* 110,000. Famous university town with automobile industry.

P

Pacific Ocean, covers third of world. *a* 64 million sq. mi. Deepest spot, 37,800 ft.

Pakistan, Islamic republic in S Asia. *c* Islamabad; *a* 365,529 sq. mi.; *p* 114,150,000. Languages: Urdu, Bengali, English. W. and E. Pakistan are separated by about 1,000 miles of India. The W is a dry semi-desert, the E rainy, fertile and densely populated. Indus river flows through W. Pakistan. Brahmaputra and Ganges flow through E. Pakistan. Products include cotton, jute, wheat. East Pakistan set up as independent state of Bangladesh after civil war with West Pakistan in 1971.

Pamirs, mtn range in central Asia

Panama, republic in Central America. *c* Panama; *a* 29,209 sq. mi.; *p* 1,460,000. Bordered by Caribbean Sea, Colombia, Pacific Ocean and Costa Rica. Products include bananas, mahogany and rice. Won independence from Colombia in 1903.

Panama, *c* and port of Panama. *p* 373,000.

Panama Canal, 51 mi. long, links Atlantic and Pacific Oceans across Panama, Central America.

Panama Canal Zone, Central America. *a* 553 sq. mi.; *p* 60,000. Leased to US.

Papua, Australian territory, SE New Guinea. *c* Port Moresby; *a* 90,540 sq. mi.; *p* 841,096. Copra, gold, rubber, timber.

Paraguay, landlocked republic in S. America. *c* Asunción; *a* 157,047 sq. mi.; *p* 2,329,000. Languages: Spanish and Guaraní. Bordered by Bolivia, Brazil and Argentina. Chief products: cattle, timber, maté (Paraguay tea). Won independence in 1811.

Paraguay, S. American river, 1,500 mi. long.

Paraná, S. American river, flows 2,450 mi. through Brazil, Paraguay and Argentina.

Paris, *c* of France. *p* 7,750,000. One of world's leading cultural, educational and social cities. Famous for fashions, food and night life.

Peak District, hilly area in Britain, mainly Derbyshire.

Peking, *c* of China. *p* 4,010,000. Cultural, intellectual and industrial city. Famous for architecture and landscapes.

Pemba, island belonging to Tanzania, E Africa. *a* 380 sq. mi.; *p* 134,000. Copra.

Penang, Malaysian state consisting of island of Penang and Province Wellesley on mainland. *a* 400 sq. mi.; *p* 671,000. Rubber.

Pennsylvania, E state, US. *c* Harrisburg; *a* 45,333 sq. mi.; *p* 11,728,000. Coal, lumber, oats, textiles, tobacco, wheat. Named after William Penn, the founder.

Persian Gulf, NW arm of Indian Ocean between Iran and Arabia. *a* 90,000 sq. mi. Sometimes called Arabian Gulf.

Perth, *c* of Western Australia. *p* 558,821. Market and manufacturing city.

Peru, mountainous republic in S. America. *c* Lima; *a* 496,223 sq. mi.; *p* 13,520,000. Half the people are of Amerind descent, the rest are *mestizos* (mixed Amerind and European). Language: Spanish. Location: N of Chile, on Pacific Ocean. Main products are cotton, copper and fish-meal. Land of Inca people, conquered by Spain in early 1500's. Won independence in 1824.

Part of the ruins of Machu Picchu, an Inca city probably built in the 1400's. It remained undiscovered until 1911.

Petrified Forest National Park, Arizona, US. 147 sq. mi. Six forests of petrified wood.

Philadelphia, port in SE Pennsylvania, US. *p* 4,690,000. Petroleum refining, shipbuilding, sugar and textiles. City's name (in Greek) means 'brotherly love'.

Philippines, republic, group of islands in SW Pacific. *c* Quezon City; *a* 115,507 sq. mi.; *p* 38,120,000. People are called Filipinos. They are of mixed origin. Main languages: Filipino, English, Spanish. Most people are Christians. Main groups of islands: Luzon, Mindanao and Visayan. Most islands are mountainous and volcanic, having earthquakes. Main products are coconuts, fish, minerals, pineapples and rice. Independent from US since 1946.

Phnom Penh, *c* of Cambodia. *p* 404,000.

Phoenix, *c* of Arizona, US. *p* 831,000. Hot springs resort. Electronics, metals.

Pierre, *c* of South Dakota, US. *p* 10,000.

Pietermaritzburg, *c* of Natal, S. Africa. *p* 111,000. Industrial city. Named after two Boer leaders.

Pin-chiang, city in NE China. *p* 1,552,000.

Pitcairn Is, British territory in S Pacific. *a* 2 sq. mi.; *p* 185. Founded by mutineers from HMS Bounty.

Pittsburgh, city in Pennsylvania, US. *p* 2,376,000. Coal, gas, steel industries.

Poland, republic in central Europe. *c* Warsaw; *a* 120,359 sq. mi.; *p* 33,247,000. Poles are a Slav people and most are Roman Catholic. Main river is the Vistula. Nearly half the people are farmers. Forestry, manufacturing, mining. Exports include cereals, coal, ham, sausages. An ancient country, Poland regained independence from Austria, Germany, Russia in 1919.

Polynesia, one of 3 main divisions of Pacific islands, includes Cook, Easter, Ellice, Hawaii,

Samoa, Society, Tokelau, Tonga islands. *a* about 10,000 sq. mi.

Popocatepetl, extinct volcanic mt. in Central Mexico, 17,887 ft.

Port Louis, *c* of Mauritius, in Indian Ocean. *p* 130,000. Commercial and industrial city. Mainly French speaking.

Port-au-Prince, *c* and chief port of Haiti. *p* 240,000. Fishing and food industries.

Port-of-Spain, *c* of Trinidad and Tobago, W. Indies. *n* 94,000.

Porto Novo, *c* of Dahomey, Africa. *p* 105,000.

Portsmouth, city in S England, *p* 219,000.

Portugal, republic in SW Europe. *c* Lisbon; *a* 35,216 sq. mi.; *p* 9,479,000. Most Portuguese are Roman Catholics. Portugal, with Spain, forms the Iberian Peninsula. Chief exports: cork, fish, fruit, pottery, textiles, wine. Portuguese sailors began exploring much of the world about 500 years ago.

Portuguese Guinea, territory in W Africa. *c* Bissau; *a* 13,900 sq. mi.; *p* 533,000.

Portuguese Timor, territory in E. Indies. *c* Deli; *a* 7,330 sq. mi.; *p* 594,364.

Prague, *c* and largest city of Czechoslovakia. *p* 1,023,000. Engineering, glove-making, metalworks, smoked meats.

Pretoria, *c* of Transvaal, S Africa. *p* 479,800. Industrial city and trading point. Administrative *c* of S. Africa.

Prince Albert National Park, central Saskatchewan, Canada. *a* 1,496 sq. mi.

Prince Edward Island, province, SE Canada. *c* Charlottetown; *a* 2,184 sq. mi.; *p* 110,000. Farming and fishing.

Providence, *c* and port of Rhode Island, US. *p* 736,000 (Includes Pawtucket). Machinery, silverware and textiles.

Puerto Rico, island E of Hispaniola, under protection of US. *c* San Juan; *a* 3,435 sq. mi.; *p* 2,877,000. Manufacturing industries.

Purus, river flowing 1,850 miles through Peru and Brazil.

Pusan, large port in Korea. *p* 1,420,000.

Pyongyang, *c* of N. Korea; *p* 653,000. Metals, sugar refining, textiles.

Pyrenees, mtns dividing France and Spain.

Q

Qatar, Arab sheikdom on Persian Gulf. *c* Doha; *a* 4,000 sq. mi.; *p* 94,000. Petroleum.

Quebec, *c* of Quebec, Canada. *p* 166,984. Grain and fur trade, metalworking.

Quebec, oldest and largest province, E Canada. *c* Quebec; *a* 594,860 sq. mi.; *p* 5,984,000. Asbestos, cattle, forestry, manufacturing, metals. Largest city is Montreal, in south.

Queensland, state, NE Australia. *c* Brisbane; *a* 667,000 sq. mi.; *p* 1,751,800. Crops, livestock, minerals, petroleum. Great Barrier Reef (mainly coral) off coast.

Quezon City, *c* of Philippines. *p* 482,000. Contains University of the Philippines.

Quito, *c* of Ecuador, in the Andes. *p* 402,000. Cultural and industrial city.

R

Rabat, *c* and port, Morocco, NW Africa. *p* 355,000. Handicrafts.

Raleigh, *c* of North Carolina, US. *p* 196,000. Trading point.

Rangoon, *c* and port of Burma. *p* 822,000.

Recife, port in NE Brazil. *p* 1,010,000. Fruit, metal, sugar industries. Rail hub.

Red Sea, almost divides Arabia and Africa. *a* 170,000 sq. mi. Flows into Indian Ocean.

Regina, *c* of Saskatchewan, Canada; *p* 131,000. Foundries, petroleum, sawmills.

Réunion, French island in Indian Ocean. *c* St Denis; *a* 970 sq. mi.; *p* 464,000. Sugar.

Reykjavik, *c* and chief port of Iceland. *p* 92,000 (nearly half of Iceland's people). Fishing.

The River Rhine has been a great highway of commerce for centuries. It is navigable by river barges as high up as Basle.

Rhine, river in Europe. Rises in Switzerland and flows 800 mi. to North Sea in Netherlands.

Rhode Island, smallest state, NE US. *c* Providence; *a* 1,214 sq. mi.; *p* 914,000. Agriculture, fishing, silver, textiles.

Rhodesia, self governing country in S Africa. *c* Salisbury; *a* 150,333 sq. mi.; *p* 4,991,000 (including 220,000 Europeans). Tobacco and minerals. Declared itself independent of Britain in 1965.

Rio Grande, river flowing 1,885 miles through southern US and northern Mexico.

Rio Muni, now part of Equatorial Guinea.

Riyadh, *c* of Saudi Arabia. *p* 225,000. Fruit, grain and handicrafts.

Rocky Mtns, range in western N. America, running through Canada, US, Mexico.

Rome, *c* of Italy. *p* 2,560,000. Once capital of the Roman Empire and still one of the world's leading cultural cities. Contains many famous buildings including Colosseum, Pantheon, numerous churches and Renaissance palaces. The Vatican City in the W contains St Peter's Church.

Giraffes gather at a waterhole in Wankie National Park, Rhodesia.

Richmond, *c* of Virginia, US. *p* 493,000. Chemicals, metals and tobacco.

Riding Mountain National Park, SW Manitoba, Canada. *a* 1,148 sq. mi.

Rio de Janeiro, port in SE Brazil. *p* 3,909,000. Largest city and former capital of Brazil.

Rio de Oro, part of Spanish Sahara.

Rumania, republic in E Europe. *c* Bucharest; *a* 91,669 sq. mi.; *p* 19,685,000. The Rumanian language comes from Latin. The country is mountainous, and rich in forests. Minerals include petroleum. Products include cereals, corn, fruit, grain, livestock and minerals.

Rushmore, Mt., 5,725 ft., in S. Dakota, US, has rock carvings of four US presidents.

Russia, see USSR.

Rwanda, densely populated, landlocked re-

public in E Africa. *c* Kigaii; *a* 10,166 sq. mi.; *p* 3,616,000. Coffee, minerals and tea. Gained independence from Belgium in 1962.

Ryukyu, island group near Japan. Some islands administered by Japan, some by US. *a* 1,800 sq. mi.; *p* 1,998,000. Largest island is Okinawa.

S

Sabah, state of E Malaysia, in Borneo. *c* Jesselton; *a* 29, 387 sq. mi.; *p* 518,000. Hardwoods, rubber, tobacco.

Sacramento, *c* of California, US. *p* 192,000. Fruit and meat packing, lumber.

Sahara, N Africa, largest desert in world. *a* about 3 million sq. mi.

Saigon, *c* of South Vietnam. *p* 3,000,000. Chief industrial city. Food processing.

St Elias, mt. on Alaska-Yukon border, 18,008 ft.

St Helena, British island in SE Atlantic. *a* 47 sq. mi.; *p* 5,000. Flax, lace.

St. John's, *c* and port of Newfoundland, Canada. *p* 80,000. Fishing, trade.

St Kitts-Nevis-Anguilla, W. Indian islands. State in association with Britain. *c* Basse-Terre; *a* 138 sq. mi.; *p* 64,000.

St Lawrence, Gulf of, Arm of Atlantic in SE Canada. *a* 100,000 sq. mi.

St Lawrence, important N. American river flowing 2,100 mi. from Gt Lakes to Atlantic. Forms part of US–Canada border.

St Lucia, W. Indian island state in association with Britain. *c* Castries; *a* 238 sq. mi.; *p* 109,000. Agriculture.

St Louis, city in Missouri. US. *p* 750,000. Furs, livestock market. Food processing.

St Vincent, W. Indian island state in association with Britain. *c* Kingstown; *a* 150 sq. mi.; *p* 97,000. Cotton, sugar.

Salween, river flowing through Tibet, China, Burma, 1,750 miles to Indian Ocean.

Samoa, group of islands in S Pacific. W. Samoa is independent state. E. Samoa belongs to US. *a* 1,210 sq. mi.; *p* 151,000.

San Antonio, city in S Texas US. *p* 588,000. Famous for Alamo (American fort besieged in Mexican War, 1836). Many missions.

San Diego, port in California, US. *p* 1,168,000. Aircraft, fish canneries.

San Francisco, port in California, US. *p* 2,958,000 (including Oakland). Famous for Golden Gate Bridge.

San José, *c* of Costa Rica. *p* 178,000.

San Marino, republic near Florence, Italy. *c* San Marino; *a* 24 sq. mi.; *p* 20,000.

San Salvador, *c* of El Salvador, Central America. *p* 281,000. Cigars, textiles.

San'a, *c* of Yemen, Arabia. *p* 100,000. Ancient trading city.

Santa Fe, *c* of New Mexico, US. *p* 33,000. Founded by Spanish in 1610.

Santiago, *c* of Chile. *p* 248,000. Food, metal and textile industries.

Santo Domingo, *c* of Dominican Republic, West Indies. *p* 561,000.

São Francisco, Brazilian river, 1,800 mi. long.

São Paulo, port in SE Brazil. *p* 4,098,000. Food processing, textiles.

São Tomé and Príncipe, Portuguese islands in Gulf of Guinea, Africa. *a* 372 sq. mi.; *p* 62,000.

Sarawak, state of E Malaysia, in Borneo. *c* Kuching; *a* 47,071 sq. mi.; *p* 820,000. Pepper, petroleum, rubber, timber.

Sardinia, Italian island in Mediterranean. *c* Cagliari; *a* 9,302 sq. mi.; *p* 1,419,000. Cork, grapes, livestock, metals, olives.

Sark, see Channel Islands.

Saskatchewan, province, south-central Canada. *c* Regina; *a* 251,700 sq. mi.; *p* 959,000. Farming and farm machinery.

Saudi Arabia, kingdom in SW Asia. *c* Riyadh; *a* 870,000 sq. mi.; *p* 7,349,000. Most

people are Moslem and speak Arabic. Bedouins can be found in the large areas of desert. Saudi Arabia, covering most of the Arabian Peninsula, is an important producer of petroleum. In the cities of Mecca and Medina, Islam began.

Scandinavia, general name for Denmark, Norway, Sweden. Sometimes includes Finland and Iceland. See separate entries.

Scotland, mountainous country, north UK. *c* Edinburgh; *a* 30,411 sq. mi.; *p* 5,194,000. Shipbuilding, whisky.

Seattle, port in Washington, US. *p* 1,214,000 (including Everett). Aircraft, fish canning, lumber.

Senegal, republic in W Africa. *c* Dakar; *a* about 77,000 sq. mi.; *p* 3,939,000. On Atlantic between Mauritania and Guinea. Fish, peanuts, phosphates. Gained independence from France in 1960.

Seoul, *c* of S Korea. *p* 3,800,000. Cultural city. Brassware, pottery, silk.

Seychelles, 92 islands in Indian Ocean, British territory. *c* Victoria; *a* 156 sq. mi.; *p* 47,000. Coconut, oil, spices, phosphates.

Shanghai, port and largest city in China. *p* 6,900,000. Chemicals, machines, textiles.

Sheffield, city in England. *p* 532,000.

Shenandoah National Park, N Virginia, US. *a* 302 sq. mi. Near Blue Ridge Mtns.

Shenyang, city in NE China. *p* 2,411,000.

Shetland Islands, part of Zetland County, Scotland. *a* 551 sq. mi.; *p* 18,000.

Shikoku, Japanese islands S of Honshu.

Siberia, USSR Asian terr. *a* 5 million sq. mi.; *p* 4,210,000. Developing rapidly.

Sicily, Italian islands in Mediterranean. *a* 9,926 sq. mi.; *p* 4,712,000. Contains Mt Etna, 11,122 ft. Farming, fishing.

Sierra Leone, Commonwealth republic in W Africa. *c* Freetown; *a* 27,699 sq. mi.; *p* 2,520,000. Bordered by Guinea and Liberia. Products include cassava, diamonds, iron-ore. Gained independence from Britain in 1961.

Sikkim, independent state between China and India. *c* Gangtok; *a* 2,744 sq. mi.; *p* 193,000. Copper, forestry, rice.

Singapore, island Commonwealth republic in SE Asia. *c* Singapore City; *a* 224 sq. mi.; *p* 2,154,000. Majority of people are Chinese. A free port, Singapore is one of the most important trading points in Asia. Independent from Britain since 1963, it left Federation of Malaysia in 1965.

The Tiger Balm Garden in Singapore was built by the manufacturer of an ointment called Tiger Balm.

Sinkiang Uighur, autonomous region of China. *a* 705,962 sq. mi.; *p* 6,000,000.

Snowdonia, national park, Wales. 800 sq. mi.

Society Islands, groups in S Pacific. Includes Tahiti and Morea. *c* Papeete; *a* 646 sq. mi.; *p* 66,000. Copper, phosphates.

Socotra, island, part of Southern Yemen in Indian Ocean. *a* 1,382 sq. mi.; *p* 9,000.

Sofia, *c* of Bulgaria. *p* 793,000. Spacious city with interesting churches and mosques.

Solomon Islands, British territory in SW Pacific. *a* 11,500 sq. mi.; *p* 152,000. Minerals.

Somalia, republic in E Africa. *c* Mogadishu; *a* 246,201 sq. mi.; *p* 2,949,000. On Gulf of Aden. Agriculture, livestock and uranium. Gained independence in 1960 from Britain and Italy.

South Africa, republic in southern Africa. *c* Cape Town (legislative), Pretoria (administrative); *a* 472,733 sq. mi. (including Walvis Bay); *p* 20,133,000. S. Africa's many peoples are classified by the Government's segregation policy into 4 groups: Africans, Asians, Coloureds (mixed origins), Europeans. Official languages: Afrikaans, English. Main religions: Dutch Reformed and other Protestant groups, Roman Catholicism.

S. Africa is mainly plateau surrounded by narrow coastal plain. Mts include Drakensberg, bordering the SE coastal plain. Rivers, which include Limpopo, Orange, Vaal, are not navigable. Warm and sunny, S. Africa has large national parks where wild life is preserved. Farming and mining are important, especially gold (half world's production), coal, diamonds, uranium. Manufacturing is developing fast.

European settlements began in 1652. As the settlers moved northwards, they met African peoples migrating southwards. United as a country in 1910, S. Africa left the Commonwealth in 1961.

South America, see under separate countries.

South Australia, Australian state. *c* Adelaide; *a* 380,070 sq. mi.; *p* 1,118,000. Agriculture, cotton and wool, electrical equipment, mining, quarrying.

South Carolina, S state, US. *c* Columbia; *a* 31,055 sq. mi.; *n* 2,664,000. Cereals, cotton, livestock, lumber, tobacco. Chief port is Charleston.

South Dakota, N state, US. *c* Pierre; *a* 77,047 sq. mi.; *p* 656,000. Agriculture, gold, lumber, silver.

South Island, New Zealand. *a* 58,093 sq. mi.; *p* 813,583. Dairy products, sheep.

South West Africa (Namibia), S. African administered territory. *c* Windhoek; *a* 317,887 sq. mi.; *p* 630,000. Cattle, diamonds, sheep.

Southern Ocean, between Australia and Antarctica. See also, Antarctic Ocean.

South Yemen, republic in SW Asia. *c* Medina-as-Shaab; *a* 112,000 sq. mi.; *p* 1,500,000. Port of Aden provides much of its income. Won independence from Britain in 1967. Bordered by Yemen, Saudi Arabia, Muscat and Oman, Arabian Sea.

Soviet Union, see USSR.

Spain, monarchy in SW Europe. *c* Madrid; *a* 194,884 sq. mi. (including Balearic Is., Canary Is); *p* 32,903,000. Language: Spanish. Religion: Roman Catholic. Bordered by France, Mediterranean Sea, Gibraltar, Portugal, Atlantic, Bay of Biscay. Meseta plateau covers central Spain. Mts include Cantabrian and Pyrenees ranges in N and Sierra Nevada in S. Rivers include Ebro, Guadalquivir, Tagus. Mild climate becomes more extreme near Madrid. Industry and tourism have developed since disastrous civil war, 1936-39.

Spanish Sahara, Spanish territory in NW Africa. *a* 105,000 sq. mi.; *p* 48,000, mainly nomadic.

Springfield, *c* of Illinois, US. *p* 153,000. Once home of Abraham Lincoln.

Stewart Island, southernmost of 3 main islands of New Zealand. *a* 670 sq. mi.; *p* 540.

Stockholm, *c* and port of Sweden. *p* 1,262,000. Cultural, industrial city. Noted for modern architecture.

Stoke-on-Trent, city in England. *p* 273,000
Sucre, official *c* of Bolivia. *p* 58,000.
Sudan, largest republic in Africa. *c* Khartoum; *a* 971,450 sq. mi.; *p* 15,568,000. Most people are Arab Moslems living in N. Christian Negroes live in S. Location: S of Egypt, W of Red Sea. Cotton, gum arabic, hides. Independent since 1956.
Suez Canal, running 101 miles across UAR, N Africa, links Mediterranean and Red Seas. The Canal was blocked during the Arab-Israeli war in 1967.
Sumatra, island of Indonesia. *a* about 163,000 sq. mi.; *p* 15,739,000. Coal, coffee, gold, rice, sugar, tin.
Superior, largest of Gt Lakes, N. America. *a* 31,820 sq. mi. Ports include Duluth, Fort William, Marquette.
Surabaya, city of E Java. A leading naval base of Indonesia. *p* 1,008,000.
Surinam, Netherlands territory in NE South America. *c* Paramaribo; *a* 55,143 sq. mi.; *p* 349,000. Farming, food processing, bauxite mining. Once called Dutch Guiana.
Svalbard, Norwegian islands in Arctic Ocean. *a* 23,957 sq. mi. The only people are visitors.
Swaziland, independent Commonwealth state in Southern Africa. *c* Mbabane. *a* 6,704 sq. mi.; *p* 390,000. Agriculture, mining.
Sweden, monarchy in Scandinavia, N Europe. *c* Stockholm; *a* 173,666 sq. mi.; *p* 8,029,000. Language: Swedish. Bordered by Norway, Finland, Baltic Sea, Kattegat. Mountains cover Sweden's border with Norway. Eastwards, forested land sweeps down to the Gulf of Bothnia. Most people live in the southern plain where the industrial cities and ports lie. Products

Women in traditional Swedish costume preside over a table set with appetizing hors-d'oeuvres, known as smorgasbord.

include aircraft, automobiles, matches, ships, steel. A Viking kingdom, Sweden once ruled much of N Europe. Neutral since 1815, Sweden joined EFTA in 1959.
Switzerland, European republic in Alps. *c* Bern; *a* 15,491 sq mi.; *p* 6,221,000. Swiss people are of mixed descent. Most speak French, German or Italian. Bodies of water include: lakes Geneva, Constance; rivers Inn, Rhine, Rhone, Ticino. Large cities include Zurich, Geneva. Exports include cheese, chocolates, light engineering products, watches. Switzerland has been neutral and independent since 1815. Its ski slopes draw many tourists.
Sydney, *c* and port of New South Wales, Australia. *p* 2,647,000. Commercial, cultural and educational city. Sydney Opera House stands on Benelong Point.
Syr Darya, river in southern USSR, 1,770 mi. long.
Syria, Arab republic in SW Asia. *c* Damascus; *a* about 71,000 sq. mi.; *p* 6,134,000. Most people are Moslems who speak Arabic. Important rivers include Euphrates, Jordan, Orontes. Main products include cement, cereals, cotton, leather, petroleum, wool.

T

Taipei, *c* of Nationalist China's island of Taiwan (Formosa). *p* 1,135,000.
Taiwan, island republic near China. Also called Formosa. *c* Taipei; *a* 13,885 sq. mi., *p* 14,564,000. Headquarters of Nationalist China since 1949. Taiwan, which includes the Pescadores Islands, has many forests and mountains. Earth tremors are common. The island is rich in minerals. Other products include bamboo, camphor, fish, rice, tea and textiles.
Taiyuan, city in E China. *p* 1,020,000.

Talien, city in NE China. *p* 1,590,000. Once called Dairen.
Tallahassee, *c* of Florida, US. *p* 58,000.
Tananarive, *c* of Malagasy Republic, Madagascar. *p* 322,000. Commercial city.
Tanzania, republic in E Africa. *c* Dar-es-Salaam; *a* 363,708 sq. mi.; *p* 11,917,000. Lakes Victoria, Tanganyika and Nyasa lie on its borders. Mt Kilimanjaro lies in NE. Agriculture is the chief occupation. Exports include sisal, diamonds, cloves. Tanganyika became independent in 1962, Zanzibar in 1963. The two countries joined in 1964 to form the unified state of Tanzania.
Tashkent, city in Uzbekistan, USSR. *p* 1,295,000.
Tasmania, island and smallest Australian state. *c* Hobart; *a* 26,383 sq. mi.; *p* 386,000. Cattle, fruit, grain, minerals.
Tegucigalpa, *c* of Honduras, Central America; *p* 171,000. Food processing, minerals.
Tehran, *c* of Iran. *p* 2,317,000.
Tennessee, S state, US. *c* Nashville; *a* 42,244 sq. mi.; *p* 3,957,000. Chemicals, food and metal products, textiles. Copper, iron, marble and zinc.
Texas, S state, US. *c* Austin; *a* 267,339 sq. mi.; *p* 10,977,000. Beef, chemicals, cotton, fishing, gas, meat packing, petroleum. Famous for Alamo, Texas Rangers.
Thailand, monarchy in SE Asia. *c* Bangkok; *a* 198,456 sq. mi.; *p* 35,412,000. The people and their language are called Thai. Most are Buddhist. Thailand is bordered by Burma, Laos, Cambodia, Malaya and the sea. Main products are fish, rice, rubber, sapphires, silk and timber. Once called Siam, Thailand has many beautiful temples. An ancient country, it has never been taken as a colony by Europeans.

Tibet, autonomous region in SW China. *c* Lhasa; *a* 471,660 sq. mi.; *p* 1,274,000, in mid 1960's, since increased by Chinese immigration.

Tien Shan, mtn range in N China.

Tientsin, port in NE China. *p* 3,220,000.

Tigris, river flowing 1,150 miles through Turkey and Iraq. Flows through Baghdad and site of ancient Babylon.

Timor, E part of island is Portuguese, W part Indonesian. *c* Dili; *a* 7,330 sq. mi.; *p* 570,000.

Timor, Sea of, between Australia and Timor

Tirana, *c* of Albania. *p* 180,000. Leading commercial and industrial city.

Tocantins, Brazilian river, 1,700 mi. long.

Togo, republic in W Africa. *c* Lomé; *a* 20,400 sq. mi.; *p* 1,869,000. A thin strip of land bordering the Atlantic between Dahomey and Ghana. Products include coffee, cocoa. Gained independence from France in 1960.

Tokelau Islands, New Zealand Pacific territory. *a* 4 sq. mi.; *p* 8,000. Copra.

Tokyo, port and *c* of Japan, on Honshu island. *p* (including Yokohama) 14,000,000. World's most highly populated city. Once called Yedo, or Edo.

Although most of Tokyo was destroyed during World War II, much traditional Japanese architecture remains, for instance the gaily coloured Asakusa Gate.

Tonga, islands in S Pacific. British-associated state. *c* Nukualofa; *a* 270 sq. mi.; *p* 84,000. Also called Friendly Islands.

Topeka, *c* of Kansas, US. *p* 119,000.

Toronto, port and *c* of Ontario, Canada. *p* 1,882,000. Business city for mining industry. Machinery, shipping.

Transvaal, S. African province. *c* Pretoria, *a* 110,450 sq. mi.; *p* 6,273,000. Agriculture, brewing, diamonds, wool.

Trenton, *c* of New Jersey, US. *p* 296,000. Metals and pottery.

Trinidad and Tobago, island Commonwealth monarchy in W. Indies. *c* Port-of-Spain; *a* 1,980 sq. mi.; *p* 1,126,000. Products include asphalt, rum. Independent since 1962.

Tripoli, port in Lebanon. *p* 214,000. Petroleum refinery, sponges, textiles.

Tripoli, *c* and largest city of Libya. Leading port. *p* 195,000. Products include hides, wool.

Tristan da Cunha, British island in S Atlantic. *a* 40 sq. mi.; *p* 262.

Trucial States, W Asia. *a* about 32,300 sq. mi. Seven sheikdoms on Persian Gulf. Includes (W to E) Abu Dhabi, Dubai, Sharjah, Ajman, Umm Al-Qaywayn, Ras Al-Khaymah, Rujairah.

Tsingtao, port in E China. *p* 1,121,000.

Tunis, *c* of Tunisia, N Africa. *p* 662,000. Ruins of Carthage near.

Tunisia, republic in N Africa. *c* Tunis; *a* 48,332 sq. mi.; *p* 4,688,000. People are mainly Arab or Berber Moslems. Bordered by Algeria, Mediterranean, Libya. Income from agriculture, phosphates and tourism. Independence from France, 1956.

Turin, city in NW Italy. *p* 108,000. Automobiles, engineering, textiles.

Turkey, republic between Mediterranean and Black seas. *c* Ankara; *a* 301,381 sq. mi.; *p* 35,327,000. Turks are a Moslem people, and most are farmers. The Dardanelles and Bosporus straits separate the European and Asian parts of Turkey. Main products are cereals, chromium, figs, mohair, nuts, olives, textiles and tobacco. Turkey was the site of the Byzantine and Ottoman empires.

U

Uganda, republic in central Africa. *c* Kampala; *a* about 93,000 sq. mi.; *p* 8,543,000. People are mainly of Buganda tribe. Bordered by Lake Victoria and five countries. Products include coffee and copper. Gained independence from Britain in 1962.

Ukraine, republic of USSR. *c* Kiev; *a* 225,000 sq. mi.; *p* 41,893,000. Leading coal and iron region. Fertile 'black earth' agricultural area.

United Kingdom, island monarchy in W Europe. *c* London; *a* 94,214 sq. mi.; *p* 55,289,000. The UK consists of England, Northern Ireland, Scotland, Wales. Britain's people now include many immigrants from Europe and Commonwealth. Main religions: Protestantism and Roman Catholicism. Language: English, with Welsh in some parts of Wales.

Apart from the Pennines in N England, most of Britain's low mts are in Scotland. Most people live in or near the great industrial and commercial areas such as Glasgow – Edinburgh, Liverpool – Manchester, Birmingham and London. Main rivers include Clyde, Humber, Mersey, Severn, Thames. Coal, iron and fertile soil, allowed Britain to become prosperous and develop huge overseas trade and empire in the 1800's. British engineers pioneered industrialization in all its forms. In the 1900's, Britain decreased its overseas commitments and became increasingly involved in Europe.

Chigaco is the second largest city in the United States.

Language: English. Main religions: Protestantism, Roman Catholicism.

From the Pacific to Atlantic Oceans, 48 of the 50 states lie between Canada in the N and Mexico and the Gulf of Mexico in the S. Alaska borders NW Canada. Hawaii lies 2,400 mi. W of California's coast. The US developed fast during the 1800's. Settlers pushed the 'frontier' westwards across the five main regions. These are: *E coastal plain* where great ports like New York and Boston lie; *Appalachian Mts; interior plain* which stretches W to Rocky Mts; *western highlands* which include Rocky Mts and Sierra Nevada-Cascade range; *Pacific slope* where newer cities like Los Angeles and San Francisco lie. The US shares with Canada the Great Lakes in the midwest. Longest rivers are Missouri (2,714 mi.) and Mississippi (2,350 mi.). Only Russia, China and Canada are larger than the US.

More than 40 million immigrants joined US-born people to develop the US into the world's wealthiest farming and industrial country. Each of the 50 states has limited self government under president elected for 4 year term.

This peaceful scene in the Cotswolds is typical of many parts of the United Kingdom.

United States, federal republic in N. America (except for Hawaii state, in Pacific). *c* Washington D.C.; *a* 3,615,211 sq. mi.; *p* 209,816,000.

Upper Volta, landlocked republic in W Africa. *c* Ougadougou; *a* 105,869 sq. mi.; *p* 5,448,000. Products include cotton, livestock and rice. Gained independence from France in 1960.

Ural Mountains, in USSR. Traditional border between Europe and Asia.

243

Uruguay, smallest republic in S. America. *c* Montevideo; *a* 72,172 sq. mi.; *p* 2,907,000. People are mostly of Spanish descent. 80% live in towns. Language: Spanish. Uruguay is bordered by Brazil, the Atlantic and Argentina (by Rio de la Plata). Chief products are hides, meat and wool. Independence from Spain won in 1830.

USSR (Union of Soviet Socialist Republics), also called Russia or Soviet Union, is a federation of 15 republics. *c* Moscow; *a* 8,649,500 sq. mi.; *p* 247,489,000. Stretches from E Europe across Asia to the Pacific. Russia, the world's largest country, is a land of great contrasts in people, places, climate and products. It borders 11 countries and the Pacific and Arctic Oceans. Main language: Russian (there are 80 other languages). Religion: Russian Orthodox, now in decline.

The Urals partly divide European from Asian Russia. Russia's great water-ways include Caspian and Aral Seas, L. Baykal, L. Balkhash, and Don, Lena, Ob, Volga, Yenisey rivers and linking canals. The USSR produces about every kind of crop, mineral, and manufactured item.

Throwing off Mongol rule in 1480, the Russian state of Muscovy expanded in all directions to cover a sixth of the world. Communist since 1917, Russia is second only to the US in production of goods.

Utah, US state in Rocky Mts. *c* Salt Lake City; *a* 84,916 sq. mi.; *p* 891,000. Agriculture and mining.

V

Vaduz, *c* of Liechtenstein. *p* 4,000.

Valetta, *c* of Malta. *p* 18,000. Resort.

Vancouver, Canada's main Pacific port, SW British Columbia. *p* 892,000.

Vatican City, independent Papal state of Roman Catholic Church, part of Rome, Italy. *a* 108·9 acres; *p* 1,000.

Venezuela, republic in S. America. *c* Caracas; *a* 352,143 sq. mi.; *p* 10,440,000. People are mainly *mestizos* (of mixed European and Amerind descent). Language: Spanish. Bordered by Caribbean Sea, Guyana, Brazil, Colombia. Angel Falls are among the world's highest. Products include coffee, minerals, petroleum. Independence won from Spain in 1821.

Venice, port in Italy. *p* 360,000. Historic city with many canals.

Vermont, NE state, US. *c* Montpelier; *a* 9,609 sq. mi.; *p* 425,000. Farming, livestock, lumber, machinery, textiles.

Victoria, SE state of Australia. *c* Melbourne; *a* 87,884 sq. mi.; *p* 3,356,900. Farming, coal, iron, oil, textiles. Two-thirds of Victoria's people live in Melbourne.

Vienna, *c* and largest city of Austria. *p* 1,637,000. Historic and manufacturing city on Danube river.

Vietnam, in SE Asia, has since 1954 been divided into two countries, North and South. North Vietnam (Democratic Republic of Vietnam): *c* Hanoi; *a* 61,293 sq. mi.; *p* 20,700,000. South Vietnam (Republic of Vietnam): *c* Saigon; *a* 65,948 sq. mi.; *p* 17,414,000. People are mostly Vietnamese. Vietnam's religions include Buddhism, Christianity, Confucianism, Taoism and combinations of these. Long coastline on South China Sea. Vietnam came under French rule between about 1858 and 1870. After fierce fighting, the French left Vietnam in 1954 and the country was divided. Internal fighting continued into the 1960's, and war spread into Laos and Cambodia by 1970. Products include apatite, cement, coal, copra, processed food, rice, rubber.

Virgin Islands, group of W. Indian islands, divided between Britain and US. *a* 192 sq. mi.; *p* 74,500. Resort.

Virginia, E state, US. *c* Richmond; *a* 40,815 sq. mi.; *p* 4,595,000. Agriculture, coal, manufacturing. World famous for tobacco. First permanent English settlement in N. America was made at Jamestown in 1607.

Vladivostock, Pacific port in SE Siberia, USSR. *p* 325,000. Petroleum refining.

Volga, Europe's longest river, flowing 2,290 miles entirely through the USSR.

W

Wagga Wagga, town in New South Wales, Australia. *p* 26,000. Education, industry.

Wake I, central Pacific (US). *a* 3 sq. mi.

Wales, principality in Western UK. *c* Cardiff; *a* 8,016 sq. mi.; *p* 2,720,000. Languages: English, Welsh. Metalworking, mining.

Warsaw, *c* of Poland. *p* 1,261,000. Commercial and culture city. Largely destroyed 1939-45, but old part of city restored when rebuilt in modern style.

Washington, NW state, US. *c* Olympia; *a* 68,192 sq. mi.; *p* 3,276,000. Largest apple crop in US. Farming, fishing, mining. Largest city and port, Seattle.

Washington DC, *c* of US, on Potomac River. *p* 2,615,000. Administrative area. Government industries include printing and engraving.

Waterford, port in Republic of Ireland. *p* 30,000. Dairy products, glass, paper.

Wellington, *c* of New Zealand, on North Island. *p* 175,000. Communications, cultural and industrial city; port.

West Indies, several groups of islands between Florida and Venezuela. See separate entries.

West Irian, Indonesian administered part of New Guinea and smaller islands. *c* Sukarnapura; *a* 162,915 sq. mi.; *p* 758,000. Foods and spices, fishing, timber.

West Virginia, E state, US. *c* Charleston; *a* 24,181 sq. mi.; *p* 1,802,000. Agriculture, coal, iron, glass, lumber, salt, steel.

Western Australia, largest Australian state. *c* Perth; *a* 975,920 sq. mi.; *p* 931,000. Large area is desert. Asbestos, cereals, coal, gold, livestock, silver.

Western Samoa, independent state in S Pacific. *c* Apia; *a* 1,097 sq. mi.; *p* 135,000. Four islands. Farming and fishing. Independence from NZ, 1962.

White Sea, inlet of Arctic Ocean, USSR.

Wight, Isle of, English island off south coast. *a* 147 sq. mi.; *p* 98,000.

Windward Islands, group in W. Indies. Includes Dominica, Grenada, St Vincent. *a* 821 sq. mi.; *p* 336,000. Agriculture, fishing.

Winnipeg, city in Manitoba, Canada. *p* 509,000. Wheat market. Rail hub.

Wisconsin, midwest state, US. *c* Madison; *a* 56,154 sq. mi.; *p* 4,221,000. Beer, dairy

Above: Beautiful mountains and vast pine forests typify Yugoslavia's dramatic scenery.

products, farm machinery, iron, paper. Fishing resort. Largest city, Milwaukee.

Wollongong, town in New South Wales, Australia. *p* 177,000.

Wood Buffalo National Park, Alberta and NW Territories, Canada. *a* 17,300 sq. mi.

Wyoming, US state in Rocky Mts. *c* Cheyenne; *a* 97,914 sq. mi.; *p* 315,000. Agriculture and mining. Famous for Old Faithful geyser, Yellowstone National Park.

Wuhan, city on Han river in central China, formed by integrating Hankow, Hanyang and Wuchang. *p* 2,146,000.

Y

Yangtze, Asia's longest and most important river, flowing 3,100 mi. through China.

Yaoundé, *c* of Cameroon, Africa. *p* 101,000.

Yellow Sea, part of Pacific Ocean between Korea and N China.

Yellowstone National Park, Wyoming and Montana, US. *a* 3,458 sq. mi. Canyons, geysers and hot springs.

Yemen, desert republic in SW Arabian Peninsula. *c* San'a; *a* 75,000 sq. mi.; *p* 5,328,000. Yemen lies along the Red Sea. Its people are Arabs, mostly Moslems. Products include coffee, cotton, grains and hides.

Yenisey, Asian river flowing 2,360 miles through central Siberia, USSR.

Yokohama, port, part of Tokyo, Japan.

Yosemite National Park, E California, US. *a* 1,183 sq. mi. Famed for sequoia trees.

Yugoslavia, federal republic in SE Europe. *c* Belgrade; *a* 98,766 sq. mi.; *p* 20,721,000. People and languages include: Serbo-Croatian, Macedonian, Slovene. A Balkan state, Yugoslavia lies along the Adriatic Sea. Half its people are farmers. Products include fruit, grain, livestock, metals, petroleum. N part of country won independence from Austria in 1918, and joined with Serbia and Montenegro.

Yukon, territory in NW Canada. *c* Whitehorse; *a* 207,076 sq. mi.; *p* 15,000. Fishing, forestry, furs, minerals.

Yukon, river flowing 1,979 miles through Yukon (Canada) and Alaska.

Z

Zambia, landlocked republic in E Africa. *c* Lusaka; *a* 288,130 sq. mi.; *p* 4,319,000. Languages: English, Nyanja. Bordered by Congo (Kinshasa), Rhodesia and five other countries. Zambia is one of the world's largest copper producers. Gained independence from Britain in 1964.

Zanzibar, island, part of Tanzania. *c* Zanzibar; *a* 1,020 sq. mi.; *p* 325,000. Copra.

Zululand, region in eastern S. Africa. *a* 10,427 sq. mi.; *p* 544,000. Once a warrior state, incorporated into Natal in 1897.

Index

246

250

255

Acknowledgements

We gratefully acknowledge the assistance of the following organizations in assembling photographic material for this encyclopaedia:

Air India, Anglo-American Corporation of South Africa Limited, Arab Information Centre, Sir William Arrol & Company Limited, Australian News & Information Bureau, Bowaters U.K. Paper Company Limited, The British Petroleum Company Limited, Canadian Film Board, Canadian Government Travel Bureau, Central Office of Information, Ceylon Tea Centre, Consolidated Gold Fields Limited, Thomas Cook & Son Limited, Courtaulds Limited, French Government Tourist Office, French Line, German Embassy, Granada Television, Greek Tourist Office, Houston Chamber of Commerce, I.C.I. Plastics Division, Imperial Government of Iran, Infoplan Limited, Israel Government Tourist Office, Italian State Tourist Office, Japan Airlines Company Limited, Japanese Embassy, The Mansell Collection, Middle East Airlines, A. Monk and Company Limited, Moroccan Embassy, National Portrait Gallery, New Zealand High Commission, Novosti Press Agency, Pan American Airways, Peruvian Embassy, Port of London Authority, Shell Chemicals United Kingdom Limited, Science Museum, South African Airways, Sun Alliance and London Insurance Group, Trans Antarctic Expedition, Uganda High Commission, Union Castle Line, United States Embassy, United States Naval Forces in Europe, Walker Art Gallery, Liverpool, Zambian National Tourist Bureau.